Paternalism Incorporated

PATERNALISM INCORPORATED

Fables of American Fatherhood, 1865–1940

DAVID LEVERENZ

Cornell University Press

ITHACA AND LONDON

First published 2003 by Cornell University Press

Printed in the United States of America

Library of Congress Cataloging-in-Publication Data

Leverenz, David.
  Paternalism incorporated : fables of American fatherhood, 1865–1940 / David Leverenz.
    p. cm.
Includes bibliographical references and index.
  ISBN 0-8014-4167-6 (alk. paper)
  1. American fiction—20th century—History and criticism. 2. Fathers in literature.
3. American fiction—19th century—History and criticism. 4. Corporate culture—United
States—History. 5. Paternalism—United States—History. 6. Fathers and daughters in
literature. 7. Fathers and sons in literature. 8. Father figures in literature. 9. Corporations
in literature. I. Title.
  PS374.F35L48 2003
  813'.4093520431—dc21

2003005529

Cloth printing   10 9 8 7 6 5 4 3 2 1

To Anne,
who once called me "the pregnant monk."

Contents

Preface

After twelve years of intermittent labor, I'm amazed that I've finished this book. When I began it, I had a nice, tidy project: I wanted to write about daddy's girls and daddy's boys as figures of upward mobility in early corporate America. Then I started to think about the changing public meanings of "father" and "daughter." Soon I was hip deep in issues of honor and shaming that I'd assumed were peculiar to the American South and other preindustrial cultures. That turn led me to wonder what connection white racism had with paternalistic values based on honor and shame. And on and on.

At various points I considered abandoning the project as too incorporative, too diffuse, too implausible, too overreaching, or just too much. But the ideas kept coming around again. Then, in the Fall of 2000, thanks to Dean Neil Sullivan, Provost David Colburn, and especially John Leavey, who chairs the English Department, the University of Florida (U.F.) not only matched a tempting outside offer, but also gave me a year's leave to keep me at U.F. At last this book gained momentum.

My thanks to Steven Feierman for many conversations, and for trying to persuade me that paternalism is a hot topic. Thanks also to colleagues and friends who have commented on various chapters, especially Paula Bennett, T. Walter Herbert, Gordon Hutner, Lee Clark Mitchell, Vivian Pollak, Eric Savoy, and my U.F. colleagues Anne Goodwyn Jones and Malini Johar Schueller. Evelyn Bishop, Lee Person, and Augusta Rohrbach have welcomed me to conference panels where I could try out some of my ideas and readings. Many students and colleagues have engaged me in spirited discussions about these texts and issues. At talks from San Francisco to Poland, members of the audience helped me to clarify my ideas, while usually suggesting five or ten more daddy's girl novels that I should have read.

I'm also grateful to the University of Florida for granting me a semester-long sabbatical in Fall 1993, when I slowly overcame my terror of computers. I thank Bernie Kendler, once again my editor at Cornell University Press, for sending the manuscript to an exceptionally generous and thoughtful reader, for nudging me about length, and for suggesting that "Fables" might be part of the title. Also at Cornell University Press, Karen Laun and Susan MacKay have been exceptionally scrupulous editors. A few paragraphs in chapter 4, on boy books, revise part of a review essay, "Tomboys, Bad Boys, and Horatio Alger: When Fatherhood Became a Problem," published in *American Literary History,* vol. 10 (Spring 1998), 219–236. The rest of this book hasn't been published before.

Finally, I have a life-long indebtedness to Anne Rutledge and our four children, Allison, Elizabeth, Trevor, and Nell, our family of six with five last names. They continue to teach me about the reciprocities of fatherhood.

Paternalism Incorporated

Introduction

"Are you lost, Daddy?" I asked tenderly.
"Shut up," he explained.

Ring Lardner, *The Young Immigrunts* (1920).

Paternalism has become a pejorative word. In ordinary speech it usually signifies an outmoded management style that treats adults as children. It's a bad thing; end of story.

In this book I try to restore a sense of its complexity in the early corporate era. After the Civil War, paternalism became a normative management style, used to foster upward mobility as well as to control work forces. The "Great White Father" became a staple of the nation's imperial rhetoric. More broadly, as my title implies, paternalism was incorporated into American narratives as well as into Big Business and the nation-state.[1] Surprisingly, these fables of fatherhood often undercut their own fabulations, by exposing a shaky narcissism in representations of male authority. Many narratives also register the looming threat or promise of social equality, whether personified in the black man, the immigrant, the New Woman, or the youngster bent on rising to the top.

Paternalism is a huge subject, almost a field. Its bibliography includes philosophical and legal studies as well as histories of preindustrial societies, the antebellum South, and imperialism. Yet if my conversations about it are any guide, the word is a shut-off valve, partly because paternalism seems so opposed to American individualism. W. E. B. Du Bois dismissively writes about the Freedmen's Bureau's "paternalistic methods which discouraged self-reliance[.]"[2] This book tries to complicate that binary, sometimes by writing about paternalism from the inside. For most privileged people, it's impossible to act in the world without some paternalistic aspects in one's behavior and thinking.

I

To make the topic manageable, I've narrowed it to representations of paternalistic rhetoric and experience in early corporate America, which I take to be from Reconstruction to World War II. For my generalizations about corporate practices, I rely on various historians rather than archival work. Though touching on imperialism and the treatment of Native Americans in the 1887 Dawes Act, I focus primarily on American narratives, including narratives about the corporation, from after the Civil War to 1940, or from *Ragged Dick* and *Little Women* to *Tender Is the Night,* Shirley Temple, and Robert Nathan's *Portrait of Jennie,* with glances before and after. I used to claim that prose narrative is a uniquely useful medium for exposing social tensions and transformations. I still think literature offers intimate access to shareable public meanings of private experiences, though it's only one of many refracting lenses. In any case, it's what I know.

As dictionaries define it, paternalism is a practice of care, management, and control modeled on the relation of a father to his dependent children. The term derives from the Latin word "pater," meaning father. Fatherly care becomes a legitimating metaphor to define how those in authority should treat individuals and groups not connected to one's family, usually employees, students, citizens, or natives of occupied territories. Antebellum white Southerners invoked paternalism to characterize their management of their slaves. The term presumes a stable, small-scale hierarchy of deference and mutual obligation, expressed through gift giving of various kinds more than through contractual relations. In a relatively small and closed social system, such a hierarchy often promises and sometimes delivers reciprocal rewards over time.[3]

The negative view of paternalism has a long, complicated history in philosophy and legal thought. In the eighteenth century, Immanuel Kant opposed paternalism because it affronts human dignity and interferes with a person's rational agency. John Stuart Mill's *On Liberty* (1859) argues that laws should protect people from each other but not from themselves, since such governmental paternalism blocks people from asserting their own autonomous choices. John Rawls's *A Theory of Justice* (1971) is a more complex version of Mill's argument. Other philosophers and theorists of the law have argued for the usefulness and rightness of such legislation. Donald VanDeVeer's *Paternalistic Intervention: The Moral Bounds on Benevolence* (1986) usefully if dryly discusses the complex tensions between individuals' rights and appropriate interferences with those rights.[4] In practice, paternalism continues to shape many institutional requirements, from general education courses to seatbelts and smoking regulations, whether of cigarettes or marijuana, usually with the justification that people will be better off, even if they don't think so. Some elite universities, for instance, continue to oppose graduate student unions on the classically paternalistic grounds that students should be grateful for their privileged institutional place and their distinguished professors' personal mentoring.

More broadly, paternalism inheres in any social structure that features inequality. The term includes attitudes of benevolence as well as charitable or philanthropic acts. Beyond helping people down on their luck, paternalists often aim at social improvement, sometimes even reform. In its more admirable aspects, paternalistic behavior says to oneself and others, *I'm helping less fortunate people to uplift themselves.* Less admirably, paternalism is an enforceable attitude that says, *I know what you need better than you do,* and *Remember, I am your superior.*

From a radical point of view, paternalism supports and mystifies structural inequalities by highlighting what individuals can do at both ends of the scale. From a liberal point of view, it shows how individuals can make a social difference. From a conservative point of view, it helps to reinforce a sense of social duty among the justifiably privileged classes, and to expand their control. Historically, philanthropic paternalism helped members of the new industrial class to consolidate their cultural as well as marketplace dominance. By imitating an older gentry model, rich men could gain honor among their peers by giving without immediate expectations of exchange.

After the Civil War, executives appropriated paternalism to explain their management practices and justify the corporation's social usefulness. The term evoked civic and domestic forms of nostalgia for deference, whether to the preindustrial gentry or within domestic patriarchy. Both associations idealized responsible, humane care of inferiors by their superiors. The term also implied a practice of providing for people's needs without giving them much responsibility. Finally, it emphasized developing the moral character of inferiors, without considering the social structure that pushes them toward the bottom. Though paternalism invokes idealized domestic patriarchy as its ground for social meaning, its corporate and cultural practices of benevolence, mentoring, and philanthropy tend to presume short-term rather than long-term human relationships. In that respect, postbellum paternalism has less to do with the family than with the limited personal liability that legally enabled the rise of the corporation.

My subtitle uses "fables" and "fatherhood" rather loosely. "Fatherhood" includes mentors, philanthropists, sugar daddies, and other nonbiological father-figures who preach or practice paternalism. By "fables," I want to highlight the irony that so many seemingly childlike idealizations of fatherhood reveal the father-figure's inadequacy. Why do so many stories during this period turn ambitious young adults into daddy's girls and daddy's boys? Why do so many midlife men want to play daddy outside the home? Such stories uplift the father-figures as well as the aspiring, deferential youngster. Yet typically, the storytelling destabilizes the fable's traditional moralizing or legend making. Instead, in texts as different as *The Gilded Age, Sister Carrie,* and *Up from Slavery,* narrators play with the midlife, middle-class white male's need to be depended on. Putting a fatherly face on the power of money and mentoring reinvented the possibilities of paternal authority, just as idealized domestic patriarchy seemed to be disappearing into company flow charts. Yet these fables and fictions acknowledge that young women and men can rise beyond paternal controls.

This introduction and my first chapter sketch some connections between the rise of daddy's girl and daddy's boy narratives and the rise of managerial work, which accelerated the capitalist redefinition of middle-class fatherhood. Chapters 2 and 3 consider a wide range of daddy's girl narratives, in part to show their sudden profusion after the Civil War. Chapter 2 surveys the rise of the daddy's girl in tension with the more threatening specter of the upwardly mobile career woman, whose story could no longer be contained by traditional narratives of women rising through spirituality, scandal, or marriage. Chapter 3 focuses on Mark Twain and Charles Dudley Warner's *The Gilded Age*, Theodore Dreiser's *Sister Carrie*, Willa Cather's *O Pioneers!*, and Jean Webster's *Daddy-Long-Legs*, all briefly compared with other contemporary texts.

Chapters 4 through 6 argue that a nostalgia for traditional ideals of honor and civic status provides a broader social frame for the construction of fatherhood, paternalism, and white racism after the Civil War. Chapter 4 turns to the motif of the daddy's boy in its sacrificial and theatrical modes. This narrative complements the daddy's girl, though the daddy's boy has less cultural centrality. After considering stories of filial sacrifice by Stephen Crane, Twain, Herman Melville, and Henry James, I highlight the theatricality of daddy's boy self-presentations in Horatio Alger's *Ragged Dick* and Booker T. Washington's *Up from Slavery*, along with Hank Morgan's relish for androgynous Clarence in Twain's *A Connecticut Yankee in King Arthur's Court*.

Chapter 5, "Narrating the Corporation," explores seven critiques of corporate development from 1869 to 1932, from Charles Francis Adams, Jr. to Adolf A. Berle, Jr. and Gardiner Means. These critiques mix laments for paternalism's inadequacy with attempts to articulate the corporation as a strange new power. Chapter 6, "Giving and Shaming," considers some dynamics of giving and shaming as responses to the transformation of social scale and the intensification of class divisions. Looking at Andrew Carnegie's *The Gospel of Wealth*, William Dean Howells's "Tribulations of a Cheerful Giver," Washington's *Up from Slavery* again, and Jane Addams's "A Modern Lear," I also consider how Marcel Mauss's ideas might apply to the philanthropy of Carnegie and John D. Rockefeller. I conclude that philanthropic benevolence and shaming help to consolidate class-linked whiteness as a cultural base for honor and resurgent paternalism. White racism serves as a collective shaming to shore up that base.

Chapters 7 and 8 explore two literary narratives in more detail. James's *The Golden Bowl* dramatizes the strains as well as the triumph in Maggie Verver's incorporation of two implicitly racialized outsiders into white paternalism, while F. Scott Fitzgerald's *Tender Is the Night* mourns for Dick

Diver's fall from paternalistic control to social irrelevance. The Epilogue takes a brief look at Shirley Temple's *The Little Colonel,* which opens up possibilities for regional, gender, and racial crossovers, while sentimentally reinforcing paternalistic presumptions. In several chapters I cross over to British texts, notably Edmund Spenser's "Mutability Cantos" in chapter 2 and George Eliot's *Middlemarch* in chapter 6, to consider "Mutability" as an upwardly mobile woman and Eliot's uses of honor and shaming.

Paternalism and Upward Mobility

After the Civil War, the corporate transformation of work in the United States created widespread desires for higher social status along with widening class divisions. As cultural fictions, the daddy's girl, the daddy's boy, the Great White Father, incorporative whiteness, and "the firm" emerge at the intersection between hopes for upward mobility and pervasive paternalistic controls. Although such hopes presume class hierarchy, they also undermine traditional status groups by creating a national imaginary, an endlessly expansive middle class. For the first time in modern history, status equality became conceivable on a large scale—a promise for those below, a threat for those above.

Since the United States has recently claimed to be an equal opportunity employer, it may seem odd to say equality was a threat. Yet from 1865 to the 1920s, white middle-class Americans encountered a modern version of a Contact Period, a term usually applied to encounters between explorers and natives in Columbus's era. Surging into the workplace, many African Americans, immigrants, and women dreamed of rising to respectability, and some achieved it. Paternalistic rhetoric and philanthropy encouraged those dreams, while more disciplining paternalistic practices tried to preserve class and racial hierarchies. That social tension frames the narratives I'm considering.

The rise of corporate and professional work threatened traditional norms of fatherhood and honor, two linked ideologies that for centuries had emboldened and constrained men's behavior. By offering the promise of upward mobility, paternalism helped to preserve a deferential society's emphasis on personal honor in the midst of class conflict and burgeoning bureaucracies. Yet a new impersonality characterizes both the firm's hierarchical authority and the federal government's imperial role as Great Father. Localized traditions of hierarchical reciprocity conflicted with the corporation's large-scale bureaucracies, its impersonal emphasis on contracts and profits, its multiple sites of employment, and its production of class divisions between white-collar and blue-collar employees. The age of paternalism on a national scale was also an age of its discontents.

In a great variety of ways, executives and cultural authorities invoked paternalism to control the democratic threat and promise of greater human diversity—a diversity stimulated by the corporate need for workers. From the 1830s onward, the U.S. government declared itself a Great Father to Native Americans, Filipinos, and other peoples who might yield to what William McKinley called "benevolent assimilation." In rhetorical strategies for imperial conquests, whether of Native Americans or other precapitalist peoples, the United States often used the rhetoric of fatherhood to justify its national self-image of rightful dominance. I argue in chapter 7 that James's *The Golden Bowl* dramatizes an elite version of benevolent assimilation, enforced by a daddy's girl. In American literary realism, benevolently omniscient narrators gave readers the pleasures of super-vision, while offering imaginative engagement with an increasingly variegated social scene.

Yet most of the narratives I consider register how these "uplifting fictions" didn't quite work. I would have put that term in the title, but, as with paternalism, "uplifting" has lost its cultural resonance. Once beckoning ambiguously to the uplifter and the upliftee, it now evokes bras, Prozac, Viagra, and other temporary boosts.

Unfortunately, "uplifting" is also an ungainly and redundant word. What would "downlifting" mean? At the turn into the twentieth century, the term gained a special cultural intensity for African Americans.[5] Yet the drive for racial uplift was part of a wider zeal to push the lower classes toward white middle-class standards of behavior, and to raise the middle-class self toward moral purification. More covertly, the term intimates the erotic charge that daddy's girls and daddy's boys could provide for their mentors or spectators, whether in Alger's pederastic engagements, Clarence's prancing before his Connecticut Yankee, Captain Vere's chaste yearning for Billy Budd, the considerably less chaste yearnings of "the portly gentlemen in the first row" for Sister Carrie, or Lawyer Royall's pursuit of his ward "Charity" in Edith Wharton's *Summer.*

Many corporations used paternalism not to foster upward mobility but to organize their work forces along gendered lines. Typically, corporations divided male managers from female clerical workers, and made the managers superior.[6] Still more ubiquitously, paternalism became a basic management style, from the executive and philanthropic behavior of Andrew Carnegie and John D. Rockefeller to the company town of George Pullman—"a modern Lear," Jane Addams called him. As Addams contends, paternalistic attempts to stabilize social inequalities opposed a more democratic respect for human heterogeneity. John Patterson has gained ambivalent respect from historians for using his National Cash Register Company to develop "welfare work." Across the Atlantic, George Bernard Shaw's play, *Major Barbara* (1907), presents a sympathetic English munitions manufacturer whose company town creates happy middle-class lives for his workers.

Paternalism was not simply a way of managing and disciplining lower-class and immigrant laborers, though it was sometimes only that. Neo-

Marxists tend to see it as what Mary Jackman calls "the velvet glove."[7] Yet it also structured various kinds of hopes. At the bottom of society, continuing patterns of deference both stimulated and constrained desires for upward mobility. At the top, eagerness to gain honor, or avoid shame, helped to motivate the extraordinary gifts by Carnegie, Rockefeller, and other philanthropists to help people from poor and immigrant groups rise—if such people could be incorporated into middle-class respectability. That mixed cultural signal resembles the development of "inclusive whiteness" that Matthew Jacobson has analyzed.[8] As many critics have said, this partially assimilative class and racial dynamic explicitly excluded African Americans, who had to develop their own middle class as a parallel but disparaged universe.

In retrospect, corporate and cultural paternalism provided a mediating structure of perception, at least for people of privilege. It linked residual longings for patriarchy and honor with progressive hopes for reform and social uplift. It put a simple fatherly face on the emerging complexities of a national and international credit economy. As Andrea Tone puts it at the start of *The Business of Benevolence,* "capitalism and paternalism have matured in tandem[.]" Yet it also prompted calls for social or moral reform as a solution to class conflict. Reformers were eager to bring the lower or immigrant classes toward spiritual uplift as well as upward mobility. In the introduction to *The Dangerous Classes of New York* (1872), for instance, Charles Loring Brace argues that "the cheapest and most efficacious way of dealing with the 'Dangerous Classes' of large cities" is to "change their material circumstances, and draw them under the influence of the moral and fortunate classes, that they shall grow up as useful producers[.]" By telling his stories of the poor, he also hopes to "bring the two ends of society nearer together in human sympathy."[9]

To our eyes, the reformers' paternalism betrays an unconscious arrogance. They assume that the white "race" not only is superior to people of color, but also has the right and duty to colonize them in its own respectable image. That attitude took many forms, in keeping with what Edward Said has called "the high-handed executive attitude of nineteenth century and early twentieth century European colonialism."[10] Yet one can consider that attitude somewhat differently, as the first response by people of privilege during what I've called a modern Contact Period. For W. E. B. Du Bois, American racism emerged so virulently after the Civil War because "this is an age when the more advanced races are coming into closer contact with the less developed races, and the race-feeling is therefore intensified[.]"[11]

Progressive reformers believed that any social problem could be solved. As Judith Sealander observes, one of the most astonishing aspects of Progressives a century ago is their "relentless optimism"—"a fierce kind of optimism we now find peculiar."[12] Much of that optimism now looks like an imperial expectation that the "better class" of individuals, such as superior races and nations, should take on the responsibility of governing and uplifting inferior peoples. Yet Sealander has a point. Our charge of presumption can license a diminished sense of engagement with social problems that late nineteenth-century reformers felt entitled to fix.

On the other hand, contemporary critiques of corporate paternalism expose its uneasy blend of moral zeal, narcissistic grandiosity, and economic exploitation. Jane Addams wrote and spoke "A Modern Lear" in 1894, yet she couldn't get it published until 1912, in part because her challenge to George Pullman's paternalism was so sharp. For Addams, Pullman regulated his workers' lives and built workers' communities for narrowly commercial ends. He never considered gaining the workers' consent. Fundamental to such benevolence, Addams declares, is an "almost feudal" desire for gratitude, and a failure to see that industrial relationships are no longer personal or parental. Like Lear, Pullman was astounded and outraged to find his self-image vilified by his dependents in the Pullman Strike of 1894. When he died in 1897, his burial vault was fortified so it couldn't be blown up.[13]

Unlike Lear, Pullman combined paternalism with racism to expand his realm. The Pullman Palace Car combined luxurious efficiency with nostalgia for the Southern gentry ideal. As Sara Blair summarizes, from 1867 onward, Pullman cars featured only former slaves, and soon only former male slaves, as servants. The effect reconstructed white mastery in the midst of Reconstruction. Pullman paid black men to perform the faithful darky, so that white men would pay to indulge their resurgent paternalistic fantasies.[14] These plantation yearnings were compensatory as well as nostalgic. Racial othering, or race-ing, served to prop up male self-images of privileged white control as well as shaky class and gender hierarchies. Even Twain's *The Adventures of Huckleberry Finn* (1885) slides from Huck's dangerously democratic equality with Jim to Tom Sawyer's pointless paternalism, his presumptuous adventure of freeing a black man who is already free.

Today, when stories about paternalism appear in the *New York Times,* they usually refer to a thankfully vanished past or an "Orientalized" present. In the summer of 1999, for instance, a front-page story on East Asia's "struggle for democratic openness" focused on Thailand's tensions "as a bolder, better-educated middle class begins to rise up against the paternalistic order of the past."[15] In that same summer, a front-page Sunday *New York Times* story on honor in the Arab world quotes a young Egyptian journalist who recalled a moment in his high school biology class. After sketching the female reproductive system, the teacher pointed out the entrance to the vagina and said, "This is where the family honor lies!" Another front-page Sunday *New York Times* story, about Serbian rapes in Kosovo, highlighted the "lifelong shame to a woman and her family." Until the defeat of the Taliban regime in Afghanistan, almost every Western reporter emphasized its repression of women, and several stories about Pakistani immigrants to northern England featured families that hired people to kill sexually transgressive daughters. In the summer of 2002, newspaper stories emphasized brutal gang-rapes of daughters in Pakistan, or the killing of a Kurdish daughter in Sweden.[16]

These articles usually highlight the pressure on daughters in many preindustrial societies to embody the patriarchal honor of their families, while giving much less attention to their varied modes of agency and resistance. The stories' prominence in the *New York Times* also suggests the ongoing need of well-educated Americans to feel superior to "primitive" peoples, and to take pleasure in "before and after" stories of capitalist triumph. Perhaps such responses harbor our own paternalism. As Gayatri Spivak has suggested, white men like saving brown women from brown men.[17]

Daddy's Girls and Daddy's Boys

As with paternalism, the daddy's girl and the daddy's boy begin nestled in the family. In the late nineteenth century they turn into more paradoxical fictions, reflecting tensions in middle-class families. Parents often expected filial dependence, yet hoped that their sons would rise beyond their father's station. Daughters, too, should choose their own life paths, though much more constrained by traditions of family honor and status display.

I'm using "daddy's girls" and "daddy's boys" somewhat ahistorically, since these terms don't come into mainstream usage until the 1920s, after the word "daddy" gained national currency. I also focus primarily on the daddy's girl, whose infinite variety centers several chapters, since that motif most intimately articulates the changing social meanings of "father" as well as "daughter." From the 1870s onward, daddy's girl narratives proliferated in tandem with representations of the New Woman. Yet these daddy's girls, such as Laura Hawkins and Sister Carrie, are often upwardly mobile young women. In containing the dangers associated with young women's independence, the narratives also acknowledge the threat of career women, a new social category engendered by corporate capitalism and the rise of specialized professions.

By the early 1920s, the modern daddy's girl story had become comfortably marketable. After Harold Gray's Little Orphan Annie finds Daddy Warbucks, Shirley Temple stars in a series of films about spunky young girls who spar and bond with crusty fathers or grandfathers.[18] By 1934, Fitzgerald's *Tender Is the Night* juxtaposes Rosemary's starring role in a film called *Daddy's Girl* with Nicole's childhood abuse by her incestuous father. Those twinned aspects of the daddy's girl trope persist.

Daddy's girl and daddy's boy stories appealed to men not only because they exalt father-figures, but also because the stories also intimate men's tensions about workplace subservience or even failure. By helping a few Ragged Dicks or Sister Carries along, older men could feel like remasculinized protectors. In *A Connecticut Yankee in King Arthur's Court,* Hank Morgan uses Clarence to rise from his nineteenth-century position as an obscure factory superintendent in Connecticut to become "The Boss" of Arthurian England—"with my hand on the cock," as Hank puts it.[19] With a similar though more unconscious appeal, Booker T. Washington's fund-raising makes each Yankee donor feel like a big strong daddy whose hand "uplifts" the entire black race.

For middle-class white men who defined themselves ever more obsessively through their work, daddy's girl or daddy's boy narratives also provided a knowable self modeled on familiar norms and yearnings. They reawakened a nostalgia for themselves as ambitious young men on the make, while affirming their personal benevolence.[20] To plot the independent paths of young men and women on a fatherly grid made life seem more cozy and familiar. Conversely, these narratives provided young men and women with fantasies of autonomy, ambition, upward mobility, and an often theatrical recognition for one's abilities beyond parental and class restraints.

These narratives also intimate a more radical transformation of social value. As the daddy's girl started to look like a potential career woman, value began to float free of its base in patriarchal entitlements. From Adam Smith to Karl Marx, many economists have contrasted "use-value" and "surplus value." In chapter 1, I suggest that traditional use-value implies paternity or paternal control, manifested as artisan labor, property ownership, and the husband's domestic authority. During the antebellum period, when the United States was composed primarily of what Robert Wiebe has called island villages, social value presumed those small-scale norms for masculinity.[21] But corporate capitalism opened up a more fluidly gendered and contending diversity of possibilities, stimulated by subjectively uplifting fictions. Fictions of upward mobility paradoxically reinforced, yet undermined fatherhood's social centrality, by making paternalistic help a transient step toward young people's independence and success. Still more ironically, consumer fantasies of self-uplift through shopping also diversified value. Ultimately, I argue, value itself became an uplifting fiction, to enhance fantasies of aspiration.

Turn-of-the-century fiction absorbs and refracts these family and cultural tensions. The ubiquitous paternalism in various male authors' narrations reflects both a presumption of privileged position and a sense of depersonalization. We can see that tension in Theodore Dreiser's avuncular sentimentalities, Frank Norris's passionately Olympian condescensions, Henry James's paternalistic prefaces, or William Dean Howells's anxious sense of omniscient nobodyness, an outsider on the inside. Narrations by James, Kate Chopin, and Edith Wharton articulate the daughterly strains and costs of paternalism in a world where ladies were still not allowed to make nondomestic work central to their lives.

In the last decade or so, critics have complicated the cultural contexts for fiction after the Civil War, particularly for realism. Following Alan Tracht-enberg, Amy Kaplan has added imperialist romances to her previous argument that realism assuaged middle-class feelings of unreality. Brook Thomas has explored the intersections and disjunctions between realism and contract law. Nancy Glazener has argued that realism consolidated bourgeois class entitlements.[22] Paternalism needs to be added to that critical ferment.

Implausible Arguments

One of my more implausible arguments considers race-ing as a form of social shaming. After the Civil War, race-ing helped white people to manage the transformation of their lives from small-scale relations among family and neighbors to more diverse possibilities of interaction and mobility. In preindustrial patriarchal families, the sexually transgressive or violated daughter is a primary site of kinship shame and dishonor. During the early corporate era, the daughter remains a potential site of localized kinship shame. But she also represents the more ambivalently imagined potential of the independent New Woman, who rejects a family role as her primary self-identification.

Chapter 6, on giving and shaming, argues that shaming also expands in scale, from trying to define the daughter to trying to define whiteness. If the daughter's sexuality continues to signify family honor, race-ing African Americans helps to preserve the imagined superiority as well as the social control of white Americans, who faced burgeoning cultural diversity. Racist hierarchy blatantly prevents African Americans from achieving the kinds of upward mobility that would allow them to mix with "respectable" white people. It also protects a residual ideology of honor, previously dominant in localized family and village relationships, and now threatened by expansions of scale.

Yet race-ing functions as a collective rather than individual mode of social shaming. It situates white middle-class self-respect in an abstract category, incorporative whiteness, rather than in individual achievements or authority. In that respect, race-ing parallels managerial self-identification with the "firm." Racist hierarchy replicates as well as solaces middle-class men's felt loss of independence as they accept the hierarchical self-subordinations and categorizations required by corporate work.

My most implausible argument is that corporate capitalism progressively diminishes the functional importance of manhood. Several years ago, when I submitted an earlier version of "Narrating the Corporation" to *PMLA*, that essay concluded just as chapter 5 now does: "Manhood still bestrides the world like a colossus, but its feet are planted firmly in mid-air." The essay made it to the editorial board, until an incisively dismissive third reader's report said I was simply wrong, wrong, wrong. Corporate capitalism "did not destabilize patriarchy and gender hierarchies." Instead, "the tycoon, the corporate manager, the technological wizard, the financial speculator filled the historical vacuum" left by the corporate displacement of the eighteenth-century gentleman and the man of right reason. Manhood "reasserted itself" through "corporate/managerial authority, technical efficiency, technological knowledge and 'genius,' and the 'work-ethic,' Protestant or otherwise." Not until "the new ideological and economic conditions of post-modernity," abetted by "feminist and gay critiques," does manhood start to crumble. "Under modernity, manhood did just fine."

That's rather well put. Michael McKeon makes a similar argument for the reinvention of patriarchy in early capitalist England, and Stephen Frank's *Life with Father* argues that as nineteenth-century American fatherhood moves from patriarchal hierarchy to spousal partnership in the North, "patriarchal power became less personal and more institutional."[23] The usual thing to say is that though a variety of masculinities get contested, challenged, and shifted around, some version of masculinity is always dominant. Chapter 1 takes up that issue in more detail, by considering several reinvigorations of patriarchal modes.

Nevertheless, despite the many ways that manhood is still revered in the United States, I hold to my argument that corporate work ultimately undermines hierarchies of gender, class, and race. In transforming the nature of work, corporate capitalism and the allied professions potentially mandate a lessening of gender as a prescriptive channeling for entry and advancement in the workplace. The mental and decision-making skills demanded by managerial or professional work don't require the categories of gender, race, and class. In theory, the greatest profits should come from employing the most talented managers and experts in every group, not from looking to only one group of white middle-class males. Moreover, the logic of corporate expansion mandates marketing products and services to increasingly diverse customers.

So why is it that my *PMLA* reader is right, at least in the short term? Why have the upper echelons of U.S. corporations remained a nearly exclusive enclave of waspily white male privilege and power? One answer lies in the adaptability as well as the tenacious hold of paternalistic practices. From the late 1860s onward, as chapter 5 details, writers registered unease about the corporate erosion of manhood. Corporate paternalism became a major strategy for preserving white male entitlements. Although industrial capitalism offered many low-level workplace opportunities drawing young women away from the home, paternalistic controls forced many, perhaps most of these women to lose their jobs when they married, especially if they were white. The belief that men should be providers and protectors while "their" women should be wives and mothers held sway into the 1970s and beyond. Yet corporate capitalism ambivalently welcomed more and more women, immigrants, and African Americans as employees, if only because they could be paid less than white men.

More radically, the corporate transformation shifted the locus of social value from individual male production to diverse varieties of consumer subject positions, implicitly identified as female. From 1880 to 1920, many corporations shifted their emphasis from production, imagined as male, to service, imagined as female.[24] These transformations made white male paternalism a defensive, transitional cultural style to manage a profound cultural change, from what James Livingston calls the age of necessity to the first age of surplus. Manhood's appeal became more compensatory than functional. By the 1920s, traditional images of manly independence, patriarchal authority, and physical prowess were being outsourced to a variety of cultural formations, such as spectator sports or the "den" in the modern home.[25] Even the new norm of manly providing, as Andrea Tone points out in *The Business of Benevolence,* functioned as a fall-back position to remasculinize men at home, while they grudgingly adapted to a workplace that minimized their independence and individual authority.[26]

Only in the last decade or so has corporate culture begun to give women, African Americans, and members of other excluded or marginalized groups access to power, responsibility, and serious money. For the *PMLA* reader, the causes for that shift should be sought outside corporate culture. Yet the potential loss of white male privilege in new patterns of self-subordination, diversity, and human mixing has been inherent in corporate work from the beginning. It's a measure of how threatened white men felt about that heterogeneous prospect that the corporation as paternalistic white male enclave has persisted for so long.

Promptings

My arguments have been prompted by two ideas and several discontents. Over a decade ago, a basic question occurred to me: why is it that upward mobility structures so few American narratives before the Civil War, and so many afterward? After the Civil War a few writers even dare to dramatize young middle-class women who gain upward mobility through wage-earning work rather than marriage. In Twain and Warner's *The Gilded Age* (1873), Laura Hawkins rises from orphanhood to become a Washington power broker, while Ruth Bolton tries to become a doctor until she sees a black man's corpse in the laboratory and slowly shifts her sights toward marriage. In Dreiser's *Sister Carrie* (1900), Carrie Meeber rises from her rural Indiana family beginnings not because of her lovers but because of her career as an actress. And in Willa Cather's *O Pioneers!* (1913), Alexandra Bergson's extraordinary success in managing the family farm makes her what Howard Horwitz has called the first wholly admirable capitalist in American fiction.[27]

These are intriguing social as well as narrative changes, I thought, but upward mobility has been done again and again. Then came my second idea, when I realized that Laura Hawkins, Carrie Meeber, and Alexandra Bergson are all presented as daddy's girls.

The aha! moment for me came with *Sister Carrie*. Carrie rises with less narrative punishment than Twain and Warner deal out, partly because she performs daddy's girl roles on stage with an arousing mixture of dependence and insouciance, and partly because she leaves her lovers instead of killing them. Yet the narrative relentlessly punishes Hurstwood, who turns to Carrie not only because of his wife's indifference to him, but more immediately because he senses his growing separation from his daughter. "There was a time when he had been considerably enamored of his Jessica, especially when he was younger and more confined in his success. Now, however, in her seventeenth year, Jessica had developed a certain amount of reserve and independence which was not inviting to the richest form of parental devotion" (83).[28]

Dreiser's language is marvelously charged with narcissistic ironies. To have been "considerably enamored" seems almost oxymoronic, as if Hurstwood had been an aging suitor who kept his passion in the "reserve" he attributes to Jessica. Whether father or suitor, he seems rather ponderous and self-absorbed. More subtly, the passage implies that his fatherly love used to compensate for his feelings of being "confined in his success." Now, when Hurstwood sees his own "certain amount of reserve and independence" mirrored in his seventeen-year-old daughter, he turns to an exaggerated language of paternalism to shore himself up. Yet musing that Jessica's independence "was not inviting to the richest form of parental devotion" seems petulant as well as pretentious. That formulation also seems contradictory, since Hurstwood's devotion requires his daughter's initiative rather than his own. Moreover, her initiative has to be restricted to displays of submissiveness and need.

In the passage's most subtle irony, Hurstwood's nostalgia for his "richest" period of parenting inflates Jessica's "certain amount," even as he mourns for the implicit reduction of his fatherly self-image to the money he can provide. The meditation exposes how profoundly Hurstwood's paternalistic self-construction depends on preserving his daughter's dependence—or the dependence of someone like his daughter. A little later, after their first seductive carriage ride, Hurstwood says to Carrie, "You're my own girl aren't you?" (126). Overtly, his "my own" announces that he has bested Drouet. Covertly, "girl" implies that he has found Jessica's replacement. By letting her head drop onto his shoulder, Carrie accepts her new daughterly dependence. By not answering his question, she keeps her own independence in reserve.

More simply, men such as Hurstwood turn to daddy's girl fantasies when their sense of themselves as adored and adoring fathers starts to run up against the reality of maturing daughters heading out the family door. Daddy's girl fantasies compensate for midlife male anxieties about powerlessness, most intimately dramatized as the King Lear scenario: aging men's fears of formerly dependent daughters' unresponsiveness or uncontrollability. At the same time, as Lynda Zwinger has emphasized, the daddy's girl plot articulates a sentimental form of women's patriarchally conditioned desires.[29] For both fathers and daughters, the narrative reflects tensions between dependence and independence. These tensions signal the sense of limitation, unmanliness, and sometimes failure among middle-class white men in bureaucratic hierarchies, as well as the frustrations and desires of young women seeking options beyond the home.

Once I saw that possibility, a variety of texts and passages invited a broader meditation on paternalism. Just to cite one: near the beginning of Edith Wharton's *Summer,* Lawyer Royall ineptly attempts to solace himself for his sense of failure in the world beyond North Dormer by propositioning his young ward, whom he has paternalistically named "Charity" after his own charity. At the end, after Charity has agreed to marry him, he gives her two twenty-dollar bills and says, "I want you to beat 'em all hollow."[30] The hollowness, the charity, and the desire to dominate are all his, not hers. And it's the "hollow" that reverberates.

Several intellectual discontents have also helped to prompt this book. During the past decade I've been bothered by an absence at national MLA and American Studies conferences. There are many panels about border crossings, hybridities, regional and ethnic constructions of subjectivity, the intersections of literature and popular culture, and the transgressive interplay of desires. What's missing is the metropolitan center for all these energies: not an urban place, but rather corporate capitalism, which generates mobilities, consumer desires, social hierarchies and heterogeneities, desires for upward mobility, and nondomestic options for middle-class women. Corporate capitalism also funds and entitles the professional-managerial class in which we academics all work and live.

So why aren't more of us writing about literature and corporate capitalism? One reason is very simple: many of us went into literature so we wouldn't have to go into business. So who wants to write about business? That's a false binary, of course. Yet if critics such as Alan Trachtenberg, Walter Benn Michaels, Mark Seltzer, Martha Banta, Brook Thomas, and Cecilia Tichi have begun to collapse that binary, cultural studies critics have often reinforced it.

A second reason is that current critical frameworks tend to block our perception of the complexity and the progressive aspects of corporate capitalist dynamics. Following Fredric Jameson, those who invoke the post-Marxist trinity of alienation, reification, and commodification present "late capitalism" as if a funeral were in the offing. Critics on the left avidly imagine theoretical revolutions against global capitalism. Other critics who focus on desire, whether sexual or consumerist, tend to minimize or miss the centrality of work as a structuring site of desire in modern middle-class lives. A few recent critics such as Philip Fisher, Christopher Newfield, and Evan Watkins have been addressing these issues, and several historians of business, notably Angel Kwolek-Folland, Andrea Tone, and Clark Davis, have highlighted gender and race issues in studies of corporate organizations. For most of us, however, work beyond the academy remains invisible. Perhaps that's because all we knew of our fathers' work, and for a younger generation our mothers' too, is that they brought home money and looked tired.

A third reason is that many if not most of us still hold on to a small crafts or artisan ideal that social value inheres in individual labor and production. Again, there may be a simple reason for that: in the humanities, academics tend to work alone. Though situated in bureaucratic institutions, those of us with tenure-track positions have a considerable degree of independent control over our teaching and our writing. Paradoxically, our privileged individualism may make us more responsive to the neo-Marxist valuing of producerist or labor-oriented models of social value. Yet that perspective blocks awareness of the appeal of corporate work, which is collaborative and collective. From Olivier Zunz to Clark Davis, historians of corporate capitalism have emphasized the choices and trade-offs inherent in corporate work, especially managerial work. Though irked at being commanded by a hierarchy of bosses, managers relish being part of a group beyond themselves, a large, important organization with a useful social mission. How many academics can say the same about our writing?

This book differs from prevailing modes of scholarship in at least three ways. First, most historians continue to associate paternalism with the social functions of honor in antebellum South or preindustrial societies.[31] I argue that corporate culture writes the gentry South into the national imaginary, with racial as well as literary consequences. Second, this book continues my indebted resistance to the strand of feminism that highlights the persistence and reinvention of patriarchy. Third, an issue I've already touched on, the current emphasis in queer theory and postcolonial theory on desire, hybridities, and border crossings makes corporate capitalism the undiscovered center of cultural studies. To highlight the play of eroticisms misses the constriction of male middle-class desire—and now many women's desires as well—to a drive for upward mobility in workplace hierarchies. Until recently, that drive has been uniquely intense in the United States. More broadly, to resurrect an audacious observation by Philip Fisher over a decade ago, multiculturalism may be our contemporary form of regionalism.[32] There's a germ of usefulness in that problematic claim, since corporate capitalism both regulates and stimulates our circulating social energies.

Finally, several chapters draw on James Livingston's *Pragmatism and the Political Economy of Cultural Revolution* (1994). Among his many intriguing arguments, Livingston suggests that the figure of the consumerist New Woman supplants class-based formations of the laborer as an allegorical representation of national capitalist dynamics. I try to complicate and qualify that argument by claiming that diversely self-uplifting subjectivities supplant traditional associations of social value with patriarchy and property owner-ship as well as productive labor. Paradoxically, as explored in chapter 7, Maggie Verver becomes more modern than Charlotte Stant, the New Wom-an in James's *The Golden Bowl,* or than Alexandra Bergson in Cather's *O Pioneers!,* because Maggie exposes the arbitrary construction and contin-gency of value in the first age of surplus rather than necessity.

It wasn't just value that started to look less useful and more created. To twist Marx's aphorism, the grounds of value in production, paternity, and ownership of landed property also began to melt into air. And, despite Marx's followers, that's not a bad thing.

1 Middle-Class Fatherhood and the Transformation of Work

In the 1880s, the U.S. federal government acted as "the Great Father" to guide, push, and coerce Native Americans into owning property independently. Federal officials and humanitarian reformers shared a paternalistic belief that owning property would encourage the Indians' competitive individualism and diminish their tribal loyalties. At the same time, in an enormous cultural irony, thousands of white men abandoned their independence to join collectively owned corporations. This chapter traces some of the tensions between resurgent patriarchal rhetorics and the ambivalence of white middle-class men about hierarchically organized work.

The government's attempt to reconstruct Native American subjectivities egregiously failed, in part because bureaucratic paternalism reduced Indians to childlike wards rather than treating them as entrepreneurial equals. The corporate reconstruction of middle-class white men's subjectivities partially succeeded, in part because managerial employees could affiliate themselves with the corporation's collective force. Paternalism became so pervasive not only because it imposed discipline on immigrant and lower-class workers, but also because it mediated middle-class male tensions among subordination, loyalty, and individual responsibility. Whether through personal mentoring or vicarious identification with a firm, practicing paternalism helped to restore a white-collar worker's knowable self. It provided a comfortably empowered self-image based on traditional ideals of benevolent authority and civic responsibility. Yet paternalism's social entitlements ultimately reflected a man's institutional position in the workplace, not his fatherly control at home.

The Dawes Act

In the mid-1880s, Senator Henry Dawes of Massachusetts visited what he considered the "Five Civilized Tribes," the Cherokee, Creek, Choctaw,

Chickasaw, and Seminole Indians. In one of his encounters, the Senator reported, "The head chief told us that there was not a family in that whole nation that had not a home of its own. There was not a pauper in that nation, and the nation did not owe a dollar. It built its own capital and it built its own school and its hospitals." Nevertheless, Dawes concluded, "the defect of the system was apparent. They have not got as far as they can go because they own their land in common, and under that [system] there is no enterprise to make your home any better than that of your neighbors. There is no selfishness, which is at the bottom of civilization."[1]

Therefore the Dawes Severalty or Allotment Act of 1887 imposed a traditional U.S. model of property ownership to force Indians toward competition. It divided tribal land into 160-acre parcels for each head of the family, or eighty acres to each single adult. As the bill said, "Once an Indian had received his allotment, he would become a citizen of the United States." The Dawes Act also drastically reduced the amount of tribally owned land, opened reservations to homesteading, and dissolved Indian tribes as legal entities. The government wanted to reinforce individuality, not groups. Soon the U.S. government changed the land division specifications to give equal allotments for all adult tribe members, female as well as male, and to establish a national school system for the Indians. As Francis Prucha notes in his two-volume history, *The Great Father,* no longer did the U.S. government consider Indians "as a relatively few tribal units, but as thousands upon thousands of individual wards of the federal government."[2]

Reformers as well as land-grabbers enthusiastically supported this flagrantly paternalistic imposition. So did some Indians, perhaps out of desperation. In response to a second 1887 Dawes bill dividing the Great Sioux Reserve, 4,463 of the 5,678 eligible Sioux voters approved the measure, opposing their own chiefs, in part because the alternatives were so much worse.[3] Among the lesser ironies of the Dawes Act, the bill made no provision for children yet unborn, because Senator Dawes thought the race would die out. As Prucha concludes, the Dawes Act exacerbated what the reservation system had already established. As Indians "now became in fact the wards and dependents of a paternal government . . . the bureaucracy of the Indian Service dominated every aspect of the Indians' lives." Finally, in 1934, the Dawes Act was repealed.[4]

The government's expanded role as "Great Father" is an extreme instance of what Stephen Frank has called the "relocation" of patriarchy outside the home, in medical, legal, and other institutions.[5] The phrase makes the president a metonym for awe-inspiring governmental power. In 1804 Lewis and Clark used "The Great Father" to refer to the U.S. president. John Marshall invoked the phrase in his 1831 Supreme Court ruling restricting Indian sovereignty to that of "domestic dependent nations." Though Marshall's ruling supported the Cherokee Nation's case against Georgia, the Great Father of the moment, President Andrew Jackson, contemptuously and unconstitutionally refused to enforce it.[6] The phrase soon extended beyond the President to legitimate a federal paternalism that treated Indians as children. As Secretary of the Interior Carl Schurz wrote in an 1881 article for the *North American Review,* the Indian "is overcome by a feeling of helplessness, and he naturally looks to the 'GREAT FATHER' to take him by the hand and guide him on. . . . That guiding hand . . . can only be that of the government which the Indian is accustomed to regard as a sort of omnipotence on earth."[7] Having inflated their power to near godlike proportions, government officials and reformers imagined Indians as childlike dependents who somehow could grow into independent strivers by simply owning property.

Dawes' earlier report displays a more subtle contradiction. When President Grover Cleveland signed the Dawes Act, he noted that the amount to be allotted "reflected the strong tradition of a quarter-section homestead for the yeoman farmer." Yet the language of Dawes' report presumes that the ideal male self in the United States isn't a yeoman farmer; rather, he's a competitor for upward mobility. Equating "selfishness" with "enterprise," Dawes declares that enterprise begins with the desire not just to improve your home but "to make your home . . . better than that of your neighbors." By implication, the drive to rise beyond one's present social station structures civilized male subjectivity. If the desire to be "better than" grounds the individuality that Indians should aspire to, "home" becomes a cozy patriarchal metonym for using superior domestic property to display competitive triumph at work. The definition seems unrealistic as well as contradictory, since for those advancing beyond their neighbors, a change of address seems more likely than a fancier parlor. Dawes's symptomatic, prescriptive definition of male subjectivity as the desire for upward mobility becomes an animating paradox within the more welcoming American ideals of democracy, equality, and citizenship.

The Great Father?

The Great Father became an exportable imperial posture, available for colonizing work in the Philippines, or for missionary work in Africa.[8] In the United States, however, the pressure for upward mobility at work was taking its toll on middle-class fatherhood. As one result, the image of the family patriarch took on dated, Old Testament connotations. In *Innocents Abroad* (1869), Mark Twain mocked the Middle Eastern cultures that "still live as their fathers live . . . in the same, quaint, patriarchal way[.]" Symptomatically, starting with William McKinley in 1896, U.S. presidents lost their beards.[9]

Conventional expectations for white middle-class children still reflected enduring presumptions that the father should control family property, sons should be primary heirs, and daughters should be "given away" in marriage. But money and workplace hierarchy were becoming more important than landed property and paternity for defining a middle-class white man's sense of social worth. At work, landed property had become another form of capital, useful for enhancing one's credit—that is, if credit didn't make a man feel feminized.[10] At home, though fathering styles have always been as various as fathers, the normative middle-class man's role was shifting from disciplinarian to provider.

The corporate transformation of work also undermined the rhetoric of male independence. While the federal government induced or coerced Indians to become "civilized" through owning property and competing with their neighbors, corporate work required explicit self-subordination, often experienced by middle-class men as feminization. As Angel Kwolek-Folland emphasizes, corporations restored a mystique of patriarchy partly by making male managers superior to female clerical workers. Nevertheless, a middle-class man's position at "the office," rather than in the home or community, became the primary signifier for his social status.

By the 1920s, as Kwolek-Folland notes, "one fourth of the male laboring population" were white-collar workers.[11] That precipitous transformation of middle-class work established new norms of efficiency, rationality, and specialized expertise. The transformation also created an impasse between personal self-subordination and national images of collective patriarchy, whether governmental or corporate. It's no accident that so many corporate executives took to identifying their first names impersonally, using their initials rather than their first names. By implication, their individuality should be absorbed in the company's power and authority.

A new workplace abstraction acts as a magnet for men's desires and identities: "the Firm." Yet the firm differs from "the Great Father" in being depersonalized and collective. The term manifests and stabilizes the power of pooled capital. But capital is a different kind of property, fluid rather than tangible. Its power lies in its potential exchangeability, not in the intrinsic material value of actual money. Though a company may incorporate many buildings, machines, and employees, it measures whether it is "better than your neighbors" by calculating its profits and convertible assets, not by displaying its properties and personnel.

The firm, then, is a metonym with a difference, and the difference undermines previously individuated signifiers of manhood. A manager's productivity within the firm usually remains invisible to outsiders, and even to his own family. A manager's corporate position, more than his domestic or civic authority, signals his cultural status. A manager's property ownership is a by-product of his corporate salary. In effect, for white-collar corporate workers and specialized professionals, the traditional metonyms for manhood were localized, or even quarantined.

The growing gap between patriarchal rhetoric and post-patriarchal diversities of manly images and fathering styles had been growing since the birth of the Republic, except perhaps in the South. By the end of the nineteenth century, the disjunction between national rhetoric and middle-class practices emerges in a great many cultural instances, great and small. When Lydia Maria Child published her well-known Thanksgiving song, "Over the River and Through the Woods" in 1844, her next line originally read, "To grandfather's house we go." Subsequent generations of schoolchildren sang, and still sing, "To grandmother's house . . ." Another seemingly small instance: in 1872, Ward McAllister organized the first of his annual "Patriarch" balls for the elite families of New York City. As Blanche Wiesen Cook tells the story, twenty-five prominent men were each asked to invite four ladies and five gentleman to make up the 250 members of the Knickerbocker Society. The label and display of patriarchal power quickly yielded to "The 400," a name flaunting the capacity of Mrs. William Astor's ballroom.[12]

The new cultural prominence of Santa Claus as a distant, loving, gift-giving workaholic also signals the decline of patriarchal control as a domestic norm. In Stephen Frank's cogent analysis, Santa Claus becomes

> a consummate father figure, the protector and rescuer of children, laden with toys and treats. A protean figure (successful factory owner, philanthropist, and secular saint), Santa Claus absorbed the dual aspects of modern fatherhood. Demanding goodness but seldom chastising children, he was the embodiment of nurturant male love, an ideal Victorian parent. At the same time, he reflected the work-centered life of American fathers, a man whose business . . . seemed much more important than his own home life.[13]

The hugely popular 1897 newspaper editorial, "Yes Virginia, There Is a Santa Claus," contrasts the eight-year-old daughter's imaginative belief in Santa Claus with those who reflect "the skepticism of a skeptical age." "Papa," who has told her, "'If you see it in "The Sun," it's so[,]'" becomes the primary skeptical foil. "You might get your papa to hire men to watch in all the chimnies [sic] to catch Santa Claus on Christmas Eve," but not even "the united strength of all the strongest men that ever lived" could tear apart the "veil" covering "the unseen world[,]" the "supernatural" reality of "childlike faith[.]" Though Virginia O'Hanlon's quickly maturing friends say Santa doesn't exist, and though rational Papa can't trust anything that's not visible or in the newspaper, the enduring child-like spirit knows that "in all the world there is nothing else real and abiding."[14] Santa Claus wins, Papa loses, perhaps loses twice, since Papa's delegation of authority advertises the *New York Sun* as more trustworthy than himself.

In an 1862 letter to T. W. Higginson, Emily Dickinson writes more ambiguously about fatherhood. After noting that "My Mother does not care for thought—and Father, too busy with his Briefs—to notice what we do[,]" she declares, "They are religious—except me—and address an Eclipse, every morning—whom they call their 'Father.'"[15] Her joke, of course, refers to the family's morning recitation of the Lord's Prayer. Yet the joke has a double edge. If this Great Father's eclipse is temporary, the possibility of God's reappearance undercuts her own skepticism, or the blinders of her already skeptical age. If permanent, the disappearance of the ultimate father mockingly extends the remoteness of her own father to its vanishing point.

In literature, the marginal male provider becomes a peripheral staple of James's and Wharton's upper-class fictions. Mr. Bart, Lily's father in Wharton's *The House of Mirth* (1905), comes into view only when he goes bankrupt. More ominously, fathers who remain present and dominant in the home become dangerous. In England, as Claudia Nelson's *Invisible Men* argues, middle-class men were expected to be invisible providers, and stories of incestuous working-class fathers functioned as cautionary tales to keep respectable men at work rather than trying to meddle with the child rearing.[16] Yet English nineteenth-century fiction dramatizes the ongoing struggles of several caring fathers or father-figures who raise children by themselves, notably Anthony Trollope's *Dr. Thorne* (1858) and George Eliot's *Silas Marner* (1861). Conversely, in *Dombey and Son* (1848), Charles Dickens portrays Dombey as a widowed husband and father whose heartless distance from his children nearly destroys him.

I'm not aware of any analogues to Dr. Thorne or Silas Marner in American fiction during the early corporate era, except perhaps for Oliver Wendell Holmes's *Elsie Venner* (1861), where the father "could influence, but not govern" his wild witch-child.[17] A brief introductory interlude in Lydia Maria Child's *A Romance of the Republic* (1867) presents a white Southern father benignly raising his two mulatto daughters on his plantation. But he suddenly dies, leaving them unfree. Much more typically, fathers who try to raise their children by themselves, either by patriarchal discipline or more nurturing attentiveness, become dangerous or degenerate, as in Nathaniel Hawthorne's "Rappaccini's Daughter" (1844). It's telling, for instance, that in James's *The Portrait of a Lady* (1881), when Madame Merle first tells Isabel about Osmond and his " 'little girl' " of sixteen, she says: "He's devoted to her, and if it were a career to be an excellent father he would be very distinguished. But I am afraid that is no better than the snuff-boxes; perhaps not even so good. Tell me what they do in America . . ."[18] Clearly readers, and Isabel too, should be on guard. A man who claims distinction through leisured fathering rather than work is bad news.

More sympathetically, in Wharton's *The Custom of the Country* (1913), one measure of gentlemanly Ralph Marvell's lack of manly force is that he cares much more for his son than his wife does. This inversion of the "natural" domestic order reflects Undine's appropriation of traditionally masculine entrepreneurial energy for her own social advancement. Similarly, in Fitzgerald's *Tender Is the Night* (1934), when Dick Diver starts to pay more and more attention to his two children, that's a sign of his deterioration. As his wife Nicole thinks, Dick seeks his children "not protectively but for protection" against his increasingly uncontrollable desires, which can't quite fend off his awareness of his fading powers.[19]

More oppressively patriarchal fathers lose control of their children, or become hapless failures. In James's *Washington Square* (1881), clever Dr. Sloper tries to control his unclever daughter's affections, but fails to understand or love her except as she conforms to his expectations. In Frank Norris's *McTeague* (1899), Mr. Sieppe looks merely comic as he barks his wrong-headed orders to his family. In Stephen Crane's *The Monster* (also 1899), Dr. Trescott's complacent paternal control leads only to his final helpless contemplation of fifteen empty teacups. Most tellingly, in *The Adventures of Huckleberry Finn* (1885), Pap's rage against his son because Huck has outstripped him in learning signals a pervasive cultural shift in father-son expectations. Twain knows that middle-class readers will expect a son to try to advance beyond his father's station, not dutifully follow the father's calling. Pap's rage represents the silliness of an outmoded patriarchal era. Moreover, all these fathers fail. They become almost as helpless as M. Nioche in James's *The American* (1877), who throws up his hands and lets his daughter market her body for upward mobility.

Four Etymologies: Daddy, Businessman, Corporation, the Firm

According to the Oxford English Dictionary (O.E.D.) and various dictionaries of slang, "Daddy" traditionally is a word spoken by a baby, or a very young child, as in the nursery rhyme,

> Bye Baby bunting,
> Daddy's gone a-hunting
> Gone to get a rabbit skin
> To wrap the baby bunting in.

By the late eighteenth century, adolescents and younger adults in the United States sometimes used "daddy" to express familiarity or affection for an elderly man, especially an older black man. During the mid- to late-nineteenth century, some adolescents appropriated the term to refer to their fathers with more intimacy and less formal deference. The term also took on some nonfamily associations, oscillating between respect and contempt. An 1871 issue of *Harper's,* for instance, defines "daddyism" as "respect for distinguished men," but a 1902 usage defines it as a recent word for "slavish adulation of high parentage or noble birth."[20] By the early part of the twentieth century, "daddy" could also connote an older man with money and a younger mistress, as in "Sugar Daddy." The daddy as older lover, originally a term from African American jazz culture, was ambiguously immortalized in Cole Porter's 1938 song, "My Heart Belongs to Daddy."

These shifting definitions register the change in the norms for fatherhood from disciplining and distance to more companionable intimacy. Visiting Europeans were appalled at the seemingly egalitarian comradeship between American fathers and their sons, even in antebellum times.[21] Although the social reality was more various and often authoritarian, the trend continued. As my epigraph to the introduction notes, near the start of *The Young Immigrants* (1920), Ring Lardner nicely encapsulates the impasse between a father's old-fashioned gruffness and a son's modern familiarity: "'Are you lost, daddy?' I asked tenderly. 'Shut up,' he explained."[22] The second line has become famous. In context, the son's patronizing solicitude undermines the father's traditional shut-upness.

In the 1820s, "businessman" meant a man who was exceptionally busy.[23] That valuing reflects a denigration of work by provincial gentry. Only in the 1780s, Gordon Wood has argued, does the United States begin its shift from manifesting high status through the display of leisure to manifesting respectability through the work ethic, since goods signifying gentility became available in substantial quantities for "the middling sort" to buy. For the first time in history, hard work paid off in upscale emulation, and the first substantial capital surpluses were born.[24]

In 1840, Edgar Allan Poe satirizes the speculations of "The Business Man," who finally succeeds by raising cats so that he can sell their tails. By the 1880s, "business man" had "turned into a generic term" in financial chronicles, Sven Beckert notes, much as "capitalist" replaced "merchant." In 1893, William Dean Howell's "The Man of Letters as a Man of Business" tries to bring authors into that expanding circle. Howells still writes "business man" as two words. Expanding the term still further, William Jennings Bryan's "Cross of Gold" speech at the 1896 Democratic Convention in Chicago affirms that the "broader class of business men" should include not only corporate executives, but also wage laborers, country attorneys, small merchants, farmers, and miners—in short, anyone who works.[25] Soon "businessman" became a normative label, and the United States seemed the busiest culture in the world. In the early 1930s, Antonio Gramsci's prison diaries record his astonished admiration that American millionaires don't retire to live a life of leisure, as any rich European man would do.[26]

As the eighteenth-century ideal of the landed gentleman yielded to the new American ideal of the hard-driving businessman, work became all-absorbing for many middle-class men. In *A Modern Instance* (1882), Howells nicely catches the new spirit of masterly but disengaged fatherhood: "A man is master in his own house generally through the exercise of a certain degree of brutality, but Squire Gaylord maintained his predominance by an enlightened absenteeism. No man living always at home was ever so little under his own roof." Instead, after he bought a large house, "he thenceforth made his home in the little detached office."[27] The convergence of "home" with "office" seemingly doesn't affect his quasi-patriarchal mastery of the household, until the daughter that he dotes on starts to exercise her own will.

Toward the end of *Up from Slavery* (1901), Booker T. Washington notes with pride that for nineteen years he never took a vacation. Earlier, he mentions in passing that his first two wives worked themselves to death for the success of his Tuskegee Institute. Washington's workplace practices exaggerate the workaholic zeal as well as the paternalism of white northern businessmen. In George Lorimer's *Old Gorgon Graham* (1904), a collection of fictionalized letters from a Chicago businessman to his son, the father notes proudly that he works ten hours a day, six days a week, to run his pork-packing firm of 10,000 men.[28] In that respect, when James portrays Christopher Newman, Mr. Touchett, and Adam Verver as American businessmen who retire to develop their tastes as leisured gentlemen, he is being nostalgic as well as polemical.

Two other related words become transformed during this period: the corporation and the firm. The word "corporation" comes from the Latin "corporare," to embody. Paradoxically, the rise of corporate capitalism comes from the corporation's disembodiment. Before the mid-eighteenth century, "corporation" referred primarily to municipal authorities, with a broader signification of any group of persons legally authorized to act as a single individual. The word also evoked a large or "corpulent" human body. In the *Dartmouth College v. Woodward* case of 1819, Chief Justice John Marshall incisively shifted the matrix by defining the corporation as an artificial person, created only in law. By 1886, when the Supreme Court applied several aspects of the Fourteenth Amendment to corporations, constitutional law was fine-tuning the similarities and differences between these artificial persons and human persons.[29]

By 1904, according to one business history, "corporations accounted for three-quarters of all of America's industrial production[.]"[30] The key to their economic dominance was that actual, embodied persons incurred only limited liability for their incorporated risks. Ambrose Bierce memorably defines the term in his *Devil's Dictionary:* "Corporation, *n.* An ingenious device for obtaining individual profit without individual responsibility."[31] Corporate paternalism, one could say, is daddying with limited liability.

A paternalistic ideal of benevolence played at least a peripheral role in Marshall's decision. As Daniel Webster successfully argued, the Supreme Court should affirm the immunity of incorporated charitable institutions so that rich men would continue to act as benefactors. Slowly but inexorably, especially in the Northeast, state and federal courts invoked the benefits of unrestricted philanthropy to free corporate management of property from direct public constraints. One of the primary justifications for enabling corporations to act as individuals, the Supreme Court ruled in the 1830s, was to ensure corporate freedom to do charitable acts.

Most legal historians now hold that property rights, not philanthropy, provided the primary impetus for these and other nineteenth-century court decisions. Corporate personhood became a convenient legal fiction that enables courts to protect the property rights of actual individuals.[32] Nonetheless, courts protected corporations in part because development-minded judges thought corporate enterprises provided significant contributions to the commonweal, including charity. Corporate rhetoric swiftly appropriated conventions of paternalistic benevolence to justify their civic usefulness and improve their moral image. Although the rise of the large-scale corporation depended on employing "individuals socialized to modes of dependable autonomy and internal control[,]" as Peter Dobkin Hall has said, its social justification equally depended on the paradox that groups of men, aggressively competing with each other and with rival firms, should foster collectively benevolent behavior.[33]

Similarly, though surprisingly unstudied, the word "firm" comes from a Latin word for an authorizing signature. For over a century, "the firm" has been the primary metonym for corporate power and stability. Yet until the mid-eighteenth century, according to the O.E.D., "firm" was interchangeable with "name," a signature affixed to an aristocrat's orders or a general's commands. Slowly it shifted to the "style" or name under which the business of a commercial house is transacted, or simply a multiple partnership or commercial house. By the mid-nineteenth century the word evoked an image of collective invulnerability to the risks and instabilities inherent in any capitalist enterprise. The term plays a prominent role in Dickens's mid-century English novel, *Dombey and Son,* and by the end of the century it was beginning to be featured in American magazine titles.

As with the corporation, the firm's legitimacy as well as power depend on a linguistic paradox that shifts identity, authority, and vulnerability from personal bodies, subjectivities, and properties to the group management of shared capital. Both words took on the impersonal personhood that legally enabled the rise of corporate capitalism. By the end of the nineteenth century, large firms and corporations could act as single individuals, incorporating many names, signatures, and bodies into one disembodied signature-body of unshakably manly firmness.

The most obvious critical move here would be to analyze the firm as a symbolic imaginary for the phallus. Yet the phallus can't quite stand as a metonym for the firm's social meaning, because the firm is so conspicuously impersonal and collective. Moreover, firms can go bankrupt. Most important, the term's impersonality manifests physical absence as much as symbolic phallic presence, since firm-ness depends on the availability of large amounts of capital, not bodies or synecdochic body parts. As a badge of identity—"what firm do you work for?"—the label gives each employee reflected authority and status in both public and private spheres. But the employees' individual labors have little or no visibility in either sphere. Corporate work remains mysterious except within the firm.

Upward Mobility and Class

Before the 1860s, aside from a few autobiographies and slave narratives, upward mobility takes a distant back seat to lateral mobility as a plotting device in American narratives. The Benjamin Franklin motif of rising from low to high social station has surprisingly little circulation in antebellum fiction written by white males, except as a spiritual journey. For Hawthorne's Hester Prynne, James Fenimore Cooper's Natty Bumppo, Harriet Beecher Stowe's Uncle Tom, Melville's Tommo and Ishmael and Ahab, Poe's Arthur Gordon Pym, Whitman's persona in "Song of Myself," and a host of less familiar protagonists, moving from place to place seems incidental, in several senses. Some characters, such as Hester Prynne or Henry David Thoreau's persona in *Walden,* build their complex individuality in relation to one locale, with and against the grain of their small community. From 1820 to 1850 a good many writers dramatize outward mobility to some sort of frontier, whether in Cooper's Leatherstocking series and Melville's *Typee* or in travel narratives by Caroline Kirkland, Richard Henry Dana, Margaret Fuller, and Francis Parkman. Of all the antebellum narratives by white writers, only Fanny Fern's 1855 novel *Ruth Hall* tells a jaunty story of a resourceful and witty woman's rise from poverty to fame through her writing. Augusta Jane Evans's *Beulah* (1859) tells a more ambivalent saga of a southern woman who rises to triumph as a writer, then suddenly reverts to wifely submission.[34]

Moreover, when major writers such as Stowe, Emerson, Thoreau, Whitman, and even Melville appropriate slavery as a metaphor for spiritual conformity, they narrate freedom as a moral expansion of the self—or immoral expansion, for Melville's Pierre. These narratives ignore the upward mobility so central to slave narratives. For white Northern writers, freedom connotes a lateral or inward mobility that enables them to challenge, escape, or transcend social norms. For African Americans such as Harriet Jacobs and Frederick Douglass, freedom means not only escape from enslavement, but also access to respect, dignity, and social entitlement. Where narratives by former slaves expose the intimate links between freedom, respectability, and high-class status, white-authored narratives tend to present class hierarchies as peripheral givens or constraints.

Perhaps that came naturally to the privileged writers who constituted New England literary culture. For those born to some measure of social entitlement, climbing the social ladder can seem as superfluous and external as the money Poe's nameless narrator gets from Ligeia's "will." Better to evade or overcome the constricting civilities of upper-class behavior through individual self-development, going into oneself or out to a wilder environment, or preferably both. It's an old story, replicated in more recent theoretical tensions between ethnic or gendered agency and social construction. Those who are out want to get in, while those who are in want to get out or, as a woman once defined transcendentalism to Emerson, "A little beyond."[35]

All that changed with the Civil War. Almost immediately thereafter begins a parade of stories about men rising or attempting to rise in the world. Among the most well known: Horatio Alger, Jr.,'s *Ragged Dick* (1868),

Henry James's *The American* (1879), William Dean Howells's *The Rise of Silas Lapham* (1885), Mark Twain's *A Connecticut Yankee in King Arthur's Court* (1889), Frank Norris's *McTeague* (1899), Booker T. Washington's *Up from Slavery* (1901), Theodore Dreiser's novels about Frank Cowperwood, and Abraham Cahan's *The Rise of David Levinsky* (1917). More radically, a few writers narrate the stories of young women who gain upward mobility through work rather than marriage. In *The Gilded Age* (1873), co-authored by Twain and Charles Dudley Warner, Laura Hawkins becomes a prominent Washington power broker. In Dreiser's *Sister Carrie* (1900), Carrie rises not as a mistress but as an actress. And in Willa Cather's *O Pioneers!* (1913), Alexandra faces down her patriarchal brothers to turn her father's farm from a failure to an expansive, almost imperial triumph.

Why does this plot move from the wings to center stage? The traditional answer would be that as realistic writers paid more attention to social dynamics, American plots converged with the long English tradition of empathetic, ambivalent, or satirical narratives about upward mobility. Another version would be that "outsiders"—first Howells and Twain, then a flood of midwestern writers—gained greater access to the centers of cultural power. Their novels chronicle the trials, triumphs, and tragedies of protagonists who strive for higher social status. A third version would be that after the Civil War, the newly consolidated nation-state became a nation-stage for secular success.

My version focuses on corporate capitalism as the primary generative context for widespread dreams as well as narratives of upward mobility. Before the Civil War, for ordinary white Americans, upward mobility seemed much less realizable than maintaining a precarious place among "the middling sort." To expand Mary Ryan's observation about native-born residents of Utica, New York, "Their story is not a dramatic case of upward mobility but rather a sustained battle to maintain middle-range occupations for themselves and their children." Ryan suggests that the antebellum American male's "vaunted autonomy and egotism" was a home-nurtured strategy to preserve and protect his family in the midst of great economic insecurity.[36]

After the Civil War, that economic insecurity certainly continued. Nonetheless, the greater prospects for managerial and professional work, the widening class divisions, the diversification of employees, and the more widespread accessibility of upper-class markers fostered dreams of rising to riches or respectability. "A terrific drive upward," as Miles Orvell puts it, was "the spirit of the age . . . with the *appearance* of elevated status serving just as well, almost, as the real thing." Yet upward mobility, real and imagined, came with an inward price. To quote Orvell again: "The culture of consumption was making it possible for the American to jump several rungs in the social ladder in a single generation, . . . but it was also generating a sense of the 'real' self as a remnant one left behind[.]"[37]

Paradoxically, the narrowing of desire in the corporate transformation of work, especially for white men and more grudgingly for white women, had an impact at least as profound as the production of excess desire that Walter Benn Michaels and other critics have emphasized. Moreover, as capitalism stimulated desires for what Philip Fisher has called "the anticipatory self," it bound those desires to class-linked fantasies of aspiration more intensely than at any other period of American cultural history.[38] But hopes of raising one's social status through money, manners, and culture brought a volatility at odds with traditional stabilizations of class.

As respectability came to characterize the broad middle class coming to social and corporate dominance in the northeast United States, ideas of class took on connotations of otherness, either above or below. Conflicting with its residual European signification as a hierarchy defined by gentlemen who display their leisure, class shifted toward its new American meaning: an industrial middle-class consolidating its social dominance, defining itself through respectability, and looking hungrily or anxiously to the top and bottom end-points for mobility. To be upper class or lower class became fantasy sites for aspiration or fear. Anxiety about being really poor whetted fantasies of being really rich. Class was coming to signify who you were not: either a member of the New York 400 or a New York tenement dweller. It meant a melodramatic future, beyond a respectable present. The "Americanization" of class provided closure to imagined narratives of prospective upward or downward mobility, beyond one's present social location. And hard capitalist work was the way for a man to stay afloat on fantasies of rising.

Middle-Class Men's Work and Desires

"Where does the real life of most American men lie?" says Charles Bowen, midway through Wharton's *The Custom of the Country*. "In some woman's drawing-room or in their offices?" The answer is obvious, he says. Moreover, unlike a European man, the American husband is so "indifferent" to his wife that he won't even talk to her about his passion for business. That has become "the custom of the country." The only solution Bowen can think of is paternalistic: "Why haven't we taught our women to take an interest in our work?" Because business has become so all-absorbing that men don't even take the time to talk to their wives about it. The result: for men, passion means "the passion for making money[,]" and their romance of "real life" happens at the office. Meanwhile, their women "pretend to themselves and each other" that shopping is "what really constitutes life[,]" though "money and motors and clothes are simply the big bribe she's paid for keeping out of some man's way!"[39]

Wharton frames this chapter with a delicious irony. Bowen begins his speech on "the whole problem of American marriages" by saying, "the average American looks down on his wife." At the end of chapter 15, Ralph

Marvell is indeed looking down from a New York City window on his wife, but only to see her returning from her affair with Peter Van Degen. As he starts to reproach her, first for missing their son's birthday party and then for lying about where she had been, "she became something immeasurably alien and far off," and his potential accusations "died on his lips."[40] Undine's insouciance stymies Ralph's attempt to reassert control. Ralph's unmanly ineffectuality as a caring husband and a gentleman of leisure becomes an ironic yet reinforcing counterpoint to Bowen's incisive pronouncements about workaholic men indifferent to their wives.

I don't think Bowen's perspective has been sufficiently attended to in recent cultural criticism. Critics tend to emphasize the aspects of corporate capitalism that proliferate consumerist desires, not the aspects that narrow men's desires—and now women's too—to work, work, and more work. From the early corporate era to the present, work has become a middle-class American passion. For men, it satisfies several converging social pressures, including the homosocial need to feel validated and respected by one's peers and bosses, the satisfaction in identifying oneself with a useful or at least powerful collective effort, the drive to prove one's worth and value by upward mobility within the company, and, not least, the measurement of manhood by the size of a man's salary and stock options.

The work ethic became both an obsessive satisfaction in itself, and a way of bonding with other men. As William Dean Howells notes rather mournfully in "The Man of Letters as a Man of Business," "at present business is the only human solidarity, we are all bound together by that chain."[41] The work ethic also served as a means to satisfy consumer-driven desires for purchasable images of upward mobility. Embodied in consumer goods, these images signified what used to be called gentility, and now might be called celebrity cool. The separate spheres of office and parlor came together in shared inward narratives of imagined pseudo-aristocracy, which could be brought into the home as luxury goods for status emulation.

People bought these commodities less for their use-value than for their capacity to beget fictions of self-remaking. Anxieties about feeling fraudulent, uprooted, and unreal stimulated fantasies of self-refashioning through imitation or assimilation upward. Both elements encouraged men to redouble their work for the firm, in part because the workplace gave men a place to escape these domestic contradictions. There one could feel special, performing tasks that required manly expertise rather than the feminized tasks of housework or child rearing. There one didn't have to choose between being effete Bromfield Corey or bumptious Silas Lapham at a dinner party.

As John Locke theorized in *An Essay Concerning Human Understanding* (1689), desire is really an "uneasiness" inherent in wanting what we don't have. Especially when the imagined delight seems attainable, that uneasiness is "the chief, if not only spur to human industry and action." For later Enlightenment theorists, the safest as well as most useful way to manage the threatening resentments and cravings of ordinary men was to channel their desires toward making money. The capitalist workplace could absorb the passions into one all-consuming interest: to better one's lot.[42] Corporate capitalism therefore expanded, yet narrowed male desire. While expanding speculative desires for an anticipatory self, corporate and professional employment narrowed the arena for pursuing those desires to the work ethic and the workplace.

In the process, corporate work undermined the social value of the leisured gentleman, while accelerating the long-term capitalist redefinition of the "pursuit of happiness" from leisure to work. Here a generative paradox emerges. In Locke's original version, "pursuit" meant the pursuit of property. "Property" was a kind of shorthand, a metonym for the dream of gentlemanly ease. Work was only a necessary evil, a means for rising to the state and estate of a propertied gentleman, for whom others work.

Arguably from its beginnings, and certainly since Benjamin Franklin's "Information to Those Who Would Remove to America" (1784), America was the land of opportunity for white men of "the middling sort." They judged each other by a new binary of hard work or idleness, not by complex gradations of class status. The American question that Franklin noted still surprises many Europeans: "people do not inquire concerning a stranger, *what is he?* but, *what can he do?*"[43] Especially in the Northeast, American men felt most vital when they were working, not when they were at ease. After the Civil War, that Yankee style became the national corporate style. Nowhere else in the world did men find more pleasure in their work.

To apply Locke's definition, such delight means to remain in a constant state of productive yearning, or uneasiness. The craving for "more"—to do more, get more, be more,—seems more real, more animating, than the contemplation of one's achievements or one's estate. To twist William Blake's aphorism, from "Several Questions Answered": "What is it men in work do require? The lineaments of Ungratifiable Desire." Dreiser became the prose chronicler of men's ungratifiable desire, while Fitzgerald became its poet.

In social terms, then, the American Dream seems narratable as class-linked upward mobility. Hard work can raise one's class status, or at least raise oneself above one's neighbors, as Senator Dawes defined capitalist desire. Yet that formulaic narrative constrains the dreaming. For Nick Carraway, Jay Gatsby represents a fantasy of upward mobility as an endless green light, a state of wonder at the possibilities for self-remaking. The fantasy of what Emerson's friend called "a little beyond" continually transgresses its class containments. It remains unlocatable except in imaginative play and imaginative unease. For less transgressive men, work paradoxically binds desire to imaginative excess as a permanent state of obsessive or delicious unfulfillment.

That paradoxical source of workplace energy still helps to drive corporate capitalism toward global triumph. It also helps to generate stories of daddy's girls and daddy's boys. These narratives domesticate or eroticize male desire beyond men's work. If relocating the metonymic site for men's yearning uneasiness from the landed estate to the workplace transformed the social valuation of labor, it also transformed the traditional social meanings for "father," "daughter," "son," and value itself.

Undermining Patriarchy, Property, and Production

Corporate paternalism, I've suggested, tries to preserve daddying with limited liability. To put that more formally: corporate paternalism preserves the traditional norms and privileges of daddying, but more collectively, in a credit economy and a workplace hierarchy, at a spectatorial and philanthropic distance. The shift undermines individual labor and production as sources of social value.

Neo-Marxists still hold to a precorporate valuing of the small-scale producer or laborer who makes or grows something. Adam Smith and Karl Marx agree in making a man's labor the basis for a product's value.[44] An implicit metonym of paternity inheres in such product-centered conceptions of value, presuming the intrinsic worth of a man's autonomous making or laboring. Critiques of consumerism such as Richard Ohmann's *Selling Culture* preserve a nostalgia for small-scale production values by arguing that large-scale marketing processes, dependent on packaging and advertising for women shoppers and domestic uses, alienate buyers from the product's attachment to the more manly process of giving it social life.[45]

But corporate capitalism undermines paternity as a central social metaphor, by reducing the father's domestic role. As Adam Smith noted, patriarchy was grounded in the scarcity of luxury goods. Once luxury goods became more broadly available, fathers had less success in controlling their sons with hopes of receiving a patrimonial estate.[46] In many respects, corporate capitalism reinforced traditional norms of manly self-control, stoic prudence, and collective male dominance by establishing a homosocial workplace, with more overt hierarchies of male dominance, and more stringently homophobic proscriptions against physical intimacy between men.[47] As argued in chapter 4, the motif of the daddy's boy ambiguously de-eroticizes the potential for workplace intimacies between older and younger men, partly by highlighting the young man's sentimental search for a father. In other respects, corporate capitalism unsettled the gendered grounds for men's self-perception. Even traditional ideals of moral character sometimes inhibited workplace performance. "[M]en wholly developed in all the attributes of manhood can not become accumulators[,]" wrote George E. McNeill in 1886. "It is only towards those possessing special qualifications of management, of speculation and of foxcraft that the flow of accumulated wealth centres."[48]

Recent criticism by Martha Banta, Mark Seltzer, and others has emphasized Taylorization and man-machine relations as alienations that define
the corporate transformation.[49] More crucial, I argue, are the daily man-to-
man relations in the corporate workplace, including the pleasures of what
McNeill called foxcraft. Physical labor and fatherhood signified less; mental work, hierarchical collaboration, and the manipulation of capital signified more. When small-scale production yields to large-scale integrations of
production, consumption, and national marketing, efficient management
matters far more than autonomous productivity. Typically, the work of a corporate manager has more to do with circulating paper and assessing subor-
dinates than with making a visible product. Personal craftsmanship began to
look a bit provincial. Such representations of symbolic paternity seemed of
a piece with the vanishing world of rural childhood.

Despite the Dawes Act's faith in property ownership as the basis for civilization and upward mobility, landed property also receded in importance.
In the Anglo-American eighteenth century, as J. G. A. Pocock has said,
"Property was the foundation of personality" and the base for civic virtue.
But that ideology had already become a defensive argument against the rise
of "public credit" and speculation.[50] By the late nineteenth century, landed
property still had its patriarchal mystique, but it had become just one temporarily stabilized form of capital flow. And access to capital depends more
on credit than on the ownership of tangible property and goods. Early in *Up
from Slavery,* Washington tells of a white mentor who said, "in his fatherly
way: 'Washington, always remember that credit is capital.'"[51] To rise from
being a white man's property to becoming a black plantation patriarch, as
Washington did, he had to learn how to gain credit as well as capital from
whites who liked to be "fatherly."

At home, a father's legacy, calling, or decree no longer determined a child's
future. Stephen Frank highlights the "dramatically declining birth rate" as
hopes for elevating the family's social position led to higher and more varied expectations for sons and daughters as well as men at work.[52] Even a
daughter could gain or seize some independence beyond her traditional role
as patriarchal property to be given in marriage. Her prospects no longer
seemed reduced to her role as a human signifier of the father's dynastic
power. Until the 1960s, particularly for families at the higher end of the social scale, the daughter's virginity still secured her family's honor and her
own marketability as a marriageable young "lady." But the middle-class
daughter's range of choices, for work as well as sexual activity, slowly expanded beyond the traditional gentry goal of being given away by her father
to be an unsalaried wife, mother, and domestic manager.

All that was in social motion long before the advent of corporate capitalism. Nonetheless, the consolidation of the American nation-state after the
Civil War and the corporate reach for national markets accelerated the destabilization of small-scale manhood and its metonyms for social meaning.

Boy Books

The corporate transformation of work provides a key context for the sudden appeal of boy stories after the Civil War. In tomboy, bad boy, and Horatio Alger stories, childhood paradoxically comes to signify not dependence, but a yearning for the imagined independence lost in the fall from play to adult work, as well as an innocent past displacing the bloody years of sectional carnage. As with other modes of regionalism, depictions of playful rural or village childhood flourished just after a war between regions had left over six hundred thousand people dead. In the 1870s and 1880s such representations suddenly became enormously popular, from *Little Women* (1868) and *Tom Sawyer* (1876) to Winslow Homer's early 1870s paintings of white rural life. While corporate capitalism united the states through national markets and managerial bureaucracies, stories about tomboys and bad boys in small-town settings displayed a nostalgic site of otherness. They provided a latter-day version of romantic pastoral, familiar yet remote.

Yet celebrating the insouciant adventures of tomboys and bad boys was also a way of saying, *Let the past be past.* The loss of adventurous self-display seemed as natural as growing up, to enter a world of business or domestic duties. To be sure, some men looked back on their childhood as a site of pain. As David Levinsky begins his story, "My wretched boyhood appeals to me as a sick child does to its mother."[53] More typically, retrospective fictions of boyhood evoked idealized memories of freedom, spontaneity, and roads not taken.

If childhood simultaneously represented a national future and a localized past, it also represented the pleasures of theatrical subjectivity, for boys and girls alike, seemingly constrained by the workplace roles expected of adults. It's easy to forget that tomboys and bad boys were roles, too, staged in part for more dutiful peers, but also for adults caged in their own conventions of goodness. For that matter, character itself was a role, staged for an imagined audience of lifetime neighbors. As developed in chapter 4, the transition from "character to personality" that Warren Susman has described was really a transformation in the stability and scale of the audience.[54] This change accompanied the corporate transformation of scale that reshaped how people looked at themselves through the eyes of others. If conscious role-playing seemed fraudulent, yet necessary to adult life, stories about Ragged Dick or Jo March or Tom Sawyer could make theatricality feel "natural" again, meaning local, protected, spontaneous, indulged. It could be remembered as "play," not felt as "work."

Although paternalistic traditions shaped new corporate and professional hierarchies of power, most if not all of the boyhood books show fathers failing their sons. Again and again, as Marcia Jacobson points out in *Being a Boy Again,* fathering seems both crucial yet inadequate as a cultural signifier. In Hamlin Garland's *Boy Life on the Prairie* (1899), Jacobson notes, "It is the changing nature of prairie life . . . that separates father and son[,]" particularly "the advent of new farm machinery[.]" A widening technological and cultural discontinuity between fathers and sons undermines traditional rites of passage for becoming a man. As Jacobson observes, corporate capitalism made small businessmen and farmers "frequent casualties[.]" If "the boy book explicitly served the needs of a developing capitalist society[,]" it did so not just by taking people's minds off present difficulties, but also by presenting father-son relations as a vexed and inadequate stabilization of male identity.[55] Perhaps the boy books also stabilized time itself. In that respect, as with narratives reinforcing paternalism, these stories evade accepting the accelerating pace of social change.

Today's patriarchal polemics frequently call for the renewal of men's dominance in the home. At a more subtle and personal level, these rhetorics and the postbellum boy books may share a quiet desperation. Perhaps the boy books spoke so keenly to adult men as well as younger readers because the tales registered a felt loss of fatherhood as well as childhood. In conventional middle-class families, work has separated men not only from nature and domesticity, but also from day-to-day fathering. To such men, childhood becomes a nostalgic register for loss, not only of outdoor play, but also of the power and reciprocities inherent in daily parenting.

The Transformation of Value

Critics such as Gail Bederman, Christophe den Tandt, Steven M. Gelber, and Amy Kaplan have linked the widespread crisis of white middle-class masculinity to the corporation's destabilization of manliness.[56] They emphasize compensatory cultural recoils, and rightly so. Corporate capitalism reinvigorated traditionally manly rhetorics and behaviors, from paternalism and self-control to the Great Father and the warrior ethos. Abstracted loyalties to gender and race intensified, and gestures of remasculinization saturated American culture. Nor have they slackened much in our own postmillennial atmosphere of white male pathos and bathos.

Yet it's not enough to say that manhood developed new forms of contestation and patriarchal performativity as men's work alienated their gender codes from their gendered bodies. The rise of large-scale organizations threatened manhood's usefulness as a goad to make men risk danger and combat for personal honor and small-group survival. Nor were character and hard work sufficient to ensure success. As Olivier Zunz notes, "The pursuit of profit required both the habit of order and a penchant for flexibility, even deception."[57] In the new world of white collars, bosses, and foxcraft, the congruence between a man's work and traditional signs of a man's individual value no longer could be presumed. Here James Livingston's *Prag-*

matism and the Political Economy of Cultural Revolution provides a way beyond equations of capitalist value with alienation.

Where can capitalist value be situated—in producers, consumers, or, as Catherine Gallagher has argued, in the exchange relation itself?[58] To emphasize the late nineteenth-century shift from producer to consumer capitalism, as current criticism tends to do, isn't quite enough. Why is it, Livingston asks, that the New Woman rather than the "proletarianized" laboring man comes to represent the possibilities for reconstituting a "social self"? To simplify his answer: what capitalism gave, corporate capitalism took away.

Capitalism first established, then undermined, the priority of the principle of class. By the late nineteenth century, class had become a culturally dominant category of social organization. Yet in the twentieth century, in the United States, class has given way to race and gender as primary categories, because relations of production no longer regulate other social relations. For Livingston, the New Woman represents "not only the principle of consumption but the promise of subjectivity" in the first age of surplus rather than necessity.[59]

As Livingston's answer implies, those who invoke proletarianized labor as a site of resistance to corporate culture are nostalgic for the autonomous producer. They look back longingly to a time when the relations of production created modern class structure and consciousness. In contrast, the New Woman evokes the more open-ended subjectivities becoming available beyond class categories. Her cultural appeal opposes the reductive "managed self" that critics of consumer and corporate culture construct, whether imagined as David Reisman's other-directedness or Michel Foucault's force field of ideological controls. To accept the play of desires and performances in oneself means at least partially relinquishing paternity and production as grounds for constituting male subjectivities and gender difference.

The New Woman is a term invented by the British writer Sarah Grand in 1894, and popularized in a hostile magazine rejoinder by another woman writer, Ouida. Critics have applied it to middle-class and elite women from the 1880s to the 1920s who sought lives beyond the home. In Livingston's argument, the cultural fascination with the New Woman expresses "dissatisfaction with the *priority* of the principle of class" (his emphasis). Partly through her transgressive adventurousness, and partly through her continuing freedom from the male world of work, she represents a sense of "possibilities waiting to be discovered in the regions beyond the realm of necessity, where consumption and its connotations would matter more than production and its requirements." Once corporate capitalism makes consumer demand more important than productivity as "the key variable in economic growth," value becomes "constituted by the varieties of subject positions or social relations required to appreciate goods, not measured by the quantities of labor-time required to produce commodities[.]" As one consequence, "the integrity of the self finally becomes a function of the modern subject's fragmentation and reconstruction." In part through the varieties of shopping experience, to twist William James, the culture of corporate capitalism "supersedes the categories of necessity, production, and class."[60]

That analysis needs to be qualified in at least five ways. Livingston doesn't give enough emphasis to the corporate workplace as a major factor in the transformation of middle-class male and working-class female subjectivities. There class continues to be a shaping and regulative force, especially toward the extremes. Also, "fragmentation" evokes alienation, whereas "mobilities" offer more open-ended possibilities. Third, white people used racialized binaries to fend off threatening new mixings as well as "varieties of subject positions or social relations[.]" Fourth, the realms of necessity and surplus perpetuated traditional gender stereotypes, just as they relied on traditional class stratifications to stabilize their cultural significations.

Finally, Livingston gives too much centrality to the New Woman's role as the major cultural figure for subjective diversities and possibilities in the first age of surplus. To be sure, men as well as women felt the contrary tugs of independence and dependence represented in the New Woman, particularly in narratives of the upwardly mobile daddy's girl. If middle-class white male managers felt that they were losing their manly independence and visibility as they disappeared into the hierarchic, bureaucratic corporate workplace, their wives felt a converse yet reciprocal itchiness while they managed the home and displayed their husbands' status. But the New Woman was only one aspect of the transformation of value from normative producerism to more heterogeneous subjective imaginings. Dreams of a more fashionable self, or of a self able to be refashioned, animated a great variety of desires for consumer goods.

Nonetheless, Livingston is on to something big and new. In a December 1999 speech, Alan Greenspan put it more simply. During the early part of the century, steel mills and skyscrapers were "manifestations of America's industrial might[.]" Now "ideas have replaced physical bulk and effort as creators of value," he said. "Today, economic value is best symbolized by exceedingly complex, miniaturized integrated circuits and the ideas, the software, that utilize them . . . Most of what we currently perceive as value and wealth is intellectual and impalpable."[61] For the chairman of the Federal Reserve, ideas are like "software." Another word for those "intellectual and impalpable" ideas is fiction.

Highlighting corporate capitalism's production of commodification and alienation misses the play of mind that creates the surplus value constituting the imagined self. A freedom inheres in detaching value from production, labor, and the small-scale marketing of artisan goods. If an anticipatory self drives the desire to work hard, make money, and exchange money for goods, such desire detaches value from simply making or using a product. Value becomes an add-on, attached to tangible products or property by advertising or more private desires. It nurtures intangible dreams of a higher, cooler, richer, sexier, or more sophisticated self. That can be liberating for novelists as well as advertisers. It was becoming possible for ordinary people to create selves on spec.

In short, corporate capitalism transformed not only village traditions of valuing and evaluating character, but also the nature of value itself. A high-culture example can illustrate the union of fiction making with paternalism. Henry James's 1908 preface to the New York edition of *The Portrait of a Lady* patronizingly savors how he created value from "the conception of a certain young woman affronting her destiny." "Affronting" carries a condescending charge, since it connotes a confrontational attempt to reduce someone else to shame or confusion. That's difficult to do with one's destiny. How can the novelist make this "mere slim shade of an intelligent but presumptuous girl . . . endowed with the high attributes of a Subject?" The task was especially daunting, he muses, since "Millions of presumptuous girls, intelligent or not intelligent, daily affront their destiny, and what is it open to their destiny to *be,* at the most, that we should make an ado about it?"

Yet James found himself "in complete possession" of this "vivid individual[,]" as if he were a "wary dealer in precious odds and ends" holding a "rare little 'piece'" whose "'value'" was apparent only to him. He had the power to transform this "thin" character into a Subject, by raising Isabel into conscious "relation to herself." The possibility of "organising an ado about Isabel Archer" lay in the novelist's capacious, possessive, uplifting hands. The "extravagance" and "charm of the problem" was to create formal value from the inexplicable "wonder" that "the Isabel Archers, and even much smaller female fry, insist on mattering."[62]

Many ordinary women, and ordinary men too, inexplicably insisted on mattering. It wasn't just for climbing the social or corporate ladder, or for spending money. Narratives of upward mobility stimulated the convergence of advertising and fiction as constituents of subjectivities that aspired to be more than what they were, whether in men hoping for promotion or in women shopping for upscale goods.[63] Value no longer held tightly to the natural, the functional, or the necessary. As a widely shared imaginary, the dream of upward mobility used class categories to frame and stabilize the volatility of emulative desires. Amid proliferating fictions of aspiration for the many instead of the few, the trope of the New Woman became one of many signifiers for tensions between the emergent realm of choice and the residual realm of necessity.

In novels, characters rise by the performability of their emulative fictions, from Ragged Dick and Laura Hawkins to Simon Rosedale in *The House of Mirth* and James Gatz, reborn as Jay Gatsby. Or, from McTeague and Hurstwood to Edna Pontellier and Lily Bart, they fall by becoming trapped in the desires and discontents of an immobilized, intractable self. The daddy's girl and daddy's boy emerge as ways of using familiar domestic figures to narrate the self's unfamiliar potential for surplus value as well as for upward mobility. If corporate capitalism co-opted as well as unsettled traditional constructions of manliness, no wonder a good many middle-class white men felt powerful yet unreal. No wonder such men turned to plucky, resourceful young women and men to make themselves feel more spontaneous and adorable as well as more daddy-like.

In the early corporate era, then, narratives of upwardly mobile daddy's girls and daddy's boys become the first stage of a broader transformation from narrating conditions of necessity to narrating subjective possibilities in an age of surplus choices. Beyond its traditional links to the uses or making of a product, value begins to reflect the product's ability to stimulate the imagined self's fictions of upward mobility. Value inheres in the surplus of desire on both sides of a capitalist exchange, not in the "nothing" that establishes equivalence at the moment of exchange. Value becomes a volatile fiction of aspiration and longing, much as the son or daughter can create an adult future beyond the father's control.

2   Daddy's Girls and Upwardly Mobile Women: An Overview

Until the Civil War, most narratives of upwardly mobile women in English and American literature show them rising through spirituality, scandal, or marriage. Postbellum American culture begins to feature a fourth possibility: rising through respectable work outside the home. Partly to secure a patriarchal frame for ambitious young women, at least in fantasy, a great variety of daddy's girl narratives appear in the early corporate era. In seeking to contain the threat, they also voice its lure. Surprisingly, many of the stories portray considerable shakiness in the stabilizing role of the father figure. Perhaps less surprisingly, the professional woman often becomes a demonized version of the writer's creative double, for women as well as men.

At least five kinds of daddy's girls became prominent in twentieth-century American culture. In the 1920s, the daddy's girl emerged as a popular figure for dependent independence, most enduringly with Harold Gray's Little Orphan Annie and Daddy Warbucks. Soon its second and third manifestations also gained wide cultural circulation. In 1938, playing an available yet unavailable young woman, Mary Martin became a star in her Broadway debut by singing Cole Porter's saucy song, "My Heart Belongs to Daddy."[1] More ubiquitously, throughout the 1930s Shirley Temple appeared in a series of films about spirited little girls who manage hapless, grouchy, or bemused fathers or grandfathers.[2] In a fourth version, dramatized in Philip Barry's *The Philadelphia Story* (1939), a vigorously transgressive daughter rescues her father from his philandering and his fears of growing old, after he tells her that he needs her loving. Until the last few decades, the final variant has been more difficult to sell. In *Tender Is the Night* (1934), F. Scott Fitzgerald parallels Rosemary's starring role in a film called *Daddy's Girl* with Nicole's sexual abuse by her father during her childhood.[3] Today "daddy's girl" evokes a range of possibilities from indulgence to incest.

In an age when images of the New Woman threatened and fascinated women as well as men, stories about daddy's girls served as a mediating cultural compromise. Though permanent domestication remained the primary social pressure on middle-class girls, the roles of wife and mother no longer seemed the only options. Respectable young women could rise through wage-earning work, at least if they became members of a profession rather than of the "working" class. They could even ride the new safety bicycles leaning over the handlebars, despite doctors who accused them of masturbating in public.[4] The first short story written by an African American woman, Frances E. W. Harper's "The Two Offers" (1859), sharply contrasts the happiness of a self-reliant, self-regulated woman writer with the suffering of a friend who chose marriage. As G. Stanley Hall noted in *Adolescence* (1904), almost half of adolescent girls in the United States rejected the role of wife and mother, and preferred the privileged role of the male sex.[5]

Yet conventional disparagements of working women as "unladylike" or even "whores" persisted. Stories about the self-uplifting workplace achievements of Laura Hawkins, Sister Carrie, Alexandra Bergson, and many others make ambitious young women seem less threatening by emphasizing their yearning for father-figures (Laura), their ability to play daughter-like roles (Carrie), or their ability to fulfill father's hopes (Alexandra). At the same time, these characters embrace the New Woman's spirit of adventurous independence.

For men, images of daddy's girls prop up traditional images of themselves as paternal care-givers. Such stories offer solace and nostalgia to men preoccupied with workplace advancement, or afraid of aging, or nervous about the impasse between idealized patriarchy and the middle-class father's diminished presence and authority in the home. As a man told me recently about his delight in becoming a grandfather, "It's the ultimate mulligan." That golfing term for do-over suggests part of the appeal of daddy's girls for midlife men. Mentoring an ambitious young woman also confirms a man's powers, sometimes with erotic intensities. Other more ominously patriarchal narratives serve as cautionary tales, implying that men should remain more focused on competing at work than on dominating at home.[6]

The simplest goal of this chapter is to show that narratives of father-like men and daughter-like women pervaded American culture in the early corporate era. Yet most of these stories and images undermine the patriarchal grounds for paternalistic practices and expectations. Almost all the daddy's girl stories considered here expose instabilities in the father's role. On one hand, stories such as Henry James's Pansy and Gilbert Osmond in *The Portrait of a Lady*, Catherine and Dr. Sloper in James's *Washington Square*, or Kate Chopin's Edna Pontellier and her father in *The Awakening*, inflate and undercut patriarchal controls. On the other hand, in presenting freely ranging characters such as Noémie Nioche in *The American* or Undine Spragg in *The Custom of the Country*, James and Edith Wharton satirize the father's new place as a sideline supporter for the daughter's autonomous rise.

In the most comfortable popular usage, a daddy's girl seems much less threatening than an upwardly mobile woman. The term suggests a daughter whose loving father doesn't impose much discipline. He thinks his daughter is special, perhaps even a "princess." Perhaps thinking of her that way makes him a king. If she is "the apple of his eye," that might make him the serpent. Yet such fathers tend to play the role of cheerleader, not seductive or auto-cratic authority. A variety of Disney movies, particularly *The Little Mermaid* (1989) and *Beauty and the Beast* (1991), feature spunky, motherless daugh-ters doted on by their fathers. Even King Triton in *The Little Mermaid* not only lets himself be controlled by Ariel, but also sacrifices himself—until he is resurrected—so his daughter can live. Nancy Drew and Veronica Lodge of the Archie comic books are both daddy's girls. They're adventurous, in-dependent, unconditionally loved, and almost unconditionally funded, with no mother to cramp their style.

More surprisingly and ambiguously, Grant Wood's *American Gothic* paint-ing depicts a sternly protective rural father and his daughter, whom many viewers mistake for his wife. Robert Hughes nicely highlights the "not very alluring daughter, the pitchfork-grasping father protecting her against all comers, the carpenter-Gothic house doubling as the church of domestic virtue."[7] The painting has gained such iconic status in part because it seems on the edge between parody and elegy, and partly because the woman re-mains on a more intimate edge between wife and daughter. Once the viewer learns she's his daughter, the scene becomes an undecidable mix of paternal protection and incest. Beyond those ambiguities, Wood's depiction of em-battled rural domesticity half mourns and half mocks the decline of a long patriarchal history in which the daughter's chastity functions as a prime sig-nifier of paternal and familial honor.

Beginnings: A Longer View

The upwardly mobile woman has been an intermittent feature of Western narratives at least since the Virgin Mary. Until the advent of corporate cap-italism, such characters usually demonstrate their worthiness to rise through their potential for spiritual uplift within symbolic patriarchy. In European poetry, Dante Alighieri's Beatrice remains the pole star for allegories of spir-itual perfection that celebrate female adoration of the Father and the Son. For women who rise in secular terms, a heterosexual rather than spiritual form of patriarchal dependence awaits them. Typically, they either marry up or take on the role of mistress. Cinderella remains the fairy-tale prototype for marrying up, while Samuel Richardson's *Pamela* (1740) keeps a servant girl on the edge between prospective mistress and prospective wife, before she finally succeeds in marrying Lord B.

The *Pamela* plot all but vanishes in the Victorian era, in part because middle-class women readers were threatened by the prospect that a servant girl might rise above their own class status. It reappears with paternalistic brio in George Bernard Shaw's *Pygmalion* (1916).[8] Though in Shaw's play, Eliza marries the aristocratic Freddy Eynsford Hill, the 1957 musical brings her relation with Professor Higgins considerably closer to a daddy's girl romance. Recent movies such as *Pretty Woman, As Good As It Gets,* and *Maid in Manhattan* play variations on the Pamela plot, as a prostitute, a waitress, and a hotel maid not only rise to equality and intimacy with very rich men, but also bring them back to more healthy manhood.

Though many of these secular narratives evoke considerable empathy for the young woman's precarious and subordinated position, they also reflect male fascination with ambitious women as threatening embodiments of what Renaissance writers called "the woman on top." The ur-narrative is probably Edmund Spenser's "Mutabilitie Cantos," published posthumously in 1609. Spenser's appropriately unfinished and changeable poem allegorizes Time as a self-centered woman hellbent on conquering Jove. Though one would think that Spenser's loyalties clearly favor the patriarchal side of this binary, instabilities pervade his text. Sometimes his narrative of a strong woman's vertiginous upward mobility from earth to heaven approaches high camp. When Mutability ascends to "molest" the moon by blotting out its light, Jove seems hilariously baffled and befuddled. What has caused this "strange astonishment," he cries. Someone, anyone, please "arrest / The Author"![9]

The disorientingly conflicting meanings of "author" (first cause or published writer), not to mention the double meaning of "arrest" (stop, hold in custody) suggest that Spenser has entered into the spirit of Mutability's creative changeability. In using "author" as first cause, Jove implicitly undermines his status as prime mover. Still more subversively, in what might well be called The Birth of the Author, Jove calls for stopping Spenser's own imaginative powers before they really get out of control. Mutability is probably the first in a long line of covert female doubles for an Anglo-American male writer's powers of invention.

Subsequent cantos further undermine Jove's control by making him descend from Paradise to a field in Ireland, where Mutability and Jove debate at length. Moreover, the female goddess of Nature rather than a male deity finally decrees that Mutability has to yield to eternal order. Throughout, the "author" treats Mutability's insatiable desire for power with an uneasy mixture of trepidation, contempt, and admiration. A modern reader might wonder, why does Spenser invent this outrageous attempt at a hostile takeover, by a woman no less? Given his more conventional moralizing about mutability, why is he recounting her transgressions with such panache?[10] If this were a movie, the spirit of Charles Ludlam would be directing it, and Mutability would be played by Madonna, Cher, and Bette Midler in alternating scenes.

A modern variant of "the woman on top" uses ambitious women to dramatize the changeableness and exchangeabilities in capitalism. Typically, women represent what twentieth-century commentators have called capitalism's production of "creative destruction" or "insatiable desire." In English fiction, Daniel Defoe's Moll Flanders first links female audacity and social climbing to capitalist flux and marketplace exchange.[11] William Thackeray's Becky Sharpe, whom Twain and Warner draw on to portray Laura Hawkins in *The Gilded Age* (1873), follows in Moll Flanders's wake. In *The Custom of the Country* (1913), Wharton recasts Defoe's narrative of Moll's crass capitalist hustle as a national allegory personified by Undine Spragg (U.S.), who ceaselessly enacts her countrymen's fluid self-refashioning for social advancement. As with Spenser's Mutability, these women seem born from their own brains, without any parenting or fathering dynamics. That's part of their transgressiveness.

In a traditional marriage, even today, the daughter is "given away" by her father. At least in expectation, the father's gift of an obedient daughter is a loss repaid with several kinds of nonmaterial gifts from his community. Giving the daughter away, especially in an arranged marriage, establishes alliance with another clan or kinship group. The gift also displays the father's power to tell his daughter what to do. The ritual exchanges a tangible daughter for intangibly augmented patriarchal honor. In a great variety of Mediterranean and post-Mediterranean societies, as reemphasized in chapter 6, the gift of a daughter helps to secure or enhance the family's ownership of property when property is scarce. Conversely, an independent or sexually active daughter becomes a prime signifier of family shame. Some families try to injure or kill daughters who have been unchaste, or who leave home to avoid arranged marriages.[12] The ceremony of traditional marriage affirms that until the father gives away his daughter, her virginity has been his property, to protect and preserve.

With the development of capitalist societies, more diverse opportunities for mobility and upward mobility among strangers threatened the gift-giving rituals binding patriarchal kinship groups, just as increased mobility threatened the long-term reciprocities that helped to manage economies of scarcity. Not coincidentally, many young women began to seek footholds in the world beyond the family. As Amartya Sen has argued in various writings, global development and population control require post-patriarchal expectations of freedom and equality, so that women can find roles outside as well as within the home.[13]

Semi-Gothic Incest and Modern Male Weakness

In England, as the onset of industrial capitalism put patriarchal fatherhood under considerable strain, a new literary genre challenged traditional images of paternal honor and protectiveness. From Hugh Walpole's *The Castle of Otranto* (1764) onward, Gothic novels often dramatize overt tensions and covert attractions between strong young women and willful father-figures whose attempts to dominate or control mix cruelty and terror with chivalry and intimations of supernatural powers. As in Grant Wood's painting, the mothers are either absent or dead. If Wood uses an architecturally Gothic yet churchly house to frame his blend of protective rural fatherhood and subliminal incest, the novelistic strain of daddy's girl Gothic plays more directly with the threat of incest always latent in the genre.

Several of Wharton's narratives, from *The House of Mirth* (1905) through *Summer* (1917) to her "Beatrice Palmato" fragment and *Twilight Sleep* (1927), dramatize the predatory sexual dangers in young women's dependence on middle-aged men of money and power. In *The House of Mirth,* for a moment at least, Lily Bart feels ambivalently attracted to Simon Rosedale when she sees him playing, daddy-like, with a little girl. Much more disturbingly, Wharton's explicitly pornographic "Beatrice Palmato" excerpt shows an Italian Renaissance father manipulating his daughter's body and erotic desires for his sexual benefit, and also to prove to himself that he is more sexually adept than her new husband. In the fragment's last line, after they have full intercourse for the first time, he triumphantly whispers to Beatrice, "Was it . . . like this . . . last week?"[14]

As Wharton's fragment subtly implies, the father's sense of male rivalry and incipient inadequacy impels his incestuous desire. If, as John Updike has observed, incest is "self-love turned heterosexual," that male narcissism has shaky underpinnings.[15] In the wake of Fitzgerald's Dick Diver in *Tender Is the Night* (1934), a great many novels, movies, and memoirs about incestuous or quasi-incestuous desire highlight the father-figure's sense of failure or lack. Even earlier, men like Wharton's Lawyer Royall in *Summer* seem to be saying to themselves, *I've done all right, but I could have done so much better, and I'm getting old* . . . Faced with this narcissistic impasse, they look toward little or not-so-little girls, who can make them feel strong, tall, and youthful again. *Eve's Bayou* (1997) is one of the best movies on that theme, and Toni Morrison's first novel, *The Bluest Eye* (1970), culminates with a disturbingly sympathetic representation of Cholly Breedlove's incest. Typically, while the daughter struggles with the conflict between her feelings of horrified violation and her yearning for father's approval, the father abuses family trust and intimacy to assuage his imagined need for more respect, more adoration, more power, either at home or more commonly in his work.

A more decorous version of the father's incestuously narcissistic needs for his daughter surfaces midway through Philip Barry's 1939 play, *The Philadelphia Story*. Out of the blue, Seth explains to Tracy that his "philandering" is her fault, not his wife's, and certainly not his own. It comes from his "reluctance to grow old." To fend off that fear, "the best mainstay a man can have as he gets along in years is a daughter—the right kind of daughter. . . . One who loves him blindly—as no good wife ever should, of course.—One for whom he can do no wrong— . . . I think a devoted young daughter gives a man the illusion that youth is still his." Without such a daughter, he says, a man "is inclined to go in search of it again" with other women. "But with a girl of his own full of warmth for him, full of foolish, unquestioning, uncritical affection—" "None of which I've got," Tracy rejoins. Right, Seth replies; "you have everything it takes to make a lovely woman except the one essential—an understanding heart." Accepting her father's critique, Tracy changes herself from "goddess" to "human being" as the play moves toward a happy paternalistic ending. "I love you," father and daughter say to each other at the end, before he escorts her down the aisle to give her away in marriage.[16]

Seth is unusual only in not blaming his wife for his anxiety about limitations and aging. In *Sexual Violence and American Manhood,* T. Walter Herbert suggests that male fantasies and practices of pederasty, incest, and sexual abuse of women are all forms of "compensatory pornographic enchantment" to evade feelings of inadequacy, inferiority, or belittlement.[17] A mordant line in Margaret Atwood's *Bodily Harm* sums up the dynamic psychologically as well as physically. As Jocasta says, men tell her again and again that their wives don't understand them. "What they usually mean is that their wives won't go down on them[.]"[18]

The desire to have a woman "go down" to make a man feel "up" again doesn't have to be explicitly sexual. As Seth's speech implies, it can be reflected in an aging man's pleasure in looking down at little girls who make him feel lively as well as loved.[19] Late in his life, Mark Twain lived out a chaste version of that delight by collecting twelve adoring prepubescent girls, ages ten to sixteen, whom he named his "Angelfish." In their many affectionate and reciprocated letters, their frequent imagined kisses are called "blots." An example from Gertrude Natkin, in thanking Twain for telephoning her: "I am just overflowing with love for you and there is likely to be an inundation at any time, . . . Oh, that I could give you a real blot right now, well I will have to make the best of it and store it up for the eventful evening. Good Night, Sweet Dreams[.]" Twain's favorite seems to have been Dorothy Quick, who later wrote fifteen volumes of poetry and fiction as well as a reminiscence of him. In his edition of the letters, John Cooley reprints several pictures of Dorothy snuggling on Twain's lap. As soon as the girls became sixteen, which for Twain was the age of sexual awakening, they became "honorary" angelfish, and his intimacy with them precipitously waned.[20]

In the alternative tradition of Vladimir Nabokov's *Lolita* (1955), an independent teenager uses an older man to learn about sex, adventure, and the pleasures and pains that come from erotic intimacy with a man of the world. This tradition twists the Taming of the Incipient Shrew convention so central to nineteenth-century Anglo-American women's fiction about young girls growing up. Typically, the proud, imaginative, hot-tempered, or rebellious young heroine reluctantly submits to wise male guidance, whether Emma to Mr. Knightly in Jane Austen's *Emma* (1816) or Verena to Basil Ransom in James's *The Bostonians* (1886), or Jo to Professor Bhaer in Louisa May Alcott's *Little Women* (1868). Little eroticism surfaces in Jo's story, except perhaps in a masochistic mode, though there's a great deal of female anger that has to be controlled. When Jo worries about what she calls her "dreadful" and "savage" temper, her mother responds, "I am angry nearly every day of my life, Jo, but I have learned not to show it; and I still hope to learn not to feel it[.]"[21] G. M. Goshgarian nicely sums up the eroticized discipline in various mid-century American women's novels as "To Kiss the Chastening Rod."[22]

Nabokov complicates the expectation of the adolescent girl's reluctant yet necessary submission to male control by making Humbert Humbert a bumbling, pederastic fool as well as a handsome, lustful schemer. Only Humbert's obsessive desire for his imagined angelfish, or what he calls "nymphets," makes him feel exceptional. Otherwise he is just an ordinary humbled Humbert, humiliated by his first wife's Parisian lover, a Russian taxi driver. During their three-way discussion in the apartment, Humbert recalls, Mr. Maximovich peed in the toilet and left it unflushed. But Humbert talks himself out of rage by musing that what looks like an "insult" was just "middle-class Russian courtesy," because the flushing sound would have exposed "the small size of his host's domicile[.]"[23] Equally outrageously, Humbert's first erotic act with Lolita is to lick her eyeballs, ostensibly to remove an irritant. Even after Humbert becomes Lolita's quasi-incestuous father by marrying his landlady to seduce her daughter, his sexual hunger for his not so little girl makes him more dependent than controlling.

From a daughter's vantage point, Dolores Haze accepts a highly erotic daddy's girl role to grow toward emotional complexity and independence as well as to gain sexual experience. Indifferent, contrary, funny, or aroused by turns, she also cries herself to sleep almost every night before she finally leaves her increasingly hapless lover. Recently a comic book artist, Phoebe Gloeckner, has been playing variations on themes of adolescent incest, sexual exploitation, and sexual exploration.[24]

Three much less threatening novels from the early part of the twentieth century portray noneroticized, headstrong daughters with more admiration than ambivalence. Irving Bacheller's *Keeping Up with Lizzie* (1911) dramatizes what happens when fathers unstintingly fund a competition between a daddy's girl and a daddy's boy to see which one can rise higher in social status. The novel eventually makes the boy a "real man" (22), meaning a farmer rather than a lawyer, while the girl regains "true womanhood" (77) by retreating from unwomanly ambition, and lives the simple life as his happy wife. But the interim is a spirited romp of a story, in which Lizzie's father taxes the community to pay for her education, Lizzie and Dan duel with automobiles, and Dan starts a ham price war. The novel seems to be the origin of the phrase, "Tin Lizzie."[25] In many ways, Bacheller reinforces paternalist controls, with the comic twist that fathers have to get control of themselves before they can rein in their children.

A virulently racist novel has a similar competition between a daughter and a young man. Gene Stratton-Porter's *Her Father's Daughter* (1921) presents Linda Strong, the daughter of a great doctor who has died in a car accident.[26] Linda's rival has an equally allegorical last name, Donald Whiting, and Linda incessantly taunts him about "a little brown Jap" (6) who is head of their class. But where Lizzie wants to best Dan, Linda becomes a friendly goad for Donald, since she knows she has "to wound his pride, to spur his ambition" (192). Young white men have to excel, she tells him, or the "yellow peril" will win: "it's the deadliest peril that ever has menaced white civilization" (118). The "honour and glory of . . . the white race everywhere" depends on this contest, she declares (164–65). An older man, Peter Morrison, writes an article declaring that his country is "threatened on one side by the red menace of the Bolshevik, on the other by the yellow menace of the Jap, and yet on another by the treachery of the Mexican and the slowly uprising might of the black man" (247).

Eventually, after many passages of equally flagrant racism and xenophobia, Linda makes a real white man of Donald, the Japanese rival dies in a cliff fight with someone else, and she accepts a proposal from Peter, who will "teach me what you would like me to know yourself" (486). Until then, she'll continue to compete to be first in her senior class, but she won't go to college, since she yearns for the fatherly care that she lost with her father's death.

Finally, Booth Tarkington's *Alice Adams,* also published in 1921, is a much more touching story of a theatrical daughter who rescues her father's manhood from his workplace subservience and firing.[27] Here Alice isn't quite a daddy's girl, because her father is too conspicuously weak throughout the story. "Men were just like sheep," she thinks, "and nothing was easier than for women to set up as shepherds and pen them in a fold" (42). She's the "business-like" one (55), but that's just one of her talents. Relishing her performances and reveries, she can be gentle, arch, mocking, and emotional as it suits her (200). After a series of twists involving a suitor and her father's secret invention of a glue-making process, the novel ends by getting her father another job and sending Alice to business college, "the end of youth and the end of hope" (433). This muted conclusion rescues the father at the daughter's expense.

All three of these novels portray fathers who are either weak or dead, and daughters who are brimming with independent energies. All three conclude by leading the spirited daughter back to some measure of dependence, with varying degrees of submission. Bacheller's happy ending leads Lizzie all the way back; Stratton-Porter's happy ending leads Linda part way back; Tarkington's ending leaves a quiet impasse in Alice between desire and duty. In those respects, despite their great differences, each story both undermines and restores patriarchal controls.

Patriarchal Instability

Lynda Zwinger and others have emphasized the incestuous dynamics and heterosexual enforcements in all daddy's girl narratives.[28] I see the motif as less patriarchal and more complicated. In the early corporate era, daddy's girl narratives provided a contradictory middle ground for narrating the stories of ambitious women framed by paternalistic constraints. The daddy's girl plot features spirited yet accommodating daughters such as Pen Lapham in Howells's *The Rise of Silas Lapham* (1885). Mark Twain's satire of Emmeline Grangerford in *The Adventures of Huckleberry Finn* (1885) mocks such a daughter's creative ambitions. Kate Chopin's Edna Pontellier shows a much more complex mixture of rebellion and accommodation. Occasionally a more admirable heroine uplifts herself by responding to her father's high hopes and expectations. That motif has been a factor in the rise of many American women to public prominence, from Anne Bradstreet through Margaret Fuller to Jane Addams and beyond.

More typically, novels satirize ambitious daughters who uplift themselves not by using work to fulfill paternal hopes, but by manipulating their trailing fathers for social climbing. Characters such as Wharton's Undine Spragg or James's Noémie Nioche in *The American* exemplify an adaptive amorality, and their negative portraits reflect the upper-class bias of their authors. Wharton and James narrate an uneasy mixture of fascination and disgust at how elite, gentlemanly, old-money norms are losing their transcendent value. The daughter's virtue, a primary metonym for family honor, seems to be vanishing into the black hole of capitalist exchange and self-promotion. As Noémie memorably says to Christopher Newman, "Everything I have is for sale."[29] Christopher Newman is far more upset at the danger to male honor in her father's lack of moral character than he is with the daughter's uses of her body for upward mobility. Eventually both Noémie and Undine succeed in uplifting themselves by mistressing a Lord or (re)marrying a billionaire. Yet the desire of an incessant role-player can never be fully satisfied. In the last sentence of *The Custom of the Country,* Undine muses that to be an Ambassador's wife is "the one part she was really made for."[30]

Popular nineteenth-century Anglo-American stage plays dramatize considerably less patriarchal instability. To simplify Elaine Hadley's arguments about class and gender formations in nineteenth-century English melodramas, these plays evoke sympathetic exchanges based on conservative models of patriarchal deference and honor. As market forces undermined status hierarchies, kinship-based bonds, and benevolent patronage, melodramas nostalgically restored honor and community through sympathy, exalting patriarchal domesticity as the ground of human feelings as well as of deferential communities. Yet they also used these modes of sympathetic feeling for social protest.[31]

An 1871 melodrama on the American stage, Charles Foster's *Bertha, the Sewing Machine Girl; or Death at the Wheel,* keeps patriarchy in abeyance through most of the play, while the working class heroine struggles through various dangers and misadventures. At the end, the long-lost father's bequest suddenly lifts Bertha from rags to riches. It's as if a paternal legacy becomes the American version of the handsome prince. Throughout, as Heather Nathan argues, Bertha gains the audience's sympathy by being remarkably passive and helpless during her trials, then by being remarkably bountiful rather than selfish with her money. The play resolves the audience's ambivalence about women working by having Bertha use her upward mobility in traditional ways. She quickly forsakes the workplace for happy domesticity, mixed with benevolent charities. As she gives lots of money to the women she worked with, she never considers using part of her inheritance to organize a union.[32]

In many nineteenth-century novels, by contrast, daughters gain sympathy for their complex mixtures of accommodation and resistance, while fathers provoke varying degrees of suspicion. Henry James can be taken as an Anglo-American instance. The implicitly incestuous aspect of the adolescent daddy's girl story emerges rather tamely in James's first novel, *Watch and Ward* (1871, revised in 1878). This tale of a man who adopts a twelve-year-old girl and eventually gets engaged to her anticipates Jean Webster's *Daddy-Long-Legs* (1912) as well as Wharton's *Summer* (1917), perhaps a downscaled homage to her late friend's first literary production. With more eroticized and semi-Gothic amplitude, James's narration of Pansy Osmond in *The Portrait of a Lady* (1881) emphasizes Osmond's desire for eroticized control.

James takes the name of Osmond from one of the earliest Gothic villains, and the description of Osmond's stifling villa evokes a small-scale Gothic castle in a state of incipient decay.[33] "I am convention itself," he says to Isabel, and like a conventional patriarch, he hungers to augment his honor and status by arranging his daughter's marriage to Lord Warburton, without regard for Pansy's feelings. In a modern world that values a man's work rather than a man's gentlemanly leisure, that hunger betrays an unpatriarchal sense of inadequacy. Worse, Osmond knows it, and solaces himself with young women he imagines he can control. "He was a failure, of course[,]" Osmond muses, in James's indirect rendition. Nonetheless, he could still "impress himself not largely but deeply; a distinction of the most private sort. . . . if he wished to make himself felt, there was soft and supple little Pansy, who would evidently respond to the slightest pressure." Not surprisingly, to get in touch with his inner Lord, Osmond likes to make Pansy "stand between his knees[.]"[34]

Isabel too is a daddy's girl, but one who seeks dangerous adventures. Her father's laissez-faire permissiveness has left her with an undisciplined imagination, a conscious desire for independence, and perhaps a more hidden yearning for paternal controls. Isabel feels drawn to Osmond in part because she thinks he won't force her to choose between dependence and independence. He also seems sexually safe, unlike Caspar Goodwood, whose last name is now the term of choice in pornographic movie-making for a male actor who can sustain his erection. Besides, after Mr. Touchett's bequest, Isabel takes pride in her newly enriched capacity for benevolence; she thinks she can give what will enable Osmond's genius to shine. More unconsciously, Isabel may feel fascinated with Pansy's submissiveness as an image of her own daughter-like desire. Or perhaps Pansy's portrait, like Isabel's marriage, signals a certain Osmond-like sadism on James's part, as he births Isabel's consciousness from her pain.

In any case, if Isabel begins as a seemingly independent woman who strangely wants to experience suffering, her disastrous choice puts her in a psychological version of a Gothic setting, where she has to raise her own consciousness to make her way through hidden passageways of treachery and potential imprisonment. As she discovers in her night-long meditation in chapter 42, Osmond's "egotism lay hidden like a serpent in a bank of flowers." ("Bank" is a nice, Osmond-like touch, intimating the money he had received from her.) Now "her husband's personality, touched as it never had been, stepped forth and stood erect."[35]

Instead of going down on her husband to save her marriage, Isabel gets down and dirty, while never tainting her new status as a lady. Despite the latent threats of Pansy's incestuous submission and Isabel's masochistic desire, Isabel blocks the arranged marriage, while Pansy too develops a quiet independence within her dependence. Subtly stimulating Lord Warburton's sense of honesty and honor to stop him from proposing to Pansy, Isabel turns Osmond's phallic oppressiveness into a helplessly exposed desire with nowhere to go. His craving to use his daughter for aristocratic affiliation turns into impotence and lack. "He was going down—down; the vision of such a fall made her almost giddy; that was the only pain."[36]

Jack London invokes an Osmond-like ideal of fathering to justify the opposite behavior, his flagrant neglect of a daughter. As he wrote to Joan London in 1914, when she was in high school, "I was ever a lover of fatherhood. I loved fatherhood over love of woman. I have been jealous of my seed, and I have never wantonly scattered my seed." But her "stupid" mother "prevented me a guiding hand in your upbringing." Therefore, since his daughter is "a colt" who has been "ruined by your trainer[,]" London tells her that "in whatever you do from now on, I am uninterested." For him, fatherhood has to be either all or nothing. "Years ago I warned your mother that if I were denied the opportunity of forming you, sooner or later I would grow disinterested in you, I would develop a disgust, and that I would turn down the page." This is not "my strength, but my weakness." Nonetheless, "I am so made." Steeped in a narcissism worthy of Osmond, London betrays the "weakness" inherent in that will to patriarchal power. Though he prides himself on loving independent comrade-women, he can't bear the thought of loving an independent child.[37]

Persistent Patriarchy, with Lemons

The Gothic novel is not the only genre that has dependent yet independent daughter-figures facing the dangers of incestuous desires or paternal control. Sentimental fiction, poetry, and even children's literature often feature young women who learn how to escape or manage oppressive, indifferent, or benignly attentive father-figures. These genres usually reward young women's capacity for spiritual rather than secular upward mobility, though the latter sometimes follows hard upon the former. In many of these stories, a young woman's moral and social progress exposes weakness or inadequacy in a seemingly patriarchal figure. When the heroine is given lemons, she makes lemonade.

In Charlotte Brontë's *Jane Eyre* (1847), for instance, orphaned Jane moves from servitude through angry verbal tussles to a power shift, then rapport and marriage with her formidable employer, Mr. Rochester. Jane's progress, not quite a Pamela plot because she comes from a respectable background, becomes a Cinderella story with several twists, as Jane's appealing anger forces this tyrannical older man beyond his paternalistic presumptions toward respect as well as desire. More tellingly, Cinderella's generic prince becomes Jane's man in need, after the fire that reveals his hidden past leaves him mutilated and dependent.[38] Other spirited young girls such as Ellen Montgomery in Susan Warner's *The Wide, Wide World* (1850), or Jo in *Little Women,* find love through the disciplining attentiveness of an older man, after their fathers prove to be indifferent or ineffectual. Still other girls lead weak-willed fathers toward more humane values. Here Harriet Beecher Stowe's five-year-old Eva becomes the American prototype of a spiritual daddy's girl, guiding her father toward moral strength.

In *Uncle Tom's Cabin* (1852), Augustine St. Clare is a kinder, gentler version of Brontë's Mr. Rochester. Yet what remains memorable about these two male characters is their ultimate weakness and dependence. St. Clare seems sympathetic in part because he doesn't share his brother Alfred's patriarchal ways. He's bored by his manly responsibilities as lord of his wife, his child, and his Louisiana plantation. Delegating the plantation's management tasks to Uncle Tom, he detaches himself from his wife's manipulative hypochondria. Delegating his conscience to Eva, he uses irony to mask his baffled shame at his complicity with oppression. Nonetheless, he remains master of his domain, in control of everything except what he should do about slavery. As a prisoner of his paternalistic contradictions, he evades them by looking to Eva to lead him toward moral clarity about slavery, love, and justice. Even after Eva's death, he can't find time to act on his new-found resolve to free his slaves before he is killed.

As an inattentive patriarch, St. Clare manifests his moral weakness in his indifference to his slaves. To him they are somewhere between toys, animals, and things. When Eva asks her father to buy Uncle Tom, St. Clare seems perplexed, though Tom has just saved the little girl from drowning. "What for, pussy? Are you going to use him for a rattle-box, or a rocking-horse, or what?" (151). Later St. Clare presents Topsy to his sister Ophelia as a "purchase . . . rather a funny specimen in the Jim Crow line." "Here, Topsy," he calls, whistling for her as if she were "a dog" (239), and commanding her to sing and dance. Later, after his sister Ophelia has locked the little girl in a dark closet, St. Clare says Ophelia can whip her too; "I'll give you full power to do what you'd like" (248).[39]

If Topsy plays the bad-girl or trickster opposite of angelic Eva, she is also Eva's double as a daddy's girl. Even if we rule out the ambiguously sexual connotation, "What for, pussy?" suggests that Eva too is St. Clare's paternalistic pet. The doubling persists in the girls' upward mobilities. While Eva rises to her angelic home, the orphan black girl becomes a proper New England missionary to Liberia. But unlike Eva's hold on readers, Topsy's appeal disappears with her conversion. Until then, her contradictory mix of performances makes a spectacle of herself, for the paternalistic amusement of readers as well as St. Clare. The spectacle also mirrors and exaggerates the white liberal contradictions animating St. Clare's perceptions of her.

When St. Clare commands Topsy to sing and dance, her eyes "glittered with a kind of wicked drollery, and the thing struck up . . . [some] native music of her race[.]" Then she suddenly "stood with her hands folded, and a most sanctimonious expression of meekness and solemnity over her face," while "cunning glances . . . shot askance from the corners of her eyes" (239–40). As the narrator intimates, her "cunning" and her "glittering" or "glassy eyes" (239, 247) shield her while reflecting the expectations of her audience. At one point Topsy even confesses to stealing a necklace from Eva that she never stole. While the incident brings out "an air of command" in the little white girl, who tells another slave not to whip Topsy, Topsy simply says, "Missis said I must 'fess; and I couldn't think of nothin' else to 'fess" (246–47).

Throughout, "St. Clare took the same kind of amusement in the child that a man might in the tricks of a parrot or a pointer" (253). Others are even worse. His sister Ophelia thinks of her as a "black spider" (241). As Topsy says later, Ophelia would rather "'have a toad touch her!'" (283). Even the narrator compares her to a "cat" or a "monkey" (249). Sensing that at least her patronizing master indulges her pranks, Topsy uses St. Clare as her protector, and his chair becomes her "refuge" (253). While Topsy angers underlings, she knows how to please the boss. Yet everyone but Eva thinks of her as a pet, a specimen, a toy, a thing, or an unconvertible criminal, and Topsy's feelings about herself faithfully reflect those presumptions. What redeems this "monkey" for St. Clare (283) is her amusing "drollery" (239), from her mistakes with language to her purposefully solemn performances of confession for her thefts and practical jokes. Finally St. Clare rightly calls her an "image": "I do like to hear the droll little image stumble over those big words!" (252). Protecting herself while satisfying her audience, Topsy settles into "her usual air of careless drollery and unconcern" (283).

As Pen Lapham's droll remarks do in Howells's *The Rise of Silas Lapham* (1885), Topsy performs the verbal postures of meekness and solemnity expected of her, while making them look like parodies. If St. Clare perceives her as a toy "top," she spins white stereotypes about blackness until she turns dichotomizing categorizations of Topsy as "sanctimonious" or "devilish" into topsy turvy confusion.[40] At times the mirroring goes both ways, as she induces St. Clare's own oscillations between good and evil. "St. Clare, after all his promises of goodness, took a wicked pleasure in these mistakes, calling Topsy to him whenever he had a mind to amuse himself" (252).

In *Uncle Tom's Cabin*, the doubled daddy's girl thrives on the father's weakness. Though the novel has frequently been called melodramatic, nineteenth-century stage melodramas typically end with patriarchal closure. Stowe's emphasis on instabilities in the peculiar paternalistic institution of slavery, from Mr. Shelby's failures as a speculator to St. Clare's failures of moral commitment, brings out the contrasting strength of girls and women, particularly black women, from Eliza to Topsy to Cassy. A more simplified version of that dynamic structures Lydia Maria Child's *A Romance of the Republic* (1867), which begins with the visit of Mr. "King" to Mr. "Royal." Mr. Royal is a Southern gentleman who has been raising his two adolescent daughters, Rosabella and Floracita, since the death of their quadroon mother two years before. Both the daughters seem to be stereotypically happy daddy's girls. Of Flora the father says, "You see I spoil her, . . . But how can I help it?" Like St. Clare, however, the father has failed to manumit either his wife or his daughters, while raising the girls as beautiful entertainers and objects of male pleasure.[41] When the father soon dies, all sorts of racist complications, victimizations, and trials of spirit ensue.

Two highly canonical daddy's girl poems, a century apart and seemingly as opposite as poems can be, show patriarchy persisting without instability, for better and worse. Henry Wadsworth Longfellow's "The Children's Hour" (1860) reflects a stereotypic nineteenth-century paternalism, while Sylvia Plath's "Daddy" (1966) uses images of the Holocaust to rage against her dictatorial father. Yet the poems are curiously similar not only in their pervasive use of war imagery, but also in their picture of work-preoccupied fathers who relish their sadistic power over their daughters. In Longfellow's poem, an affectionate father recounts his delight as his three young daughters steal up to capture him as he works in his study. In Plath's poem, a daughter uses a repetitive rhyme and rhythm, much like a nursery rhyme, to express her enraged sense of being captured by the mixture of hate, fear, and desire that constitutes her memories of her father. As she says in her most famous lines,

> Every woman adores a Fascist,
> The boot in the face, the brute
> Brute heart of a brute like you.[42]

What might that feeling have to do with Longfellow's poem?

For Longfellow's first six stanzas, the answer seems to be, nothing whatsoever. Father loves to be vanquished. As the daughters invade his room, his "study" becomes a "castle[,]" and his chair becomes a "turret" that the daughters capture. Then comes the key transition:

> They almost devour me with kisses,
> Their arms about me entwine,
> Till I think of the Bishop of Bingen
> In his Mouse-Tower on the Rhine!

Longfellow's happy exclamation point belies the covert thrust of the allusion, which refers to a cruel tenth-century German archbishop who called poor people "mice," and burned a great many beggars during a famine. As Robert Southey dramatizes the story in "God's Judgement on a Wicked Bishop" (1838), an army of actual mice then swam across the Rhine to attack and devour the bishop in his island castle.[43]

Longfellow's melodramatic fantasy in response to the little girls' kisses and twining arms might simply reflect a father's suppressed resentment at not being able to continue his work. Yet immediately, in his mind at least, the power relation dramatically shifts. First, by capturing the "blue-eyed banditti," father proves that this "old mustache" is "a match for you all!" "Match" can be taken in at least two ways, as a worthy opponent, or as a potential husband. Amid that restoration of patriarchal power, a subliminal third meaning anticipates a horrifying return of Longfellow's powerlessness. It seems highly unlikely that Longfellow consciously intended "match" to suggest a tool for setting the girls on fire. Nonetheless, a year later, in 1861, Longfellow's beloved wife Fanny would burn to death by dropping "some burning wax, or perhaps a lighted match, on her summer dress," as she was sealing her daughters' hair into keepsakes.[44] To knowledgeable modern readers, Longfellow's "old mustache" evokes the beard he grew to hide the scars he got as he desperately tried to put out the fire.

In the last two stanzas, the father gains the upper hand with a different kind of prospective ambiguity. At first his domination seems complete. "I have you fast in my fortress," and he won't let them "depart[.]" Instead, he will "put you down into the dungeon / In the round-tower of my heart."

> And there will I keep you forever,
> Yes, for ever and a day,
> Till the walls shall crumble to ruin,
> And moulder in dust away!

The sentimental closure restores the father's power through the capturing force of his love. He transforms the daughters' mock invasion into a mock imprisonment, holding them fast in his heart and memory, just as they are. To put it more negatively, he arrests their development at the moment they want only him. To put it still more negatively, his metaphors suggest his delight in putting the girls into a torture chamber.

Yet, as so often happens in Longfellow's poems, the ending also meditates on his own death, when the walls of his fortress-like heart will "crumble" and "moulder in dust." The poem's last word, "away!," puts a smiling face on the inevitability of everyone's departure—especially his own disappearance, but also his daughters' growing up. When he dies, his girls will be women, turning "away" from focusing on father. A severe reading of the last stanza's logic would say that the three young women will be free to live as independent adults only when the father's death lets them go. More benignly, the last stanza suggests that he will hold fast only to their images, since he can't hold back their lives. Either way, in this happiest and simplest of paternalistic literary productions, the last lines convey the father's taste of bitterness, or at least a quiet sadness, about his inevitable future.

Career Women and Female Doubles

I've been arguing that daddy's girl narratives in the early corporate era articulate instabilities in paternal roles, even when they dramatize idealized patriarchy. These stories also moderate or counter more directly threatening models of young women's independence, particularly the career woman and the woman who chooses to be sexually active outside of marriage. Sexually active lower-middle-class characters such as Sister Carrie were dismissed as whores by many middle-class readers in 1900, and the narrative's sympathy for Carrie and her success brought a ten-year censorship by Dreiser's publisher. Charity Royall's torrid affair in Wharton's *Summer* could also be explained as the behavior of a lower-class mountain girl without a proper mother. In *O Pioneers!*, Cather punishes Marie Tovesky's adultery by making her die, as Chopin does more ambiguously with Edna Pontellier in *The Awakening* (1899). But respectable career women posed a more difficult threat to both manly providing and paternal self-images. Henrietta Stackpole in *Portrait of a Lady,* Mlle. Reisz in *The Awakening,* Dr. Merkle in *Summer,* or, more centrally and heroically, Alexandra Bergson in *O Pioneers!* each represents a road not taken by more conventional middle-class women.

Despite those middle-class examples, working-class women led the way in overcoming prohibitions against young women working for wages outside the home, since daughters of higher social status still felt intense pressure to be a domestic "lady."[45] From Susanna Rowson's Charlotte Temple, in *Charlotte: A Tale of Truth* (1794), to Wharton's Lily Bart, a lady should choose death rather than work for pay. In chapter 21 of *Uncle Tom's Cabin,* Mrs. Shelby and Aunt Chloe agree that Chloe should leave her children and go to work as a cake-maker in Louisville for four or five years to buy Tom back, since rescuing her husband is even more important than mothering. But they also agree that Mrs. Shelby should never work for wages to achieve the same end. A white lady mustn't do that sort of thing.

Ridicule was the first line of male defense against the seemingly oxymoronic possibility of a lady laboring at anything except birthing and domestic duties. To provide comic relief, and to turn readers' expectations for Isabel toward marriage rather than work, *The Portrait of a Lady* presents the gently mocking portrait of a woman who would rather be a professional journalist than the lady of the book's title. Henrietta Stackpole represents James's sustained version of the female visitor who wrote a novel reducing Mr. Touchett to a caricature.[46] Many years later, when James reread his own novel, he was embarrassed by Henrietta's excess. He takes several pages of his 1908 preface to apologize for her "superabundance" of comic energy. Though Henrietta is his writerly double as well as his imagined inferior in genre and gender, James can't quite believe how flamboyantly she escapes his architectural constraints.

From a more sympathetic perspective, Henrietta becomes an intermittent center, almost an auxiliary heart. She supplies energetic audacity and unstinting friendship for Isabel, along with her complacently stereotypic American reactions to Europe. But James seems astonished that he could have let this runaway train take his narrative so far down the wrong track. As his preface implies, Henrietta deflects attention from the more important narrative issue, how to uplift an ordinary young and headstrong girl to consciousness. To solve that problem, James puts seemingly independent Isabel into an imprisoning marriage that raises her to reflectiveness as well as ladyhood. In perfunctorily marrying Henrietta to Mr. Bantling at the end, James gestures toward uplifting the journalist into ladyhood too, but mostly to pull the rug out from under her America-first pronouncements. Until then, Henrietta's amiably comic and caring force eludes his paternalistic narrative controls.

Sometimes privileged women writers depict their creative doubles with more bite. *The Awakening* turns Edna Pontellier away from a possible career as a painter through the spectacle and specter of Mlle. Reisz, a brilliant concert pianist who is repulsively ugly as well as imperious. More egregiously, *Summer* turns Charity toward motherhood through the specter of Dr. Merkle, the abortionist whom Wharton insistently links to blackness, fraudulence, and lower-class associations. Dr. Merkle's hair and dress are black, her sign is black and gold, and her servant is "a mulatto girl with a bushy head[.]" Charity recoils from "the false hair, the false teeth, the false murderous smile[.]"[47]

In *The Rise of Silas Lapham* (1885), William Dean Howells chooses a non-career woman for his writerly double, and his portrait of "Pen" Lapham is therefore much more sympathetic. Yet he too punishes her when the prospect of marrying Tom Corey threatens to give her entry into the Boston elite. Penelope is her father's favorite daughter. In fact, Silas thinks he has moved to Beacon Hill to further the social advancement of Pen and her sister, Irene. More unconsciously, as his wife recognizes, he too wants to gain access to elite society, and much of the comedy comes from his lugubrious attempts to climb socially without forsaking his manliness. The rest of the comedy comes from Pen. In the first half of the novel, before the danger of her upward mobility becomes vividly present, her humor reflects Howells's own narrative position, poised midway between realistic mirroring and wry, detached commentary.

Like Topsy, Pen has a "droll" sense of humor, expressed more decorously in verbal twists. "She never says anything that you can remember[,]" Tom Corey tells his mother (93). "But it's a sort of droll way of looking at things; or a droll medium through which things present themselves. She tells what she's seen, and mimics a little." Yet mimicking doesn't quite catch it, he muses later. "[S]he mimicked a little, but not much; she suggested, and then the affair represented itself as if without her agency" (124). "She's very droll, you know," he tells his mother still later. "She's everything that's unexpected" (148).[48] So far, so relatively comfortable. Like a good realist, she exposes conventions while accommodating to them. Her unexpectedness requires her ongoing twisting of expected conversational norms. Pen's attractiveness as a marriageable daughter as well as a mocking mirror depends on giving her reflectiveness an absence of "agency," or a strong, ambitious, perhaps contentious self.

As the narrator of the class conflict between the Laphams and the Coreys, Howells links his own realistic mimicries to a similar state of suspended in-betweenness. He feels a certain absence of agency himself, just as Silas says of himself at the end of the novel. An elite insider, Howells is also a provincial outsider, what he calls an "adventurer in Boston society." In ostensibly meditating on the adventurer's terror of offending Boston's elite kinship networks, Howells balances on a tightrope between melodramatic exaggeration and self-pity for his rootless dislocation. Such a man "finds himself hemmed in and left out at every turn by ramifications that forbid him all hope of safe personality in his comments on people[.]" Though there is "little danger" so long as he keeps his mouth shut, he remains an "alien" who "must feel keenly the exile to which he was born" (160). Pen Lapham's humorous lack of agency provides a "safe personality" for dramatizing the class tensions inherent in upward mobility. She finds a way of resisting upper-class forms of respectability from within.

After Tom proposes to Penelope, everything changes. Expressing the novel's most eruptive energies of demonization, Tom's mother viciously disparages Pen. Earlier, during Mrs. Corey's condescending visit to the Laphams, Pen's deliberately literal yet ironic responses to Mrs. Corey's platitudes have already set her teeth on edge. Now, revenging herself on someone who made her feel socially at sea, Tom's mother at first just calls the Lapham girl disagreeable, sly, and "'pert'" (157, also 320). Later she becomes more frankly racist. "'To think you could prefer that little, black, odd creature,'" she says to Tom (320). Her husband's positive response to Pen's irreverence eventually puts his wife's prejudice on hold. But even Tom racializes Pen's attractiveness. Not only is she "'black,'" as Pen says of herself (244), but her face, "topped by its mass of dusky hair, . . . had a Japanese effect" on him (202). To all the Coreys, her unconventionality evokes an attractive or unattractive otherness.

Moreover, Howells himself participates in Pen's punishment for rising above her station, by changing her genre from droll realism to sentimental angst. Suddenly Pen experiences a protracted moral impasse, since both she and her sister thought Tom would propose to Irene. As many critics have noted, Pen's tedious agonizing about hurting Irene imitates *Tears, Idle Tears,* the book she mocks just before Tom's surprising proposal. Faced with Pen's imminent upward mobility, Howells reduces her from an intelligent comic commentator to a generically tearful daughter-sister. He puts her imitative ironies on permanent hold.

Instead, after narrating Pen's suffering as a kind of protracted hazing, he allows her to marry Tom, but only to slip the couple off to Mexico. There her social ascent can be relocated in distant, colonial surroundings that confirm the Coreys' sense of Pen's exoticism. As Howells sums up, "the differences remained uneffaced, if not uneffaceable, between the Coreys and Tom Corey's wife." Perhaps Pen will "form herself on the Spanish manner," Tom's sister Nanny says to Mrs. Corey. Perhaps she'll have "the charm of, not olives, perhaps, but *tortillas,* whatever they are: something strange and foreign, even if it's borrowed." In any case, as Nanny concludes with a wonderful pun, "I'm glad she's going to Mexico. At that distance we can— correspond" (331–32).[49]

While Pen gets uplifted to a separate and not quite equal social station, her father suffers a fortunate fall to rural Vermont, where his "moral rise" that so many critics have emphasized no longer threatens the Boston elite. The class conflicts get displaced into what Amy Kaplan has called "class tourism."[50] Only Howells is left as the outsider-insider, and his nervous breakdown shortly after finishing this novel betrays the tensions his narration bottles up.[51] As the novel becomes the Rise of Penelope Lapham, Pen's new role as a sentimental icon of womanly tears and virtue avoids confronting not only Howells's conflicted class negotiations as a realistic writer, but also the conflicts inherent in portraying a daddy's girl who reaches beyond her class and daughterly role.

Finally, unlike Pen, Nathaniel Hawthorne's creative double in *The Marble Faun* (1860) neither seeks nor gains upward mobility. But Miriam, and her friend Hilda too, do lead vigorous lives of independence and achievement. Where Chopin's Edna Pontellier chooses to explore heterosexual passion at home instead of moving to Paris to further her career as a painter, Miriam and Hilda have moved to Rome to further their dreams of artistic success. To contain the threat of independent career women, Hawthorne insistently frames Miriam and Hilda with a traditional moral allegory, much as Spenser does with Mutability.

The Hawthorne-Spenser connection is well known. He named his first daughter Una, after the heroine in Book One of *The Faerie Queene,* and "Young Goodman Brown" transposes Una, Duessa, Archimago, and the Red Cross Knight to Salem at the time of the witch trials. Linking the Mutability Cantos to *The Marble Faun* is more of a stretch. Nonetheless, if Spenser's last unpublished work inaugurates the Anglo-American tradition of ambivalent allegories about female upward mobility and patriarchal instability, Hawthorne's last published romance exposes the inability of paternalistic allegory to subdue those cultural energies. Much as Henrietta Stackpole's more conventional exuberance escapes James's paternalistic controls, Miriam's passionate subjectivity exceeds the bounds of Hawthorne's moral critique.

With an initial bow to convention, the romance presents Miriam and Hilda as classically light and dark women. Whereas Hilda is a blonde Protestant New Englander "not overflowing with animal spirits" (63), Miriam is an inscrutable foreigner of seemingly cosmopolitan and European origins, Italian and Catholic, with hints of Jewish antecedents in her mixture. Only near the end do readers learn that Miriam's mother was an Englishwoman who died when Miriam was a child, while her father is a "princely" southern Italian with a vaguely Jewish background (429–30).[52] Neither Hilda nor Miriam is a daddy's girl, though Hawthorne's Gothic variation portrays Miriam as enraged and enthralled by her "Model," whose pursuit traps her in a mysterious family history she is trying to escape. Until the end, readers know only that Miriam's mother died when she was young, leaving her father and this strangely compelling father-like pursuer. Readers know even less about Hilda, who seems to have had no childhood at all. Once, glancingly, the narrator mentions her mother (357). Emerging from these skimpy and contrasting backgrounds, each woman has chosen a life of "liberty" and artistic ambition, without "the shackles of our present conventional rules" about female propriety (54–55).

Hawthorne's narration first constrains their threat as career women by tilting the moral scales toward Hilda. Early in the romance, Hilda gives up the dangerously unfeminine dreams of originality that impel Miriam's creativity. Instead, she becomes "the best copyist in Rome" through her capacity for "sacrificing herself" as she "religiously" reproduces the paintings of the Old Masters (59–60). More complexly, Hawthorne insistently contrasts Hilda's calm and virginal purity of soul with Miriam's eruptively changeable intensities, while intimating ambiguous taints in Miriam's background. When the two contemplate Hilda's copy of what was then thought to be Guido Reni's portrait of Beatrice Cenci, the woman in Renaissance Rome who allegedly killed her father after he raped her, Hilda sees "character" while Miriam sees "history," perhaps her own (66). While Miriam contemplates the possibility of sin and evil in herself, she wonders if Hilda's character will remain so pure that the Catholics would "make a Saint of you, like your namesake of old" (53).⁵³ At the end, a compatriot sculptor does it instead. After Hilda marries Kenyon, she retreats to the United States to become a good wife and mother. There she becomes "worshipped as a household Saint, in the light of her husband's fireside" (461).

Yet Miriam's creative ambitions can't be contained so easily. Alive with fancies, Miriam frequently seems "between" states of feeling, as the faunman Donatello wavers between animal and human. The allure of her embodied ethnic miscegenation makes people conjecture various fictions about her background. Is she Jewish? Does she have "one burning drop of African blood" (23)? Is she an English lady? Whatever her mixture is, it gives her "magnetism" (36) as well as mutability. As Hawthorne's creative shadow, she gains a considerable degree of narrative empathy, before she is finally scapegoated, called a "hysteric" (429) and imprisoned for murder. "[T]here was something in Miriam's blood, in her mixed race, . . . which had given her freedom of thought, and force of will" (430) to resist an arranged marriage with the marchese who becomes the Model, and to resist a life like her mother's. Even Hilda doesn't remain immune from Miriam's influence. While copying a portrait of Beatrice Cenci, she sees Beatrice in her own face (205), and she too has a "hysteric" flirtation with Catholicism (357).

In her more Gothic aspects, Miriam's art and life resist Hawthorne's paternalistic allegory by enacting a contradictory fusion of antipatriarchal rage and involuntary patriarchal submission. The rage first manifests itself obliquely, as recurrent preoccupations with her guilt and sin. Her rage surfaces more directly in her contradictory relation to the Model, who chains her subjectivity to her mysterious history. In one aspect he seems to be a slavish follower, like Donatello; in another aspect he seems to be an enslaver. It's disappointing when the mystery fades into the light of common patriarchal day: Miriam has fled from the prospect of an arranged marriage, only to be shadowed by the man her father has chosen for her husband.

Until then, the narrative invites speculations that the Model is Miriam's father, perhaps an incestuous father. Or he might be an allegorical embodiment of generic maleness. Or he might be a male version of Miriam's in-betweenness, half man and half demon, even her demon-lover. Along with bringing the weight of history to Miriam's consciousness, he brings Death into Arcadia.[54] After Miriam's gaze induces Donatello to kill the Model, the corpse undergoes still another transformation to become the corpse of a Capuchin monk. Beyond or because of his oscillating identities, the Model holds her in some kind of "thraldom" from her girlhood onwards (93). He is Miriam's constant "Shadow." Yet he is also her double, as she is Hawthorne's "model" of the original artist. As she says to him, "I am your evil genius, as you mine!" (95).

Hawthorne's narration shares that contradictory energy. Throughout, the novel simultaneously attempts to impose and resist patriarchal closures. The patriarchal turns are rather obvious, particularly the progress of Donatello and Miriam toward the statue of Pope Julius III, where they confess their guilty bond. Later Hilda seeks out a father-confessor, and at the end, by voluntarily relinquishing her artistic ambitions to become Kenyon's wife, she accepts the patriarchal closure that Miriam tries to resist. But Miriam's fate is more complex. After inducing the Model's fall from the Tarpeian Rock, Miriam continues to be shadowed, this time by several kinds of guilt. Not only has she failed to fulfill her family's traditional expectation that she will marry her betrothed, but she has murdered him instead. She is also shadowed by her narrator's insistent expectations for a woman's proper domestic role. In Hawthorne's allegory at least, a woman can't escape that historical fate, nor should she try, however strong her character.

Nonetheless, what's best in his narrative returns again and again to Miriam's contradictory passions of in-betweenness, like an allegorical moth to a psychological flame. Ambivalently, the narrator half endorses and half recoils from her rage against oppressive, incestuous fathers, figured in the recurrent motif of the Beatrice Cenci painting. Not coincidentally, Hawthorne began writing *The Marble Faun* just after his daughter Una had a nervous breakdown in Rome, in part because Hawthorne didn't want her to be a copyist. Tensions between a controlling father and an eruptive, sexually maturing daughter pervade this romance.[55]

As in *The Scarlet Letter* and *The Blithedale Romance*, Hawthorne is fascinated with dangerously transgressive heroines. But Hawthorne also shadows his narrative with Spenserian thoughts of his own mutability. More subtly than Longfellow does in the last stanza of "The Children's Hour," *The Marble Faun* displays an aging father's quiet nervousness about death in the offing. Unlike Longfellow, Hawthorne usually displaces this nervousness into snorts of disgust—at Rome, beggars, trickeries, Jewish tenement dwellers, laboring women, even Italian towns and frescoes. The hysteria he occasionally lodges in Hilda and Miriam more appropriately describes his own sudden outbursts, rages with no clear object. Italy's aging becomes an unwanted mirror.

Hawthorne's biliousness against a great culture in decline climaxes in his lengthy tirade against modern Rome. The city is "a long decaying corpse . . . with accumulated dust and a fungous growth overspreading all its more admirable features . . . indescribably ugly[.]" Moreover, every night he meets with "a ravenous little populace" of bugs "feasting with our own substance" as he tries to sleep in a Roman bed. And yet, "hating her with all our might," cursing her "crimes" and trickeries, he finds himself "attached . . . to the Eternal City" despite himself (325–26). Much as he felt about Salem, one might say. And, I would argue, much as he felt about his own mutable body. At these points, thoughts of young working women as creative doubles or dangers seem far away.

It may seem perverse to frame a chapter on daddy's girls with Spenser and Hawthorne, especially since neither Mutability nor Miriam has much to say about her father. Yet juxtaposing these two allegories shows the persistence and the insufficiency of the long-running Anglo-American literary effort to bring independent women toward patriarchal closure. Both the Mutability Cantos and *The Marble Faun* show how attempts at patriarchal resolutions betray male instability and lack. Both texts gain much of their narrative energy from the covert doubling of a dangerously creative female character and the not quite controlling male author.

What's missing from these two allegories is class, particularly the threat that female upward mobility might transgress class-linked lines of cultural authority. In the early corporate era, the daddy's girl figure becomes a way of dramatizing class and gender conflicts psychologically, while the career woman becomes a spectral double. As empowered and entitled men confront ambitious young women from a lower social station, they also confront patriarchal ideals they can't quite measure up to. In depicting young women's complex mixtures of accommodation and resistance to fathers and father-figures, daddy's girl stories also reveal the discontents and the precariousness in men's paternalistic desire.

Though Pen Lapham and Isabel Archer seem to accept their narrative humbling, their authors leave them with unresolved and contradictory subjective possibilities. Each woman retains the capacity for displaying a challenging transgressiveness, and most modern readers hope that they will. When James rewrote *The Portrait of a Lady* for the 1908 New York edition, he had to add a few more sentences at the end to check readers who think that Isabel will leave Osmond for Goodwood, much as Hawthorne grudgingly appended a new last chapter that blocked any hopes for Miriam's future rise by putting her in a convent. Unlike Miriam, Pen and Isabel do retain some capacity for independence. Yet their new self-constructions remain dependent on both a higher class position and a husband. With greater social daring, stories about Laura Hawkins, Sister Carrie, and Alexandra Bergson sympathetically present possibilities of upward mobility for daddy's girls on the make.

3 Daddy's Girls as Upwardly Mobile Women: Four Novels

When the daddy's girl appears *as* an upwardly mobile woman, paternalistic tensions become more exposed. Particularly in Twain and Warner's *The Gilded Age* and Dreiser's *Sister Carrie,* my prime daddy's girl texts, fatherhood loses cultural authority, even as the young women uplift themselves by stimulating older men's paternal and erotic desires. Although Cather's *O Pioneers!* idealizes traditional rural values associated with strong character and farm production, the favored daughter rather than her struggling father or conventional brothers turns the land's potential into abundance. Finally, in Jean Webster's *Daddy-Long-Legs,* the implicit erotics of corporate paternalism shape the reading experience. Unlike Wharton's *Summer,* where Lawyer Royall's desires for his young "Charity" seem more pitiable than arousing, Webster's epistolary structure encourages readers to identify with both the maturing independence of a creative orphan girl and the benevolence of her secret philanthropist. Curiously, as the man she calls "daddy" starts to want her as his wife, his control and even his health temporarily lapse into need.

This chapter consists of four close readings, briefly contrasted with other narratives. After juxtaposing *The Gilded Age* with María Amparo Ruiz de Burton's *Who Would Have Thought It?* and Louisa May Alcott's *Work,* all published in 1872 or 1873, I compare *Sister Carrie* (1901) with Wharton's *Custom of the Country* (1913). *O Pioneers!,* also published in 1913, contrasts with Cather's next novel, *The Song of the Lark* (1915). I then compare *Daddy-Long-Legs* with Robert Nathan's *Portrait of Jennie* (1940) and Wharton's *Summer* (1917).

The Gilded Age

In *The Gilded Age* (1873), by Mark Twain and Charles Dudley Warner, Laura Hawkins is both a ruthless Washington lobbyist and a daddy's girl four times over. Since Laura is mostly Twain's creation, except for the chapters on Laura's romance with Col. Selby, why does he concoct this unresolved narrative tension between a young woman's realistic political manipulations and her sentimental romance longings for father-figures?

In chapter 5, Laura enters as a little orphan after three fathers or father-figures have already been undermined. First Silas Hawkins gets inwardly seduced by his dreams of riches, then Uncle Dan'l's authoritative pronouncements turn into comic flight, and finally Laura's own father and mother die in a steamboat wreck, precipitating her adoption by the Hawkins family. Later, while she rises to power as a Washington lobbyist, the young woman's narrative identity oscillates between her relish for ruthless manipulations and her recurrent desire to find the father she lacks.

Ostensibly Laura's daddy's girl yearnings parody the sentimental treatment of orphan girls in women's fiction. Twain may also have been thinking of Louisa May Alcott's *Little Women* (1868), where Jo relinquishes her independent career as a writer of sensation fiction by responding to Professor Bhaer, first as her moral mentor, and eventually as her husband, with whom she runs a boys' school. During a small dinner party in the winter of 1872, Twain and Warner were mocking the success of Alcott and Harriet Beecher Stowe, whereupon their wives challenged them to do better.[1] The two men launched their novel—Twain's first—as a satire of sentimental fiction as well as of Washington politics, since Laura's desire seems shaped as much by her readings of romances as by her experience.

Yet Twain's heroine has the paradoxical qualities of independence and dependence that Alcott gives to young Jo, and that Theodore Dreiser presents with more ambivalent sympathy in Sister Carrie. Each character is both a yearning little girl and a tough, ambitious woman. In making Laura Hawkins and Sister Carrie daddy's girls and mistresses as well as highly successful professionals, Twain and Dreiser contain the threat of young women who rise through their work, not through the more respectably male-dependent roles of wife and mother. But Twain and Dreiser do more than that. Laura and Carrie perform the mobilities, improvisations, and self-creations that unsettle traditions of value based on character, property, and labor. Even when they enact their daughterly roles, Laura and Carrie play with men's paternalistic fantasies. In the process, each heroine uplifts herself by taking advantage of a national capitalist economy that detaches social value from productivity and use.

The first five chapters of *The Gilded Age*, all written by Twain, establish a great many paternal, racial, gender, and class-linked instabilities that frame Laura's entrance. The novel begins with Squire Hawkins on the fence or on the rocks, in several senses. A man of gentlemanly style, he sits on a "'stile[,]'" really a "pyramid of large blocks," in a tiny Tennessee town that "stood on top of a mountain" (23), though no one can see the mountain.[2] Already, in the first two sentences, dreams of grandeur contend with flat pedestrian realities. As readers soon learn, the "mountain" is part of an unprepossessing range called the Knobs, a name that reaches for stylish or "Nobby" pretensions to inflate its lumpy physical contours. Even Mr. Hawkins's title of "Squire" isn't quite deserved, though the narrator continues to call him by his changing titles, while his wife calls him "Si." He has been given the title of Squire because he is postmaster of Obedstown, which receives mail once a month. True, the title doesn't "properly belong to the office," but the villagers think the "chief citizens" have to have "titles of some sort" (24). Surrounded by these yokels, who appear to him "like a company of buzzards" (25), he fears that "I am becoming one of these cattle" (26). In pursuit of the high status he thinks he deserves, he decides to move to Missouri, where his friend Col. Sellers has grander dreams to offer.

In any event, as he says to his skeptical wife, his 75,000 acres of Tennessee land will be worth a fortune some day, and those who can seize the opportunity will "live like the princes of the earth; they'll be courted and worshiped; their names will be known from ocean to ocean!" (28). "I am an honored woman to be the wife of such a man" (29), his wife responds, keeping her doubts to herself. Their reverential use of terms like "princes," "courted," and "honored" signals the Squire's allegiance to an idealized image of the leisured gentleman, and therefore his susceptibility to the status fictions proffered for profit by speculators such as Col. Sellers.

More common than he thinks he is, the Squire will soon suffer the fate of a great many American dreamers. After ascending to the title of "Judge" and even "General" (55), he suffers his "first bankruptcy" (57). As with Twain's own father, also a Judge, the Squire's faith that owning a large tract of land will lead to quasi-aristocratic rank as well as riches soon brings failure, desperation, and early death. Long afterward, at the end of the novel, one of his children lets the land be auctioned to pay the $180 they owe in taxes, at least twice its market value (427). By then the cultural authority of landed property as well as fatherhood has given way to what the authors' preface calls a "fever of speculation," brought on by an "inflamed desire for sudden wealth" (xxi).

Chapter 2 swerves from a relatively complex and realistic account of a sympathetic man's inflated aspirations into mawkish melodrama. While travelling to Missouri, the family sees a ten-year-old boy crying in front of a log cabin, where his mother has just died. Twain piles on the quick switches: within minutes the Hawkins family has adopted the boy, and by the next morning he is "almost healed" as he walks "hand in hand" with his "new mother" (35). The boy's name, Clay, suggests contradictory possibilities: either an identity capable of being molded by his new family, or an intractably base fleshiness associated with death rather than transfiguration. Twain never does much with either of these associations, or with Clay's uncertain family status as alien son. Instead, chapter 3 sets up a more explicitly parodic set of instabilities. There, on the banks of the Mississippi, Twain dramatizes a perceptual impasse.

Though two adult slaves sit with the children doing unpaid child care, this "little company . . . were all children," Twain says, and they see a mystery that fascinates and appalls them (37). Through childlike eyes, readers watch a muddle of disconnected attributes coming down the river—a "deep cough-ing sound[,]" a "fierce eye of fire[,]" "a huge shape" that "developed itself out of the gloom," and "tall duplicate horns" spewing "volumes of smoke, starred and spangled with sparks." The horns suggest the devil, while the "starred and spangled" sparks evoke the American flag held high in battle. The "coughing," the wild eyes of fire, and the "spots" might also suggest a contagious disease, perhaps measles or smallpox.[3] To the children, the "huge shape" becomes first "the thing[,]" and finally "the monster[.]" To Uncle Dan'l, one of the family's slaves, "It's de Almighty! Git down on yo' knees!"

Of course it's simply a steamboat, and the rest of the chapter recounts Un-cle Dan'l's comic failures as a paternalistic authority. First he prays at length for the Lord to take him rather than the children. Then, as the "flaming and churning steamer" gets closer, he snatches up two of the children and flees into the woods, "feebly" shouting, "Heah I is, Lord, heah I is!" (38). Then, after "the august presence had gone by," he proclaims his "ficiency in prah[,]" a nice Twain touch that poises Uncle Dan'l's praying skills midway between efficiency and deficiency. When Clay asks him why he ran, he says he was "under de influence ob de spirit," like "de Hebrew chil'en that went frough the fiah[.]" (39). Here Uncle Dan'l's relatively conventional address to the Lord suddenly swerves to a more original charge of double meanings, as he takes a crack at Clay's capacity for irony. "Sometimes a body can't tell whedder you's a sayin' what you means or whedder you's a sayin' what you don't mean, 'case you says 'em bofe de same way."

Then, with more audacious panache, Uncle Dan'l invents gender instabil-ities in the Bible. Those Hebrew children were boys, he says, because "if dey'd ben gals dey'd missed dey long haah (hair), maybe" (39, Twain's civi-lizing parenthesis). But since they were boys, they never felt the fire. Wait a minute, says Clay, "they *were* girls[.]" Both Clay and Uncle Dan'l are wrong, since the "children" are Shadrach, Mesach, and Abednego, adult males in the first book of Daniel, a namesake whom he doesn't seem to know. A con-ventional rejoinder might be to call them "children of God," but Uncle Dan'l takes a far more original tack. Nonsense, he replies; "don't it call 'em de *he*-brew chil'en? If dey was gals wouldn't dey be de she-brew chil'en? Some peo-ple dat kin read don't 'pear to take no notice when dey *do* read."

Suddenly, as another steamer appears, Dan'l says "Dey ain't two, mars Clay—dat's the same one. De Lord kin 'pear eberywhah in a second." At last he takes flight: "ole Uncle Daniel gwyne out in the woods to rastle in prah[.]" As the chapter concludes, "he went so far that he doubted, himself, if the Lord heard him when He went by." The nonexistent "he" asserted for the Hebrew children returns as the omnipresent two-in-one yet equally far-fetched "He" of God himself, converging with the five "he" and "him" des-ignations for Uncle Dan'l.

This dizzying sequence of instabilities undermines more than the paternal authority Uncle Dan'l tries to presume in Squire Hawkins' absence. A fearless protector is also a coward. God is everywhere and nowhere. An uncle is not an uncle. Girls are boys and boys are girls. Adults are children, here and in the Bible. Saying what you mean and saying what you don't mean may be the same thing. Reading means nonreading. Reality may be real, though the steamboat never gets acknowledged except by the narrator, or reality may be no more than everyone's divergent perceptions, including the narrator's. Uncle Dan'l is Twain's minstrel-like literary commodity to provide comic relief, or a faithful family slave who later provides momentary narrative pathos as he and his wife get auctioned off because of the Squire's involvement in Col. Sellers' failed sugar speculation (67). In genres and styles as well as themes, Twain's narration has already become a kind of bait-and-switch game, undermining its own coherence and authority in pursuit of new events, new pretensions, new melodramas, new mockeries, new stimuli, anything to keep readers on the hook. As the novel shifts from sympathetic yet satirical realism to fake melodrama to vernacular burlesque, narrative controls on meaning itself start to disintegrate.

The shift back to melodramatic realism in chapter 4 temporarily stabilizes the story. But the explosion of the Amaranth in its race to catch up with the Boreas shows male competition run amok. Moreover, raced words about black smoke erupt from one pilot's mouth as his competitive excitement intensifies: "nigger roosting on the safety-valve! . . . Bully! Every time a nigger heaves a stick of wood into the furnace he goes out the chimney with it!" (46).

Blackness remains the one narrative component whose ongoing subordination shores up the pleasures and powers of white paternalism, and not just in Twain's uses of Uncle Dan'l to show how human property is linguistically exploitable. When the Squire whispers to his wife of their land's potential for profit, his first example is the possibility of turning "that black stuff" on his Tennessee land into marketable coal (28). Similarly, the first scheme of Col. Sellers that the Squire's dubious wife recalls is his idea of "buying up whole loads of negroes in Delaware and Virginia and Tennessee" (29), delivering them to Alabama, then getting a law passed to stop any further sales of negroes to the south, thus nearly monopolizing the slave market. These initial examples prefigure Col. Sellers's later, still grander plan to get the U.S. Government to buy the Hawkins' Tennessee land for a Tuskegee-anticipating "Knobs Industrial University" that will ostensibly uplift the black race. Throughout the novel, blackness becomes an abstracted signifier that secures white respectability, much as Uncle Dan'l's vernacular confirms Clay's superior language and literacy while entitling the irony of Clay and Twain.

From all these rhetorical swerves and indeterminacies, Laura Hawkins emerges as their synecdochic embodiment. This "little black-eyed girl of five years" (49) already has a mysteriously mobile and polyglot past. As the Hawkins family welcome a second orphan, they learn only that her family boarded at New Orleans, "where they had just arrived in a vessel from Cuba; that they looked like people from the Atlantic States; that the family name was Van Brunt" (50). Much like the seemingly unplaceable past of Hawthorne's Miriam in *The Marble Faun,* Laura's background uneasily joins Southern, Cuban, mid-Atlantic and Dutch strains, while her body hints at possible miscegenation in her family history. As readers learn a little later, "her complexion was pure white and contrasted vividly with her black hair and eyes" (63). She embodies the fractures in the nation's attempt to reunite after the Civil War: Southern, yet Northern; white, yet black; family, yet "of alien blood" (56). Soon, as if replicating Uncle Dan'l's biblical exposition, she will also be an adult "she," a beautiful lady, yet implicitly "he" in her enjoyment of work and power.

From the start, Laura is also an amalgam of contradictory roles. Like a good daddy's girl, she latches onto Squire Hawkins immediately, but with a strange mixture of desire and decisiveness. "Something in the face of Mr. Hawkins attracted her and she came and looked up at him; was satisfied, and took refuge with him." The Squire's response—"He petted her" (49)—blends fatherly comfort with condescension to a pet animal, much as St. Clare treats Topsy in *Uncle Tom's Cabin.* But Laura's sense of being "attracted" has a latent erotic charge, and leads to a more mysterious process of assessment and choice, as if she were already a little adult. To juxtapose being "satisfied" with taking "refuge" intimates her independence in the midst of enacting her dependence. Moreover, she chooses to take "refuge with him," not "within his arms," almost as if the Squire were a companion who sought common refuge with her.

Laura's enigmatic reserve constitutes part of her own attractiveness, to adults and readers alike. Like the steamboat in chapter 3, she continually generates diverse responses and perceptions. Arriving as a destitute orphan from a middle-class family, she provokes enough pathos to justify Mr. and Mrs. Hawkins' protective response. Yet her bearing intimates a social status much higher than their own. "The child's manners were those of a little lady, and her clothes were daintier and finer than any Mrs. Hawkins had ever seen before" (50). Soon this little lady takes charge even of Col. Sellers: "the Colonel took the lead, with Laura astride his neck" (53). That startling word "astride" makes the Colonel seem like a horse, with Laura the rider.

These contradictions take somewhat different forms as Laura enters adulthood. At the age of eighteen, Laura has "a proud bearing[,]" and speaks "like a princess" (63). Yet this young lady dares to talk about working for pay, to help herself and the family. In "fond reproof[,]" Mrs. Hawkins responds, "we will hope that we haven't got quite down to that, yet." While Laura's eyes "beamed affection under her mother's caress," she "straightened up . . . and became a splendid ice-berg" (63). Soon, performing opposite roles of iceberg lady and sentimental icon, the adopted daughter supplants Hawkins's wife at his deathbed. By now Clay is calling her "the

Duchess" (81), because she seems so imperious in commanding that she be at the Squire's bedside all the time. When he dies, it's Laura, not his wife, who "bent down and kissed her father's lips as the spirit left the body" (82). Has the daughter become both wife and vampire, sucking in her father's spirit at the moment he dies? Less oddly, while everyone else is crying, she remains mutely self-possessed, as if she were a stoic male who does what has to be done: "she did not sob, or utter any ejaculation" as she closes his eyes and crosses his hands (82).

The end of Laura's first daddy's girl role begins her second. Hard upon the death of the man she thinks is her father comes the death of Major Lackland, whose last name undermines the Squire's fantasies of land as the ground of his dynasty. Finding some letters from Major Lackland to the Squire, Laura learns that Hawkins was not her real father after all.[4] The Major has discovered that her father may still be alive but in a delirious state. The letters describe Mr. Van Brunt as an "aristocratic gentleman," with a "fine presence" and "a slight limp in his walk" (85–86). Faced with this new mixture of information and speculation, Laura sits "thinking—and unconsciously freezing. . . . An undefined sense of injury crept into her heart" (86–87).

In yet another narrative swerve, Laura's oscillations between her freezing pride and her yearnings for dependence on a father-figure get reduced to literary romance. The discovery of her unknown origins makes her think she has "romance secreted away" in her "composition." "She was a heroine, now, with a mysterious father somewhere" (87). As she reads more romances, "her mind preyed upon itself, and the mystery of her birth at once chagrined her and raised in her the most extravagant expectations." Besides, she has "imbibed" some "crude" ideas about "the emancipation of women" (140–41). At that point she finds a third father-figure, Col. Selby, a man whose aristocratic bearing suits her "exaggerated notions" of her possible powers and status. Though Twain and Warner forget to give him a limp until much later, Laura precipitously marries him anyway, or thinks she does, until he tells her he already has a wife. Her status as wife/not wife parallels her previous knowledge of herself as daughter/not daughter.

Laura's recovery from a melodramatic faint leads to rhetorical questions that uncertainly repackage her psychological state. "When she came to herself . . . Did she come to herself? Was there anything left in her heart but hate and bitterness, a sense of an infamous wrong at the hands of the only man she had ever loved?" (143). One might ask, what happened to Laura's love for Squire Hawkins? Or her search for her father? Having erased these daddy's girl roles, the narrator gives Laura a quasi-incestuous third version, in which the father-lover's sexual exploitation and betrayal leaves her with a passionate mixture of desire, dependence, and rage. Yet that mix of feelings gives her all the more beauty and power. More unresolved questions follow: "Is there a beauty in the knowledge of evil" that gives her an "added fascination"? Does she resemble a "Beatrice Cenci" figure (143), the Renaissance Italian aristocrat who allegedly killed her father for raping her, and who so fascinates Miriam in *The Marble Faun*? For the narrator, it's all too much. "The lovely woman had a devil in her heart. That was all."[5]

Such narrative reductions won't stay put, though the Selby relationship turns rather flat. The narrator doesn't do much to develop its erotic father-figure possibilities, perhaps because Warner, who wrote those sections, casts them in the more conventional mode of "He done her wrong."[6] Instead, the novel's satire of sentimental romance jostles with its realistic satire of Laura's workplace rise as a Washington lobbyist and power-broker. Her fourth role as daddy's girl begins when Senator Dilworthy tells her that she "could be useful in the great cause of philanthropy, . . . uplifting the poor and the ignorant[.]" She sees that invitation as the high road to the full use of her powers. No longer will she feel like "a large-size pigmy among these pigmies here, who tumble over so easily when one strikes them" (215).

What she wants, she says to herself, "is to go to Washington and find out what I am. I want money, too" (216). There she gains entry to the political stage not simply through her beauty, but also through the credit people give her for seeming to be "a great landed heiress" whose "whole heart was devoted to . . . the uplifting of the down-trodden negro" (229). Privately, the only uplift she cares about comes when "many eyes were uplifted toward her face" (226). In pursuit of influence and power, she also becomes a superb actress, leading Congressmen, Harry Brierly, and even Philip Sterling to believe she has eyes and feelings only for them (e.g.,150).

Soon Senator Dilworthy calls her "my daughter" (229, 250) while she calls him "uncle" (248), and a newspaper later calls her the Senator's "niece" (324). Their relationship seems to be all business, veiled in the language of paternalism and philanthropy, though perhaps the hundreds of dollars in "pin money" he gives her intimate some sexual dalliances (229). Later, as part of her manipulations, Laura tells Senator Trollop—an ostensibly moral opponent—that she has set him up with her "agent," a woman who has either bribed him or given him sexual services, or both (290–91). Has she become a Madam to further her plans for the Hawkins land?

Laura's search for a limping father persists, but now in a more punitive mode, as a succession of crippled men people the stage. Even before the letters about Mr. Van Brunt appear, Squire Hawkins's wife muses that Col. Sellers had already "crippled us" at least twice with his schemes (29). Now, after Senator Trollop lives up to his name by saying he will prostitute his vote for money, then decides to oppose the Knobs University bill after all, Laura makes him a "crippled man" (291) by withholding a page from his speech. His "break-down in the House" (298) brands him as "Crippled-Speech Trollop" (303). By the end, Senator Dilworthy has been "ruined" (401), and Clay's business in Australia has also been "crippled" (423), though not by Laura. Most centrally, Col. Shelby's suddenly prominent limp (268–69) helps to reignite Laura's passion for him, leading to her Beatrice Cenci-like murder of the lover she chose as husband because he seemed like the father she imagined.

Throughout, Twain and Warner reserve the image of romance heroine to describe Laura's private, desperate desire for Col. Shelby (e.g., 268–73), while they keep recirculating negative sound bites for her public image as a proudly independent woman. "Duchess" and "ice-berg" recur many times, along with "queen" (148, 225, 318, 326) and "devil" (297, 336), sometimes in the narration, sometimes in the dialogue. Though three father-figures have abandoned her in different ways, the narrator's image of her vacillates between sympathy and satire. When she seems dependent on her womanly desire for Col. Shelby, the narrator expresses patronizing pity for the struggling heroine. When she relishes the "power" that women's fiction shows can be hers (147–48), or flashes into "'spite'" at what men have done to her (298), she gets reduced to a calculating villain, asserting feminist cliches that she doesn't even mean. As she says to Harry Brierly, "I'm angry with the cruel world, which pursues an independent woman as it never does a man" (281). But she says that to cover up her rage at what she has just learned from Harry, that Col. Selby is once again taking his wife and children rather than herself. That information brings on the pistol shots that land her in jail.

If her longing for a father begins as romance, it ends as farce. At her murder trial, Col. Sellers explains that Laura had always yearned for limping men with scars, since they reminded her of her father. But she kept getting the wrong mix of scars and crippled legs. "[I]f his legs were right, his scar was wrong, if his scar was right his legs were wrong. Never could find a man that would fill the bill" (387). The jury's only question to the Judge is if Col. Sellers is "related to the Hawkins family" (391). As Laura is declared not guilty by reason of insanity, so by implication Col. Sellers's more engagingly crazy speculation, like all of his speculations, can be absolved of any guilt for the consequences of his schemes.

The Laura-Sellers connection runs deeper than most critics have allowed.[7] Though the narrator tries to reduce her to contradictory stereotypes of romance and satirical realism, Laura parallels and complicates the speculative mania that Col. Sellers represents more endearingly. She too knows how to create value and manipulate public opinion. "We must create a public opinion," says Senator Dilworthy (276), and Laura and the Colonel know just how to do it. Laura also understands Col. Sellers's guiding principle, that value must be created from appearances. As his family huddles around a tallow candle in their stove, he memorably declares, "What you want is the *appearance* of heat, not the heat itself—that's the idea" (70).

"Sellers" sells dreams, not products. In his own appearance, he presents himself as a classic Southern gentleman, at home in "'aristocratic'" hotels. "We Southern gentlemen don't change our ways, you know[,]" he says to Philip and Harry (107). But his patrician rhetoric is an act to gain their credit, so that they will pay his bill. On a larger scale, he performs his gentlemanly status as a defeated patrician Southerner to enhance his social capital during Reconstruction. "He was one of the Southerners who were constantly quoted as heartily 'accepting the situation.' 'I'm whipped,' he used to say with a jolly laugh" (275). For him, speculation becomes a national unifier.

Moreover, he believes in every one of his grandiose ideas. That's part of what makes him a great salesman, and most of what makes him more than a con man to his readers. He represents the nation's innocent, hungering faith in the grand future that awaits its recovery from its war-torn recent past. Every white man can realize his fantasies of uplift through the Colonel's confident plans for developing the country. Every white man also wants to be "conspicuous" (194), not common, in the know rather than out of the loop. For Col. Sellers, Washington, D.C., is a "paradise" of speculation (179), putting him "at the centre of the manufacture of gigantic schemes, of speculations of all sorts, of political and social gossip" (274). Near the close of Reconstruction, he reconstructs the Southern gentleman's pseudo-aristocratic style as capitalist panache, available to any man able to sell believable fictions of prospective self-uplift. These fictions have replaced production as the basis for social value.

Laura's life represents the underside of that national allegory. As the narrator suggests, she mirrors the "uprooted" condition of national institutions after the Civil War. Will the nation, like a woman, become a "vestal of a holy temple" or a "fallen priestess" (137–38)? Laura becomes both possibilities, and more. She embodies a nation trying to heal its self-fracturing injuries by creating itself anew. In Laura's passion for a limping Southerner, the narrative transforms her search for her father into a mixture of romance and allegory, joining near-incestuous passion with a rescue fantasy of nursing the half-crippled white South back to health. Then, as if her Northern side erupts at the South's betrayal of her dreams, she kills Selby in the hotel where "the Southerners all go" (327).

At another level, the recurrent narrative charges of "devil" signal an eruption of male anxieties that capitalist dynamics might be creating strong women. Carol Karlsen's *The Devil in the Shape of a Woman* suggests that in colonial New England, growing expectations for men to be mobile, profit-oriented individuals required women to subordinate themselves into a "helpmeet role[.]" When "demons" were in a woman, she could act out both "her *desire for* independence and power . . . and her rage at the man who taught her that independence and power were the ultimate female evils. When possessed, she could assert the witch within[.]"[8] The witch figure expresses social instabilities in scapegoat form, as men tried to preserve patriarchal power while responding to new economic imperatives.

By *The Gilded Age,* capitalist dynamics have muted the patriarchal pull, except in sentimental rhetorics and practices that continue to constrain women such as Laura. In partially scapegoating Laura while almost wholly exonerating Col. Sellers, the narrative revels in the Colonel's imaginative powers, while turning Laura's workplace ambitions and man-killing rage into a cautionary spectacle. At the end she dies, ostensibly from a sentimentally broken heart, but also because she fails as a lecturer, she looks "worn and old[,]" "my pride is all gone," and she never has found her father (420–21). Always split between father-identification and a will to power, Laura ends in that self-divided mode. Trying to connect opposed explanations of her subjectivity, the narrator periodically says that Laura's desires for power and money are only a kind of unwomanly self-freezing, a spiteful rage at being victimized by a fatherly man. Yet Laura's proud energy, her zest in combat, and even her amoral calculations are Col. Sellers's dreams put into practice. Both pursue the "beautiful demon of money" (343), though only one is demonized.

In the sections of the novel written by Charles Dudley Warner, Ruth Bolton's progress through the novel from medical school ambitions to loving wife inverts Laura's self-divisions. At first she is a "sweet rebel" who strikes a strong feminist pose: "What a box women are put into . . . Father, I should like to break things and get loose" (114–15). But it's clear that her sweetness destines her for a domestic role by Philip Sterling's side. Ruth's dream of becoming a doctor gets a rude awakening when she sees a black man's corpse in a medical laboratory. She turns "pale as the white sheet" at the "repulsive black face[.]" Perhaps his look simply shows the "agony" of a painful death, she thinks. Or perhaps its "scowl" says, "Haven't you yet done with the outcast, persecuted black man, but you must . . . send even your women to dismember his body?" (122).

Recoiling, Ruth begins to follow her heart rather than her ambitions, in the binary that Warner genially imposes on her subjectivity. Much later, when Philip suggests that Laura Hawkins is "a devil[,]" Ruth vehemently defends the right of women to enter the professions, but her faint blush at the possibility that he cares for her signals her own preference (336–37). Not coincidentally, Philip's manly aggressiveness immediately takes the form of "running a tunnel into the breast of the mountain" to discover coal (337).

His success with that tunnel encourages Ruth to reject the devil within. "Good Money! beautiful demon of Money, what an enchanter thou art! Ruth felt that she was of less consequence in the household, now Philip had found coal; perhaps she was not sorry to feel so" (343–44). For Twain and Warner, that renunciation of independent desire makes her a good woman. At the novel's end, with all the sentimental stops pulled out, Philip becomes her white knight and rescuer. As he "drew her back to life" from a serious illness, she feels a new "dependence on another's nature, . . . a new but a dear joy, to be lifted up and carried back" for love (436–37). In the words of William Congreve's Mrs. Millament, she rather likes it that "I may by degrees dwindle into a wife."[9]

More generally, good women and black people provide a converging base that justifies white men's superiority as capitalist speculators. The "niggro" is an idle, "speculating race," Col. Sellers declares to Senator Dilworthy. "Nothing practical in 'em." But education would only give the black man "a wider scope to injure himself. A niggro has no grasp, sir. Now, a white man can conceive great operations, and carry them out; a niggro can't" (152). Once the Hawkins land comes into play, of course, the Colonel changes his tune. Nevertheless, it's clear to him as well as to various Senators that Knobs Industrial University will succeed only as a scam. If the black man's incapacity for fruitful speculation confirms white men's confidence in their special gifts, women function in much the same way. While Philip and Col. Sellers take suitable risks, "[i]t is probably on account of the lack of enterprise in women that they are not so fond of stock speculations and mine ventures as men. It is only when woman becomes demoralized that she takes to any sort of gambling" (352). Such glancing, dismissive observations firm up the raced and gendered hierarchy of power that Laura undermines.

Yet *The Gilded Age* also subverts these diffusely patriarchal resolutions. Laura gains her upward mobility by mastering the speculative spirit of the age, and turning it to her advantage. Her political career is much more transgressive than the social success of amoral Becky Sharp in Thackeray's *Vanity Fair* (1847) or the more chillingly amoral Undine Spragg in Wharton's *The Custom of the Country* (1913). Even as a figure of satire, she remains poised on the edge between readers' sympathy and condemnation. Her contradictions set her beyond the frame of romance that the narrative sometimes imposes, and that Twain and Warner set out to mock. Nor can Laura quite be reduced to national or political allegory. History, not fiction, licenses the writers to present an early version of the New Woman, and they play with the paradox. As they write near the end, if this were a regular novel, Laura would be locked away in an insane asylum, since "The novelist who would turn loose upon society an insane murderess could not escape condemnation." But "this is history and not fiction" (401), so readers can't be so comforted. Laura remains in the public sphere in part because there are no hospitals for insane criminals, but also because she is now a hot commodity, suitable for a lecture tour. Once more she displays her capacity for self-invention as an aspect of creating speculative value.

To summarize my arguments: first, *The Gilded Age* exposes the shakiness of patriarchal dreams based on landed property. Though men continue to derive cultural authority from class status and political office, the novel shows how speculative ventures in pursuit of money and status get greater attention. White men's respect now flows more from anticipatory desire than from deference. Second, Laura Hawkins is much more than the melodramatic satire of romance that critics usually take her to be. She is also the female counterpart to Col. Sellers in her manipulations of value. Her sometimes scapegoated contradictions express various tensions between North and South as well as between independence and dependence, or in her case between upward mobility and the daddy's girl. Third, as Ellen Goldner has argued, the novel not only satirizes the greed animating speeches for public philanthropy, but also subverts paternalistic rhetoric as a moral basis for subjectivity.[10] Last, and conversely, Twain and Warner use race to prop up the white paternalism that the novel usually mocks.

Of those arguments, my claims for Laura's complexity may seem the most problematic, so I've taken considerable space to justify them. Two other novels can serve as brief foils for Laura's originality. A satirical novel published a year earlier, María Amparo Ruiz de Burton's *Who Would Have Thought It?* (1872), conventionally dichotomizes good and bad women, though it addresses racial hierarchies more forthrightly. Lola, a little orphan girl of "pure Spanish blood" is taken for black by the main character, Jemima Norval, who calls Lola "this horrible little negro girl[.]"[11] Plotting to possess Lola's wealth, Jemima becomes a much more one-dimensional devil than Laura Hawkins is, while the orphan girl grows into a woman with a heart of gold, and eager for love. While Laura exploits her insanity plea, Jemima's money lust drives her genuinely insane, a simple if satisfactory punishment for a mother's will to power.

To exorcise Jemima's devilish desires, *Who Would Have Thought It?* brings her to moral sanity through patriarchal closure, since the narrative relies on white patricians to restore social order as well as Jemima's health. Tellingly, Lola has also whitened her skin to marry the man she loves without any taint of miscegenation. Instead of complicating these sentimental modes of patriarchal resolution as Twain and Warner do, Ruiz de Burton turns Jemima into a cautionary tale. Traditional female virtue and character triumph, as Lola's white makes right. The author reserves her wit and her ironies for the U.S. government's imperial corruptions and for a mother's parallel self-disfigurement by greed.

Finally, comparing *The Gilded Age* with Louisa May Alcott's *Work,* also published in 1873, shows how Laura Hawkins subverts traditional interpretive frames for securing female identity and social value. Here yet another orphan girl seeks what the first sentence calls "a new Declaration of Independence[.]"[12] Accepting her uncle's dismissive indictment of her as "discontented, proud and ambitious" (10), Christie Devon takes a series of jobs, from servant, actress, and governess to companion and seamstress. Slowly discovering the true meaning of work, she turns toward the more rewarding roles of wife and mother. As companion to a half-mad invalid woman and her family, Christie has already learned the narrator's conclusion that "Submission and self-sacrifice are stern, sad angels, but in time one learns to know and love them" (99). Moreover, her various jobs never alter her disposition, which remains "sound and sweet . . . a touchstone for the genuineness of others" (59). Her virtuous character and dedication to service sustain her in the face of adversity, especially when she becomes a Civil War nurse to care for her wounded husband. At the very end, after her husband dies, Christie hesitantly ventures beyond the home as a public speaker.

Although Christie's recurrent aloneness resembles Laura Hawkins's, Alcott's celebration of traditional female values blocks exploration of the pervasive tensions between her solitude and her need to serve others. Alcott doesn't let the contradictions out. Instead, although she exalts Christie as an independent woman who discovers the joys and trials of feminine duty, she also secures Christie's class entitlement as a lady. Even in her first job, Christie's presumption of paternalism guides her with Hepsey, an ex-slave. Eager to "pay a little part of the great debt which the white race owes the black[,]" she satisfies her "sense of obligation" by giving Hepsey part of her wages to free her "ole mammy" in Virginia (26–27). As Lynne Pulliam has pointed out, Christie never defines herself through her work roles. Instead, she always thinks of herself as the daughter of a gentleman, and therefore a lady. As she says to herself early on, "My father was a gentleman; and I shall never forget it, though I do go out to service" (24).[13]

Paternalistic class entitlement cradles Christie's subjectivity with an increasingly visible hand. Like Laura, Christie has long since lost her father. Though she doesn't seem to be a yearning daddy's girl, she does marry a slightly older man who takes in homeless girls such as herself. Having already subsumed her self-reliance in defining herself as the daughter of a gentleman, she now finds a temporary haven in the shelter of her husband's benevolence, until she finds more independent fulfillment as a mediator between two projected sides of herself, the lady and the working woman. She will act as a "mediator to bridge across the space" that separates "ladies" such as herself from the "women" whose work she had shared (333–34).

None of that fits Laura. Though both Lola and Christie experience abundant social fluidity, neither disrupts class and paternalistic hierarchies by making that fluidity an inward resource. Warner, too, uses an Alcott-like frame of elite domesticity and virtuous character to rein in Ruth Bolton's liking for work. More adventurously, Twain brings Laura forward with the contradictions that bedevil and enable middle-class white women in the early capitalist era.

Sister Carrie

Twenty-seven years later, in *Sister Carrie* (1900), Carrie's upward mobility begins as the train carries her past "the flour mill where her father worked" (7), and past the productive working-class manhood he represents.[14] If Laura Hawkins seems obsessively father-identified, Mr. Meeber is irrelevant. Father, mother, and home get discarded in the first paragraph. Even as Twain attempts to contain Laura in a daddy's girl narrative, his narration of Col. Sellers prefigures Dreiser's narration of Carrie by exulting in the Colonel's inventive, groundless fantasies of making it big. Carrie, too, has a rootless desire to rise by imitating upwards. Through buying things and acting parts, Carrie perpetually reaches for a classier self.

Like Laura, Carrie becomes a mistress, though neither character rises by that traditional means. Rather, Carrie succeeds as an actress, while Laura succeeds more briefly as a behind-the-scenes political manipulator. Yet despite the continuing sexual taint attached to women in the theater, Carrie receives much less narrative punishment, and not only because she abandons rather than kills her lover. More basically, by playing daddy's girl roles in private and public, she awakens protective, paternalistic responses in nearly everyone, from Drouet, Hurstwood, and Ames, to her narrator and her readers. Most deeply, she seems a sympathetic "sister" to everyone's inchoate longings. If Laura's contradictory character constitutes much of her appeal, Carrie succeeds by having no character at all. Or rather, as Walter Benn Michaels has said, Dreiser identifies her character with the speculative desires that corporate capitalism excites in everyone.[15] Throughout, the pathos of Carrie's uprootedness becomes part of her buoyancy.

In the last fifteen years, the most influential criticism of *Sister Carrie* (1900) has focused on either Carrie or the narrator's voice, or both, as contradictory manifestations of unsatisfiable capitalist desire. I'm more interested in exploring how Carrie arouses paternalistic desires in various men, including the narrator.[16] Carrie is not a daddy's girl; that would make her desire too knowable. But she has the knack of stimulating men's desires for daddy's girls, not least in Dreiser. Her social ascent comes from her ability to awaken protective as well as sexual feelings in men of higher status than her own, first brotherly Drouet, then fatherly Hurstwood, then "portly gentlemen" (411) in her theater audiences. The manager of the Casino is "secretly pleased with this pretty, disturbed-looking young woman" (353). She makes such men feel more manly and powerful, while inwardly she continues to float and drift. Yet their paternalistic and erotic feelings surge up from unacknowledged fears of being like her, dependent on external status for power, authority, and a sense of self. Men too are adrift.[17]

For Dreiser and his heroine, manliness comes from playing distinguished roles in corporate and cultural hierarchies of consumption, not from making things or fathering children. Manliness has become ungrounded, much as Carrie's assessments of men never stay fixed. In the world of the city and the firm, Drouet first seems admirably kind and sophisticated, then just an amiable provincial salesman as Carrie lifts her imagination of possibility. Hurstwood first seems to be a consummate manager of consumption, then an increasing drag. Where Carrie floats, he sinks into his fix, and finally becomes self-consumed. By implication, the only way to rise is continuously to detach oneself from any stabilizations of identity or desire.[18]

Sister Carrie also shows a shift in the representation of daddy's girls. Where Twain and Warner satirize the daddy's girl by playing with the sentimental motif of the orphan daughter, Dreiser more daringly narrates the daddy's girl as a compensatory male fantasy. As commodities temporarily give Carrie a lift, so daddy's girl fantasies give men a lift in several senses, by erecting a temporary paternalistic frame for their self-images. Carrie's hunger for upward mobility and men's hungers for daddy's girls are two sides of the same anxious yearning to be somebody special, somebody above your ordinary self, worthy of being respected or even adored.

With Hurstwood's entrance, the daddy's girl theme takes center stage. As I've argued in the introduction, Hurstwood's sense of narcissistic injury about losing his adolescent daughter's adoration helps to prompt his turn to Carrie. Now, on their first carriage ride, he passionately "seized" her hand. "A breath of soft spring wind went bounding over the road, rolling some brown twigs of the previous autumn before it" (126). Dreiser has not often been associated with stylistic subtlety, but the twigs are a deft touch. Like the vigorous verb and participles—"seized," "bounding," even "rolling"—the twigs suggest an inward "spring" that rolls away his autumnal feelings. Perhaps in his mind as well as his body, his aging brown "twig" turns white and firm again, lifted by the wind of his desire. Then, after he kisses her, he proclaims rhetorically, "you're my own girl aren't you?" To repeat my introduction, the "my" takes possession of Carrie from Drouet, the "girl" substitutes her for Jessica, and the "own" goes both ways.

In the next chapter, Dreiser muses on the delicate dance of power and powerlessness in Carrie's mute acquiescence. Given Hurstwood's "dignity and grace" and "his consuming affection for her[,]" she thinks she has "yielded sufficiently" (127–28). Beyond her calibration of what degree of submission might be appropriate, other ironies come into play. What "consumes" Hurstwood is "affection," not passion, and what attracts Carrie is his style, not his force. She feels no passion of her own. Instead, "It was the first time her sympathies had ever been thoroughly aroused, . . . She had some power of initiative, latent before[.]"

Carrie's "aroused" sympathies, a nice oxymoron, respond to Hurstwood's weakness rather than his strength. In the midst of their carriage ride, she realizes that he needs her at least as much as she needs him. Though Hurstwood thinks he's displaying his powers of persuasion, Carrie begins to yield to him because she thinks he "needed her aid . . . She truly pitied this sad, lonely figure. To think that all his fine state should be so barren for want of her," just as "she herself was lonely and without anchor" (125). Drifting between dependencies, she senses the possibility of independent agency, since now she has something to give. As Carrie's sentimental fantasies respond to Hurstwood's fears of being "barren" and alone, the narrator's doubled identification hovers between satire and sympathy, again with considerable subtlety.

Moreover, as Hurstwood induces her fantasies of sentimental agency rather than sexual ecstasy, he also represents "a drag in the direction of honor." That phrase tugs in two directions, by ambiguously joining her uplifting dream of "honor" with the potentially downward pull of Hurstwood's "drag." For Carrie, honor connotes more than her immediate hopes of "freedom" from the "dishonor" of being Drouet's mistress, thinly masked as his wife (128). Though she continues to play the daddy's girl role by deferring and seeming to adore, she more unconsciously wants the power, free-dom, and status that bring other people's deference.

Eventually Dreiser reduces Hurstwood's daddy's girl needs to his fears of aging, with its accompanying attenuation of sexual passion. In one of his most notorious passages, Dreiser says Hurstwood's inadequacy as a lover ex-plains Carrie's quiet independence of mind. "[F]or all her leaning toward Hurstwood, he had not taken a firm hold on her understanding."

> This was due to a lack of power on his part, a lack of that majesty of passion that sweeps the mind from its seat, fuses and melts all arguments and theories into a tangled mass, and destroys for the time being the reasoning power. This majesty of passion is possessed by nearly every man once in his life, but it is usu-ally an attribute of youth and conduces to the first successful mating. (207)

As Dreiser dismissively concludes, "Hurstwood, being an older man," could induce Carrie's "leaning[,]" but only because she wants "to be shielded, bet-tered, sympathized with," and she mistakes that for "love" (207–8). Pater-nalism becomes a fall-back position, once the powers of "mating" fade. At least, that's the view taken by the paternalistic narrator.

Startlingly, at this point in the narrative, Hurstwood is "slightly under forty" (45). That's younger than Humbert Humbert at the onset of his pas-sion for Lolita. For me at least, Dreiser's tone of Olympian or Darwinian judgment claims a pseudo-scientific authority to disguise a young man's gloating. It's his own form of posing. Yet it also registers a touch of nostal-gic mourning at the passing of his own first mating.

A good many critics have taken Dreiser's emphatic pronouncement about fears of aging as the key to Hurstwood's desire, or lack of desire. But as Amy Kaplan astutely argues, it's Hurstwood's "precarious position as manager and husband[,]" not his diminishing testosterone, that makes him feel "pow-erless[,]" and therefore more needy than passionate. At work he can't even touch the money in the cash register, and at home he has signed over all his property to his wife. Although he plays a controlling role in both places, he has no control in either.[19] Even in Hurstwood's famous last line, "What's the use?" (462), he still defines himself through his use-value to someone else. When he loses the roles that others want him to play, he has no self left, and falls to a "nameless" burial in Potter's Field (464).

Earlier, Dreiser's more ambiguous formulation of Hurstwood's desire un-dercuts another reductive pontification. Carrie has "a something childlike in her large eyes which captured the fancy of this starched and conventional poser among men. It was the ancient attraction of the fresh for the stale" (103). Though succinctly defining Carrie's appeal as a prospective daddy's girl, these two sentences don't quite go together. The "fancy" of the "poser" can't be reduced to an "attraction" that banishes his feelings of being "stale." It's the role-playing that makes Hurstwood feel not old but unreal.

At the end of the novel, Dreiser reintroduces a younger and more "stalwart figure" (294), Ames, who promises a higher level of paternalism as well as a more vigorous mating. Not only does he suggest several times that Carrie try "good, strong, comedy-drama" (447), but he also tells her to read Balzac's *Père Goriot,* which she does with an "aroused" interest in more serious reading (457). More profoundly, this boyish father-figure says of her "large, sympathetic eyes and pain-touched mouth" that her "natural look" evokes someone who is "about to cry."

Ames usually prompts readers' mockery, and for good reason, since he seems so wooden and one-dimensional. Yet he serves an important narrative function, by rescuing Carrie from incipient self-satisfaction. His charm lies in his impersonality, not his character. Always "so interested in forwarding all good causes[,]" Ames now makes Carrie his latest civilizing mission. As James muses about Isabel Archer in his preface to *The Portrait of a Lady,* so Ames muses about how to make Carrie a compelling focus of public attention. He seems much less concerned with attracting a daddy's girl for himself than with analyzing how her face attracts audiences. "It's a thing the world likes to see, because it's a natural expression of its longing." These pronouncements are "abstractedly" analytic, but they are also "preachments" to "stir her up." If Carrie chooses to "live to satisfy yourself alone," he says, her "power to act will disappear."

Paradoxically, the high seriousness of Ames's attention to Carrie's professional demeanor makes her feel "wholly aroused[,]" perhaps for the first time. Ironically, she feels aroused not by him, and not by the prospect of a higher level of being privately pursued or loved, but by a "new desire" to be "equal to the feeling written upon her countenance" (447–48). Carrie's desire is now one with her role-playing.[20] As Ames instructs her on how to make herself a better commodity, she thrills to imagine how she might rise to her public image. Although Hurstwood's role-playing makes him feel unreal, for Carrie it's the only thing that matters.

Twenty-first century readers may not understand Ames's gendered distinction in being, as he says, "connected with an electrical company" (296). It doesn't help that Dreiser uses this vague occupation as an excuse for some heavy-handed punning. After "connected" come three couplings of "bright" with "electrical knowledge" (301). Nonetheless, that knowledge makes Ames a real man among posers. As Irving Babbitt declared in 1908, while deploring the sissified image of the humanities, "The really virile thing is to be an electrical engineer."[21]

Yet Ames serves the narrative less as a higher level of manliness than as a personification of the urbane middle-class reader, really the author's ideal self. Ames both writes and reads "this feeling written upon her countenance[,]" and teaches Carrie to read it too. He also confirms that Carrie's daddy's girl appeal has moved from the private to the public sphere. Privately, Carrie's upward mobility has depended on her natural gift for combining a big girl's pluck with a little girl's neediness. That makes men feel strong and protective as well as erotically aroused. At a more subliminal level, her mixture of aloneness, bravado, and unsatisfiable yearning mirrors men's half-known feelings about themselves. As she discovers that she can use that gift in public, she rises from private dependence to public independence. Providing a kind of coda for that transformation, Ames articulates Carrie's new ability to perform the "'longing'" inherent in anonymous theater audiences, and in anonymous readers.

Many critics have missed the contradictions that constitute much of her appeal. When she plays a melodramatic heroine for an Elks Club audience, her acting becomes arresting only in the last act. Then, faced with being an "outcast" from society, she "dawned upon the audience, handsome and proud, shifting . . . to a cold, white, helpless object" (174). Her pathos at the end makes Hurstwood and Drouet cry at her empathetic power, especially when she "tenderly" says, "'love is all a woman has to give'" (180). She wholly inhabits these "shifting" states of feeling. Yet immediately afterward, the narrator's language for her becomes abrupt and crisp. "The little actress was in fine feather. She was realizing now what it was to be petted. . . . The independence of success now made its first faint showing" (181).

Carrie's first big break puts these contradictions into her acting. As she is being "paraded" across the stage as part of an oriental harem, the star suddenly departs from the script and demands of her, "Well, who are you?" Improvising, Carrie spontaneously curtsies and says, "I am yours truly" (396). Her curtsy and words imply that her heart belongs to Daddy, body and soul. Yet her "daring" challenges and diminishes the star's peremptory preeminence. She gains a space that Dreiser, playing the role of avuncular narrator, can't quite articulate: "something in the way she did it caught the audience, which laughed heartily at the mock-fierce potentate towering before the young woman." She is "droll," later audiences comment. As with Topsy, Pen Lapham, and Ragged Dick, three "droll" characters from previous decades, Carrie's wit seems deferential, yet parodic. Her role-playing gives her an insouciant independence as well as a permanent line in the play.[22]

On her opening night as a leading actress, Carrie's frown steals the show. Again it is a deferential taunting, "sweet-faced, demure, but scowling," that arouses male spectators. "The portly gentlemen in the front rows began to feel that she was a delicious little morsel. It was the kind of frown they would have loved to force away with kisses. All the gentlemen yearned toward her. She was capital" (411).

The language here is wonderfully rich in the nuances of capitalist paternalism. A "sister" has become a "delicious little morsel." Her mysterious mixture of anger and unhappiness invites "portly gentlemen" to eat her up, "force" kisses on her, and "yearn toward her." All of that is "capital." Carrie anticipates Fitzgerald's Daisy Buchanan; her frown is made of money. Men of substance and girth can gorge themselves on their contradictory desires to be protective, possessive, and rapacious. The next day, a review praises her as if her appeal were a tempered version of Topsy's antics, Ragged Dick's tall tales, or Pen Lapham's imitative wit: "It is a bit of quiet, unassuming drollery which warms like good wine" (411–12).

Although Laura Hawkins's role-playing helps her maneuver for power, the contradictions in her character finally bring her down. Much more unsettling, Carrie seems to lack a character of any kind. She doesn't calculate and scheme; she insensibly leans, so that as she rises, she seems not to maneuver at all. Fulfilling her last name of Meeber, the meek amoeba takes the shape of each man who desires her. At least as presexual as Ragged Dick, she wants only to shop and to rise on the tide of upward mobility.[23] Yet Carrie's success on stage also fulfills her first name's ambiguity. "That girl knows how to carry herself," as the stage manager says (367), while her large, timid, "childlike" eyes (103) invite men to carry her. Her face pleases them so because it mutely sends two contrary messages: "Take care of me" and "I can take care of myself, thank you." A tension between her solicitation of fatherly men and her seemingly selfless self-possession makes gentlemen spectators feel powerful, and powerfully aroused.

Again, a brief comparison can highlight Dreiser's audacity in representing Carrie not as a firm character, but as a convergence of desire with role-playing. In Wharton's *Custom of the Country* (1913), Undine Spragg is considerably more of a daddy's girl than Carrie is. Her hapless, indulgent father calls her "Undie" as he funds her and follows her about.[24] Like Carrie, her name has contradictory allegorical resonances. Though Undine was named after a chemical, "a hair-waver father put on the market the week she was born . . . from *un*doolay, you know, the French for crimping" (70), "Undine" is a soulless water sprite in mythology. Her initials also represent the crass materialism of the "U.S.," while her name repeatedly evokes a French phrase, "*divers et ondoyant*" (e.g., 70), an unattributed allusion to Montaigne's meditation about mankind: "Certes, c'est un subject merveilleusement vain, divers, et ondoyant, que l'homme."[25] Like Carrie, she's "capital" in several senses, fluid and convertible. Like Carrie, Undine always wants "something still better beyond" (48).

But unlike Carrie, Undine has a strong, ruthless self, "fiercely independent and yet passionately imitative" (17). Though she can play the daddy's girl role when she chooses to, she does so not to please men but to entangle them in the "glittering meshes" of her hair (51). Even a paternalistic gentleman and a patriarchal aristocrat, Ralph Marvell and Raymond de Chelles, become disposable assets to further her upward mobility. While Carrie is very much a girl-woman, Undine sometimes seems almost gender-neutral, not in Laura Hawkins's mode of flip-flopping between exercising power and yearning for daddy, but in the universalizing mode of Montaigne's "l'homme," so "vain, diverse, and undulating." Where Dreiser protectively sympathizes with Carrie, even identifies with her as "a waif amid forces" (7), Wharton depicts Undine from her own ruthlessly cold upper-class position, old money staring down at new money, disowning any hint of affinity with her character's crass ambition. Instead, Wharton relentlessly exposes the soullessness inherent in Undine's personification of capitalist liquidity, exchangeability, and manipulation.

It's a much more traditional satire, in which the narrator's superior position is never threatened. Nor do readers ever feel aroused by Undine, paternalistically or erotically. Though she allegorically embodies the incessant mutability at the center of capitalist dynamics, as a character she strikes one note and holds it for five hundred pages. If Carrie's progress induces a complex spectrum of sympathetic, judgmental, and analytic responses, we watch Undine's relentless machinations with a simpler blend of amusement and repulsion.

O Pioneers!

At first reading, Willa Cather's *O Pioneers!* (1913) seems a distinct step backward in the daddy's girl tradition I've been sketching. Alexandra Bergson, whose name evokes both Alexander the Great and Henri Bergson's "élan vital," resurrects traditional rural values based on land ownership, moral character, and agricultural production, though in a gender-neutral or even matriarchal mode. Yet though the men see the land only as a means to produce profits, Alexandra sees it as a place for creating value by birthing possibilities. Her vision of the land's potentiality supplants the labor-based practices and presumptions of her brothers and even of her failing father, who knows from the start that his daughter has managerial genius.[26]

Alexandra inherits not only a third of her father's farm, but also the spirit of her grandfather, without the desperate desires brought on by his fears of aging. "Alexandra, her father often said to himself, was like her grandfather; which was his way of saying that she was intelligent." Toward the end of his life, the Stockholm shipbuilder married a "much younger" woman of "questionable character" who shamefully manipulated him. What Dreiser takes a book to complicate, Cather takes a sentence to dismiss: it was an "infatuation, the despairing folly of a powerful man who cannot bear to grow old" (18).[27]

In contrast, from her youth onward, Alexandra welcomes a strong fantasy-lover that she finally comes to know as Death. Though she thinks of herself as a practical, down-to-earth person with "not the least spark of cleverness" (46), throughout her "girlhood" she has one recurrent "fancy[,]" usually on Sunday mornings as she dozes in bed. Then she feels herself "lifted up bodily and carried lightly by some one very strong," much "larger and stronger and swifter" than any man she knows, who "carried her as easily as if she were a sheaf of wheat." Though she never sees him, he resembles a

Corn God, "yellow like the sunlight," with "the smell of ripe cornfields about him." This "reverie" makes her get up, "angry with herself[,]" and "prosecute" a cold bath, "pouring buckets of cold well-water over her gleaming white body which no man on the Divide could have carried very far" (153).

That "gleaming white body" invites some lingering. Though "girlhood" governs the paragraph, "gleaming" makes Alexandra seem fully a woman. Is she over six feet tall, so men couldn't pick her up in any sense? Or is it that even as a little girl, her gleaming eyes would intimidate men? In the very first scene, when the "shabby little travelling man" is awe-struck by "the shining mass of hair she bared[,]" the girl wearing men's clothing "stabbed him with a glance of Amazonian fierceness" (6). More intriguingly, though Alexandra's hair rivals Undine's, she lets her sensuality emerge only privately, momentarily, and in a self-punishing mode, not in relation to men. Finally, an implied tension exists here between writer and readers. Although Cather may be relishing Alexandra's naked body as a fleeting homoerotic vision for herself, or of herself, she also throws down the gauntlet to heterosexual male readers, as if to say, You too can dream, but you wouldn't dare.[28]

Even as a girl, Alexandra mixes a practical independence with a strange yearning for dependence on a man much stronger than her father or anyone else she knows. Much later, she realizes that her dream of being uplifted by a godlike natural man is really her prospective encounter with Death itself. As she dozes off, "[s]he longed to be free from her own body, which ached and was so heavy. And longing itself was heavy: she yearned to be free of that." Then comes "the old illusion of her girlhood, of being lifted and carried lightly by some one very strong." Now this man "was with her a long while," and when the dream-figure sets her down, she sees him for the first time, though "his face was covered." He has a "white cloak[,]" and "[h]is shoulders seemed as strong as the foundations of the world[,]" while his "right arm, bared from the elbow, was dark and gleaming, like bronze[.]" At that moment, "she knew at once that it was the arm of the mightiest of all lovers. She knew at last for whom it was she had waited, and where he would carry her" (210–11).[29]

As Alexandra moves from youth to maturity, so the Corn God becomes a youthful aspect of Death. Unlike her grandfather, and unlike her brothers, she experiences growing old in the same spirit as she experiences the land.[30] Ostensibly she welcomes being released from her body, her longings, and her managerial cares. More deeply, joining the spirit of Spenser's Mutability with the spirit of capitalism, Alexandra understands that incessant change and creative destruction are the twinned sources of creativity, whether the land's or her own. Though Cather gestures toward a conventional wrap-up by marrying the heroine to her weak but faithful friend, Carl Lindstrom, Alexandra's passionate vision of a stronger, more natural father-lover grounds her visionary management of the land.

For a cautionary counterplot, Cather presents a traditional daddy's girl whose sexual passions lead to disaster. Marie Tovesky lives and dies in what Jessica Benjamin has called "the bonds of love."[31] She likes to flirt with men who can hurt her, and her dependent femininity develops into a self-destructive and perhaps masochistic sexual obsession. Cather's contrasting daddy's girl plots celebrate visionary female independence while punishing women who reduce their desires to male-dependent sexuality.

In the first chapter, Marie appears as "a little Bohemian girl . . . a dark child" with hair like "a brunette doll's" and "a coaxing little red mouth[.]" She "made no fussy objections" when a stranger, Alexandra's little brother Emil, fingers her tippet. Then her Uncle Joe holds her up for his friends, who demand that she "choose one of them for a sweetheart[.]" After she "archly" looks them over, she "delicately" caresses Joe's "bristly chin" and says, "Here is my sweetheart." Delighted, Joe "hugged her until she cried, 'Please don't, Uncle Joe! You hurt me.'" When Joe's friends give her candy, "she kissed them all around, though she did not like country candy very well." Finally she leaves her "lusty admirers" to give some of the candy to Emil (8–10).

These daddy's girl erotics rather patly prefigure Marie's adult subjectivity, torn between patriarchal submission and adulterous desire for Emil, and shaped by men who give her pain. The youngest child of a father for whom she was "the apple of his eye[,]" she marries Frank Shabata, a grouchy and possessive man with "interesting discontent" in his eyes (107). Much as Edna marries Léonce Pontellier in Chopin's *The Awakening,* Marie does so in part to spite her father. Though her father tries to prevent their marriage, he soon "forgave" his daughter and "bought her a farm" (109). Marie's subsequent story serves primarily as a counterpoint to Alexandra's, but it also might be Cather's commentary on *The Awakening,* which she reviewed very negatively.

Soon Marie begins to feel attracted to Emil, who has a "sharp young bitterness" in his eyes (97). Though he seems American on the surface, "underneath he is more Swedish than any of us[,]" Alexandra says. "Sometimes he is so like father that he frightens me; he is so violent in his feelings" (87). As a child, he's proud of killing a duck, though Marie gets upset as she "looked at the live color that still burned on its plumage" (96). Later, at the University dances, "[a]ll the girls were a little afraid of him" because of his "brooding" intensity (134). Though Alexandra cherishes her brother in part because he represents the world beyond the Divide (92, 158), Emil has imperious dreams of destroying anything that imposes separation. He wants to "pull the corners of the Divide together[,]" he tells Marie "in a low tone, so intense that it was almost threatening" (117), and he wants to possess her beyond her divided, married identity.

Marie's seemingly opposite feelings for her husband and her lover both build heterosexual desire from fear. As Alexandra says of a servant, "most of my girls have married men they were afraid of. . . . I guess we think a cross man makes a good manager" (170). Though Alexandra welcomes being lifted by a strong and caring fantasy-lover, Marie's loving feeds on conflict and brutality. For Cather, such female sexuality leads to violence and death. Ultimately, Cather represents both lovers' passion as a form of narcissism, especially Emil's. At the moment when he takes Marie in his arms under the white mulberry tree, he "saw his own face" in her eyes (193). Disturbingly, after Frank kills his wife and her lover, Alexandra empathizes with him, while she "blamed Marie bitterly" (220) for breaking her marriage bond to indulge her desire.

In contrast, Alexandra is most intimate with the land. Unlike Crazy Ivar, she doesn't subsume herself in the prairie. Like Carrie and Undine, she longs for a beyond, and sometimes feels stuck or trapped on the Divide. But she doesn't feel their desire for More, or their desire for upward mobility in social terms. Rather, her self-uplifting takes a more traditionally proprietary form, in which her expanding land holdings signify her success. Although the novel comprehensively undermines patriarchal controls, it exalts her rural individualism, which Cather opposes to the impersonality and interchangeability associated with cities. There, as Carl tells her, "we own nothing[,]" we "pay our rent, . . . We have no house, no place, no people of our own." To be one's "own" carries a price, Alexandra rejoins; "our minds get stiff" (92). Yet whenever she engages with the land, her mind takes on a natural fertility and authority. Though not as inventive a speculator as Col. Sellers is, she can make her speculations bear fruit.

The key is what President George H. W. Bush once called "the vision thing." In corporate terms, Alexandra knows the difference between management and labor. Her brothers don't grasp that, because their minds are stuck in a conventional male view valuing physical work and property ownership. "The property of a family belongs to the men of the family, because they are held responsible, and because they do the work[,]" Oscar says, repeating his brother's formula. "And what about my work?" Alexandra responds. "You liked to manage round, and we always humored you[,]" Lou replies. "But, of course, the real work always fell on us" (126–27). For Alexandra, and for Cather, the "real work" isn't labor but the thinking needed to direct labor. Alexandra also understands that the land isn't an inert site for displaying ownership and mastery, but a resource for creating value.

Although *O Pioneers!* certainly critiques the heterosexual desire that defines Marie's conventionally feminine subjectivity, the novel doesn't turn to lesbian erotics as an alternative. Cather's passion was for work, not sex, and the Alexandra-Marie divide enforces that larger dichotomy.[32] Instead, Alexandra's individualism takes on a more Emersonian selflessness, as her mind receives and births the land's possibilities. As the narrator rhapsodizes, "[f]or the first time, perhaps, since that land emerged from the waters of geologic ages, a human face was set toward it with love and yearning" (50). Alexandra "had a new consciousness of the country, felt almost a new relation to it." As her heart snuggles down into "hiding . . . with the quail and the plover and all the little wild things[,]" her whole being "felt the future stirring" (54).

Cather's next novel, *The Song of the Lark* (1915), offers a more traditional individualism, in which paternalistic men mentor female genius. At the start, various hovering men see something special in eleven-year-old Thea Kronberg—her doctor, her professorial piano teacher, a traveling man who falls in love with her, a Mexican villager, almost everyone but her own father, a rigid and pretentious Methodist minister. These men are her "Friends of Childhood," as the first chapter titles them; she seems to have no friends her own age. Soon, on the way to becoming a world-class singer, Thea muses about why so many men have been so helpful. "Perhaps each of them concealed another person in himself, just as she did. Why was it that they seemed to feel and to hunt for a second person in her and not in each other?" (172).[33] Music, she thinks, brings out their hidden selves, as it brings out her own. Occasionally these men have to stifle erotic desires that she arouses in them, especially Dr. Archie. A rival music student starts calling her "the savage blonde" (142). More deeply, her mentors share her sense that art serves as a "vessel" or a "sheath" for the "stream" of life (242) that otherwise would pass them by.

Even as the narrative ostensibly affirms multicultural crossovers, especially in Thea's musical celebration with Spanish Johnny and her later performance for a Jewish patron, Cather insistently contrasts ordinary people with others who have artistic sensibilities, if only as foils for genius. Ordinary people, even some successful singers, are simply stupid, the narrative says again and again (e.g., 350, 363). Thea's own family is among "her natural enemies" (190), she realizes. In fact, as she is told by Fred Ottenburg, the young German-American "beer prince" (212) and patron who eventually becomes her husband, "most people in the world are not individuals at all . . . Everything is second-hand with them" (281–82).

Fred's *Übermensch* philosophy shapes the narrative as well as Thea's ascent. No wonder she stars in Wagner's operas. Charitably, this modernist dichotomy may have helped Cather to ruminate on artistic genius. *O Pioneers!* has a little of that dichotomizing edge in portraying Alexandra's brothers. Yet its vision of receptive genius is more ample and strong, even loving. Perhaps part of the difference is that Thea is not a daddy's girl, whereas Alexandra is. If Alexandra's pioneering grows from a relaxed sense of natural and spiritual entitlement, Thea's music uplifts her to the more self-isolating state of temperamental diva.[34]

Daddy-Long-Legs

The last novel featured in this chapter, Jean Webster's *Daddy-Long-Legs* (1912), turns the sentimental tradition of the orphan daddy's girl into a more titillating paternalistic surveillance. Through breezy, thoughtful, and irreverent monthly letters required by her unknown benefactor, whom she names Daddy-Long-Legs, an adolescent orphan girl narrates her progress. Her name for him shows her knack for imaginative fiction, prompted by a brief glimpse of his departing shadow, which has "grotesquely elongated legs and arms" (8). Since her own name of Jerusha Abbott comes from a tombstone and a telephone directory, she also renames herself "Judy" (33).

Throughout this book for children and young adults, the reader's double pleasure comes from juxtaposing the destitute young girl's growing independence with the rich older man's voyeuristic access to her mind. The epistolary form puts readers into the position of the recipient, Daddy-Long-Legs, as well as Judy, the writer. After readers detect that Daddy is Jervis Pendleton, whom Judy eventually meets, the intimate mix of spontaneity and surveillance intensifies, since her letters recount her changing feelings about Jervis without any knowledge of her benefactor's double identity, while he attempts to exercise control with increasing insistence and mixed results. As her interest in Jervis increases, she also starts calling her benefactor "Daddy," or the more caressing "Daddy dear," though with a touch of writerly brio: "I like to call you Daddy dear; it's so alliterative" (275). At the end, when she discovers his identity and agrees to marry Jervis-Daddy, this Cinderella/Pamela plot gets uncomfortably close to pederastic submission, though Jervis's loneliness and ill-health complicate the patriarchal wrap-up.

As a trustee of the orphanage, the man she nicknames Daddy-Long-Legs is very taken with what the matron calls an "impertinent paper" that seventeen-year-old Judy writes about the institution (13), and decides to fund her as a budding writer. Once Judy reaches college, she meets Jervis as the uncle of one of her friends, and he invites her to spend several companionable summers on his Connecticut farm, where they stroll through the woods and she writes stories "in a corner of the attic where Master Jervie used to have his rainy-day playroom" (168). Fourteen years older than Judy, he never reveals that he is her "Daddy-Long-Legs," who she imagines is in his fifties and probably bald. Though Judy finds Jervis "an unusually rich and desirable uncle" (88), she gets increasingly testy about the two men's attempts to rule her life. As her benefactor's letters try to keep her from meeting potential boy friends or making money on her own, her angry sparks show her growing self-reliance. Meanwhile, when Jervis insists that she go to Europe with him, she refuses because he is "so dictatorial" (239).

Judy also stands up to her Daddy-Long-Legs about money. She accepts a scholarship and tutors freshmen to start to pay him back, and goes to Princeton against his decree for a dance. In her relation with Jervis, too, she starts to feel equal and sometimes superior, despite the age and class difference. Though he is considerably older and wiser, she tells her benefactor, he is "just an overgrown boy, and he does need looking after" (291). Men require tactful manipulation, she says earlier: "They purr if you rub them the right way and spit if you don't" (123). Finally, still in college, Judy exultantly becomes "an AUTHOR" (194), winning prizes and money and getting published. When her first novel gets rejected, she melodramatically burns the manuscript "as though I had cremated my only child!" (252). Next morning she plots a new novel, and then writes still another, until she sells a story for $1000 and proudly sends Daddy-Long-Legs a check, after commenting on his illness and his "pretty wobbly hand" (289).

While Daddy-Long-Legs' lengthening letters intimate his lonely need as well as his habits of command, Judy comes to feel grateful for the freedom from convention that her own lonely life has forced on her. Though she used to feel "robbed of the normal kind of childhood[,] . . . I regard it as a very unusual adventure. It gives me a sort of vantage point" (270–71). Judy's letters also show increasing ambivalence about her anonymous benefactor's role in her life. She relishes "the life and freedom and independence that you have given me. My childhood was just a long, sullen stretch of revolt" (147). She also feels angry and hurt by his mixture of control and inscrutable distance: "It's the impersonality of your commands that hurts my feelings." Yet Judy also yearns to be his daddy's girl. "If there were the slightest hint that you cared, I'd do anything on earth to please you. . . . I'm so awfully lonely. You are the only person I have to care for, and you are so shadowy. You're just an imaginary man that I've made up" (166–67).

As a model for female authorship, and as an indirect reflection of Judy's conflicts between feminist independence and patriarchal dependence, Emily Dickinson haunts this book. One poem in particular, put on the board by her teacher, fascinates her, though the narrative never indicates it's by Dickinson. "I asked no other thing" implicitly voices Judy's ambivalent yearning to be mastered by a "mighty merchant." As she reports her interpretation of the first stanza to her merchant benefactor, "[t]he Mighty Merchant was a divinity who distributes blessings in return for virtuous deeds." The second stanza strikes her as "blasphemous[,]" since it displays this divinity as an imperious salesman just "twirling a button," patronizingly indifferent (76–77).[35] The ambiguities of this poem and her response shape many of her later letters to him. Annoyed, she flares up at him: "it is very humiliating to be picked up and moved about by an arbitrary, peremptory, unreasonable, omnipotent, invisible Providence[.]" Yet in the same sentence, she acknowledges that her Daddy-Long-Legs is "kind and generous and thoughtful[,]" so he "has a right" to act like a Calvinist God (167).

Surprisingly, even though Judy loves Jervis by the time he proposes, she refuses him because she thinks he would "regret" their difference in class, not age. "It didn't seem right for a person of my lack of antecedents to marry into any such family as his" (292), she writes to her still anonymous benefactor. And yet, she muses, Jervis is a socialist, so perhaps it's all right for him to marry into the proletariat—what does Daddy think? Webster probably intended this comic swerve to show Judy's love for Jervis, and also to show that she's not a gold-digger. Finally, her long last letter to him retrospectively describes their meeting and the onset of their mutual love. As part of their near equalization, Jervis's isolation has converged with recurrent bouts of serious illness, one of which almost kills him (297). Nevertheless, though Judy has loosened him up, it remains ambiguous whether her sparky self-confidence will survive his controlling temperament as he uplifts her to his class position.

In fact, the sentimental daddy's girl closure evokes several touches of pederastic submission, perhaps in the spirit of Dickinson's "Master" letters. "My very dearest Master-Jervie-Daddy-Long-Legs[,]" she begins her last letter to him (297). "'Dear little Judy[,]'" Jervis addresses the twenty-one-year-old woman in return, at the moment when he reveals his identity in person (302). Just before ending her "first love letter" as well as the novel, she asks, "Doesn't it seem queer for me to belong to some one at last? It seems very, very sweet" (304). More archly, after the doctor has told her that being in love makes Jervis look ten years younger, she wonders if that might happen to her. "Will you still care for me, darling, if I turn out to be only eleven?" (299).

The path from that conclusion to Nabokov's *Lolita* is a short one, progressing through Robert Nathan's *Portrait of Jennie* (1940). In Nathan's novel, a struggling young New York artist meets Jennie Appleton, a poised and paintable little girl who mysteriously seems considerably older every time she appears in his life. More explicitly titillating than *Daddy-Long-Legs,* the novel contrasts Jennie's mixture of self-reliance and childlike need with the unfeminine women who seem to pervade Depression-era New York. To prospective buyers of his paintings of her, Jennie evokes a look of a past "not altogether belonging to today" (61). What belongs to today is Miss Spinney, a tough art bargainer who "swore at me like a truck driver" (129). She represents new urban women who lack a "timeless" quality, and resemble "present-minded" men (55, 61).[36]

To the artist, Jennie's intermittent and ultimately supernatural presence conveys a Poe-like yearning for Annabel Lee's ungraspable love. Jennie represents death in life, the past in the present, and total love amid unreachable distance. Upward mobility is not an issue here, at least for her, since she seems of a higher class than his own. Yet Jennie seems orphan-like, detached from other human connections. Her growing dependence on the artist gives him a feeling of "inexpressible one-ness" (185) that rescues him from his own orphan-like depressions. As the not-so-little girl lies on his bed after one posing, he holds her "cold" hand while she says gravely, "You're all I have now, Eben" (105–6). Clearly supernatural to him by now, she tells the artist to "wait for me" until she completes her accelerated growing up (108). Soon, as she approaches "vigorous young womanhood" (110), they hold hands, she leans her head against his shoulder, and at last, on the "one clear day of happiness" that he ever has had, "[s]he lifted her lips, trusting and innocent, to mine" (156–57). Finally, her ghost-self appears to Eben on a Cape Cod shore during a storm, and "I kissed her full on the lips" (209). At that moment she dies in a shipwreck one hundred miles away (212).

Hovering between sentimentalism and a depressive's wet dream, *Portrait of Jennie* makes the narrator's paternalism increasingly needy as well as erotic. Jervis's relatively peripheral physical illness in "Daddy-Long-Legs" expands into the artist's psychological craving, and his mixture of need, protectiveness, and desire stimulates male readers' voyeuristic identification. In sharp contrast, throughout Wharton's *Summer* (1917), Lawyer Royall's desire for his "Charity" repels both her and the reader. Yet like Nathan's narrator, the middle-aged lawyer's hapless sexual hunger for his ward solaces his sense of failure in the world beyond North Dormer.

Only shame and aloneness make Charity turn to Lawyer Royall's protection at the end. Pregnant by a lover who has abandoned her, and repelled by her return to her animal-like beginnings on the Mountain, she accepts Lawyer Royall's proposal of marriage as a less disgusting refuge. Far from fulfilling a Cinderella or Pygmalion fantasy, Charity's upward mobility is a desperate last resort, and it remains ambiguous whether they will ever be sexually intimate. Their marriage rescues her, and soothes his own loneliness.

Among the issues that bring these narratives together into a daddy's girl tradition, almost all of them show how business, domestic, or physical weakness stimulates men's paternalistic desires, especially in Hurstwood and Lawyer Royall, and to a lesser degree in Alexandra's father and Daddy-Long-Legs. These texts depict varying degrees of symbiosis between the father-figure's lack and the daughter's progress. Narratives of the daddy's girl as an upwardly mobile woman also show the young woman's ability to create social value beyond the confines of paternity, property, and physical labor or production. Laura Hawkins puts Col. Sellers's speculations into political practice; Carrie creates an image of solitary longing on stage. In public, the seeming contradiction between daddy's girl desires and self-reliant resourcefulness becomes a convergence that animates Carrie's and Laura's successful performances, though the splitting becomes at least partially disabling in their private lives. Although *O Pioneers!* and *Daddy-Long-Legs* seem more traditional in presenting strong female characters, both Alexandra and Jennie enact the contradictions at less personal cost. Their yearning for father-figures who can carry them away helps them triumph as independent creators.

In the adult novels, as the young women's desires for upward mobility and daddy-like protectors split and fuse, their narrators oscillate between sympathy and moral condemnation. Laura and Undine Spragg remain primarily satirical figures, though Laura gains recurrent narrative empathy, whereas Carrie's seeming lack of force arouses the narrator's chastely protective powers. Where *The Gilded Age* splits Laura's seemingly contrary desires for upward mobility and father-figures, Carrie joins them in her stage role successes, and Cather splits them again into two daddy's girls. Beginning in the pain inflicted by Uncle Joe, Marie's traditionally feminine heterosexuality leads her to an early and violent death. In sharp contrast, Alexandra invests Col. Sellers' speculative mode with a fusion of self-reliance and a self-abandoning vision that is as much the land's desire as her own. Paradoxically, she finds a strong father in the mutability and creative destruction of death itself, the ultimate weakness that comes to all fathers.

With Carrie, Jennie, and Charity Royall, the eroticized daddy's girl slowly becomes a narrative possibility, though the novels shy away from making the daughter's sexuality central to her paternalistic appeal, at least for readers. Ironically, or perhaps less threateningly, the erotic appeal of an independent young woman emerges most directly in a children's book, *Daddy-Long-Legs*. As noted in chapter 2, James's first novel, *Watch and Ward*, inaugurates this tradition of shaky paternalistic surveillance and yearning. There Roger Lawrence, a conventionally weak twenty-nine-year-old patrician, gains individuality and strength by adopting a little girl, whom he is about to marry at the novel's end. As with James's protagonist, and as with Nabokov's Humbert Humbert, the artist narrating Nathan's *Portrait of Jennie* finds his weakness blending with his yearning. Strong patriarchs, too, give way to their desire for eroticized daughter-figures. A few years after her "Beatrice Palmato" fragment, Edith Wharton's *Twilight Sleep* (1927) culminates with unnarratable quasi-incest between a dominating father and his daughter-in-law, witnessed by his daughter. As Phillip Barrish argues, the horror of that private spectacle signifies the breakdown of upper-class controls on patriarchal desire.[37]

Throughout, as father-figures expose their desire, their honor diminishes. In the next three chapters I explore how a nostalgia for honor frames other forms of contemporary paternalism.

4 Daddy's Boys:
Sacrifice and Theatricality

This chapter focuses on what I'm calling the daddy's boy story, in which a powerful, benevolent man helps a young man to rise. Typically, the mentoring mode of corporate paternalism performs a double rescue fantasy. In explicitly uplifting a deserving young man, the businessman implicitly rescues his honor and perhaps his feeling of self-reliant individuality by bringing his leadership into civic life, beyond the walls of his business, and beyond the moral taint often associated with corporate profits.[1] Such paternalism makes a man feel publicly respected for his altruistic deeds. More unconsciously, it also counterbalances an executive's corporate dependence by making someone at least temporarily dependent on him.

Daddy's boy and daddy's girl paternalisms converge in many ways, and several popular characters fit both models. In *Little Women* (1868), Louisa May Alcott presents Jo as a daddy's girl, a daddy's boy, and a mama's girl, all in one. As Michael Moon has emphasized, Horatio Alger's Ragged Dick has stereotypically feminine attributes.[2] Whether the young lad's malleability reflects Dick's ambitious strategy or Alger's pederastic fantasy, similar passivities appear in other daddy's boy narratives, especially those of the sacrificial type. On the assertive side, Harold Gray's first version of Little Orphan Annie in 1924 featured "Little Orphan Otto." Quickly realizing that there were many comic strips about boys but none about girls, he changed the gender and name for his spunky hero/heroine.[3] Conversely, though Maxwell Perkins prompted Marjorie Kinnan Rawlings to write a novel about a boy and his father in the Florida scrub, her preface to a later edition of *The Yearling* (1938) says Jody reflects her own childhood, and a 1983 movie of Rawlings's life dramatizes *The Yearling*'s protagonist as a girl.[4]

Nonetheless, in an all-male managerial world the upwardly mobile daddy's boy raises worrisome specters. If the threat of young women's independence undermines their fathers' sense of control, seemingly deferential young men raise their mentors' anxieties about potential rivalry and homo-erotic intimacy. At another level, as Philip Fisher suggests, young men in the workplace exemplify the accelerating pace of change, which threatens stabi-lizations of older men's self-respect as well as authority.[5]

Perhaps because it was more threatening, the daddy's boy has less cultural prominence than the daddy's girl during the early corporate era. As with daddy's girls, these are usually not real "boys" being raised by real fathers. Rather, they are young men being mentored and favored by older men. Yet the refashioning of a young man in one's idealized self-image brings possi-bilities of rivalry and generational challenge. The hero of Alger's *Ragged Dick* (1868), or Tom Corey in Howells's *The Rise of Silas Lapham* (1885), or Clarence in Twain's *A Connecticut Yankee in King Arthur's Court* (1889), or even Booker T. Washington in *Up from Slavery* (1901) minimize the threat of ambitious young men by assuming self-subordinating or dependent roles.

Most of the narratives present paternalistic authority in a surprisingly hol-lowed-out mode, either morally or theatrically. From the top down, Herman Melville's "Bartleby, the Scrivener" (1853) and *Billy Budd* (1924, 1962), Stephen Crane's *The Monster* (1899), and Henry James's "The Pupil" (1891) dramatize how men in privileged positions lose moral authority by sacrific-ing boys or men for whom they are responsible. In *A Connecticut Yankee in King Arthur's Court* and *The Mysterious Stranger* (1916), Mark Twain turns daddy's boys into spectators of more catastrophic sacrifices.[6] Both of these narratives indulge in near-pederastic spectacles of paternalistic intimacy en route to spectacles of mass destruction, created in one case by an entrepre-neur gone mad with power, in the second case by the devil himself, the ulti-mate in hollowed-out protagonists.

The word "sacrifice" derives from a Latin term meaning to make sacred, or worthy of the gods. In the early corporate era, the gods of paternalism start to crumble, even as they try to tighten their social grip. My argument differs from Susan Mizruchi's *The Science of Sacrifice,* which focuses on the social and spiritual uses of sacrificial rites in late nineteenth-century Amer-ica to fortify borders and purify groups against the threat of heterogeneity.[7] I'm emphasizing how narratives of sacrifice during this period expose pa-ternalism's emptiness as well as its consolidating powers.

From the bottom up, or from the outside looking in, *Ragged Dick* and *Up from Slavery* flaunt theatricality, sometimes in quite campy ways.[8] These two narratives all but give readers a wink as they dramatize the art of soliciting moneyed men. In displaying the convergence of paternalistic desire with mythic upward mobility, each text conflates traditional ideals of character with role-playing and performance. Animated by a zestfully ongoing par-adox, Alger's tale shows how Dick's extravagant tall tales about his high-status connections stimulate the benevolence of rich men, who in turn ex-travagantly praise his honesty. Within more rigidly racialized constraints, Washington recounts his white audiences' pleasure in the masterful, yet deferential erectness of his body, whose oddly shifting colors destabilize the black-white dichotomy that his words reinforce.

Narratives of helping young men rise beyond a contaminating class or color compensated for various white middle-class male anxieties, from threats of class war to a sense of being subservient or exchangeable in large-scale workplace hierarchies, to similar feelings of being displaced from traditional fatherhood at home, to more Silas Lapham-like nervousness about being fraudulent or unmanly in performing genteel etiquette. An intensified middle-class preoccupation with manners and appearances put respectability and manliness at odds. As sociologists like to say, middle groups in unstable social transformations become obsessed with status.[9] Manliness becomes a converse obsession, and daddy's boy narratives become one way of reassuring patrons that personal power and benevolent respectability can be the same thing.

The narratives' submerged eroticism also intimates tensions in the heterosexual and homosexual consolidations linking gender identity to capitalist dynamics during this period, as Eve Kosofsky Sedgwick, Michael Moon, and others have argued.[10] Stories of daddy's boys safely de-eroticize the potential for workplace intimacies between older and younger men. More covertly, they encourage men at the top of the corporate ladder to think about bottoms, safely disguised as poor young men moving up or simply "the bottom line."

By exaggerating the links between respectability and theatricality, *Ragged Dick* and *Up from Slavery* expose the dreaming in the American dream, though very differently. What Thorstein Veblen called "emulative consumption," or Philip Fisher has labeled "the anticipatory self," generates the desire both for upward mobility and for myths of upward mobility.[11] Alger and Washington resolve the tension between precorporate ideals of localized character and more modern expectations of mobile role-playing, but only by flaunting assimilation upward as if that were self-mastery. The relationship between Hank Morgan and Clarence in *A Connecticut Yankee in King Arthur's Court* inflates both the flamboyant theatricality and the moral hollowing out. This impasse between feeling real and feeling fictional, and its paternalistic resolution, helped to constitute male subjectivity at the center of the dominant culture.[12]

But first, a reprise.

Fatherhood, Work, and Honor

As I've been arguing in chapters 1 to 3, paternalism in the early corporate era is not merely a corporate and imperial strategy of dominance and exploitation; it also counters threats to the norms of middle-class manliness based on independent work and fatherhood. Rhetorics of corporate and imperial benevolence subsume tensions between the weakening norms for middle-class fathers' presence in the home, the weakening status given to individual productivity, and the intensification of aspirational desires for the prestige, power, and riches that come to high-level corporate managers. Corporate capitalism also fostered heterogeneous opportunities for white immigrants and working women, and even for some women in the professions. By the end of the nineteenth century, nearly half of the adolescent women in America said they would prefer a man's career to a life as wife and mother.[13] Those tensions frame the rise and conflicted convergence of two cultural images, the daddy's girl and the upwardly mobile career woman.

In chapters 4 to 6, I explore how American paternalism after the Civil War reflects a nostalgia for precapitalist ideals of patriarchal honor and authority, as well as for earlier capitalist ideals of individualism.

Traditionally, from precapitalist Mediterranean cultures to the English Renaissance to the antebellum South, honor functions to stabilize and preserve small community hierarchies by shaping the behavior of men at the top of deferential societies. It also helps to preserve and protect property ownership and patriarchal roles in places where land is relatively scarce.[14] Women, especially daughters, become prime signifiers of family honor, as sketched in chapter 2. In the United States, particularly after the Civil War, that ideology becomes increasingly dysfunctional, partly because the corporate workplace becomes a major new site for middle-class white men's status and advancement, and partly because capitalist dynamics induce ubiquitous desires for upward mobility or outward mobility beyond family and community relationships. Also, property begins to be redefined as fluid capital, a resource less dependent on scarcity for its value.

Male honor doesn't just retreat to white nostalgia for the South's Lost Cause. Instead, its locus shifts from domestic and civic leadership to competition in the professions and corporations.[15] As emphasized in chapter 1, respect from professional and corporate peers matters much more; respect from neighbors and social friends matters much less. Honor also suffuses paternalistic rhetorics and practices that restore feelings of being recognized by an impersonal society for one's personal impact and benevolent authority. In "giving back," a phrase frequently invoked by philanthropists, a man matters in social as well as business terms. He can gain the respect traditionally due to a good and privileged citizen. For men of a certain age and station, it helps to provide what Marianna Torgovnick has called a feeling of "groundedness."[16]

A personal anecdote may illustrate the transformation. One of the more antiquated claims in Thorstein Veblen's *The Theory of the Leisure Class* (1899) is that "the usual basis of self-respect is the respect accorded by one's neighbours."[17] But neighborhoods were already yielding to workplace networking. As part of my own search for groundedness beyond professional status, I ran for our New Jersey town's school board during the early 1980s.

After I was elected, several Rutgers colleagues asked with varying degrees of bemusement or disapproval, "Why are you wasting your time doing that?"

Another story illustrates the corporate dynamics that help to foster paternalistic desires. *Liar's Poker,* Michael Lewis's memoir of life at Salomon Brothers in the 1980s, links hypermasculine corporate poses to the flux of power and powerlessness, especially in the raucous display of what he calls "Big Swinging Dickhood." When any trader, male or female, scored a big deal for the firm, a managing director would shout, "Hey, you Big Swinging Dick, way to be."[18] Such praise gave only a momentary rush of metaphoric testosterone amid the impersonal instabilities of capital. By 1991 many if not most of the praise givers, from directors to the president of Salomon Brothers, had been fired.

Corporate life in the late nineteenth-century United States had similar rhetorics of jungle prowess, and similar tensions between personal power and loss of control. As Jessica Benjamin has argued in *The Bonds of Love,* "the longing for recognition lies beneath the sensationalism of power and powerlessness."[19] Sensationalism takes macho forms at work as well as Gothic forms in the novel. Partly to mediate or escape those tensions, civic or mentoring forms of paternalism stabilized self-respect by providing the personal recognition put at risk in the corporate workplace's incessant interplay of power and powerlessness. As suggested in chapter 1, genteel paternalism gave men a feeling of being firm beyond the Firm. Alger and Washington invite well-heeled executives to feel like Big Swinging Daddies by patronizing deserving representatives of the underclass.

Conventional Mentoring: George Lorimer and Silas Lapham

George Lorimer's *Letters from a Self-Made Merchant To His Son* (1902) mockingly illustrates corporate paternalism's manly and domestic conventions. The founder of the *Saturday Evening Post,* Lorimer adopts the persona of "Old Gorgon Graham," a Chicago pork packer writing to his rather foppish son Pierrepont, or "Piggy," at Harvard. He wants to teach his son how a noncollege education "from the boys. . . . can make you a man" (5).[20] A sample of his rambling ruminations and aphorisms: you can't be "a halfway man" about business. "You've got to eat hog, think hog, dream hog—in short, go the whole hog if you're going to win out in the pork-packing business" (142–43). Usually his letters adopt that sententious tone, though occasionally they display a racist edge: "Business is a good deal like a nigger's wool—it doesn't look very deep, but there are a heaps of kinks and curves in it" (151). Earlier, he waxes nostalgic for the simple "straight sailing" days when his business was "just turning hogs into hog meat—dry salt for the niggers down South and sugar-cured for the white folks up North" (31). Nostalgic for what he sees as a simpler past, he opposes having women in the office, "though I reckon I'm prejudiced and they've come to stay" (306).

Throughout, the father urges his boy toward manliness. "Don't ever write me another of those sad, sweet, gentle sufferer letters" (157), he tells his son. "A good man is as full of bounce as a cat with a small boy and a bull terrier after him" (159). In his second volume, when he compares marriage to business, it's clear that business should have the upper hand in a man's life, just as the man should have the upper hand in the home. In both places, "the man has to be boss, and "shape the policy of the concern" (83).[21] The lines of responsibility should be clear: the husband supplies the money, while his wife does the housekeeping, admittedly a harder job (84–86). But most of a man's energy and thought should be devoted to his firm, in Old Gorgon's case a company of ten thousand men, where the norm for work is ten hours a day, six days a week. "Be the silent partner at home and the thinking one at the office" (94), he counsels. More emphatically, as his last sentence italicizes, "*Mind your own business; own your own business; and run your own business*" (308).[22]

Lorimer's persona seems modeled on Silas Lapham, who leaps at the possibility of turning Tom Corey from a young gentleman like Pierrepont into a real man who works. As Silas says to his wife, "I could make a man of that fellow" (55). Later he holds forth on that subject to Tom's father, Bromfield Corey: "His going through college won't hurt him . . . and his bringing up won't; don't be anxious about it."[23] As he continues, even more offensively, some of his army mates who developed "the most go-ahead . . . hadn't ever had much more to do than girls before the war broke out" (132). Privately, Silas considers Bromfield a prime example of the "sterile elegance" (134) that he envies and despises in gentlemen of leisure. Yet he senses that Tom's "civility" in visiting him at home to ask about his health isn't quite the same thing as the "womanish inquiries" that men in his own "circle of acquaintance" would make (139–40). By the Coreys' climactic dinner party, his uncertainty retreats to a strident defense of his manliness. When Silas gets drunk, he brags to everyone that with Tom, he knew from the first "that he could make a man of him if he had him in the business" (191).

Where Lorimer's businessman invites the reader's amused sympathy, Howells's narrator establishes a more complex mix of sympathy and irony. Although he likes Silas's manly straightforwardness, he quietly mocks Silas's attempts to override class differences. After the party, Howells further complicates his narrator's uncertain investment in Silas's use of manhood to trump class, by dramatizing Tom's class-based disgust at Silas's unmanly shame. Filled with "resentment" of Lapham's "vulgar, braggart, uncouth nature[,]" Tom also feels a deeper recoil from Silas's "abasement" (195) the morning after. Class loyalties move young Corey toward class war. He inwardly pledges "allegiance to the exclusiveness to which he was born and bred, as a man perceives his duty to his country when her rights are invaded."

Surprisingly, as if he were discovering who he really is, Tom revels in his sudden excess of disdain. He "rioted in his contempt of the offensive boor, who was even more offensive in his shame than in his trespass" (196). Here, for the first and only time, Tom's intensity seems to contradict Howells's usual depiction of him as "commonplace," a bit boring, though trustworthy and "sweet" (117–18). Yet much as Silas's braggadocio about manhood shows his own conventionality, Tom's vivid private ferocity represents a little lower layer of his class identification, angry when crossed, and perhaps given muscularity by Silas's infusions of manliness. Tom becomes "a man" by preparing to defend his class against Silas's lack of both manliness and class.

Then, as Howells does in various ways throughout the novel, incipient class conflicts yield to a sentimental resolution. Even as Tom revels in his rebellion, he senses "at the bottom of his heart" something that "must control him at last"—not his upper-class loyalties, but "the girl's voice" that will bring him from "indignant resentment" to "submission" (196). The only remaining uncertainty is whether the girl is Pen or Irene. Thereafter Tom retreats to his apprenticeship and budding partnership with Silas, dutifully learning the business, and occasionally defending moral character as more than "'the prey of mere accident and appearance'" (270). Meanwhile, Silas's fortunate fall gains him a patronizingly ambiguous approval: he behaves "like a gentleman" (276), once his threat to the upper class has vanished. As I've argued in chapter 3, the only class crossover happens with a daddy's girl, through Pen's upwardly mobile marriage. If Tom becomes a manly gentleman at last, his future lies not in Boston but in South America, where he will expand the international markets for Silas's paint.

Although both Lorimer and Howells play with the businessman's convention of the daddy's boy that they help to establish, Howells' narrative does so much less complacently. In framing Silas's complacent pride with class-based ironies, the novel undermines those ironies with sympathy for Silas's manliness. Tom Corey's relation to Silas's patronage remains conventional, of a piece with his "commonplace" character, except for his one momentary recoil. Particularly in that scene, *The Rise of Silas Lapham* shows a great deal of unresolved tension about intersections between gender and class. Yet the novel's last paragraph suggests that an emptiness underlies ideals of manliness and moral character as well as Bromfield's equally conventional presumptions of class privilege. As Silas muses, "it don't always seem as if I done it . . . Seems sometimes as if it was a hole opened for me, and I crept out of it" (336–37). Other narratives will explore that "hole" with less allegiance to conventions of class and gender.

Character to Personality?

To consider the feelings of unreality that help to prompt daddy's boy narratives, I'll briefly digress. Silas Lapham's fortunate fall from his desire for upward mobility to his restored rural character culminates with his rejection

of "the devil," personified as two ostensible Englishmen who treat their prospective deal as all show, appearances, and games. Lapham experiences their
conversation as a stage "play" in which his own "show of integrity" merely
functions as one of the roles, though he seems to miss the momentary lapse
of accent suggesting that the Englishmen are really corrupt Americans in
disguise (301). More blatantly, in *McTeague* (1899), Frank Norris's macho
riposte to what he called Howells's tea-party realism, McTeague's degeneration to his natural, primitive manhood through wife-eating and murder contrasts with the steady upward mobility of the "Other Dentist," "the poser,
the rider of bicycles, the courser of greyhounds," who wears "astonishing
waistcoats" with his "salmon-pink neckties" (43) or his "gay cravat" (215)
and reappears in "a velvet smoking jacket" (260).[24]

These passages would seem to confirm the now conventional narrative of
a capitalist fall from character to personality, allied here with a fall from
manliness to unmanly posing. First established by Warren Susman, the narrative has been taken up more recently by John Kasson in *Rudeness and Civility*. In a capitalist democracy, Kasson says rather mournfully, "[t]he self
becomes a series of stage effects, a repertoire of social roles, without any solid
and stable core of individuality."[25] Since upward mobility meant assimilation to what could be called a patrician imaginary, in which manners define
one's social entitlement, a nostalgia for rural "character" complemented
anxieties about imitativeness. All that contributed to what Amy Kaplan describes as the social construction of realism, which "both articulates and
combats the growing sense of unreality at the heart of middle-class life."[26]

Both character and personality, however, are theatrical fictions.[27] What
changes is the audience, in scale and stability. When an audience is small-
scale and long-term, self-respect and community respect become mediated
through the face-to-face predictabilities of "character." When one keeps
meeting strangers in varied settings for brief periods of time, "character"
loses much of its ability to stabilize a community's long-term gaze as self-respect. Yet the corporation itself becomes a hierarchic community demanding the continued predictabilities of character, even as it also demands the
salesmanship of personality. During the onset of this enduring paradox, corporate paternalism and realism emerged as key cultural strategies to contain
fears that the real—implying both manly and local character—was becoming an unreal fictionality. Daddy's boy narratives either ward off those feelings of unreality through the father-figure's benevolent act of sacrifice, or
make those feelings an aspect of the boy-man's solicitation through theatrical self-display.

Sacrificial Narratives: Melville, Crane, Twain, and James

Four much darker narratives sacrifice the younger or subordinated man
to preserve the paternalist's hollowed-out honor and authority. Melville's

"Bartleby, the Scrivener" (1853) and *Billy Budd* (written 1888–91, published in 1924) "unman" paternalistic controls, as Bartleby's narrator says twice of himself. The increasingly threatened status of Bartleby's narrator and Captain Vere leads each man to make an Isaac-like sacrifice to maintain the empty form of his honor and authority. In *The Monster* (1899), Stephen Crane undermines Dr. Trescott's social control as well as his moral character, when his village won't let him shelter the black servant who saved his son's life in a fire. Henry Johnson's defacing leads to Dr. Trescott's loss of face. A more unfamiliar short story, Henry James's "The Pupil" (1891), shows a genteel young narrator sacrificing his pupil rather than giving the boy the love he craves. Two other narratives, Mark Twain's *A Connecticut Yankee in King Arthur's Court* (1889) and *The Mysterious Stranger* (1916), separate the powers of paternalistic sacrifice from paternalistic desire. Their endings move through near-cosmic destruction to self-pity and other inflations of emptiness.

The anonymous narrator of Melville's "Bartleby, the Scrivener" repeatedly congratulates himself on his benevolent disposition toward his employees. Yet Bartleby's simple "I would prefer not to" slowly exposes the conflicts in the narrator's performance of paternalistic privilege. "I had thought better of you[,]" he says to Bartleby midway through the story. "I had imagined you of such a gentlemanly organization that in any delicate dilemma a slight hint would suffice." In the next breath, the narrator's own "gentlemanly organization" proves to be a sham. "'Why,' I added, unaffectedly starting, 'you have not even touched that money yet[.]'" Unaffected anger replaces affected solicitude: "What earthly right have you to stay here? Do you pay any rent? Do you pay my taxes? Or is this property yours?" (119).[28] This "title-hunter" (99) grounds his own gentlemanly entitlement on money and property rights.

As Wyn Kelley points out, these rights too are a sham, since he rents rather than owns his office. Among the story's many ironies, Bartleby's assertions of personal preference expose the narrator's inability to "occupy myself" (120) with any kind of stable personal desire grounding the role he plays. Soon, by appropriating and mirroring the lawyer's claims to proprietary space, Bartleby makes the lawyer a vagrant, before Bartleby is arrested for vagrancy.[29] At the end of the story, when the grub-man asks him if Bartleby is a "gentleman forger[,]" the narrator responds, "No, I was never socially acquainted with any forgers" (130). The gentleman forger, of course, is himself, still performing his acts of benevolent charity to Bartleby after he has allowed his employee to be evicted from his former office.

Billy Budd, too, dramatizes what Gilles Deleuze has called the American undermining of "the paternal function." For Deleuze, Captain Vere's "paternal mask" betrays a "double identification: with the innocent," whom he loves, and "the demon," which makes him destroy what he loves. Much as Bartleby's narrator sacrifices Bartleby to good business practices, Vere sacrifices Billy to his version of the Law. As Vere likes to say, "forms, measured forms, are everything" (128), and to that end, "[t]he father in him . . . was replaced by the military disciplinarian" (100). To fulfill the authority of the imperial code or the business code as they conceive it, Vere and Bartleby's boss lose their moral agency. They become reduced to what Deleuze calls "[w]itnesses, narrators, interpreters." Inwardly, further undermining their performance of authority, the older men become helpless lovers who "continue to cherish the innocent they have condemned[.]"[30] As Melville puts it, Vere may have "caught Billy to his heart, even as Abraham may have caught young Isaac" (115). Vere's last words, "Billy Budd, Billy Budd" (129), like the earlier narrator's "Ah, Bartleby! Ah, humanity!" (131), helplessly invoke the names of the underlings they have sacrificed.[31]

Most of the best recent criticism of *Billy Budd* has focused on this love in its homoerotic aspects. As Eve Kosofsky Sedgwick suggests, Claggart's homosexual desire and homophobic recoil converge with Vere's more distanced paternalistic yearning. After both men become "disempowered," Vere's "suffering male body" becomes a residual site of "theatricality[,]" encouraging readers to sympathize with Vere rather than Billy by "sentimentalizing" his subjectivity both privately and publicly.[32] Readers who extricate themselves from that sympathy, and it's difficult to do, can see more clearly that in this captain's subjectivity, organized as it is by codes of power, what Sedgwick calls phobic homoerotic desire accompanies self-pity. Both erupt as paternalism loses its authority.

In Crane's *The Monster,* Dr. Trescott begins in complacent control of himself, his family, his career, even his lawn, which he is "shaving" (190).[33] His son Jimmie and his black servant, Henry Johnson, think of him as "their moon" (192). Soon the reflected rather than inherent quality of his authority becomes apparent. Just as Dr. Trescott drives homeward, "feeling glad that this last case was now in complete obedience to him, like a wild animal that he had subdued" (206), a fire breaks out in his home laboratory, and when Henry saves Jimmie, the servant's face gets burned beyond recognition. Inexorably, as several critics have pointed out, Henry's literal loss of face leads to Dr. Trescott's social loss of face.[34] Terrified by this "monster," the more monstrous town refuses to tolerate the doctor's wish to care for Henry, though a few feel perturbed. "I wonder how it feels to be without any face?" muses the barber (223). Though the doctor's office is the first structure to rise from the "black mass" on his property (229–30), Dr. Trescott can't regain the "reflected majesty" that he used to presume, and that various other townsmen experience more momentarily (210). At the end of the story, he haplessly counts the fifteen empty teacups set out by his wife for visitors who never came.

As with Bartleby's narrator, Doctor Trescott tries to do the right and benevolent thing, especially because he feels so obligated. But the town strips him of moral authority as well as patients. Moreover, since his home laboratory was the site of Henry's defacing, one could argue that in Frankensteinian ways, the doctor's professional ambitions have created a monstrosity. As with Bartleby's narrator, Dr. Trescott thinks of himself as a genteel paternalist, but he's really a careerist, and the basis for his expertise has nearly killed Henry and his son. Now, shamed and ostracized, he finds that his honor, or "face," depends on his community, not himself. A hollowed-out man, he stares vacantly at his future. As with Captain Vere, the narrative encourages readers to sympathize with a paternalist's suffering, rather than with the suffering of the man who has been sacrificed.

Bartleby's narrator, Captain Vere, and Dr. Trescott seem relatively sympathetic, in part because each finds his benevolence stymied by his business. With more satirical detachment, Mark Twain's *A Connecticut Yankee in King Arthur's Court* and *The Mysterious Stranger* depict the destructiveness inherent in benevolence. Displaying a disturbing relish for the cruelties of power, these narratives turn daddy's boys into spectators for their masters' powers of mass sacrifice. Hank Morgan enlists Clarence as his adoring assistant in the art of killing knights, while Satan enthralls and appalls his audience of young boys with demonstrations of his murderous, yet seemingly humane powers. As many critics have said, Twain's later narratives become obsessed with amoral, godlike power, prefigured in the Col. Sherburn episode of *The Adventures of Huckleberry Finn* (1885). By the end of *A Connecticut Yankee,* and throughout *The Mysterious Stranger,* this power evokes the tyrannical grandiosities of a C.E.O. gone mad.

In *A Connecticut Yankee,* Hank acknowledges how ordinary his twentieth-century future at home had seemed. "I should be foreman of a factory, that is about all" (86).[35] Now, by modernizing sixth-century Arthurian England and playing Big Daddy to an androgynous adolescent whom he names Clarence (50), he can be a remasculinized figure of vast national power—"with my hand on the cock," as he puts it (103).[36] Clarence appears to him first as the antithesis of manliness: "an airy slim boy in shrimp-coloured tights[,]" with "dainty laces and ruggles" and "long yellow curls . . . He was pretty enough to frame." Yet this boy-girl has an insouciant self-confidence that Hank also finds appealing, and a malleable textuality as well. In their famous first interchange, when the boy tells him he is a page, Hank responds, "Go 'long, . . . you ain't more than a paragraph" (47). Thereafter Clarence proves to be a very fast learner. Soon, to mock Sir Kay, he whispers to Hank, "Oh, call me pet names, dearest, call me a marine!" (55). Though he quickly rises from apprentice to an executive manager implementing Hank's schemes, he remains an androgynous hybrid, both male and female, child and pet. At one point Clarence's real name surfaces: it's "Amyas le Poulet," (130), the last name being French for "chicken."[37] Later Morgan le Fay, Hank's double in cruelty as well as name, seems "as fresh and young as a Vassar pullet" (173).

Meanwhile Hank becomes more Clarence-like as he turns toward violence. Wearing "flesh-coloured tights . . . with blue silk puffings" (356), he shoots nine knights at a tournament, then throws down a challenge. Given fifty assistants, he will "stand up against *the massed chivalry of the whole earth and destroy it*" (364, his italics). Clarence selects fifty-two boys between fourteen and seventeen, who please Hank greatly: "a darling fifty-two! As pretty as girls, too" (394). Then they electrocute thirty thousand knights, before Merlin, "disguised as a woman" (406), sends Hank back to the nineteenth century. Though the gender-bendings keep the pederastic pleasures at a playful distance, one can see anticipations of Twain's "Angelfish" girls in the offing. More paradoxically, Hank's surge of desire to control a harem of adolescent boys accompanies his equal and opposite surge of desire to be a mass murderer.

Martha Banta has situated Hank's role as boss in relation to what she calls the second stage of industrial capitalism. As Banta frames Hank's story, workplace boss-employee relations were moving beyond the local paternalism of small-village shops writ so large in Hank's fantasies of power, toward Taylorized hierarchy, efficiency, and impersonality. It was no longer possible "to be both effective boss and larky boy[,]" though Twain longed for such doubling. His homoerotic subtext, she notes in passing, surfaces in all Twain's writings amid "relaxation or violence, those mythologized motives for eroticized male play."[38] I would add that *A Connecticut Yankee*'s barely suppressed homoeroticism is an adjunct to Hank's fantasies of aggrandized paternalistic power. When his desires for exercising power and being adored converge in destruction, they reveal a hollowness masquerading as grandiosity.

At the end of *The Mysterious Stranger,* that hollowness becomes a spectacle of cosmic self-pity. Until then, the narrative features a god-man with two complementary desires. Strangely, Satan needs approval and awe from his audience of adolescent Austrian boys in 1590. Less strangely, he needs to display his destructive powers, ostensibly to illustrate the greater cruelty of God and the "moral sense." Then Satan, otherwise known as Philip Traum, suddenly reveals that there is no reality to the universe, only dream and vacancy. "And you are but a *thought*—a vagrant thought, a useless thought, a homeless thought, wandering forlorn among the empty eternities!"[39] Homoeroticism turns into homelessness, cruel powers turn into powerlessness, and a desire for companionship with young boy-men turns into a mixture of solipsistic self-pity and self-emptying. The ending evasively abandons any grounding for paternalistic desire, whether in cruelty or love. Ambiguously—do they mean the whole story or just Satan's final lines?—the adolescent narrator's last words affirm "that all he had said was true" (253).

Finally, Henry James's short story "The Pupil" (1891) quietly exposes the emotional hollowness in the paternalistic narrator, a genteel young Englishman named Pemberton who tutors an eleven-year-old American boy, Morgan Moreen. Morgan anticipates Miles in *The Turn of the Screw* (1898), though without Miles's pleasure in power games, and with far more emotional warmth. Unlike *The Turn of the Screw,* and unlike the other narratives I've been considering here, "The Pupil" shifts the reader's sympathy from the paternalist to the boy, in part because Pemberton seems so conventional as well as self-absorbed, and in part because he becomes like John Marcher in "The Beast in the Jungle" (1902), unable to risk love or desire. Like Miles, Morgan seems preternaturally gifted, and like Miles, he lets himself die after he sees that his tutor can't respond to him except with possessiveness.[40]

Pemberton soon sees that Morgan is an "undeveloped little cosmopolite" (140) in the midst of the Moreens, a morass of crass American adventurers and affected snobbery. He also knows that the boy has serious health problems. "You had better let me finish you," the tutor says, with unconscious ambiguity; "you're too clever to live" (155). Strangely, Morgan thrives when Pemberton attends to him, and starts to wither when Pemberton disappears because the parents can't pay him. Although the tutor seems more intent on his own unappreciated "delicacy" (149) in dealing with the family about money matters, he intermittently thinks that Morgan's confidences and tears reflect his shame about his family's inability to pay, not his yearning to be with the tutor. Morgan sees more clearly. "I'm not afraid of the reality" (148), Morgan tells Pemberton. He has the capacity to look "straight . . . at the facts" (156). Thinking about money and prospects, Pemberton balks and retreats when Morgan desperately asks to be taken away. Throughout, the story flirts with homoerotic titillations, embarrassments, and recoils, not least in their discussion of living together into "our old age," before Pemberton reduces that prospect to a "high, rather tense pleasantry" that seems the "safest" tone "for their separation" (161–62).

At last, when he is fifteen, Morgan realizes that his tutor likes him only when he's sick and a potential victim, so that Pemberton can play the paternalistic rescuer. At "the bottom of Pemberton's heart[,]" the tutor thinks that Morgan is "probably . . . strong enough to live and not strong enough to thrive" (159–60). Sensing that fatalistic thought, Morgan understands that his prudish, passive tutor would rather sacrifice the boy to death than welcome their intimacy on terms that acknowledge their equality or even the boy's intellectual superiority.[41] So Morgan chooses to die rather than live without the older man's loving companionship. Faced with a last instance of Pemberton's overt welcoming and covert recoil, Morgan has a sudden heart attack. Instead of venturing toward fulfilling the narrative's intimations of homoerotic desire, the melodramatic final scene punishes Pemberton's lack of emotional courage by giving Morgan a broken heart. As with Bartleby's narrator, Vere, and Dr. Trescott, Pemberton lets his conformity to his business hollow him out. In one of the story's many ironies, the teacher becomes the "pupil" who can't learn to love.

Ragged Dick

From the bottom up, the hollowing out of paternalism takes another form: a theatrical exaggeration of its powers to create social uplift, with mentors playing near-anonymous roles. *Ragged Dick* (1868), Horatio Alger's first book and only best seller during his lifetime, shows a surprising avidity for presenting fraudulent stories of emulative aristocracy as if they displayed the hero's moral honesty. These witty fantasies awaken the paternalistic desires of Dick's interchangeable mentors.

In the Horatio Alger myth as we've come to know it, a penniless young hero rises from rags to respectability by luck and pluck, lifting himself by his connections and his bootstraps. In fact, "bootstrapping" has been lifted from the Alger myth to become a basic term in computers and mathematics.[42] In leaping from one social level to another, the deserving young lad develops traditional middle-class or petty bourgeois virtues of character, notably honesty and hard work. Yet right from the start of *Ragged Dick,* the brash orphan bootblack presents himself as a jaunty liar. He continuously tells tall tales about his former life among the rich and famous, to amuse and impress his audience.

"Ten cents!" says Dick's first customer. "Isn't that a little steep?"

"Well," Dick replies, "taint all clear profit"; there's the blacking to pay for, and the brushes. "And you have a large rent too," rejoins the gentleman, looking at a hole in Dick's coat.

"'Yes, sir,' said Dick, always ready to joke; 'I have to pay such a big rent for my manshun up on Fifth Avenoo, that I can't afford to take less than ten cents a shine. I'll give you a bully shine, sir'" (41).[43]

Mollified, the gentleman asks about Dick's "tailor," and Dick "comically" declares that his coat once belonged to General Washington, who wore it out during the Revolution. Dick's pants "was a gift from Lewis Napoleon. Lewis had outgrown 'em and sent 'em to me,—he's bigger than me, and that's why they don't fit." Finally, when the still anonymous gentleman asks if Dick has change for twenty-five cents, Dick says, "Not a cent, . . . All my money's invested in the Erie Railroad[,]" the Enron scandal of the 1860s. Rather than wait, the gentleman gives Dick the extra money, his last name, and his business address where Dick can return the change.

In withholding Mr. Greyson's name for most of their dialogue, Alger signals an obvious hierarchy of power, paralleling the conventional disparity between last name for patron and nickname for servant. Yet the contrast between "Dick" and "the gentleman" also signals the boy's heightened individuality, vitalizing the generic gentleman's interest. As Mr. Greyson walks away, he says to himself, "I wonder whether the little scamp will prove honest" (42). If so, "I'll give him my custom regularly." With unconscious ambiguity, the customer defines himself through his "custom."

Mr. Greyson's curious restriction of "honesty" to money matters persists.

Much later, Dick visits him to return the fifteen cents. Now Dick has a much better suit on, and Mr. Greyson remembers neither the money nor the boy. He vaguely recalls that the bootblack "'wasn't as well dressed as you.' 'No,' said Dick. 'I was dressed for a party, then, but the clo'es was too well ventilated to be comfortable in cold weather.' 'You're an honest boy,' said Mr. Greyson. 'Who taught you to be honest?'" (132). The weirdness of that response quickly dissipates, since Dick immediately detects his patron's meaning and mirrors it back. "[I]t's mean to cheat and steal. I've always knowed that." That's the moral character Alger preaches and Mr. Greyson teaches in his Sunday School classes. "Then you've got ahead of some of our business men," Mr. Greyson responds.

Already the gentleman has ratified the bootblack's moral progress, or rather, brought it into line with traditional probity, while criticizing the business practices of some of his contemporaries. Yet responding to Dick's flagrant lie about his clothes with praise for his honesty suggests a more covert patronage. Mr. Greyson delights in Dick not simply as a moral exemplum but also as an entertaining urban exotic, whose voice flaunts the fictions of status climbing that regulate respectable behavior.

Dick's brash patter would seem to link him with vernacular traditions of frontier tall tales, an aggressively masculine performance later appropriated and satirized by Mark Twain. His wit exaggerates an urban frontier of sharp class divisions and mixings. Yet genteel mentors, including the narrator, minimize his aggressiveness. Admiringly, one gentleman responds to his "drollery" by saying, "You're a character" (97). At several other moments, the narrative defines Dick's wit as "droll" (145) or "drollery[.]"

To call Dick droll implies that his humor is an innocuous and unthreatening form of imitation, resembling other transgressive mimicries discussed in previous chapters. As with Topsy, Pen Lapham, and Carrie, his drollery establishes an independent self subverting the deferential class lines it also presumes. Yet Dick's drollery differs from that of the three female characters in its verbal aggressiveness. Topsy remains demure and self-deprecating, while her trickster behavior contradicts her submissiveness. Pen offers verbal imitations with quietly mocking twists. Carrie's drollery lies in her wordless acting, when her face registers pathetic sadness and scowling annoyance, dependence and independence, at the same time. The humor of all three depends on the spectator's sense of contradictions. But only Dick dares to be verbally inventive in his extravagant claims. In that respect he borrows more from black minstrel shows than from genteel literature.[44]

Several working-class peers, on the other hand, see him as an uppity competitor. "It's makin' fun ye are," says "a slatternly servant" named Bridget, when Dick says she reminds him of Queen Victoria's picture—"what she gave me last Christmas in exchange for mine" (114–15). Mickey Maguire, Dick's bullying enemy, pegs him as "tryin' to be a swell" (199). A haughty gentleman's son competing with one of Dick's friends for a job calls Dick "an impudent fellow," and rightly so. When the "genteelly dressed" young man says "I've seen you before," Dick retorts, "whirling round[,] 'then p'r'aps you'd like to see me behind'" (158–59).

That incident is as close as the novel comes to class war, or for that matter to homoerotic mockery. For smiling patrons, Dick's verbal audacities entertain rather than challenge their authority. Whereas peers and young fops feel put down, businessmen recurrently find that Dick's humor awakens their "interest." Flaunting aristocratic pretensions as exaggerated fictions of upward mobility, Dick's drolleries arouse Pygmalion-like desires of bettering the boy's lot. If Dick's wit is a form of class dress-up, it both flatters and imitates his potential mentors, by signaling his double capacity for genteel mimicry and insouciant enterprise.

Why should Dick's urban tall tales give such pleasure? Transforming tatters into royal hand-me-downs, parodically dropping the names of famous friends, he seemingly lords it over whomever he talks to. Yet such transparent fraudulence pays eager homage not only to the dream of respectability, but to the more profoundly capitalistic dream of assimilative uplift and self-reinvention. Simultaneously, his exaggerations expose the dream of status-climbing as a shared social fiction of behavioral mimicry. Both capacities solicit capitalization. His upward mobility, in short, depends less on his work ethic than on being a fun-house mirror for genteel "custom" and desires. As salesman and entertainer, he flatters and distorts his audience's self-image.

Although recent critics have emphasized the middle-class or lower-middle-class ideology pervading Alger's tales, an earlier generation tended to reduce the text to the narrator's preaching. Kenneth Lynn, for instance, begins and ends *The Dream of Success* with Alger's "gospel" of hard work as a "simple, but enormously compelling" myth that has unfortunately "given way to personality selling" as a prescription for upward mobility.[45] Yet personality-selling is Ragged Dick's forte. He fully embraces what new historicists have called the speculative self-fashioning and psychic mobility produced by the circulation of capitalist energies.[46] Dick is "a capital guide," Frank Whitney says in the next chapter (108), not simply because he teaches suburban readers such as Frank how to survive in the big bad city, but because he also teaches the artful display of oneself as a "character." The contradiction between urbane performance and traditional moral character gets exposed in Dick's drolleries, which lift the "courage" of himself and others (158) by keeping appearances as "up" as he can imagine them. In his speech as in his clothes, he shows a readiness to be "so transformed in dress that it was difficult to be sure of his identity" (60).

Other capitalist contradictions remain suspended at the margins of Alger's text. After the shopkeeper hires Dick's friend instead of the snob, no one notices that the employer raises Fosdick's wages to five dollars per week nine months later rather than the six months he had promised (162, 166). Much more egregiously, neither Dick nor the narrator raises a murmur of protest when James Rockwell, who promises "ten thousand dollars" to anyone who could save his drowning son, rewards Dick with just one new suit and a clerk's job at ten dollars per week (208–14). These unvoiced inequities suggest the opposite of the book's preaching. An unbridgeable gulf separates the speculative behavior of corporation executives from the deferential work ethic required of lower-level clerks such as Fosdick, who can't lie to Jim Travis even after Travis has stolen their money. Such people should never aspire to instant riches. Dick's drolleries, as with his aggressive use of mockery against the lady on the bus or his outright fraud to counter the wiles of several con artists, suggest that he will be a quick study in executive aggressiveness, while ostensibly continuing to represent clerkish ideals of deference and moral character.[47]

A contemporary account of New York vagrants exposes the hidden economic imperatives generating the pressure on bootblacks to tell lies. In *The Nether Side of New York* (1872), Edward Crapsey briefly focuses on newsboys, bootblacks, and "other juvenile outcasts who are self-helpful, and therefore less painful to the observer[.]" "Of all street children seeking an honest livelihood," Crapsey declares, bootblacks are the "most liable to temptation"—especially gambling and smoking discarded cigar-ends found in gutters—and the most proficient in obscenities. Moreover, boot-blacks are "a much smaller class" than newsboys, because the demand for their "calling" has drastically decreased. "The rivalry of an overdone trade makes them adepts in lying."[48]

Crapsey situates these homeless children among the "collection of Bedouins" who are driving the native-born and "the middle classes" to the suburbs. His narrative mixes a voyeuristic taxonomy of criminal low life with the pleasures of amateur detection. Throughout, he emphasizes how liquor, overcrowding, and "an insatiate thirst for speculation" on Wall Street can destroy a city's moral fabric: "its middle classes in larger part self-exiled, its laboring classes being brutalized in tenements, and its citizens of the highest class indifferent to the common weal[.]" Though Crapsey's moral urgency tries to resuscitate patrician paternalism, his only specific solution, apart from family values, is to applaud an agency that has transplanted thousands of homeless children to Western families: "This is God's work."[49]

Alger's idea of God's work is to make paternalism equivalent to moral character. In the first of the novel's many gifts, Dick himself shows paternalistic solicitude by treating Johnny Nolan to breakfast (46). Later he treats Fosdick to a meal, and offers to share his room and bed in return for his friend's tutoring (134). Still later, his new habits of saving and self-denial enable him to give Tom Wilkins a "handsome" gift, which gives him "justifiable pride" (193). These moments of altruistic caring show Dick's worthiness as well as readiness to be uplifted by wealthy gentlemen, from the "stylish" young "patron" who gives him fifty cents (49, 53–54) to Mr. Whitney, who gives Dick a suit of clothes (57) and later a five-dollar bill (111). Instead of acknowledging Crapsey's intractable class divisions, Alger prescribes exemplary upward mobility through paternalistic recirculations. Instead of locating bootblacks' propensity for lying in their scrabble for a declining market, he portrays it as one deserving lad's class dress-up to solicit potential mentors. As Michael Moon puts it, Dick is a "gentle boy" who is already a chivalric "gentleman" in the making, eager to gain honor by being benevolent to his inferiors.[50]

In the first half of the novel, Dick serves a double function as an urban urchin performing for middle-class gazes, and a street-smart guide educating suburban naifs. Mixing just enough neediness with his jaunty knack for pleasing, his performances awaken paternalistic desire. In the second half, as Dick rises toward respectability, the cautionary tales of the urban jungle recede, while he demonstrates the talents necessary for class cross-over: a "steady self-denial" and its consequence, the generosity that comes with "the pleasures of property" (177). As Dick gives five dollars to poor Tom Wilkins, he reflects that he's passing along the five dollars that Mr. Whitney gave him, thus imitating the "men who do business of a more important character" (177). Fulfilling the marriage of character with elite benevolence prescribed by the Dartmouth College case of 1819 as the social justification for the corporation's legal existence, Dick feels "the self-approval" so pleasant at the high end of trickle-down economics (192–93).

Ragged Dick's happy ending features two more examples of linguistic dress-up and a wholesale self-refashioning. Asked by Mr. Rockwell if he would like to be a clerk, "Dick was about to say 'Bully,' when he recollected himself, and answered, 'Very much.'" To "recollect himself" here means to remember his audience by denying previous patterns of speech—not only "bully" but also his intermediate term, "tip-top" (149, 165). Now, restraining his body from jumping about with joy, "he exercised self-control, and only said, 'I'll try to serve you so faithfully, sir, that you won't repent having taken me into your service'" (214). Self-discipline and "service" define the patronizable self Dick has learned to perform. At last Dick's "great ambition to 'grow up 'spectable'" (215) culminates in a sea-change of clothes, job, house, and name, from Ragged Dick to "Richard Hunter, Esq.," admiringly described by Fosdick in the book's last line as "A young gentleman on the way to fame and fortune" (216). He has completed his upwardly mobile assimilation.

As Michael Moon has emphasized, Horatio Alger, Jr., was banished from his Massachusetts ministry for pederasty just before he began writing his fiction in New York City. Moon suggests that Alger's stories of genteel mentors "seducing poor children away from their underclass environments" displace homoerotic desires aroused and suppressed by the homosocial world of corporate capitalism. He notes that the two instances of Frank Whitney's physical "laying on of hands" are "decisive in [Dick's] transformation from 'street pigeon' to young gentleman." Using Alger's later novels,

Moon's essay also emphasizes Dick's gentleness, which Moon construes as a latently maternal or effeminate passivity.[51] Although I'd make Dick's verbal strutting more central to his appeal, at least in this novel, Moon is surely right to highlight the daddy side of this daddy's boy story, in which mentors seem so eager to help young boys "rise." As I've been suggesting, Alger's tale dramatizes how to seduce as well as be seduced. From either perspective, the name of Alger's first hero, "Dick Hunter," has a certain ambiguity.

Perhaps to punish his own daddy's boy eroticism, Alger contrasts Dick's cosmopolitan savvy with the teary "ejaculations" of Jonathan, a country bumpkin, for whom the narrator displays a relentless scorn. The tall, shambling yokel exhibits a sexualized unmanliness, from his "scanty" pantaloons to his "rather prominent nose" (102). He's also hopelessly dependent rather than self-reliant. "'What'll dad say?' ejaculated the miserable youth[,]" after losing fifty dollars in a fraudulent speculation. "He's a baby" who doesn't know how to "look sharp[,]" says Dick to Frank "contemptuously" (103–4). Later Dick asks if Jonathan has found the money. "'No,' ejaculated the young man, with a convulsive gasp" (107). Out-of-control sexuality slides into babyhood again, as Jonathan climaxes with "boo hoo!" and "burst into tears." "[D]ry up," Dick responds. Being an attractive rather than unattractive daddy's boy requires not only a jaunty independence but the ability to control "convulsive" desires and mood swings.

Covert homoeroticism also surfaces in Dick's fighting and friendships, though again contained by contrasting self-control with eruptive emotions. As with Jonathan but in a bullying mode, Micky Maguire is "boiling over with rage and fury" when he attacks Dick. "[A]voiding a close hug," Dick defeats Micky by tripping him up (127). Later, the only "blow" Micky receives is from the stones, as he trips again (151). That conspicuous minimization of touching has a more intimate parallel as Fosdick is about to climb into Dick's very small bed, where his equally naked friend awaits him. Just as physical contact seems unavoidable, the narrative focuses on Fosdick's prayers (140), and moralizes about the reciprocal benefits of Dick's benevolence. Inviting Fosdick to share his bed leads Dick to praying, which is a crucial step toward securing "genuine respectability" (141). Still later, Dick saves James Rockwell's drowning son by telling the boy, "Put your arms round my neck," then swimming with "[s]ix long, steady strokes" (209). Here one has to have a dirty mind to see the erotic possibilities. Once again, a rescue fantasy culminates in the reciprocal benefits of unselfish behavior, as Dick gains a steady job.

Glenn Hendler agrees with Moon that the myth of upward mobility so central to corporate capitalism represses its male homoerotic foundations.[52] Taking a somewhat different tack, I've been arguing that paternalism tames the incipient homoeroticism in *Ragged Dick,* and makes it safe for business. As Moon suggests, Alger's various novels appeal in part because they combine a relatively accurate representation of the "mild rewards" available at the lower levels of the corporate workplace, especially "fraternity" and "benevolent hierarchy" for deserving youths, with more "idyllic" narratives of a boy's life "untroubled" by parents.[53] The latter point takes us beyond erotics. Dick arouses an idealized longing for the spontaneous inventiveness of youth, accompanied by more covert pleasure in seeing one's sober aspirations reflected as verbal play.

"If you would succeed in life," said Thomas Corwin, Governor and later Senator from Ohio, "you must be solemn, solemn as an ass."[54] Along with the conjunction between benevolence and homoerotic desire, an adult yearning for play gets revealed and suppressed in *Ragged Dick*. As the narrative flirts with the homoerotics it contains in paternalistic reciprocations, it more stringently suppresses the nonerotic intensities of adult desires to gain still greater status and "position," a word given insistent prominence in Ragged Dick's own dreams of success. Yet the repressed returns in Dick's displays of wit. He parodies, yet reveres his mentors' desires to pass as more than they are. Simultaneously, he opens a brief verbal space in which the solemn, respectable male self can be freed from its accommodations to feel them once again as fictions to try on. The bootblack presents himself to potential patrons not only as a deserving inferior, but also as a nonthreatening double, the resourceful, intrepid, and verbally playful boy of their nostalgic dreams, now irrevocably lost to custom.

Up from Slavery

David Lee Miller's analysis of a seventeenth-century Dutch painting has several elements that might apply to both Ragged Dick and Booker T. Washington. In Sir Anthony van Dyck's painting of Filippo Cattaneo and his dog (1623), the little boy "postures manfully[,]" Miller observes. Yet "we gaze down on this scene of petty triumph from a superior position[.]" Endearing rather than threatening, the boy's "precocious masculinity" has a pathos that "solicits patronizing indulgence . . . the child is loved at once for impersonating a man and for not being one." Inviting the viewer's "complementary masquerade" of amused "admiration, deference, or fear[,]" the boy's "lordly attitude" is really "a form of submission as abject in its way as the spaniel's humble crouch." As Miller concludes, his "panache . . . marks his immature *me* as a wanna-be *us*."[55]

Up from Slavery (1901) presents an extreme instance of what looks like that daddy's boy abjection in a manfully posturing mode. For most people who know about him, the "T." in "Booker T. Washington" subliminally stands for Tom. In chapter 3 of *The Souls of Black Folk* (1903), W. E. B. Du Bois called him no kind of man in seven different ways, and the charge has stuck. Booker T. Washington is the wizard of accommodation, not the champion of resistance. It would be hard even to imagine a modern African American saying of him what Ossie Davis said of Malcolm X at his funeral: "Malcolm was our manhood, our living, black manhood!"[56]

In recent years, critics have begun to move toward the position Du Bois took near the end of his life, that Washington did the best that could be done for southern African Americans under extremely oppressive conditions. Why is it, then, that while many other contemporary African American men exemplified dignity and moderation as race leaders, Booker T. Washington has been singled out for charges of unmanliness? Certainly northern intellectuals such as Du Bois were keenly aware of what more had to be done to achieve equal rights. The contrast between Washington's enormous personal power and his advocacy of temporary racial subordination invites charges that he hypocritically perpetuated a regional quasi-slave culture for his own national advancement. Yet the ad hominem attacks also respond to his unusually theatrical uses of rhetorical personas.

Many American readers feel uncomfortable with manliness displayed as a deliberate performance, a means rather than an end. It seems feminized, a gendered charge that still packs a manly wallop. In *Turning South Again*, for instance, Houston A. Baker, Jr., calls Washington's life a servile, abjected, feminized "masquerade" that represented his "*personal triumph in white drag*[.]"[57] To Baker and many other readers, Washington seems inauthentic as well as hidden. He remains a Tom, an Oreo, all power on the outside, all imitative on the inside. By implication, manliness requires a strong oppositional self, not just success in managing the art of the possible with dignified self-control. As in the van Dyck painting, a daddy's boy's performance of manliness displays an abjected imitation of the spectator's superiority.

Yet Ragged Dick's theatricality is not just a seductive form of abjection. Dick's drolleries play with his patrons' abjection to fictions of high-status passing. Similarly, but at much greater risk, Booker T. Washington turns white expectations of him as a black daddy's boy into mastery and honor, through performances that mirror his audiences' ideals of manliness. Unlike Dick, Washington is almost always "solemn, solemn as an ass." Nor do his performances subvert or exaggerate that convention of public male respectability. Yet he recurrently delights in his mastery of white audiences, by presenting himself as someone who can make white businessmen thank him "for doing *our* work" (185).[58] Even more startlingly, he briefly exposes white people's desire for his glorious multi-colored body, as seen through a white man's eyes.

To focus on Washington's strategic uses of manliness implies a modification of current theorizing about gender and what Judith Butler has called "performativity." Butler's field-shifting *Gender Trouble* has stimulated many studies emphasizing that men and women perform normative gender roles with varying mixtures of imitation and transgressiveness. These studies often tend to reduce the positive side of performativity to self-discovery through self-reflexiveness. Such self-reflexiveness has been a white middle-class luxury, a privileged and private version of the tensions between accommodation and resistance that have shaped all African American lives. Washington performed manliness less for identity or self-discovery than for contradictory audiences, at the cost of considerable self-suppression.[59]

Appropriative as well as imitative and accommodating, Washington transforms his black begging body into an outsourced version of white managerial agency, at least in the autobiography he wrote for white people.[60] Yet his ultimate aim was neither power nor the traditional African American pleasure of rhetorical chiasmus, but civic service. He too had a utopian dream, not only to uplift his race, but also to exemplify how his white and black audiences might come together. "We are a mixed race in this country," he wrote in a private letter. Our business interests are "intermingled" (153) and our lives are "interlacing" (221), he emphasizes in *Up from Slavery*.[61] He strove to embody that mixture in his performances of manly dignity and public usefulness.

To place Washington in a Yankee tradition of individual upward mobility through self-reliance and lucky connections restricts his work ethic to his own ambition. It misses his Southern strategy for making uneducated African Americans useful to people predisposed to be racist. How to teach independence and interdependence without impudence? His answer was to teach hard work, cleanliness, and property ownership as the lower-middle-class tickets to manhood and womanhood, which need social respect to convey a full measure of self-respect. As their conductor on that train, Washington reached still higher for the honor conferred on him by white leaders in the next car.

At the most obvious level, Washington displays his access to paternalistic power in paying homage to his mentor and father-figure. He introduces General Samuel C. Armstrong, the head of Hampton Institute, as "a perfect man[.]" That phrase alludes to the contemporary white middle-class fascination with body-building, personified in Eugen Sandow, widely called "the perfect man." John Kasson's recent book on Houdini, Tarzan, and Sandow illuminates the sometimes bizarre theatricality and the male desires for metamorphosis underlying this cultural obsession.[62] Within sentences, however, Washington presents Armstrong as a cripple under his care. "General Armstrong spent two of the last six months of his life in my home at Tuskegee. At that time he was paralyzed to the extent that he had lost control of his body and voice . . . so badly paralyzed that he had to be wheeled about in an invalid's chair" (55–56). This reversal is a classic chiasmus, or rhetorical crossing that repeats and reverses the terms. Washington transforms his daddy's boy worship of his patron into his benevolent care, while highlighting Armstrong's loss of bodily control.

More complexly, midway through *Up from Slavery*, Washington reveals how he conducts "the science of what is called begging" (180). Elaborating on the danger of worrying about results, he declares that he has succeeded by imitating "wealthy and noted men[.]" "I have observed that those who have accomplished the greatest results are those who 'keep under the body'; are those who never grow excited or lose self-control, but are always calm, self-possessed, patient, and polite." President McKinley, he says, "is the best example of a man of this class that I have ever seen" (181).

At one level this passage flagrantly curries favor with the current president, the biggest man in the nation, who has just done him the enormous favor of visiting Tuskegee (303–10). At another level, Washington lays claim to being "a man of this class" himself. More interestingly and problematically, the phrase "keep under the body" evokes conflicting meanings.[63] Perhaps, to keep his cool among white people, he has to keep his angry or anxious feelings under a black body branded as alien and inferior. He can get his way with white audiences by imitating their self-control. Or does the phrase mean to keep under the white body, in a deferential or even homoerotic position of submission? Already the instabilities proliferate. This unstable fusion of submissiveness, mastery, and self-mastery shapes the whole of the autobiography he wrote for white people.

The phrase comes from St. Paul's first address to the Corinthians: "But I keep under my body, and bring it into subjection: lest that by any means, when I have preached to others, I myself should be a castaway" (9:27). St. Paul's context implies the restraint of sexual desires. As he says earlier, "It is good for a man not to touch a woman" (7:1), and, more infamously, "it is better to marry than to burn" (7:9). Strangely, as Washington uses it, the phrase seems on the verge of losing its own self-control, since it suggests exactly the opposite of what he says it means. "Keep under the body" might well command us to put the body above, as master. The phrase also hints at a homoerotic or conventionally feminine sexual position. By implying that it means the reverse, "keep the body under," which he translates as "never grow excited or lose self-control," Washington both affirms and denies a tension between body, subjectivity, and self-control. One has to know the Biblical context to subdue these conflicting interpretations.

Since the context is Washington's Northern fund-raising, "worry" and "excited" are probably euphemisms for shame and anger. To illustrate his self-control, he tells the story of two Boston gentlemen on whom he called. One became "abrupt," "ungentlemanly," and grew "so excited" that Washington had to leave his house. The other man wrote Washington a check, saying, "We in Boston are constantly indebted to you for doing *our* work." The second white man's paternalistic praise transforms Washington from supplicant to a field manager for a national corporate enterprise. As Washington rephrases it, "rich people" are coming to regard fund-raisers like himself "not as beggars, but as agents for doing their work" (185). Wary of seeming too proud, he lets the white man speak the reversal of his status: these benevolent capitalists are "indebted" to him. They defer to his deference, while incorporating his leadership skills into their national agenda.

Conversely, in a more subtle chiasmus, the "ungentlemanly" white man who throws him out of the house is shameful as well as shaming. It's only his loss of self-control that makes Washington feel like a beggar, or something that sounds like beggar.

Keeping under the body achieves climactic impact in the 1895 Atlanta Exposition Address, where a single sound bite about the body established Washington's national eminence: "In all things that are purely social we can be as separate as the fingers, yet one as the hand in all things essential to mutual progress" (221–22).[64] Coming just a year before the *Plessy v. Ferguson* doctrine of separate but equal, this simile attracted Northern capital to the New South by picturing a national body free of either black uppityness or—as Washington repeatedly assures his white readers—black bitterness. Tellingly, *The Story of My Life and Work* (1900), the autobiography he wrote for black readers a year earlier, never mentions black people's lack of bitterness.[65]

So desperate was the racial atmosphere of the early 1890s, that Washington merely codified what other black writers were also urging. In *The American Commonwealth* (1895), James Bryce summarizes various black spokesmen who have given up on hopes for entry into educated white society. They ask only for "a separate society" with equal opportunity, "equal recognition of the worth of their manhood, and a discontinuation of the social humiliations they are now compelled to endure." The one essay that Bryce cites, an 1891 article by the Rev. J. C. Price, emphasizes that respectable blacks want access to first-class railroad cars or restaurants to be with their black peers, not to mix with whites. Detesting the smell of tobacco, "foul men and vile women[,]" they seek "simply comfort, and not the companionship, or even the presence, of whites. . . . If he is left alone, the Negro will be contented with his own people." Washington had been saying the same thing, even with the same simile of the hand, for a decade.[66]

Washington's simile had a national impact, as Price's essay did not, because Price's essay highlights a growing black middle class wanting rights and comforts, whereas Washington's image of the national body fosters a less threatening image of black people content with separateness and subservience. Yet his image of the hand subliminally subverts what it stabilizes. To literalize it makes the hand fall apart. Is it striped, like a zebra? Blended, like a mulatto? Which fingers are black, and which are white? How many of each are there? What happens at the base of the black finger or fingers, when the black moves into the palm? Washington secures his national status by pointing to a blackness whose physicality momentarily protrudes, then all but vanishes into an abstracted racialized signifier of E Pluribus Unum. Metonymically representing a national work force, or "hands," the image promises mutual exclusiveness at the fingers and incorporation or even miscegenation in the palm as the basis for "mutual progress."

Yet as Washington spoke that simile promising compromise, his body flaunted its mastery over his Atlanta audience, his hand held high, his fingers extended. The threatening instabilities suddenly surface, not in Washington's own words, but in his reprinting of a white journalist's ecstatic report. Both *Story* and *Up from Slavery* reprint James Creelman's account, but *Up from Slavery* gives it much more prominence. *Story* tucks it away in the middle of chapter 10 (174–77), amid other newspaper accounts and a narrative of his subsequent activities. Easy to skip over, it seems no more significant than the other newspaper reports appended to his other speeches. For black readers, the positioning says this report is just one minor illustration of Washington's success.

In *Up from Slavery,* Washington gives Creelman's account top billing by placing it right at the start of chapter 15, to show "how my address at Atlanta was received" (238). As *Story* has it, Creelman simply "wrote the following for the World" (174). In *Up from Slavery,* Creelman "telegraphed" his account, intimating more eagerness and urgency. Both narratives reprint his text identically. But for white readers, resituating it so prominently says, Read this! Ostensibly, the positioning invites white readers to appreciate, perhaps even identify with Washington's delight in getting a great review.

Startlingly, Creelman presents the speech almost entirely as a spectacle of Washington's masterful body. As "the noted war correspondent" tells the story, "all eyes were turned on a tall tawny Negro sitting in the front row of the platform." Creelman comes back to the relentless gaze of the audience: "the eyes of the thousands present looked straight at the Negro orator. A strange thing was to happen. A black man was to speak for his people." Already Washington is "tawny," "Negro," and "black." At last he "strode to the edge of the stage," faced down the "blinding" sunlight "without a blink of the eyelids, and began to talk." Thereafter Creelman recounts not one word of the talk except the famous simile. He is captivated by Washington's magnificent physique:

> a remarkable figure; tall, bony, straight as a Sioux chief, high forehead, straight nose, heavy jaws, and strong, determined mouth, with big white teeth, piercing eyes, and a commanding manner. The sinews stood out on his bronzed neck, and his muscular right arm swung high in the air, with a lead-pencil grasped in the clinched brown fist. His big feet were planted squarely, with the heels together and the toes turned out. . . . And when he held his dusky hand high above his head, with the fingers stretched wide apart, . . . the whole audience was on its feet in a delirium of applause[.]

At the end the Governor of Georgia "rushed across the stage . . . and for a few minutes the two men stood facing each other, hand in hand" (239–41).

This is an eroticism of combat. As Creelman frames Washington's appearance, "a Negro Moses stood before a great audience of white people . . .

the men who once fought to keep his race in bondage" (238, 241). A commanding black man's body brings a potentially hostile white audience to an orgiastic frenzy of excitement. But whose desire is being represented? A white male audience, personified by the governor, who wants to hold hands with a black man? The "fairest women of Georgia," who seemed "bewitched"? Or the war correspondent, who seems aroused less by the audience's frenzy than by Washington's strenuous muscularity—the sinews, jaw, mouth, fist, the "bronzed neck," the more stereotypic "big feet,"—and that "dusky hand" stretched skywards? Is it Washington himself, who puts Creelman's description in his book so that he can gaze at white people gazing at his mastery? Or is it Washington's canny knack of letting the Northern reader, especially the potentially philanthropic capitalists who were this book's real constituency, gaze at all of the above with self-approval?

Creelman lingers on the various manifestations of Washington's virile erectness, twice calling him "tall," though Louis Harlan calls him "small of stature and unprepossessing of appearance[.]"[67] But the reporter dallies more uncertainly with Washington's skin of changing colors, as if it were a floating signifier that can't quite be secured. First the speaker seems "tawny," then "Negro," then "black," then "a Sioux chief" with "big white teeth," then "bronzed," then "dusky." Finally the correspondent settles on "this angular Negro," whose face never changed its "earnest" expression. Here is a body that can't even keep under its own color. Nor could white observers; William Dean Howells called Washington "this marvellous yellow man[.]"[68] For Creelman, Washington's body has an oceanic flux of changing colors. What dominates those see-changes is the speaker's unchanging face. With rigid self-control, Washington stares down the sun itself amid the "wave" and "roar" of the audience's delirium.

Just as the eroticized "supreme burst of applause came," Creelman spots a "ragged, ebony giant" who had been watching the speaker "with burning eyes and tremulous face[.]" Now, as he "squatted on the floor in one of the aisles," the man began to cry. From despair? From anger, that Washington had sold out? From relief, that a black man was doing so well in conditions of maximum tension? "Most of the Negroes in the audience were crying, perhaps without knowing just why" (241). Mirroring and reversing Washington's claim to "keep under the body," the uncontrollable tears of a nameless black man squatting at the bottom confirm Washington's exemplary rise from black unmanliness to biracial mastery.

Washington's performance displays the tactical fictions of cross-over necessary for a black man to gain power, manhood, and honor in deeply conflicting regional worlds, the white rural South and the white corporate North. We shouldn't reduce this spectacle to Uncle Tom-ism, or to suppressed black self-hatred. In the "burning" eyes of both Creelman and the ebony giant, this is Custer winning against all odds, when the Indians are white. Washington himself has become the perfect man.

Exploitation, Desire, and Lack

The theatricality of Ragged Dick and Booker T. Washington, or Twain's Clarence for that matter, is clear enough. But what of their patrons—probably not Ragged Dick's James Rockwell, certainly not Washington's Andrew Carnegie, but the Mr. Greysons, the anonymous Boston gentleman, perhaps the Whitneys, certainly Hank Morgan, the hollow men who don't quite know that they're hollow?

At this point, to explain the dynamics of daddy's boy narratives in the early corporate era, two quite different interpretations plausibly present themselves. One could be called soft liberal male; the other, tough radical feminist. For the first, Mark Carnes's provocative study of late nineteenth-century middle-class lodge rituals, *Secret Ritual and Manhood in Victorian America,* argues that middle-class male mentoring had a hidden maternal, nurturing core whose culturally coded femininity had to be disguised with mysterious patriarchal rituals initiating young men from their feminized boyhoods to the world of male work.[69] The danger here lies in a sentimental mystification of privilege, akin to what Eve Sedgwick has called "a vast national wash of self-pity" among heterosexual white males in the last decade.[70] Or, we could apply Lynda Zwinger's more radical argument, in *Daughters, Fathers, and the Novel,* that heterosexual desire itself is grounded in a patriarchal fantasy of daddy's girl incest, displaced into sentimentality.[71]

A version of Zwinger's argument that combines a daddy's boy with two daddy's girls comes near the beginning of Ralph Ellison's *Invisible Man* (1952). There a Boston banker arrives to patronize Booker T. Washington's fictionalized successor as president of a thinly disguised Tuskegee Institute. As the young narrator escorts the generic philanthropist about the campus and the town, the gentleman oddly rhapsodizes about his dead daughter, "purer . . . a work of purest art[,]" like "some biblical maiden, gracious and queenly. I found it difficult to believe her my own . . . too pure for life" (43). All of his benevolence toward the school comes from her death, he muses. "We were sailing together, touring the world, just she and I, when she became ill in Italy. I thought little of it at the time[,]" but she "collapsed" in Munich, and died. "Everything I've done since her passing has been a monument to her memory" (43–44).[72]

Intriguingly, the Boston banker is nameless until he becomes "Mr. Norton" when he approaches Jim Trueblood's cabin (47). As he hears Trueblood's lengthy story of how the black man fathered a child with his own daughter, Mr. Norton's mask of Emersonian respectability shatters. "His face had drained of color" (65), and his self-blackening desires become indirectly exposed through his horrified, shameful whiteness. Implicitly, Trueblood's tale mirrors the banker's implied incest with his too-much-loved daughter, who died because of it, perhaps because of pregnancy. This, Ellison implies, is the hidden dynamic of capitalist paternalism.

It may seem a bit much to say corporate capitalism produces pederastic and incestuous desires, whether suppressed into heterosexual monogamy or not. Arguably such desires inhere at the edges of all hierarchic social structures. Whenever needs for uncritical love and recognition abound among men of power, pederasty and incest hover nearby in a nimbus of culturally structured fantasies. Various psychological studies, notably John Crewdson's *By Silence Betrayed,* conclude that pedophilic seduction and paternal incest arise from similar narcissistic needs, sometimes with similar histories of childhood neglect and abuse in the men who turn to such intimacies. To assuage the unloved, powerless, or abused inward child in themselves, they exploit the most intimate form of patriarchal power to coerce physical affection.[73]

The issue then becomes how social structures engender and constrain narcissistic needs among people entitled to vent them through unequal relations, sexual or otherwise. For an age not quite so prescriptive about heterosexuality, Shakespeare dramatized aristocratic men of power who melancholically quest for love without equality, through doubled stories of daddy's boys and daddy's girls: Oberon and Puck, Orsino and Viola/Cesario, Lear's Fool and Lear's Cordelia, Prospero's Ariel and Prospero's Miranda. For a sexually censorious age valuing workplace obsessionality rather than aristocratic leisure, Ragged Dick dramatizes the androgynous appeal of Puck and Viola in upwardly mobile form, as class rather than gender cross-over.

Carnes is right to emphasize men's suppressed needs to be nurturing; Zwinger, Ellison, and Sigmund Freud in his first psychoanalytic phase are right to emphasize the incest latent in paternalism. The seeming contradiction articulates the most benign and malign resolutions to a suppressed male melancholy wearing several levels of masks. On the surface shimmers a display of dignity and helpful power, edged with a diffuse self-pity. At the little lower layer loom unacceptably sexual desires for dependent underlings, whether male or female. Still lower lurk feelings of fraudulence, unreality, and shame.

These feelings are not exclusively sexual. As with other obsessive compensations, paternalism can betray a disguised lack. If, as Lacanians like to say, obsessionals don't know whether they're alive or dead, and hysterics don't know whether they're male or female, current criticism tends to walk on the hysterical side.[74] By displaying extremes of social mobility in his insouciant deference to emulative status, Ragged Dick invites his mentors to feel their own fictionality vicariously, as play rather than fear. By "doing our work," Booker T. Washington can display the perfected manhood of his mind and multicolored body, to attract white philanthropists' admiring, capitalizing gaze.

5 Narrating the Corporation, 1869–1932

Faced with a new experience, people reach for familiar language. Such language usually betrays its inadequacy. In the late nineteenth century, when the rise of corporate capitalism established national markets and bureaucratized workplaces, corporate work and consumerist desires threatened individualistic, producer-centered norms as frames for social and self-interpretation. Not only did the transformation unsettle white middle-class gender expectations, as several critics have argued, but it also made traditional norms of manliness potentially dysfunctional. The six critiques of corporate capitalism considered in this chapter register various uneasinesses about the adequacy of village-based gender and class hierarchies to control or even comprehend the corporation's social impact.

At their simplest, these critiques strenuously deplore what the writers see as a national loss of self-reliance and moral character. More complexly, when corporate critics reach for what Alan Trachtenberg calls "the familiar but already outmoded language of individualism[,]" they construe gentry civility, artisan labor, and patriarchal domesticity as props for manly independence.[1] They yearn for a return of civic honor and community reciprocity as well as the competitive individual producer. With considerable rhetorical vigor, their critiques make the manly entrepreneur a metonym for the healthy nation, while blaming and shaming corporate corruption for implementing the economies of scale that threaten fairness as well as self-reliance. Still more complexly, the writers sense that when honor becomes more collective than individual, it begins to lose its cultural credibility. Gender and class, too, start to seem unstable, and for good reason. Though in the short term corporate workplaces reinforced class, gender, and racial hierarchies, in the long term the corporate transformation of work undermined these hierarchies as primary ways of organizing social value.

As I argue in chapter 1, while the newly unified nation-state continued to play the role of "Great Father" to Native Americans, especially with the Dawes Act of 1887, corporate capitalism created a disjunction in meaning systems. New patterns of white male middle-class work established norms that conflicted with traditional village norms of production, landed property, and traditional fatherhood as metonymic signifiers of the manly and the real. In introducing chapter 4, I've suggested that American paternalism in the early corporate era also reflects a compensatory nostalgia for precapitalist ideals of honor and patriarchal authority. While indulging that nostalgia, a great variety of daddy's boy texts expose the hollowness in paternalistic rhetorics and practices.

To advance these arguments, I take up six indictments of early corporate capitalism: "A Chapter of Erie" (1869), by Charles Francis Adams, Jr., included in *Chapters of Erie* (1871) with chapters by his brother, Henry Adams; Henry George's *Progress and Poverty* (1879); H. D. Lloyd's "Story of a Great Monopoly" (1881) and *Wealth Against Commonwealth* (1894), Thorstein Veblen's *Theory of Business Enterprise* (1904), and Ida Tarbell's *The History of the Standard Oil Company* (1905). I also touch on Louis Brandeis's *Other People's Money* (1913–14), and *The Modern Corporation and Private Property,* by Adolf A. Berle, Jr., and Gardiner Means (1932). Taken together, these texts attempt to restore a culture of benevolence and national honor that values individual male labor. They do so in part through rhetorics of shaming. At the same time, the critiques struggle to comprehend the power and vitality of emerging national networks connecting thousands of strangers in new hierarchies of collaborative work, requiring interdependent roles in production, marketing, and consumption.

Beyond a yearning for individualism, much nostalgia for small-scale gentry paternalism surfaces in these critiques. As late as 1905, Ida Tarbell pleads for an aroused citizenry to restore a world where "it is possible to be a commercial people and yet a race of gentlemen" (2:288).[2] Until the corporate transformation, considerable compatibility existed between elite stratification and entrepreneurial or merchant capitalism. As Olivier Zunz has pointed out, retrospective idealizations of mercantile individualists presumed a network of gentry connections between relatively isolated communities. Merchants' dominance came from their use of social status to "monopolize" connections with the outside world. When markets expanded, independent merchants "were absorbed in a new, hierarchical system of economic exchange."[3]

At the turn of the twentieth century, codes of manly autonomy and gentry stratification no longer regulated men's public and workplace interactions as they used to. As emphasized in chapter 1, corporations valued not physical prowess, independence, or even honor, but teamwork, a talent for managing, facility with words and numbers, marketing savvy, and the mastery of specialized details. These skills had little or nothing to do with gender or class, or race for that matter. What would it mean if being male or female became no more important than being left-handed or having red hair?

Narrating Corporate Progress

If my own narrative of the corporation is relatively progressive, it remains a distinctly minority view, in part because early corporate capitalism amply reinforced and even expanded the social status and centrality of middle-class white men. I've argued that the corporate transformation detached men's gendered entitlements from their metonymic roots in patriarchy, landed property, and independent physical productivity. How then have corporations managed to preserve manhood's cultural privileges? The short answer is, through smoke and metaphors.

At least five metaphors join images of manliness to idealizations of progress, power, and collective security. The first three, the ladder, the pyramid, and the firm, evolved to structure the workplace desires of middle-class white men. The emergence of the firm as a metonym joining corporate stability with masculine power has already been discussed in chapter 1. As Clark Davis says in *Company Men,* executives developed the metaphor of climbing the corporate ladder so that white middle-class male employees would feel more manly while doing bureaucratic work associated with women (9, 148).[4] Minimizing the nearly impassable gulf between clerks and executives, and minimizing the enterprise's risk-taking uncertainties, these two metaphors associate the company with upward mobility for its employees and security for employees and customers. Similarly evoking upward mobility and massive firmness, the pyramid contradicts the ladder by implying that many will serve in mid-level capacities, and many more at the lower levels, whereas few will make it to the top. That metaphor functions not simply to intensify the corporate work ethic, but also to heighten managers' competitive desires to rise above their peers.[5]

A fourth metaphor, the corporation as an intimate, interdependent, and implicitly patriarchal family, becomes ubiquitous, from early corporate advertising to one of the last scenes in *The Castaway* (2000).[6] Finally, the metaphor of man as provider served as a fall-back position for manliness. By the end of the 1920s, as Andrea Tone recounts in *The Business of Benevolence,* corporations reinforced threatened male roles not by increasing possibilities for independent work, but by transforming the social meaning of benefits. At first benefits were characterized as "welfare," and male employees linked them with emasculation and dependence. By the end of the 1920s, benefits helped to relocate manliness outside the workplace, in the role of domestic provider.[7]

These metaphors seem relatively comfortable, in part because they evade the tensions between individual manliness and hierarchic corporate interdependence. As two contemporary texts suggest, these tensions can also be evaded through a fascination with force and discipline. William Graham Sumner's often reprinted essay, "The Absurd Effort to Make the World Over" (1894), celebrates "the advance of industrial organization" and "its all-pervading control over human life," especially the "stricter subordination and higher discipline" that corporate work has imposed.[8] The current "turmoil of heterogeneous and antagonistic social whims and speculations" simply shows a "failure to understand" the benefits of organization, while the "wild language about wage-slavery and capitalistic tyranny" fends off the orderly necessity to "sacrifice" our independence and "submit" to a new, "great" thing: the "combination of force under discipline and strict coordination." Comparing "captains of industry" to generals, Sumner vigorously defends their leadership and their riches as the necessary corollary to the emergence of large-scale social organizations that require most men to be "dependent[.]" Given the corporation's "more impersonal bonds of coherence and wider scope of operations," the "value" of such leaders "has rapidly increased." That value comes not only from their leadership, but also from their symbolic manliness, which personifies corporate force. Admiring or identifying with such figures allows ordinary men to transcend their feelings of being dependent, depersonalized, or bureaucratized.

A more subtle version of Sumner's advocacy for a new, collective manliness inherent in corporate discipline comes in a 1911 Harvard Law Review essay, "Corporate Personality," by Arthur W. Machen, Jr. This essay argues that we can sort out the contradictions in court decisions constituting the corporation as a person by distinguishing the real entity from the fictional person. As an entity, he says, the corporation is just as real an assemblage as a bundle, house, school, church, or river. After all, he concludes, "[i]t is as natural to personify a body of men united in a form like that of the ordinary company as it is to personify a ship" (266).[9] To call this group of individuals a "person" only creates "a metaphor" for "some analogy or resemblance to a person" (263). The metaphor functions as a "mere means of reaching the human beings who act for the corporation" (265).

To justify that distinction, Machen makes a more intriguing and surprising one, that "the essence of juristic personality does not lie in the possession of rights but in subjection to liabilities." Less legalistically he repeats: "The essential prerogative of man does not lie in rights, but in duties" (263–64). While studiously avoiding the specific issue of limited liability for corporate partners, he curiously invokes general liabilities to define what makes anyone human. Still more curiously, he equates liabilities with duties, reducing risk-taking and personal "guilt" (265) to obedience. Not coincidentally, he recurrently supports that claim with analogies to paternity (260, 261, 264).[10] Where Sumner noisily celebrates the discipline and leadership necessary to create force on a large scale, Machen quietly goes even further. For him, being an individual or "real" person requires men to accept "subjection" to the impersonally paternal discipline manifested in the fictional personhood of the corporation.

The most basic meta-narrative in critiques of the corporation has been the Fall from ideal states of male personhood, particularly individual rights and civic honor. To simplify the story to some of its sound bites: from knowable artisan communities, the United States has created a world of rootless mobilities, exploitation, commodification, narcissism, bowling alone, and shop till you drop. As in all Jeremiads, narratives of the Fall reflect threats to a dominant group. It's no accident that Charles Francis Adams, Jr., grandson of John Quincy Adams and brother of Henry Adams, inaugurated the robust tradition of interpreting corporate capitalism as a fall from civic controls, fair pricing, and fair competition. In "A Chapter of Erie," nostalgia for gentry paternalism can't quite resolve Adams's ambivalence about the country's transformation from regional to national scale after the Civil War.

In this and later critiques, another meta-narrative emerges as a corollary to the Fall. Where Sumner invokes images of vast and progressive force, personified in captains of industry, these narratives depict corporate power as a reversion to monstrous medievalism. In 1869, the editor of the *Nation* coined the phrase, "medieval barons," to describe business leaders.[11] Thereafter, in many narratives, heartless lords, secret wizards, roving marauders, and ruthless "robber barons" tyrannize over the helpless citizen of the hapless modern state. The monopolizing Lords of Loot become the flip side or disowned double of the manly individualism that these writers champion. Though corporate critics have different genders, temperaments, and social backgrounds, their common call to restore a level playing field for entrepreneurial equals has elite regional paternalism as its idealized harbor, and the monstrous individualism of monopoly capital as its dark or shadow side.

While Adams, Lloyd, Tarbell, and Brandeis variously rage and grieve for the loss of localized individualism, they want to empower a national regulatory state, which will check large-scale corporate combinations by an even larger-scale combination of "the people." First Adams, then Lloyd, then Tarbell call for elite governing boards. Appropriating rhetorics of democratic equality and sportsmanship, they pin their tale of marketplace manhood on a traditional hierarchy of gentry deference, sometimes abstracted along racialized lines.

"A Chapter of Erie"

"A Chapter of Erie" is the most forthright about calling for gentry controls. Serialized in 1869, right after the "Erie Wars" and "Black Friday" of 1868, it vividly recounts how Daniel Drew, Cornelius Vanderbilt, and Jay Gould tried to manipulate the stock market and each other. Several of Adams's phrases have become well-known: "The stock exchange revealed itself as a haunt of gamblers and a den of thieves; . . . the halls of legislation were transformed into a mart in which . . . laws, made to order, were bought and sold" (95).[12] A little later: "Modern society has created a class of artificial beings," corporations that will be "masters of their creator" (96). As

Adams concludes, in the phrase that starts Alan Trachtenberg's *Incorporation of America,* "It is a new power, for which our language contains no name. We know what aristocracy, autocracy, democracy are; but we have no word to express government by moneyed corporations" (98). The cause, he says, and later writers ceaselessly repeat, rests with the people: the "present evil . . . springs from a diseased public opinion. Failure seems to be regarded as the one unpardonable crime, success as the all-redeeming virtue" (96).

Adams presents the rise of the corporation as a hostile takeover of the nation's financial controls by riffraff, and he doesn't disguise his disgust. "Gambling is a business now where formerly it was a disreputable excitement," he opens (2). These men are "a knot of adventurers, men of broken fortune, without character and without credit" (93). These new imperialists will make individual autonomy a thing of the past. "The individual will hereafter be engrafted on the corporation, . . . and Vanderbilt is but the precursor of a class of men who will wield within the State a power created by the State, but too great for its control" (12). In fact, he mordantly observes, these new men have encountered only one problem: "they have of late not infrequently found the supply of legislators in the market even in excess of the demand" (2). H. D. Lloyd will turn that charge into a pun: "The Standard has done everything with the Pennsylvania legislature, except refine it" ("Story," 322).[13]

What makes Adams's attack more than a conventional gentry Jeremiad is his fascination with manly wheelings and dealings, and his admiration for the ways unscrupulous men humiliate their rivals. Daniel Drew, as it turns out, lacks the gambler's pride and nerve. Because he wavers in the crunch, he is crushed by his protegees, Gould and Jim Fisk, a moment Adams gleefully dramatizes (70–71). With "a superb audacity" these gamblers corner Drew, who loses $1.5 million. At one point Fisk even takes on Samuel Bowles, the editor of the *Springfield Republican,* better known now as a candidate for Emily Dickinson's Master letters. After Bowles's editorial said Fisk's father was in a lunatic asylum, Fisk not only sued but had the editor locked up for a night when Bowles made the mistake of visiting New York (92).[14] Throughout, Adams's narration relishes what the narrator condemns.

Adams' narrative also introduces the medieval motif. This paradoxical corollary to the Fall argues that what seems like progress is really a regression to feudalism. He repeatedly indicts judges who take bribes, or, in his racist innuendo from *Othello,* "batten on this moor" (42). These courts have "reduced the America of the nineteenth century to the level of the France of the sixteenth" (88).

Finally, Adams registers the dismay of elite Northeasterners who see their creation, the limited-liability corporation, forsaking its paternalistic origins. To recap my discussion in chapter 1 of the *Dartmouth* case (1819), Daniel Webster successfully argued that the Supreme Court should affirm the immunity of incorporated charitable institutions so that rich men would continue to act as benefactors. Chief Justice Marshall's decision defined the corporation oxymoronically as an "artificial being, invisible, intangible, . . . a mere creature of law[.]"[15] Beginning in 1886, the Supreme Court granted that artificial being various rights of personhood.[16] By then various state and federal courts had invoked the benefits of unrestricted philanthropy to free corporate management of property from direct public constraints. The social justification for corporations depended on the paradox that groups of men, aggressively competing with each other and with rival firms, would foster collectively benevolent behavior.

To Adams, the monster they created seems beyond civic controls. Corporations have "a natural tendency to coalition" with "the lowest strata of political intelligence and morality; for their agents must obey, not question. They exact success, and do not cultivate political morality" (97). Such coalitions will bring class war and tyranny, since "the Erie ring represents the combination of the corporation and the hired proletariat of a great city," just as "Vanderbilt embodies the autocratic power of Caesarism" (99).

Beyond Adams's courageous exposure of corruption and his agile wrestling with the problem of explanation, his essay articulates what it feels like to be in the midst of out-of-control social transformations. The Civil War taught men how to manage operations of scale, Adams notes in a related essay (137). Erie was only "a weak combination"; soon "single consolidated lines" will span the continent (97). The state must devise moral operations on a similar scale. Yet perhaps scale itself has been the problem, he muses. The natural social order has become profoundly unnatural. As he speculates in one of his later chapters, "the corporate industrial system" may be the "result and concomitant of a complex and artificial civilization" (415). For later critics this idea of the unnatural becomes more central.

Adams's plea for regulatory controls bore quick fruit. In 1869, the year that he published "A Chapter of Erie," this grandson of John Quincy Adams was put on the Massachusetts Board of Railroad Commissioners, which he chaired from 1872 to 1879.[17] Henry George, a San Francisco printer and newspaperman, and Henry Demarest Lloyd, the son of a poor Calvinist minister in New York City, lacked Adams's connections, and they champion the little man more unswervingly. As with Adams but with more sustained protest, they mourn the passing of the "natural," which they associate with abundance, fair pricing, entrepreneurial competition, and pride in artisan labor. Sensing fault lines in property, labor, and patriarchy as social bases for manliness, they fear that without state supports for independent producers, men cease to be real.

Progress and Poverty

Like many other radical American texts, George's *Progress and Poverty* (1879) addresses capitalism's devaluation of labor and land.[18] As if facing the necessity for triage, George throws private property overboard to preserve the more basic value of labor. His fears become explicit halfway through, when a discussion of credit turns into a meditation on the loss of manly power. The laborer, George writes, spends his life "producing but one thing, or oftener but the infinitesimal part of one thing[.]" Having lost "the independence of the savage[,]" he has become "dependent." "He is a mere link in an enormous chain of producers and consumers, helpless to separate himself, and helpless to move, except as they move. The very power of exerting his labor for the satisfaction of his wants passes from his own control[.]" In such circumstances, "the man loses the essential quality of manhood—the godlike power of modifying and controlling conditions. He becomes a slave, a machine, a commodity—a thing, in some respects, lower than the animal" (256–57).

Half tract and half tome, George's best-selling book argues that the laborer's "godlike power" can be restored by demystifying the country's reverence for capital. His logic is simple: "Capital is but a form of labor" and "Labor can only be exerted upon land" (147, also 224). Though "land is the source of all wealth," only labor, what a man does to land, conveys rights of ownership (302), whereas the capitalist merely "rents land and hires labor" (145). But rent opposes labor and land: "the increase of land values is always at the expense of the value of labor" (200). The real struggle, then, is not labor vs. capital but laborers vs. land owners (282). Labor has been "shut off from nature" (244–45) by private property, associated with monopoly (149) and chattel slavery (312–21).

The remedy: confiscate rent by a "single tax" on unimproved land (365–89, 420). Making the State "the universal landlord without calling herself so" (364) liberates the true value of labor among all classes, especially those "upon whom the iron heel of modern civilization presses with full force" (257). A single tax will also reclaim society from the new "ruling class," really "the new barbarians," those "gamblers, saloonkeepers, pugilists, or worse" who "have all the power without any of the virtues of aristocracy" (480–84).

Like Adams, George intermittently imagines a time when barbarians knew their place. Unlike Adams, whose heart yearns for gentry controls, George mourns "the independence of the savage," when labor and freedom seemed one. A more crucial difference is that George can't tell a good story. The bestseller success of his reductive, lumbering book bespeaks a widespread yearning for manly labor to make a last-ditch stand against encroaching mysteries of bigness. Yet where Adams blames "public corruption" as "the foundation on which corporations always depend for their political power" (97), George senses that the rise of corporations can't be explained so easily. His readiness to jettison private property as a base for social value suggests that property ownership no longer confirms manly distinction. The rise of capital as the prime measure of social worth undermines the patriarchal signification of landed property.

Henry Demarest Lloyd

Henry D. Lloyd is the first corporate critic to settle on a satisfying villain. Corruption in the stock market, legislatures, and courts (Adams) or rent (George) or a lax popular will (both) can't quite account for the rise of corporate power. With "Story of a Great Monopoly" (1881), Lloyd frames the narrative of a Fall from good to evil as the story of the little man vs. Commodore Vanderbilt and the Standard Oil Trust.

As with Adams's relish for stories about crooked manipulators, Lloyd's relish for metropolitan power conflicts with his advocacy of the little man. In recounting the impact of the railroad strikes of 1876–77, he reveals the hierarchy subsumed in his call to civilize the corporation: "All the national troops that could be spared from the Indian frontier and the South were ordered back to the centres of civilization" (319). By "centres of civilization"—note the Anglophilic spelling of "centres"—he means Washington, Chicago, Baltimore, New York, Philadelphia, and Pittsburgh. The South and the "Indian frontier" are equivalently marginal outposts, beyond the pale. While railing against "the Standard octopus," which even "gripped itself about Mr. Vanderbilt" (323), Lloyd presents the nation-state as a benign octopus that should expand its police powers from the Southern and Indian frontiers to the corporate center.

Disconcertingly, Lloyd's villain keeps changing. First comes the God-like king of his opening sentence, Commodore Vanderbilt, who "began the world" of the railroads and then created "a kingdom within the republic" (317). Within a few pages, the villain has become the Standard Oil corporation, personified in "John Rockefeller," who has achieved "monopoly" through "conspiracy with the railroads." Indeed, "Commodore Vanderbilt is reported to have said that there was but one man—Rockefeller—who could dictate to him. Whether or not Vanderbilt said it, Rockefeller did it" (322). But the railroads created Rockefeller's monopoly by offering rebates: "The railroads create the monopoly, and then make the monopoly their excuse" (326). Already the "story of a great monopoly" has become the story of two monopolies.

The rebate itself becomes the third villain, furthering monopolistic control, idling refineries, crushing one "free man" after another (328), and worst of all, making people pay more than they should for kerosene (330). This is a "tax," Lloyd claims, and such taxation without representation should make U.S. citizens revolt. Failing that, only the discovery of oil in Germany can help restore competition. That consumerist argument for independent producers brings a fourth villain, the idea of combination itself. "It is the railroads that have bred the millionaires" through combinations. "All railroad history has been a vindication of George Stephenson's saying that where combination was possible competition was impossible" (330–31).

After other villains appear, notably state courts, judges, a craven Congress, and an ignorant citizenry, Lloyd returns to Vanderbilt and the railroads to conclude his polemic. Raising the specter of further railroad pools, Lloyd offers a list of solutions. First, the railroad combinations should be either dispersed or controlled by a national board. Second, railroad prices should be public and equal, as the law for public utilities mandates. Third, since "[t]he States have failed," the nation has to be "the engine of the people." While erasing Rockefeller's dominance over Vanderbilt, Lloyd appropriates the new language of consolidation to empower "the corporate sovereign at Washington" (334) not as an imagined community but as a greater "engine," disciplining the states, the regions, and even the people.

Norman Pollock and others have praised Lloyd for recognizing the tendency to monopoly inherent in corporate combinations. Beyond the difficulty in defining monopoly—Pollock vaguely links it to bigness and "restrictive power"—the charge has at least two problems.[19] First, as Alfred Chandler and Olivier Zunz emphasize, corporations combined primarily to control risk, particularly of overproduction, the besetting problem of the 1870s and 1880s. With heterogeneous origins, diverse organizations, and diverse visions, corporations developed what Chandler has called management's "visible hand" less to monopolize than to maximize economies of scale while minimizing the dangers of "ruinous competition[.]"[20]

Second, to champion "free men" fighting the combination, Lloyd presents monopoly control as a kind of alien bullying, the monstrous double of the manly entrepreneur. Contemporaries associated corporate power with an Asiatic or feudal collectivism threatening Anglo-Saxon individual autonomy.[21] Lloyd quotes a New York refiner: "we did n't propose to go into any 'fix up,' where we would lose our identity, or sell out, or be under anybody else's thumb" (324). Yet Lloyd inverts the binary in concluding that strong men need to be under the nation's thumb. "Our strong men are engaged in a headlong fight for fortune, power, precedence, success. Americans as they are, they ride over the people like Juggernaut to gain their ends. . . . The common people, the nation, must take them in hand" (333). To say "take them in hand" mixes a father's spanking fantasy with a more depersonalized fantasy of controlling a runaway machine.

As with George, Lloyd attacks monopoly and corporate control to preserve traditional bonds between individual labor, small-scale production, and manliness. Those linkages, however popular they remain in populist rhetoric, obscure a transformation of the social and economic framework for defining value. As Walter Benn Michaels astutely notes, Rockefeller's genius lay in his recognition that "oil production was not a source of 'tangible value'" but was instead a form of speculation."[22] The point was not to produce a commodity and hope for a sale, but to create marketing systems of production and distribution that maximized profit and minimized risk. If property, production, and labor become modes of speculation for capital accumulation, independent selves that produce and own have only temporary, negotiable value. Critics such as Howard Horwitz and James Livingston, who insightfully link the corporation's artificial personhood to Emersonian transcendence, minimize the systemic threats to the manhood that transcendent or pragmatic individualism resists and appropriates.[23]

Thirteen years later, Lloyd's *Wealth against Commonwealth* (1894) defends embattled manliness with an inchoate profusion of binaries.[24] Corporations violate nature itself, he opens; "the 'cornerers,' the syndicates, trusts, combinations" have kept oil's natural abundance from the people by an artificial policy of scarcity (1, also 152–53). That dichotomy introduces a parade of oppositions featuring manliness under duress: doughty entrepreneurial competitors vs. corporate combination; men "asserting their commercial manhood" for the public good vs. "vassals" of "empire" (65); freedom vs. slavery (82) or "business feudalization" (488); "Anglo-Saxon" manliness (299) vs. "the alien control" of "a foreign enemy" (94); "country-bred, hard-working American manhood of the last generation" (196–97) vs. secret contracts and the rebate; individuality vs. impersonality. To illustrate corporate facelessness, Lloyd now withholds the names of all the corporate executives whose pronouncements, letters, and testimony he quotes so copiously. In this 534-page book, John D. Rockefeller's name never appears.

Yet Lloyd's first sentence signals a contradiction: "Nature is rich; but everywhere man, the heir of nature, is poor" (1). The word "heir" associates nature not with abundance but with inheritable patriarchal property. Like Henry George, Lloyd interprets the corporate transformation of property as a violation of nature and human freedom. Already "the naked issue of our time" is that property has become "master instead of servant," seizing "monopoly of the necessaries of life" (494) as the unnatural possession of a few (513). Eventually, he imagines, there will be one "sole buyer of the land" (491). Unlike George, Lloyd struggles to preserve property's links to independent producers as natural grounds for manliness.

If "Story of a Great Monopoly" can't quite stabilize its villain, *Wealth Against Commonwealth* has trouble securing its hero. Lloyd's ongoing drama presents the tragic fate of entrepreneurial producers whose manly character gets them nothing. "[M]en who are merely honest, hard-working, competent, even though they have skill, capital, and customers" can't survive against secret contracts, faceless privilege, and the rebate (120). Baffled, Lloyd keeps wondering why "[t]hese almost-forgotten men, shrewd, patient, undauntable, were the pioneers of the skilful well-borers[,]" yet had to march "behind the successful men" who, "strange to say, . . . did not discover the oil, nor how to 'strike' it" (462–63). A little later: "Many other men had thrift, sobriety, industry, but only these had the rebate, and so only these are the 'fittest in the struggle for existence'" (489).

In search of a David who actually beats Goliath, Lloyd finally turns to the South he had dismissed in "Story." Now the South seems "the most American part of America" because it preserves "the original Anglo-Saxon types" without being "steeped" in commercialism or "flooded" by immigration (299). Yet the citizens of Columbus, Mississippi, defeat the trust not as independents but as citizens who act together "as one man" (299) to withstand "the oil lords" for three years. "The people were learning there was a magic in association more potent than the trick of combinations" (304).

Paradoxically, manly individualism works better as a town than as a man. Shifting to Toledo, Ohio, Lloyd's next chapter begins: "Towns, like men, stamp themselves with marked traits. Toledo had an individuality which showed itself from the start" (313). Subsequent chapters recount how Toledo gained public ownership of natural gas pipelines. Repeatedly invoking Emerson, Lloyd deplores the transformation of men into "business dependants" (498, *sic*) of other men who control production without any actual involvement in making things. "The independents . . . can produce more cheaply than the would-be Lords of Industry, as free men always do[,]" he says earlier (444–45). Yet in Columbus and Toledo citizens prevail as consumers, not producers, and by appropriating the strategy of combination.

The powerlessness of a patriarchal public sphere beyond the marketplace becomes Lloyd's basic issue. Society is no longer "making men citizens in their relations to each other" (497). "'Everything shall not go to market,' says Emerson; but everything does go to market" (492). To explain the market's logic, Lloyd invokes Cain and Abel: "the mainspring of the evil is the morals and economics which cipher that brothers produce wealth when they are only cheating each other out of birthrights" (507). Biblical patriarchy has passed into "bargainhood": "From the fatherhood of the old patriarchal life, where father and brother sold each other nothing, the world has chaffered along to the anarchy of a 'free' trade which sells everything. One thing after another has passed out from under the régime of brotherhood and passed in under that of bargainhood" (507). Now the father "breeds" children "to take his place in the factory, to unfit themselves to be fathers in their turn" (518).

If moral citizenship rests on patriarchal "birthrights" and Biblical brotherhood, those days are gone. Ominously Lloyd frames his book with a sense that bigness is here to stay. "The line of development is from local to national, and from national to international" (4), he begins. "America has grown so big[,]" Lloyd concludes, "that the average citizen has broken down. No man can half understand or half operate the fulness of this big citizenship, except by giving his whole time to it." The new world's "wealth is too great for the old forms" (520–21). So what is to be done? Perhaps there will be a natural "evolution" from status to contract to another stage of status (533). Perhaps there will be another revolution or civil war. A new Christ, or at least a "genius" (526, 524), or even his own book (528) may bring on corporate Armageddon. The socialist apocalypse will require "martyrdoms" (522) and the "readiness to die" (526).

Mixing Biblical nostalgia with Emersonian optimism and revolutionary martyrdom, Lloyd seizes at random on primitive patriarchy, chivalry, self-reliance, civic combination, revolution, and nature's gift economy of abundance to resist the market. Centering his polemic is the specter of an unseen yet omnipresent enemy, personified in the man he never names. Like a monstrous shadow-screen, John D. Rockefeller reduces Lloyd's parade of heroes and victims to insignificant players on an expanding stage.

Thorstein Veblen's *Theory of Business Enterprise*

Ten years later, Thorstein Veblen's *Theory of Business Enterprise* (1904) also summons patriarchal spirits from the vasty deep.[25] Seeking a cultural counterweight to the corporate "machine," he calls for imperial wars to bring back the ideals of honor and deference. Curiously, Robert Putnam's recent *Bowling Alone* comes surprisingly close to saying the same thing. In trying to explain why Americans have ceased to be joiners, he says the most crucial factor isn't TV or suburbanization or two-career families, but rather a generational divide prompted by the absence of a war we believe in. What we need, he rather hesitantly concludes, is what William James called "the moral equivalent of war."[26]

Most of Veblen's abstracted investigation focuses on machine technology as the basis for corporate work. Veblen notes that "remote and impersonal" business practices have undermined "handicraft and neighborhood industry" (51–53). He also argues that traditional rights of property ownership depend on "the régime of handicraft and petty trade," (79), now undermined by a machine regime based on capital and credit. Even ownership is at risk, since "the management is separated from the ownership of the property, more and more widely" (174–75). From Veblen's opening binary onward, the business man is "the only large self-directing economic factor" who can control the machine process (3). Repeatedly Veblen exalts "captains of industry" as independent heroes who control and disrupt corporate system-making (30, 122, 128). "The heroic role of the captain of industry," he asserts, "is that of a deliverer from an excess of business management" (48–49), since managers focus only on maximizing profits, rather than on product efficiency or community "serviceability" (157, also 60–61, 84–90, 175–76).

Intermittent praise for manly leaders dedicated to production and community service instead of profits becomes a call for premodern hierarchy in Veblen's grand finale, which advocates imperial warfare to restore patriarchy against the "disintegrating" effects of the machine. "The disintegration of the patriarchal tradition" in the industrial classes has led only to socialism, class conflict, and the spreading "disintegration of the spiritual foundations of our domestic institutions . . . The machine is a leveller, a vulgarizer, whose end seems to be the extirpation of all that is respectable, noble, and dignified in human intercourse and ideals" (357–58). "Warfare" is the remedy. Its "insistence on gradations of honor" will restore "the ancient virtues," including "servility" and "class prerogative." Warfare "is the strongest disciplinary factor that can be brought to counter the vulgarization of modern life wrought by peaceful industry and the machine process, and to rehabilitate the decaying sense of status and differential dignity" (393). Fortunately, "a strenuous national policy" holds some hope (393), especially since the "quest for profits" also "leads to a predatory national policy" (398). Perhaps this "discipline of prowess" may bring "a sacramental serenity to men's outlook" once more, and restore a sense of "authenticity and sacramental dignity" (399).

Can he be serious? Since Veblen praises the president's "strenuous" and "predatory national policy," perhaps he is simply angling for the ear of Teddy Roosevelt. Or he may be indulging in the irony relished by his modern interpreters. Given the patriarchal yearnings surfacing in the previous corporate critiques, however, it seems more likely that Veblen's warrior posturing represents manhood in extremis. From C. F. Adams's confident advocacy of gentry controls, through George's separation of labor from land ownership, to Lloyd's increasingly desperate foraging among premodern supports for manly independence, to Veblen's call for reinstituting "sacramental" deference through imperial warfare, "gradations" of patriarchal honor serve as a shaky prop for individual virility and social cohesion.[27]

Ida Tarbell's *History of Standard Oil*

A decade later, most critics of corporate capitalism had returned from patriarchal nostalgia to the rhetoric of small-scale manliness. "Individualism is gone, never to return[,]" said John D. Rockefeller.[28] Nevertheless, in *Other People's Money* (1913–14), Louis Brandeis enthusiastically resuscitates the ideal of small-scale individualism to attack men's unnatural dependence on nonproducers such as trusts and bankers.[29] "[T]he absorption into a great system" means becoming "subjects or satellites of the Money Trust" (126), which suppresses "manhood itself" in suppressing the "liberty" of competition (70). Women owning stock exacerbates the problem (52). Only small businesses and credit unions can preserve the nation's manhood, he concludes. One chapter title conveys his prescription for restoring manliness: "Big Men and Little Business" (108).

Yet Brandeis's confident resurrection of the now conventional opposition between manhood and monopoly comes at the end of a federal transformation that Ida Tarbell's *History of Standard Oil* (1905) had helped to accelerate. In 1911, with the "rule of reason," the Supreme Court had broken up Standard Oil into 38 companies, and in 1913 Congress had established the Federal Reserve System. As James Livingston argues, a new urban corporate elite had won the battle to alter the nation's economic discourse. It was now clear that to control commodity circulation, production had to be controlled. What John D. Rockefeller saw in the early 1870s, a host of executives had come to accept in the "wreckage" of the early 1890s, out of which the new system "almost erupted" in less than a decade.[30] The Gold Standard Act in 1900 and the Federal Reserve System provided centralized economic resources to help corporations stabilize the vicissitudes of overproduction and speculation endemic to proprietary capitalism. The new elite provided "the singular grammar" organizing everyone else's "vocabulary[.]"[31] Ironically it was businessmen, more than corporate critics or ordinary citizens, who established a national public sphere strong enough to control market capitalism.

In that context, Brandeis refurbishes small-scale individualism while taking the new national paternalism for granted. In fact he explicitly crafts an antitrust agenda for Woodrow Wilson, who later appointed him to the Supreme Court. The old complementarity between gentry hierarchy and self-reliance became benevolent central planning to preserve competition and innovation. Meanwhile the restabilized national system allowed corporations to expand far beyond individualism's scale and manhood's scope.[32] A renewed rhetoric of manliness preserved a residual faith in localized productivity while facilitating emergent structures of system-making. Abandoning previous critics' yearnings for patriarchy, Tarbell's book catalyzed the triumph of regulatory capitalism, in part by invoking manhood with a new ambivalence.

The daughter of a Pennsylvania oil-field entrepreneur outmaneuvered by Standard Oil, Tarbell celebrates the entrepreneurship of men such as her father. Yet she also voices a reluctant awareness that their day of venture speculation has passed. From the start she emphasizes the independents' "manhood" and "fair play" (1:37), contrasting their "sportsmanlike" zest and moral passion with the Trust's amoral "tricksters" (2:288) who succeed through secretive, anonymous control. The entrepreneurs "wanted competition, loved open fight[,]" especially a "fight for principle" (1:101). They held "honour" and freedom as "a cause" beyond business: "the right of men to work in their own way" (2:175). Volume 1 closes in grief, as "the audacity, the wit, the irrepressible spirit" yield to "the hush of defeat, of cowardice, of hopelessness" (1:260–61).

Unlike Lloyd, Tarbell knows why these men lost. Not the rebates alone, but the atmosphere of uncontrolled speculation and competition led to overproduction and low profits (1:54). "Such fluctuations were the natural element of the speculator" (1:31). A culture of manly daring had fostered recklessness, extravagance, "spendthrift generosity," and an inability to think beyond the day-to-day. All that exacerbated the Oil Regions' "one fatal weakness—its passion for speculation" (2:254). Though Tarbell hopes a new "spirit of individualism" might enable men to fight "A Modern War for Independence" (2:155), she acknowledges that John D. Rockefeller rightly saw the need for "permanent stability and growth" beyond "brigandage" (2:292). As volume 1 chronicles the fall of the independents, it also chronicles the rise of Rockefeller's control over production. Volume 2 tells of his control over marketing and distribution.

According to her biographer, Kathleen Brady, Tarbell saw Rockefeller as a great man who was also a greedy bully.[33] Yet her book presents Rockefeller more complexly. Ostensibly he seems an icon of monstrous yet manly daring and self-control. Though he lied to investigating committees about his role in the South Improvement Company—a role Tarbell was the first to prove—Rockefeller "always kept his word" in a deal (2:132, 24). Noting that as early as 1878 he was called "the Lord of the Oil Regions" (1:215), Tarbell repeatedly compares him to Napoleon. Reluctantly she admires his audacity, his poker face, his daring, his "imagination" and "steadfastness" (1:99), his "genius for detail" (2:241), and his "far-sightedness" (2:253). She faults him for "that lack of the sense of humour which, ethical qualities aside, is his chief limitation" (2:133).

Tarbell also tries to find words for something else: a strange absence of personality or individuality at the center of Rockefeller's calculations. He seems not monstrously manly but inscrutably inhuman. His "sphinx-like attitude" sat at the center of a vast, systematizing machine, inexorably crushing each competitor, while "an extraordinary system of competition" within the machine kept every employee "on his mettle . . . The machine was pervaded and stimulated by the consciousness of its own power and prosperity" (2:127, 126). To others he was "the soul of self-possession. His only sign of impatience—if it was impatience—was an incessant slight tapping of the arm of his chair with his white fingers" (2:261). Yet there was no self to be possessed, no human desire that could be imagined in manly terms. "To place love of independent work above love of profits was as incomprehensible to him as a refusal to accept a rebate because it was wrong" (1:156).

Tarbell senses that history is going John D. Rockefeller's way, not because of his illegal monopolizing tactics, which she exposes and detests, but because Rockefeller has subordinated himself to the idea of combination. Fascinated with Rockefeller's vision as well as his control and cunning, she portrays him as a mesmerizing genius who systematically destroys lesser men not for the sake of dominance but to advance his passion for efficiency, his horror of waste. She also mourns the cost of system-making for national markets: independent selves simply don't matter much any more in the workplace. Tarbell's portrait of Rockefeller intimates a haunting absence of the personal, a soulless nobody at the heart of the corporation's "artificial person."[34]

Adolf A. Berle, Jr., and Gardiner Means

All these corporate critiques display fears about the loss of localized framings for a man's value. What happens when bureaucratic hierarchies become primary sites for white middle-class men's self-esteem? What happens when capital flows more easily from credit than from productivity? And what to make of a world in which power no longer can be adequately personified with metonyms of individual manliness, although performances of what Michael Lewis has called Big Swinging Dickhood continue to saturate daily life?[35]

Even as late as the early 1930s, Adolf A. Berle, Jr. and Gardiner Means adopt several of these now traditional narratives to frame their insight (already mentioned by Veblen) that corporate ownership has little to do with managerial control. In *The Modern Corporation and Private Property* (1932), they affirm that separating control from ownership "makes possible tremendous aggregations of property" (5), and they note the failure of "Mr. Brandeis . . . to turn the clock backward in 1915" (viii).[36] Where Brandeis emphasizes workers' loss of individuality, Berle and Means lament a similar fate for the owners, who have lost "individual initiative" as "centripetal" power concentrates in the hands of corporate managers (9).

If earlier critics invoked medieval images of robber barons, Berle and Means imply equally un-American metaphors of fascist dictatorship. Workers and consumers alike have become "vast bodies . . . under the leadership of the dictators of industry[.]" Executives' unchecked control and "the extreme division of labor in large scale enterprise necessarily imply not individualism but cooperation and the acceptance of authority almost to the point of autocracy" (349). Adam Smith's world of competing tradesmen has long since disappeared. Now executives are like "Alexander the Great, seeking new worlds to conquer" (350). As if to echo Charles Francis Adams, Jr., who called for specific democratic and community interventions sixty years earlier, Berle and Means conclude rather vaguely that "the claims of the community" have to be asserted against the corporation's state-like power (357).

It may seem utopian at this point to return to my own progressive narrative of the corporation. Though middle-class American men's patriarchal yearnings have diminished, except in the rhetoric of the religious right, corporate capitalism stimulated new hopes for a return to patriarchal manhood. Nor have gestures of remasculinization slackened much in our own millennial atmosphere of white male pathos and bathos. Yet it's not quite enough to say that manhood developed new forms of contestation and patriarchal performativity as men's work alienated their gender codes from their gendered bodies. The rise of large-scale organizations threatened manhood's ideological usefulness as a goad to make men risk danger and combat for personal honor and small-group survival.[37] In the new world of white collars and bosses, civic and domestic metonyms for representing manliness began to lose their legitimacy.

Only recently has whites-only paternalism begun to give way to greater diversity among corporate and professional employees, who can respond more variously to diverse markets. Nonetheless, the corporate transformation of modern middle-class life has made it possible to imagine a world where value grows from local and cosmopolitan affiliations that can be chosen, rather than inherited. Lives can be lived partially unencumbered by the biological genealogy of gender, the cultural genealogy of ethnicity, and the racist genealogy of race. The corporate transformation has detached men's entitlements from their metonymic roots in patriarchy, landed property, and physical productivity. Manhood still bestrides the world like a colossus, but its feet are planted firmly in mid-air.

6   Giving and Shaming

When Andrew Carnegie's "Wealth" appeared in 1889, its assault on men who bequeath great wealth to their children seemed shockingly new. As his most famous formulation declares, "'The man who dies thus rich dies disgraced'" (29, also 49).[1] Carnegie's essay is usually cited as a key factor in the transformation of rich Americans' giving from personal charity to institutional philanthropy. Yet "Wealth" is also a highly visible public shaming, challenging elite norms for dynastic fatherhood. Attacking the tradition of localized gentry paternalism because it fosters dependence rather than self-reliance, Carnegie reconstitutes paternalism as depersonalized philanthropy on a national and international scale.

During the 1890s, few of the over four thousand U.S. millionaires practiced what Carnegie preached. In 1893, according to an article in *Review of Reviews,* the city with the most "active givers" to charities was Baltimore, with 49 percent of its millionaires actively giving. New York City, which had by far the most millionaires, ranked at the bottom of the list.[2] Carnegie and John D. Rockefeller led the way in developing new philanthropic norms and practices that emphasized institutional development rather than personal "alms-giving." By the 1990s, when Bill Gates and many other suddenly rich people in the new subculture of computer software said they were too busy to give, the media and other men of great wealth such as Ted Turner sniped at them until they grudgingly began to comply. The success of that shaming campaign implies a century-long change in social expectations for public giving by the rich. Led by Carnegie and Rockefeller, some members of the moneyed elite have used unostentatious philanthropy to "give back," to encourage moderate social reforms, or to satisfy moral or religious imperatives. Others have used philanthropic giving more publicly to enforce class cohesion and consolidate their class position, while jockeying for status and national visibility.

Carnegie's and John D. Rockefeller's concern about their extraordinary surplus wealth shows a need for honor, recognition, and reciprocal community as well as a desire to exercise power and decontaminate their social image. While pride, public image, and religious imperatives stimulated Carnegie's and Rockefeller's unprecedented scale of giving, the two multimillionaires also responded to the potential social shame inherent in possessing surplus wealth far beyond anyone's needs or wants. Moreover, localized patterns of giving could no longer address social problems with much larger scale and scope, particularly the class conflicts and social heterogeneity intensified by industrial capitalism. As Matthew Jacobson has argued, the early corporate era faced a "crisis of over-inclusive whiteness[.]"[3] The first issue of the *American Journal of Sociology* in 1895 declared that "Men are more definitely and variously aware of each other than before. They are also more promiscuously perplexed by each other's presence."[4] In *The Gospel of Wealth* (1900), Carnegie invokes a diffusely controlling category of incorporative whiteness to turn the threat of class conflicts into the promise of individual upward mobility, while containing racialized outsiders. Philanthropic giving could help to create a bounded, bonded, and beckoning new-money elite.

In the first part of this chapter, I argue that Carnegie invokes tropes of manliness and race to shame other rich men into recirculating their surplus wealth. Such giving would nurture self-reliance in others and civic leadership in themselves. Yet Carnegie challenges the patriarchal base for that tradition of paternalistic benevolence. For him, class conflicts can be alleviated and white racial uplift will thrive, not through bequeathing legacies or giving alms to the needy, but by funding institutions that can help deserving strivers rise beyond their inferior races and backgrounds. As race becomes a test of the new moneyed elite's incorporative powers, it also becomes a boundary defining the limits of entry to social entitlement.

Part 2 takes a longer view of surplus wealth, racialized shaming dynamics, and group cohesion in the postbellum United States. To show how precapitalist groups use threats of shaming to recirculate surplus wealth, Marcel Mauss's *The Gift* highlights an extreme instance, the potlatch. There a man secures honor by giving away all his possessions. Using Mauss along with Christopher Bracken's *The Potlatch Papers,* I ask how, or whether, Mauss's analysis might apply to Carnegie, Rockefeller, and other corporate benefactors in an imperial nation-state. Race-ing, I suggest, becomes a collective social shaming that prompts greater cohesion within and among white classes and subclasses.

In part 3, briefly contrasting George Eliot's *Middlemarch* (1874) with Edith Wharton's *Summer* (1917), I argue that Eliot's English novel shows how—or hopes that—dynamics of benevolence and shaming continue to shape village relations in a nation-state. In Wharton's novel, as in *The House of Mirth,* giving loses its transcendent social value. It has been reduced to expectations of individual exchanges, while shaming serves primarily to bring Charity back to a traditional woman's role under Lawyer Royall's paternalistic care.

The last part juxtaposes four early twentieth-century texts that separate shaming dynamics from a dominant class group, sometimes problematically. In Howells's "Tribulations of a Cheerful Giver" (1909), which frets about conflicts between Christian and capitalist norms for charity, a liberal's narrative of personal shame becomes a self-paralyzing moment of social shaming at the end, as the narrator confronts poverty on a scale that personal benevolence can't solve. Lincoln Steffens's *The Shame of the Cities* (1904) relies on a traditionally paternalistic rhetoric of morality and honor to expose citizens' complicity in political corruption. Steffens succeeds where Jane Addams fails, because Addams attacks paternalism itself. Her inability to find a publisher for "A Modern Lear," her caustic and incisive attack on George Pullman's paternalism (written 1894, pub. 1912), shows how middle-class institutions of publication protected the industrial elite by censoring shaming from outside or below. Booker T. Washington's *Up from Slavery* (1901), already considered in chapter 4, reveals how his art of soliciting money from wealthy capitalists not only exploits Carnegie's doctrine of benevolent stewardship, but also responds to white men's shaming of the "begging" black male body.

Empowered at the bottom, Washington turns incorporative whiteness into black agency, while resisting and accommodating white uses of race-ing for group shaming. Shaky at the top, Howells uses whiteness only to dichotomize. Addams, the most respectful of democratic diversity, ignores whiteness altogether.

Ultimately, white race-ing consolidates white people's mutual recognition and status within a quasi-colonial paternalistic imaginary. In *Imagined Communities,* Benedict Anderson argues that colonialism invented racism as a fallback strategy to establish and maintain dominance within provincial dependence. It was a way to "play aristocrat off center court."[5] Yet incorporative whiteness makes fantasies of provincial aristocracy harder to indulge, except perhaps in the postbellum South. If blackness is a shaming fiction imposed by the white gaze, then whiteness is a more comprehensive fiction of group coherence, defined in part by the colors it can absorb and affix. This whiteness implies a depersonalized collectivity as the basis for personal superiority.

In that respect at least, the rise of incorporative whiteness and the rise of the corporation reinforced each other as ways of organizing American white men's subjectivities. But large companies were creating their own metropolitan centers. By the end of the twentieth century, the pressures of workplace interdependencies and marketing diversities had begun to undermine the provincial, neocolonial basis for white racism that corporations initially strengthened.

Carnegie's *Gospel of Wealth*

Faced with corporate capitalism's production of the flagrantly rich and the flagrantly poor, Andrew Carnegie turned the American tradition of civic benevolence toward large-scale philanthropy, a word he detested for its sentimental "love-of-humanity" connotations. In 1889, Carnegie's essay on "Wealth" argued that a rich man should administer his surplus wealth during his lifetime to foster self-help among the poor. The editor rushed Carnegie's essay into print as the "finest article I have ever published in the Review."[6]

In *The Gospel of Wealth,* which reprints his essay, Carnegie begins by posing a problem: how can we administer wealth to "bind together the rich and poor in harmonious relationship" (14)? For better and worse, he says, large-scale capitalism has changed American life. On the one hand, "The Indians are to-day where civilized man then was" (14), since former "luxuries have become the necessaries of life" (16). Moreover, modern industry keeps providing such luxuries at lower prices. The great "law of competition" has been "best for the race," though "sometimes hard for the individual," because it "insures the survival of the fittest in every department." On the other hand, human society "loses homogeneity." "Rigid castes" separate rich and poor, employers and employees. Worse, "each caste is without sympathy with the other[.]" Employers cannot know their "thousands of operatives" or vice versa; and that same law of competition forces employers "into the strictest economies," especially with wages (16). What can be done to prevent class war?

Carnegie's solution is classic paternalism, but with a difference. Ostensibly his essay reflects the consolidation of businessmen's values after the 1870s to minimize class conflicts by renewing the civic leadership that would foster competitive individualism.[7] Yet Carnegie goes further. A rich man would be "most injudicious" (19–20) to give his surplus wealth to his sons, since young men need self-reliance to prove themselves in the survival of the fittest. Such legacies are inspired by "vanity" (20) and "family pride" (21), not true affection. Nor should a rich man bequeath his wealth after his death. Such bequests are another form of vanity, and besides, inherited wealth is usually administered badly. Carnegie also argues that to make the sons of the new elite become manly competitors, the State should levy a hefty estate tax, which had been enacted and repealed several times until its final passage in 1916.[8] The second part of the essay concludes by raising the shaming stakes: for a rich man, it is "but a step" from dying "disgraced" to "punishment or deprivation hereafter" (49).

Rather than hoard wealth for their families, rich men should "dignify their own lives" by acting in Christ's spirit to administer their funds as "trustee and agent" for "poorer brethren" (25). Despite howls of protest from religious leaders, Carnegie specifically enjoins "indiscriminate charity" to individuals or churches, except to rebuild church buildings in poor neighborhoods.[9] One must only "help those who will help themselves" (27). Besides, personal charity and spiritual consolations can't solve the class conflicts created by capitalism. Instead, rich men should give to institutions that can stimulate entrepreneurial initiative in thousands, even millions of young men the donor has never seen. That means universities, libraries, hospitals, parks, museums, concert halls, and public baths. Libraries are the best (36), since they provide "the ladders upon which the aspiring can rise" (28), without unmanly dependence or the "degrading, pauperizing tendency" that charity typically fosters (31). By giving back surplus wealth at three or four degrees of separation, the donor becomes both a purified capitalist and father of an imagined national community. In this "true gospel . . . to solve the problem of the rich and the poor" (29), enlightened paternalism fosters upward mobility, and everyone but the truly shiftless can live happily ever after.

Yet tensions edge Carnegie's confident prose. Why would he say "dignify their own lives" (25)? What might be the indignity in capitalist success? Surprisingly, Carnegie seems less nervous about the specter of class conflicts than about the spectacle of enormous riches beyond anyone's needs or wants. For Carnegie, hoarding great profits is intrinsically shameful. Though he celebrates capitalism's ability to make luxury goods widely available at lower cost, he doesn't make the usual case for profits as the sign of moral goodness. Neither God's grace nor the survival of the fittest justifies being excessively wealthy. Instead, only through giving back surplus wealth can a man's money benefit society or confer dignity on his reputation. Large legacies, he observes laconically, simply show that "a man is content to wait until he is dead before he becomes of much good in the world." These are men who would not have left any legacies at all "had they been able to take it with them. . . . there is no grace in their gifts" (21).

Dismissing the communistic ideal of laboring for "brotherhood" rather than for oneself (18), Carnegie vehemently asserts that only the law of competition can produce the surplus value on which modern civilization depends. But the corollary law, that a few will get revenue far beyond their needs and wants, disturbs him. He associates great wealth with unusable and wasteful excess, not with the capitalist exploitation of labor. One reason could be that "Wealth" was published three years before the 1892 Homestead massacre, which made employee resentments an inescapable part of his public life. More fundamentally, Carnegie's association of surplus wealth with shame reflects a residual ideology linking manliness with honor and civic leadership. Only those who use their wealth for public benefit should gain honor. One of his favorite words is "noble": a "nobler ambition" (22), "a noble public library" (24), "a noble use of wealth" (33), an "ennobling study[,]" "a noble work" (34), "a pure and noble" church (47). By contrast, the man who dies rich remains "the ignoble hoarder of useless millions" (49). That "requires no sacrifice, nor any sense of duty to his fellows" (48).

Another favored word is "race." As preoccupied as Booker T. Washington with "uplifting the race," Carnegie has quite a different race in mind: an ambiguous fusion or confusion of white, manly, and human, usually resolving into Anglo-Saxon dominance. Just to sample two paragraphs: "the race" will bring about an "evolution" toward an "ideal State" founded upon "intense Individualism," by voluntarily circulating the surplus wealth of the rich. But legacies and acts of charity act on too small a scale to help "the improvement of the race[.]" Instead, the law that enables a few rich men to accumulate wealth will help such men to make wealth "a more potent force for the elevation of our race[.]" Where others advocate violent or radical change that intensify social divisions, he says, donating to large projects can help "the race, as a race" (23). And so forth.

The equation of this vaguely inclusive abstraction with Anglo-Saxon dominance comes in later essays, emphatically and repetitively. Throughout *The Gospel of Wealth,* Carnegie recurrently meditates on why Anglo-Saxons deserve the supremacy they have achieved, and answers that whites have more race pride. In one essay he imagines "the ideal federation of the English-speaking people of the world" (174), and in another he reaffirms the racial bond between the two peoples. "The pride of race is always there at the bottom . . . The strongest sentiment in man . . . is racial" (198). The "race sentiment" (202) will overcome any temporary conflicts between "the two branches of our race" (208), because "pride of race" (210, 198) will bring Americans and English together "against men of other races" (198). "[M]y dream," he announces in an essay opposing U.S. imperialism, is "the coming together of the English-speaking race" (141). Conversely, as the United States contemplates the possibility of annexing the Philippines and Cuba, the Republic has to be preserved as "one homogeneous whole," and not degenerate into "a scattered and disjointed aggregate of widely separated and alien races" (123).

On the surface, Carnegie uses race to puff up traditions of paternalism and individualism. Yet the abstractedness of his terms evades tensions between self-reliance and corporate bureaucracy. "I never was quite reconciled to working for other people[,]" he remarks. "I always liked the idea of being my own master, of manufacturing something and giving employment to many men." Even the president of a company "has sometimes a board of directors who cannot know what is best to be done[,]" or stockholders who show "the property is not his own" (12–13). Middle managers shouldn't worry about that, since their manhood now has greater scale and scope: "the small, petty master in his little store has given way to the bigger, much more important manager of a department, . . . This bigger system grows bigger men, and it is by the big men that the standard of the race is raised" (85).

Carnegie's near-parodic insistence on an abstracted masculinity—being "bigger," raising a "standard"—subsumes tensions between individualism and deferential interdependence in corporate hierarchies.[10]

Carnegie intermittently inflames such tensions with his presumptuously patronizing tone. A "first-class manager" must have "the confidence and re-spect, and even the admiration, of his workmen. No man is a true gentleman who does not inspire the affection and devotion of his servants" (101). More subtly, a strange emptiness of agency looms in his argument for bigger and better benevolence. Though proclaiming himself among the biggest of the big men, Carnegie voices a late-nineteenth-century fatalism about determin-istic forces that overwhelm any one man's control. If the abyss of class in-equity and the enormity of surplus profits provide the most immediate sources for his rhetoric of shaming, Carnegie also intimates a nervousness that the bignesses of race, nation, and economic laws dwarf personal man-liness, whether self-reliant or paternalistic. Capitalist accumulation, he af-firms, manifests "overpowering, irresistible" laws and tendencies: the "aggregation of capital and increase of size in every branch of product can-not be arrested or even greatly impeded" (82–83).

Carnegie's wish to be a "true gentleman" leads him back from the prec-ipice of impersonal capitalist abstractedness to a more comfortable dream of rejuvenated civic leadership. If, as Raymond Williams has said, novels sup-plied readers with "knowable communities," paternalism supplied wealthy corporate capitalists with knowable selves.[11] In that context, "knowable" means a self that fits previously functional norms for manly dignity and gentry honor. Yet Carnegie's rhetoric of benevolence uneasily joins the small-scale manliness of self-reliance and civic fathering to the large-scale abstrac-tions of national and racial dominance. In resolving that uneasiness through institutional philanthropy, Carnegie preserves a nostalgia for "noblesse oblige" even as he depersonalizes it. He preserves the conjunction of pater-nalistic benevolence with white Southern idealizations of the gentleman, and with the racial binary on which those idealizations depended, while remov-ing direct contact with deserving but inferior beneficiaries of the rich man's largesse.

Among Carnegie's publicized or anonymous personal gifts—he gave a pension to Booker T. Washington, as well as $600,000 to the Tuskegee In-stitute in 1903—one indirectly racialized story stands out. Long after the Homestead Strike, a friend went to Mexico, where he happened to meet the skilled mechanic who had precipitated bloodshed by ordering the arrest of the Pinkertons. Accused of murder and treason, McLuckie had fled the coun-try. When the friend wrote to Carnegie about the encounter, Carnegie re-sponded that McLuckie should be given all the money he wanted, without knowing the source. The mechanic manfully refused, and the friend helped him get a job. Much later, when told who had offered the money, McLuckie responded, "'Well, that was damned white of Andy, wasn't it?'" As Carnegie concludes, "I would rather risk that verdict of McLuckie's as a passport to Paradise than all the theological dogmas invented by man."[12]

A recent critique of Carnegie highlights the conjunction between racial exclusion and fantasies of generous whiteness. Gerald Freund's *Narcissism and Philanthropy* opposes Carnegie's "narcissistic" philanthropy to John D. Rockefeller's more "selfless" philanthropic management. Though Freund idealizes Rockefeller's selflessness, he rightly notes that Carnegie's "narcissistic approach led to some disastrous consequences, such as his choice, as an officer of the Carnegie Corporation, of Charles B. Davenport, who propagated the doctrine of eugenics, used to justify racism in America." Carnegie-funded eugenics studies led directly to the immigration restriction formula written into the 1924 Johnson Act.[13] Elsewhere in *The Gospel of Wealth,* Carnegie justifies his opposition to imperialism on racial grounds, since "tropical people" simply can't be civilized and governed. "The people of the South" understand what other Americans need to learn, that we have "a 'holy duty' to keep our Republic from further dangers arising from racial differences" (152–53). When faced with "alien races, ignorant of our language and institutions[,]" we must conclude that "Americans cannot be grown there" (128).[14]

If Carnegie's racial dichotomizing simplifies a tangle of pride, privilege, and anxiety, it also defines a masterful "we" as an imagined national community. Indeed, one could argue that Carnegie's rhetoric of shaming reflects an anticipatory pride, of both the holier-than-thou and follow-me varieties. He wants to lead millionaires beyond their millions to constitute a new gentry of the moneyed industrial elite. Recent studies of elite philanthropy show how giving functions to consolidate class and subgroup boundaries as well as to mark personal status within those groupings. Francie Ostrower concludes that philanthropy supplies "a mark of class status" amid heterogeneity and change, and enables "the re-creation of a relatively homogeneous elite environment" with various hierarchies of prestige.[15] Carnegie explicitly addresses his appeal to what he calls the "millionaire class," and posits poverty as the necessary breeding ground for growing future American millionaires.[16]

For early corporate capitalist philanthropists, anxiety about class conflict probably loomed at least as large as the in-group pressures for elite class formation that Carnegie helped to set in motion. Social reformers and middle-class technocrats were challenging traditional ideals and practices of patrician benevolence.[17] If Carnegie reproduces several aspects of this code, he also registers its lack of patriarchal efficacy. He emphatically agrees that personal charity can't solve poverty and class resentments. Even as Carnegie uses shaming to restore the possibility of harmonious hierarchic community, his vehement advocacy of institutional rather than personal giving signals the inadequacy of local charitable benevolence, while his invocations of "race" and "big" signal the national divisions and corporate abstractedness he can't quite control.

Carnegie, Rockefeller, and Mauss

During their lifetimes Carnegie gave $350 million to various educational institutions, most famously libraries, while John D. Rockefeller gave $570 million, mostly to educational and medical institutions such as the University of Chicago and the Rockefeller Institute. At first glance, such unprecedented giving seems to justify Thorstein Veblen's conclusion in *Theory of the Leisure Class* (1899) that capitalist philanthropy is a form of "conspicuous waste," to display one's competitive dominance.[18] Yet "conspicuous waste" doesn't quite catch the strange appeal of giving away much of one's wealth to help strangers. Thomas Haskell's argument that capitalism expanded perceptions of causal relations, moral responsibility, and imaginative sympathies has its shadow side in capitalism's increased opportunities for exercising paternalism at great range.[19]

To many critics then and now, such benevolence functioned more to extend the power of the paternalist than to foster social change. Nonetheless, as Ron Chernow details, the medical revolution in the early twentieth century was funded largely with Rockefeller's money and initiative. Major educational gifts from Rockefeller and Carnegie, among others, helped to establish the possibility of an African American middle class, though Rockefeller focused on black women's colleges rather than helping to develop strong black citizens.[20] Although the new elite's philanthropy brought substantial social benefits, its social usefulness was always safely incorporative.

To wealthy and powerful men, used to reaping social distinction as well as profits from what they could influence or control, the idea that they might gain greater distinction by giving up control did not easily take hold. Yet the shift to institutional giving brought that prospect into view. As Carnegie and Rockefeller pioneered the institutional management of their philanthropic gifts, neither man relinquished control without a struggle, and both used philanthropy to change their Robber Baron images as well as to build a society that would favor future capitalists. Robert Bremner notes the "arrogance of [Carnegie's] language and the despotic tendencies of his philosophy[,]" and Rockefeller quietly faulted Carnegie for vanity.[21] Rockefeller himself was not immune to the charge. As Chernow puts it, "there was a well-nigh universal perception that John D. gave generously to philanthropy to fumigate his fortune."[22]

Image management on that scale counters the threat of being shamed. Publicly at least, Rockefeller succeeded. When he died in 1937, the obituaries featured his extraordinary giving, not his equally extraordinary rapacity.[23] In private, Rockefeller's national and dynastic fathering solaced shameful memories of his own father, William A. Rockefeller, a vagabond deaf-and-dumb peddler, snake-oil salesman, bigamist, and alleged rapist who brought his mistress into his home as housekeeper. John D. grew up "sandwiched" between two illegitimate siblings, before his father disappeared to pursue his huckstering and womanizing.[24]

Childhood shame does not seem to apply to Carnegie, a bantam cock of a Mama's boy. Nor does he seem concerned with charges of tainted money or worker exploitation, though no Chernow has told his full story. Instead, an uneasiness about massive private surpluses and the threat of class war, and more subliminally about the corporate threat to manly individualism, animates Carnegie's public shaming of his fellow millionaires. Honor, not guilt, generates Carnegie's manifesto. From his childhood onward, Carnegie associated honor with manly fortitude and his mother's strength of leadership. His mother, he recounts in his autobiography, gave the household a "keen sense of honor, independence, self-respect[.]" Quoting Robert Burns, he says her eye "'Beamed keen with honor'" (33). When he was 13, struggling in his first job, "it was a matter of honor" to conceal his problems from his equally struggling parents: "I must play the man and bear mine[,]" rather than "whine and give up[.]"[25] With less combative gusto and more self-control, Rockefeller also sought honor through giving.

Most studies of shame have focused on personal and familial roots.[26] Yet the threat of social shaming also stimulates ostentatious benevolence to stabilize and perpetuate small groups, whether families, clans, villages, city-states, or elites. According to J. G. Peristiany, the editor of the first major study of honor and shaming in Mediterranean societies, "Honour and shame are the constant preoccupation of individuals in small scale, exclusive societies where face to face personal, as opposed to anonymous, relations are of paramount importance[.]"[27] To understand the difficulty and the appeal of using rhetorics of shaming to solve the problems of a capitalist nation-state, we need to turn to the theories of Marcel Mauss.

Mauss's *The Gift* argues that the desire for honor and the fear of shame join to recirculate surplus wealth in primitive societies. As Mauss argues, fundamental human motives of honor and emulation generate fears of humiliation in anyone who has accepted an unreciprocated gift. Ritual gift-giving develops as a compensatory performance to restore honor: "One must act the 'great lord' upon such occasions."[28] At the ritualized extreme, in a potlatch, a man gives away all he has. Even the word "honor," as Edmund Morgan notes in his discussion of Mauss, derives from the Latin word *onus*, or burden. In premodern societies, having surplus wealth implies the burden of recirculating it, and what seem to be freely offered gifts require the subsequent burden of reciprocation. "The honor of both parties depended on the exchange."[29]

Surprisingly, as Mauss discovers, credit exists even in the most primitive society, long before money was invented, because giving establishes the receiver's obligation to reciprocate in some indefinite future. Paradoxically, the shared desire to lord it over one's peers creates lasting community bonds, at least when the group has to stay together over time. The basic motives of competition, ostentation, and grandiosity (28) act as a kind of invisible hand, to make people "feel that they are everything to each other" (36). Though a man gains honor and prestige through "antagonism and rivalry[,]" the ritual dynamics of giving remain "noble, replete with etiquette and generosity[,]" partly because the giver secures his honor by pretending not to care whether his gifts are reciprocated. When such giving "is carried on in another spirit, with a view to immediate gain, it becomes the object of very marked scorn" (37). By implication, at least in Mauss's view, modern expectations of immediate gain for any trade or exchange constitute the desiring self as a site of social shame. Perhaps, he implies, the acquisitive, capitalist self originates in the shameful repudiation of reciprocal community gift-giving.

In any case, mourning the loss of "aristocratic" reciprocity in precapitalist exchanges, Mauss polemically contrasts the "generosity" of primitive gift rituals (81–83) with the "tradesman morality" (65) of "miserly" modern business practices. Contract-based individualism (66) fosters a "cold, calculating mentality" (46–47). Even the concepts of "individual" and "profit" have been created by the victory of rationalism and mercantilism over precapitalist modes of deferential community bonding, he declares (76). One might say that Mauss's book, published in the year of his death, is his own act of aristocratic shaming, directed against what he sees as a degraded, commercial culture.

If the potlatch ensures community interdependence while elevating the giver's status, arranging a daughter's marriage secures the father's status while ensuring family alliances. To bring back a theme from chapter 2, a dutiful daughter can serve as a prime gift to secure her father's honor, whereas an independent or sexually active daughter becomes a prime signifier of her father's and therefore her family's shame. Although the reciprocal expectations in such gift-giving flagrantly constrain young women's autonomy, they help to preserve small groups that often face conditions of extreme scarcity.[30]

In larger groups, shaming also disciplines elites. From 1200 to 1500 in northern Italy, cities commissioned paintings of aristocratic men who had fled the city as accused criminals or traitors, and hung these portraits upside down on the city walls to deface their names. The specter of family dishonor lured many fugitives back to face trial and even death. As Samuel Egerton notes, those tactics worked well in "feudal, tribelike communes."[31]

In such communities, individuality as we know it is subsumed in group membership, much as various premodern societies—Vietnam and Korea, for instance—have no word for "I" separable from networks of relationships. For Mauss, only "the liberal professions of our great nations" offer faintly similar dynamics, mixing competition for rank with "honour, disinterestedness, corporate solidarity" (69). But the contrast shows modernity's fall from patriarchal and "religious" values to "prosaic" and "materialistic" values of "utility" (72). Within precapitalist groups, "individuals . . . were less sad, less serious, less miserly, and less personal than we are." For the same reasons, "they were or are more generous, more liable to give" (81).

Mauss's insights have been complicated by Christopher Bracken, whose *Potlatch Papers* shows that even the word "potlatch" was invented by Anglo-Europeans, and taken up by Canadian legislators bent on destroying the practice. By the 1870s, potlatch rituals struck law-makers in both the United States and Canada as a waste of time and property. Almost simultaneously with the U.S. Congress's 1887 passage of the Dawes Act, which opens chapter 1, the Canadian legislature passed several laws forbidding potlatch rituals in western Canada. Unfortunately for the legislators, nobody could define the word they had appropriated from early white anthropologists, and the courts struck down the legislation on those grounds or questioned it several times.[32]

Bracken quite rightly has a Derridean field day with the semiotic ambiguities and impasses that he has discovered in the Canadian archives. The postcolonial instabilities about whiteness that he finds all through the "potlatch papers" mirror the unsettled state of the settlers' language, particularly the colonizers' desire "to make the colonized subject similar but not too similar to the colonizer."[33] As "Europeans-in-Canada" attempted to define what was civilized and uncivilized, the terms kept overlapping and folding into "a tissue of contradictions" (60), in part because of contradictory desires to assimilate the natives while branding them as barbaric. The term's use to "hasten the assimilation of the British Columbia First Nations" was "part of a larger project to give Europe-in-Canada a feeling for its own whiteness and nationhood" (230). Nonetheless, it was very clear to Anglo-Europeans that wasteful giving was as abhorrent to them as unrestrained sex. As one petition by Catholic missionaries deplores, the "degrading" village rituals lure back "young men who had settled themselves upon their land, worked it industriously and built themselves a little house, after the white fashion, a step towards civilization of which a white man can scarcely appreciate the importance" (72).[34]

So we come to a basic cultural paradox. If the United States and Canada worked so assiduously to turn Indians away from extravagant giving in the late nineteenth century, why did several enormously rich white men preach and practice extravagant giving on a much larger scale? What reciprocities could a code of honor and shame address in a consolidating nation-state? Why have so many rich Americans given a considerable portion of their wealth to strangers they will never see? Isn't that a modified potlatch? Why, for that matter, does Santa Claus become such a beloved fantasy of a benevolent father-figure's once-a-year, world-wide potlatch?

The most obvious explanation for rich men's giving emphasizes religious imperatives, which have been unusually intense among many American businessmen. During the postbellum era of unregulated corporate acquisitiveness, a traditional Pauline rhetoric of stewardship for God's bounty gained renewed social vitality, especially with Carnegie and Rockefeller. Animated by Scottish Presbyterian values, Carnegie frequently declared that men of great wealth should be trustees of God's benevolence. In 1868, when Carnegie was only 33, he secretly pledged to devote each year's surplus "to benevolent purposes."[35] Rockefeller also had a deeply Christian sense of the necessity to give back and to improve his fellow man. A devout Baptist, Rockefeller gave at least 6 percent of his income to charity from age sixteen onward.[36] These two set the pace for subsequent generations of wealthy Americans.

Secular as well as religious factors animated these traditions of giving. In 1958 Merle Curti, the most eminent historian of American philanthropy, declared generosity to be a central aspect of "American character." As early as 1888, he notes, James Bryce declared that "In works of active beneficence, no country has surpassed, perhaps none has equalled the United States." Curti lists many sources for its charitable benevolence: religious traditions, unusual legal flexibility, weak governmental interventions, traditions of mutual aid among immigrant subgroups, the frontier, abundance, and the uncertainty of social status amid widespread mobilities. "In a fluid society like ours one not only has to make his place but to keep it by further achievement, such as putting success to socially approved uses."[37]

More peripherally, the resurgent rhetoric of benevolent trusteeship may reflect an incipient sense of shame about the promises unfulfilled in the legal construction of the corporation. As I've noted in chapter 1, the charitable corporation's promise of benevolence became the legal ground for the profit-making corporation, especially in the *Dartmouth College v. Woodward* case of 1819.[38] Yet that and subsequent court decisions led directly to the most rapacious age of Robber Baron capitalism. The fissure between civic expectations of corporate benevolence and the corporate practice of profit for its own sake had become a chasm.

Of all these factors, Mauss's focus on the imperatives of honor and shame in prompting the recirculation of surplus wealth best explains Carnegie's nervousness about how much money he had. "Generosity is an obligation," Mauss theorizes, because of an intimate moral connection between gifts and sacrifices. "Nemesis avenges the poor and the gods for the superabundance of happiness and wealth of certain people who should rid themselves of it. This is the ancient morality of the gift, which has become a principle of justice" (18). Cynically, one could say that Carnegie's concern about the enormity of his surplus is just another American man's way of bragging about size. But Carnegie, Rockefeller, and other American plutocrats were bothered as well as pleased with the size of their surplus wealth, which far exceeded any imaginable necessity or desire. Nemesis requires at least the appearance of sacrifice.

Besides, such wealth remains too private and inert. It signifies success, but not honor. And honor, as historians of premodern societies, Renaissance Italy, and the antebellum South have emphasized, requires rituals of public display.[39] It wouldn't have been quite enough for Rockefeller to hand out dimes and nickels. The code of elite civic leadership that framed and legitimated the legal basis for the corporation demanded more. What then to do with the surplus? How to gain honor by making it useful? How to reestablish a sense of community and reciprocity in a nation-state so starkly divided between rich and poor?

The solution, institutional philanthropy, satisfies two contrasting pressures. The first is expansive and imperial: to exercise power at a greater distance, on a national and international rather than corporate scale. The second is contractive: to establish and discipline a new corporate elite. Large-scale giving to institutions also evades an earlier danger bedeviling personal charity, that of looking shamefully duped.[40] Though Kathleen McCarthy and others have lamented the loss of mutuality and reciprocity in institutional gift giving, they are wrong in one ironic way: mutuality thrived, but it no longer crossed class lines.[41] The newly rich gave partly for civic stewardship, and partly to establish and maintain their position among similarly wealthy peers. Perhaps more fundamentally, their giving helped to create a niche group providing mutual respect and recognition as well as competition. Institutional philanthropy consolidates the new millionaire class, makes its good works visible, and dignifies it with the residual trappings of gentry honor, while delegating the management of civic leadership to technocratic underlings. In Henry Blake Fuller's 1895 Chicago novel, *With the Procession*, a female character urges, "[G]ive liberally and rightly, and nothing can bring you more credit."[42]

As with other consolidations of whiteness at this time, race functions as an abstracted, intensifying marker of the new elite's privileges and boundaries. By the 1890s, blackness had come to signify a Them who embody a shameful national past and a shamed national presence, not least in the presumptive congruence between blackness and begging. The powers and responsibilities of a benevolent white We could be constituted in part by defining which social groups were capable of being incorporated into whiteness.[43] Among the attractions of incorporative racializing, those at the top could enjoy limited liability for those people who seemed less absorbable.

Middlemarch and *Summer*

A brief look at George Eliot's *Middlemarch* (1871–72) and Edith Wharton's *Summer* (1917) can show how giving and shaming continue to secure the boundaries, cohesion, and moral hierarchies of small villages within a nation-state. At least in fiction, these communities successfully resist the lure of outward mobility. The narratives also test the limits of honor as a category of social value.

Middlemarch recounts a complex saga of benevolence and shaming in a small English village during the early nineteenth century. These dynamics shape nearly everyone's lives and subjectivities. In Maussian terms, honor accrues to those who give unstintingly and without thought of personal reward, while shame comes to those out for personal gain. The narrative sympathetically recounts the inward struggles of various characters along that moral spectrum.

Most obviously, Bulstrode finds his pretensions to evangelical piety and respectability shattered when he is shamed at a town meeting. The village has learned that the richest man in town gained his early money by taking over a "magnificent" pawnshop that received stolen goods (451), and by marrying the wealthy wife of his late boss. Moreover, he never told his wife-to-be that he had found her daughter, who had run away after discovering her father's dishonorable practices. Still worse, Bulstrode's deliberate failure to give correct instructions about drug doses ensures the death of Raffles, the man who had located the daughter. After much of this information emerges, the local lawyer and town clerk announces that Bulstrode must either justify himself or "withdraw from positions which could only have been allowed him as a gentleman among gentlemen." Realizing that he is a "dishonoured man" scorned by those he had considered his inferiors, he walks out "totteringly" on Dr. Lydgate's arm.[44] Not coincidentally, the public shaming occurs at a meeting "on a sanitary question" (532–35).

Dr. Lydgate becomes a more complex study in the "agonized struggles of wounded honour and pride" (542). He is remarkably generous and benevolent as well as skilled in his medical practice. Yet he incurs large debts to fulfill his professional ambition of building a new hospital, and he gives extravagant gifts to his wife to further her social ambitions. Those expenses lead him into increasingly shameful indebtedness. Eventually Lydgate has to seek and accept a thousand-pound loan from Bulstrode to stave off bankruptcy and the public repossession of their furniture. When he helps Bulstrode out of the meeting, the community thinks he has been bribed and perhaps complicit in Raffles's death. In contrast, Will Ladislaw refuses five hundred pounds per year from Bulstrode, to avoid dependence on tainted money. He also takes the moral high ground by keeping Bulstrode's secrets to himself, despite Will's discovery that he is the son of the runaway daughter Bulstrode had never aided or acknowledged. As Will says to Bulstrode, "My unblemished honour is important to me" (457).

Most complexly, Dorothea Brooke always tries to do the self-transcending thing. She exemplifies the loving compassion that Eliot replicates in her narrative, even for Bulstrode. "The presence of a noble nature, generous in its works, ardent in its charity, changes the lights for us: . . . we too can be seen and judged in the wholeness of our character" (558). Dorothea continually practices her duty to give—emotionally to her pedantic and self-absorbed elderly husband, financially to Lydgate, and emotionally to several other characters, particularly after her husband's death. She needs and seeks a life "filled with emotion" and "beneficent activity" (610). Yet that search finally leads her to exile in an unspecified place where she "lived faithfully a hidden life" (613).

The three couples who finally leave Middlemarch, the Bulstrodes, the Lydgates, and the newly married Ladislaws, do so to flee community shaming, not to seek upward or outward mobility. As the narrative says with empathetic dismissiveness, Bulstrode will live out his life "in the indifference of new faces" (602). Despite all of Dorothea's attempts to "save" the Lydgates' reputation and finances (579), she saves only their marriage. In his subsequent life, before he dies at 50, Lydgate publishes a treatise, and establishes "an excellent practice" alternating between London and a "Continental bathing-place[.]" Yet "he always regarded himself as a failure" (610). It also doesn't matter that Dorothea and Will move to London (601), or that Will becomes a Member of Parliament (611). It's far more crucial that her family eventually, grudgingly allows her two visits a year, and that they allow Dorothea's son to inherit the Brookes' estate.

The great surprise is that George Eliot denies readers a sentimental ending. Dorothea and Will leave Middlemarch because the community, personified by her sister's husband, thinks she is "degrading herself" by marrying a man without fortune, position, or "honour" (595). Yet Dorothea remains the most nobly unselfish and benevolent of all the characters. The impasse between her complicated subjectivity and the community's simple standards of moral evaluation detaches her personal honor from her social position. Though honor remains transcendent as a personal ideal of moral behavior, the narrative undermines honor's function as a shared social valuation. It no longer secures class hierarchy. Nor does it complement the social threat of shame to ensure community bonds and proprieties. Instead it becomes a private category of self-assessment, especially for Dorothea, Will, and their readers. Throughout, the narrative recounts this slow slippage between honor and shaming with an urbane mixture of affection and detachment, as if yearning for a world being lost, while gently satirizing that world's restrictiveness. As Eliot ambiguously observes, "It ought to lie with a man's self that he is a gentleman" (457). For that reason among many others, Henry James is right to say that *Middlemarch* "sets a limit . . . to the development of the old-fashioned English novel."[45]

Over forty years later, Edith Wharton's *Summer* (1917) shows how benevolent giving has lost its transcendent value in preserving the cohesion of a small community faced with the outward pull of national mobilities and class allegiances. Instead, as in *The House of Mirth* (1905), material gifts usually imply the expectation of sexual exchange.[46] Both novels chronicle ample uses of shaming as attempts to preserve group cohesion, whether of an international elite or of a sleepy New England town. Yet these attempts meet with only partial success.

In *The House of Mirth,* the New York elite sacrifices Lily Bart to maintain the border between them and the "dingy," after Lily rejects several opportunities to marry for money. In *Summer,* shame helps to create a bounded family, if not a community. It brings Lawyer Royall and Charity together as husband and wife, offering each other a skimpy measure of mutual consolation for their failures to fulfill more autonomous ambitions. In both novels, shaming functions with particular intensity to restrict young unmarried women's independence. For Charity, that means choosing or drifting into marriage to Lawyer Royall, instead of making her upper-class lover marry her or trying to raise her baby on her own, perhaps as a prostitute. For Lily, that means choosing or drifting into death, rather than degenerate into what Wharton presents as a near-equivalent to prostitution, an unmarried lady working for pay.

At the lower end of the social scale, *Summer* presents a town on the dependent periphery of metropolitan centers. Here shame is more starkly gendered. For Lawyer Royall, shame begins with his failure to achieve his workplace ambitions. Though fascinated with histories of American nation-building, he hasn't succeeded as a lawyer in the world beyond North Dormer, as he admits in his speech during "Old Home Week." Moreover, in a culminating moment of intense desire and shame, he tries and fails to solace his loneliness by sexually accosting the young woman he has paternalistically rescued and raised.

For Charity, the shame of being sexually active with Lucius Harney is an attribution she proudly rejects. Far from accepting the label of "bad girl" that has been fixed on Julia Hawes, Charity revels in her passionate love for the handsome young architect, whereas he revels in his more colonizing passion for this seemingly primitive mountain-girl. Eventually, after Royall shames Harney by forcing the issue of marriage, Harney leaves her to marry a woman of his own class. Being pregnant and abandoned leaves Charity seemingly without options, and passively she lets Lawyer Royall protect her with marriage, perhaps with sex in the offing, perhaps not. For both Lawyer Royall and his ward turned wife, shame compels them—in his speech's ambiguous, repetitive phrasing—to "come back for good" (193–95).

At the very end, the word "good" takes on a heightened charge. After Charity returns without the new clothes that Lawyer Royall had given her the money for, he scowls, and then "grew friendly again. . . . 'You're a good girl, Charity" (290).[47] Initially that seems ironic, since he doesn't know she has used the forty dollars to get Harney's brooch back from Dr. Merkle, the abortionist. Yet she sees in his eyes "a look that made her feel ashamed and yet secure. 'I guess you're good too,'" she responds. Here "good" carries several contradictory meanings. She's good because the baby won't be illegitimate after all, because she's not a competitive show-off, because he thinks she's frugal, because she sacrificed her claim on Harney, because she accepts his continuing role of paternalistic parent, or because he's atoning for having called her a "bare-headed whore" (151).

But the deeper meanings lie in that phrase, "ashamed and yet secure." The association highlights the necessity for a young woman to accept shame as part of defining herself as a good girl. Charity submits to a man who finally gains a lifelong companion. He also enhances his paternalistic protectiveness by gaining her as his wife, and enhances his honor by protecting her from the charge of illegitimacy. If her heart has "contracted" with that implicit contract (282), as several critics have emphasized, the novel comes to its ambiguous rest by reducing her to a passionless wife, soon to be a mother.[48] It's clear that her bond with her child will be the new love of her life, and that's just as it should be in a small town with clear gender roles.

In both novels, race glancingly helps to define the "good," at least to the community's satisfaction. Once Will Ladislaw's origins become known, various citizens of Middlemarch see him as "the grandson of a thieving Jew pawnbroker" (566), though in fact Will's grandfather met Bulstrode as fellow members of a Calvinistic church, where Mr. Dunkirk was "the richest man in the congregation" (450). Later the rector's wife declares, "It must be admitted that his blood is a frightful mixture!" (599). Those racist jibes encourage readers to separate Will's personal honor from the community's assessment of him, though the Brookes eventually accept the marriage.

In *Summer,* Charity's attractiveness to Harney bespeaks a racialized taint that makes her shameful to herself. From the start, Charity has a "small swarthy face" (8), akin to the "swarthy Mountain" she came from (182). When Harney discovers that she is "so different" because she comes from the Mountain, he is aroused for the first time. "He picked up her hand and laid a kiss on the sunburnt knuckles" (67). These descriptions ambiguously link Charity's passion for nature, and her natural passion, with racial inferiority. Without any ambiguity, as discussed in chapter 2, Dr. Merkle's black and gold sign, her false black hair, and her mulatto servant associate the abortion doctor with racial degradation.

The fact that such independent careers are more available for women than they are in *Middlemarch* may invite such conservative demonization, even by a woman author in the midst of her highly successful career. More generally, the fact that outward and upward mobility beckons beyond North Dormer, as it doesn't in George Eliot's more bounded and ethnically homogeneous locale, may also intensify Wharton's race-ing. Charity's struggles against assimilation finally yield to Lawyer Royall's incorporative paternalism, which makes her a "good girl" again, or at last.

Howells's "Tribulations of a Cheerful Giver"

Both *Middlemarch* and *Summer* try to circumscribe the increasing appeal of autonomy, mobility, and heterogeneous encounters by focusing on small village dynamics. Four very different texts highlight how shaming works or doesn't work to control the tensions in larger social settings. William Dean Howells's "Tribulations of a Cheerful Giver" (1909), Lincoln Steffens's *The Shame of the Cities* (1904), Jane Addams's "A Modern Lear" (1912) and Booker T. Washington's *Up from Slavery* (1901) variously show the difficulties and the possibilities of using shaming to create an imagined national community. Only Steffens, the most publicly successful of the urban reformers, holds fast to a rhetoric of honor, though the tangle of honor and public shaming persists from Mark Twain's "The Man That Corrupted Hadleyburg" (1899) to Martin Scorsese's movie, *The Gangs of New York* (2002).

In Howells's essay, religious and capitalist values conflict. The essay's narrator—one hesitates to call him Howells, since he performs his representativeness at every turn—seems a throwback to an earlier model of charitable benevolence, the Christian Gentleman.[49] He is affable, urbane, well-meaning, well-heeled, and scrupulously concerned to do exactly what's right toward the poor. But his two consciences give him opposite advice. His Christian conscience says "Give to him that asketh" (112). His "citizen" conscience, as if parroting Carnegie, says giving risks "pauperizing" beggars afresh, by "teaching them to trust in a fickle fortune rather than their own enterprise" (130). "So I compromise, and I am never able to make sure that either of those voices is satisfied with me. I am not even satisfied with myself" (122).[50] Every benevolent encounter with beggars intensifies his inward turmoil of doubt, self-scrutiny, and shame.

The first incident can serve for the whole. When faced with a mutilated man holding out his "stumps," the narrator finds the man's "mute appeal" "rather fine," even "impressive." "[E]xcept for his mutilation, which the man really could not help, there was nothing to offend the taste" (111). But the narrator discovers he only has a half dollar in his pocket. "This at once changed the whole current of my feelings; and it was not chill penury that repressed my noble rage, but chill affluence." Whether his "noble rage" is self-mocking or self-descriptive remains unclear. For that matter, does "rage" mean a raging desire to be benevolent or a less defined anger, in keeping with the voice "that incensed political economy gives me"? In any case, "[i]t was manifestly wrong to give half a dollar to a man who had no hands, or to any sort of beggar."

Resolving to give the man a quarter, he goes to a restaurant to get change. But "I was ashamed" to ask the young man who has walked down a long aisle to greet him, so "I pretended that I wanted a package of Sweet Caporal cigarettes," though "it was a pure waste for me to buy, since I do not smoke[.]" Then, to "encourage commerce" and satisfy "political economy[,]" the narrator buys the cigarettes. Then, to "secure myself with Christian charity," he hastens to give the quarter. But thinking that might be too much, the narrator "ended by poising fifteen cents on one of his outstretched stumps." Despite the beggar's surprised gratitude, "I came away feeling indescribably squalid" (113–14).

It seems as though one of Howells's nervous breakdowns is in the offing. Yet the incident also displays the narrator's cultural entitlement, not least in his one-downsmanship. Throughout his encounters with genuine and fraudulent beggars, he attends more to his doubly bad conscience than to their plights. Is he doing enough? Is he doing too much? Or is he a soft touch? "I was ashamed" (130) . . . "it might be embarrassing" (132) becomes a recurrent motif. Yet his investigation of his moral shame sharply contrasts with the unmanly social shame of male beggars. "I know it's a shame for a strong man like me to be begging, but—" said one beggar to him (118). Implicitly one-upping the beggar's quite describable squalor, the narrator calls his own feelings "indescribably squalid." His oxymoronic title shows the "Cheerful Giver" tormented with "Tribulations," defined by the OED as a "condition of great affliction, oppression, or misery." Yet when he touches the man's "stumps," the narrator's "poising" betrays his fastidious recoil. At the moment of physical contact, he chooses a word that connotes an elegant aesthetic of self-appreciation, and a delicate balance of engagement and disengagement, instead of the more straightforward "placing" or "dropping."

Tellingly, at one point the narrator disparagingly remarks that beggars are often "incoherent," with "very little imagination or invention; they might almost as well be realistic novelists" (116, also 125). For a moment he slips out of his anxiously benevolent persona to become William Dean Howells, a cultural eminence. His playful label for the unimaginative beggar presumes readers' knowledge of his own cultural status as "Dean" of American realists. He knows that the reader knows. If the narrator's patronizing attentiveness and self-mockery converge, the effect only widens the class divide. Strangely, he also divides respectable people like himself from the very rich, while allying himself with the least upliftable poor. "Perhaps it would be a fair division of the work if we let the deserving rich give only to the deserving poor, and kept the undeserving poor for ourselves, who, if we are not rich, are not deserving, either" (135–36). That throwaway line contradicts his earlier observation that "we give the smallest charity to those who need charity most" (115). In both these more self-referential instances, ambiguous gestures of self-mockery inflate and undercut his benevolence.

The essay ends with the narrator's "sole success" after a winter's charitable acts for an Italian family. Though both the narrator and the doctor thought "it would be little use" (138), he got a rheumatic young Italian vendor admitted to a hospital, where the young man got well. The narrator describes the young man's response at the news that the ambulance was coming for him. "It was a beautiful white spring day" (138), the narrator recalls. The strange adjective "white" functions less to abstract the day than to contrast his happy life with the implicitly black lives of the poor. Leaving the white day, "I entered the dark, chill tenement-house, where that dreadful *poverty-smell* struck the life out of the spring in my soul at the first breath." Though the young man's apartment is "clean and sweet[,]" since his poor mother "was as wholly a lady as any I have seen," the essay closes with a tableau of lower-class longing and middle-class judgment. The young man "clutched himself up from the bed and stretched his arms toward me with gasps of '*Lo spedale! Lo spedale!*' The spring, the coming glory of this world, was nothing to him. It was the hospital he wanted; and to the poor, to the incurable disease of our conditions, the hospital is the best we have to give. To be sure, there is also the grave" (139).

In these final sentences, the narrator's voice changes. For the poor, the "best we have to give" is the hospital, not the beautiful white spring day, since poverty is a "disease" leading to "the grave." What has looked like personal shame suddenly looks like contempt, edged with an implied shaming of white middle-class readers who turn away from the problem. Yet the shaming has no teeth, because the metaphor and pronoun block any radicalizing anger. To call poverty "the incurable disease" makes it seem natural and inevitable. More subtly, to say the poor are the disease "of our conditions" fudges the "we" he has just voiced. Does he mean that the poor shall always be with us, or that what makes him and his readers wealthy also produces the poor? By slipping into a more detached version of "Ah, Bartleby! Ah, humanity!" paternalism, the narrator throws up his hands, as if to say, What can anyone do? Throwing a few ambiguous phrasings across the class divide, he retreats to cynicism, the flip side of his sympathy. Both leave his privileges unchallenged, while enhancing his distinction as a realist.[51]

Carnegie's institutional focus avoids these tensions. Although Howells confronts them, his shaming and self-shaming seem to be poses, almost as fraudulent and momentary as those of the beggarly imposters he encounters. As Marcel Mauss's analysis implies, successful social shaming depends on one's fear of losing membership in a well-bounded small group. But Howells's essay portrays an urban society where the beggars are interchangeable, and where his persona holds tight to anxious urbanity throughout his contacts with the underclass. Since money and class privilege free benevolent gentlemen from the shame of being in need, the narrator seeks a moral shame to negotiate the tensions between charity and citizenship. Yet neither his persona, nor his money, nor his class, nor even the discomfort of self-scrutiny gives him a sense of recognition and belonging. Honor seems long gone, and his family, neighbors, and local community seem vestigial or unreal.

Steffens's *The Shame of the Cities* and Addams's "A Modern Lear"

Howells's essay remains a self-shaming that turns outward at the end. Much more forthrightly, Lincoln Steffens and Jane Addams seek social reform. Why then was Steffens's *The Shame of the Cities* so popular, yet Addams's "A Modern Lear" couldn't even get published? Steffens attacked many bribing businessmen and crooked politicians by name. Yet as he recounts proudly, businessmen in several of the cities thanked him for the exposés. Addams attacked just one businessman, George Pullman, and nobody would print her essay for almost two decades. The contrast may reflect Steffens's journalistic savvy, or middle-class social expectations about male and female writers. More profoundly, the difference shows Addams's more radical perspective. Whereas Steffens attacked corruption in the name of civic honor, Addams attacked a central aspect of honor, the paternalistic basis for relations between superiors and inferiors.

Steffens's *The Shame of the Cities* (1904) is a collection of six magazine articles on political corruption in St. Louis, Minneapolis, Pittsburgh, and Philadelphia, contrasted with successful reforms in Chicago and New York.[52] When he started the series, Steffens assumed that corruption was due to foreigners in "mongrel-bred" cities (2). To his great surprise, those cities (Chicago and New York) are the best. In the other, more "American" cities, the businessman "is the chief source of corruption" (3). "The commercial spirit is the spirit of profit, not patriotism; of credit, not honor; of individual gain, not national prosperity; of trade and dickering, not principle" (4–5). The rhetoric of these binary oppositions could be out of "A Chapter of Erie" (1869), the essay by Charles Francis Adams, Jr. discussed in chapter 5.

Yet where Adams calls for state regulation, Steffens calls for cold showers and virtue. For him the problem is less structural than moral: "it's all a moral weakness" (7). Ordinary citizens are most to blame, for their tolerance. The people are "not innocent[,]" nor are they deceived and betrayed. They know about the corruption, and do nothing (9). The goal of his book is "to sound for the civic pride of an apparently shameless citizenship" (1). As he concludes his introduction: "this little volume, a record of shame and yet of self-respect, a disgraceful confession, yet a declaration of honor, is dedicated, in all good faith, to the accused"—to all U.S. citizens (18).

If Steffens resembles Adams in his attempt to resurrect honor and morality as social values, he more covertly resembles Thorstein Veblen in his hopes for central state authority. He wanted to call for a dictator, Louis Joughin's introduction tells us, but his editor talked him out of it (vii). Perhaps that desire anticipates his later enthusiasm for the Soviet Union. Nonetheless, implicitly autocratic Steffens succeeds where democratic Addams temporarily fails because Steffens uses the rhetoric of a moral wake-up call to attack citizens' complicity in political corruption. He relies on a traditional language of honor, allied to civic benevolence, whereas Addams attacks paternalism itself.

Unlike *The Shame of the Cities,* Jane Addams's account of George Pullman's paternalism and the Pullman strike of 1894 has a voice more thoughtful than acerbic, with less narrative brio and more probing arguments. Though it's as close as American literature gets to Emile Zola's "J'Accuse!," "A Modern Lear" has a meditative reflectiveness, especially about father-daughter relations, and less surprisingly about class tensions. Where Howells evades confronting the class divisions that permeate his text, Addams immediately highlights the strike's "sharp division into class lines" (107), and repeatedly emphasizes Pullman's inability to comprehend "the social passion" for "the emancipation of the wage-worker" (120).[53] Deploring that class division, she argues that both sides have failed to see their common interests. Yet unlike Andrew Carnegie's "Wealth," which was rushed into print, "A Modern Lear" couldn't get published for eighteen years. Four major magazines rejected it as an ad hominem attack, and even her anticorporate friend, Henry Demarest Lloyd, said he would publish it only if she would "depersonalize" her analysis.[54] Though Addams read the essay at several clubs in Chicago and Boston, and privately showed it to John Dewey, who later said it had a profound effect on his thinking, its public influence came many years later.

For Addams, paternalism conflicts with a democratic respect for mutual consent. In improving his workers' lives, Pullman was "unusually generous" and "exceptionally liberal" (108). Yet he built the workers' community for ends that were "ultimately commercial and not social": a return on investment of "at least 4 per cent" (111). Though governing the town, Pullman "did not appeal to nor obtain the consent of the men who were living in it" (122). Instead, he "cared most for [the town] when it gave him a glow of benevolence" (112). Fundamental to such paternalism is a yearning for the "almost feudal virtue of personal gratitude (117), and a corresponding failure to see that industrial relations are no longer personal or parental (109).

Like King Lear, Pullman "rather substituted for that sense of responsibility to the community, a feeling of gratitude to himself" (117). Like Lear, he was astounded and outraged to find his imagined parental self vilified and scorned by his employees during the Pullman strike, after the company's paternalism had broken down in 1893 because of financial difficulties.[55] Like Lear, Pullman could see only "the personal slight involved; the ingratitude alone reached him" (114). To be sure, Cordelia and the employees seem "cold," "narrow," stubborn, and ungenerous (119). On both sides, the strike brought out a "barbaric" reversion to individualism and "archaic" personal ambition. The workers have been just as "dominated by a sense of possession" as Pullman has been (121). But Lear and Pullman can't comprehend that Cordelia and the workers are developing beyond their dependent relationship to the father's strength of vision and control, to embrace "the wider life" (120) of human "dignity" and mutuality (113–14).

In search of concepts to organize social perception beyond individualistic and paternalistic models, Addams invokes several contradictory metaphors. The family model no longer applies to worker-management relations, she sees. She also sees the egotism involved in philanthropic benevolence. But her attempts to describe what lies beyond corporate paternalism reveal tensions among community, class interests, and cosmopolitan citizenship. To describe workers' potential for independent thinking, Addams recurrently returns to the image of the child becoming an adult. She also invokes "class," usually associated with labor and awkwardly integrated with mutual or "common" interests. Her passion for community conflicts with her equal passion for a "wider life" of human dignity, imaged briefly in Cordelia's departure for France.

"A Modern Lear" is particularly eloquent on parallels between Pullman's paternalism and Lear's relationship to Cordelia. It is new to Lear, Addams muses, "that his child should be moved by a principle outside of himself, which even his imagination could not follow; that she had caught the notion of an existence so vast that her relationship as a daughter was but part of it." Something or someone, perhaps her suitors, "had shaken her from the quiet measure of her insular existence" so that she could feel "the thrill of the world's life" (113). Addams struggles to find words for this new vision: dignity, justice, a "larger conception of duty" (114).

These words apply to herself as well as to Cordelia. She felt profoundly respected and encouraged by her father, an eight-term Illinois state senator and independent Quaker who set a demanding standard of moral rectitude. As Louis Menand notes, "he became famous as a man who not only had never taken a bribe, but had never been offered one."[56] His daughter followed his model of public service rather than the conventional feminine model of marriage and womanhood urged by her stepmother.[57] In wondering why Pullman is not the kind of father-figure who relishes the growth of his children or workers toward mature equality, she concludes that the paternalistic model itself blocks his perception of modern social relations. Modern society is too big and interdependent to be patterned on either individualism or the deference intrinsic to child-father relations.

Addams's founding of Hull House in 1889 does reflect a "feeling of *noblesse oblige*[,]" as her biographer notes.[58] Yet she sought to bridge class lines, whereas Pullman's career exemplifies how middle-class whites used race to fend off the threat of democratic mixing and mutuality. The "Pullman Palace Car" helped to stabilize the ideal of a national Anglo-Saxon community by combining luxurious efficiency with nostalgia for the Southern gentry ideal. From 1867 onward, it featured only former slaves, and soon only male slaves, as servants. As Sara Blair says, the obsequiously bowing

and crisply uniformed black man "revived the social relations of white supremacy[,]" reconstructing white mastery in the midst of Reconstruction.[59]

These plantation yearnings for a world that was clearly and simply white
over black were compensatory as well as nostalgic. They helped to prop up
class and gender hierarchies that were starting to seem shaky, and provided
urban travelers with a transient feeling of benevolent community. To quote
Benedict Anderson again, if racism began as the European colonialists' way
"to play aristocrat off center court[,]" here was Anglo-Saxon paradise.[60]
From the outside, by 1895 a few Chicago critics were calling Pullman-style
paternalism "the Great White Plague."[61]

Coda: Shame and Race, Washington and Du Bois

As Chief Justice Roger B. Taney wrote in the 1857 Dred Scott decision,
African Americans did not deserve full citizenship because their blackness
had "stigmatized" them with "deep and enduring marks of inferiority and
degradation." In the postbellum South, as ex-slaves threatened to unsettle
white expectations of domination, many white people intensified shaming
pressures, reducing black women to Jezebels and more stringently enforcing
the humiliation of black men through terrorizing tactics such as lynchings.
Modern readers may not sense the radical shock when Huck Finn says to
himself, "It was fifteen minutes before I could work myself up to go and
humble myself to a nigger; but I done it" (*Adventures of Huckleberry Finn*,
chap. 15). In his life, too, Mark Twain sometimes tried to reverse the shaming, in part by paying for an African American student's expenses at Yale
Law School. As he wrote on behalf of Warner T. McGuinn, who later mentored Thurgood Marshall, "We have ground the manhood out of them, &
the shame is ours, not theirs, & we should pay for it."[62] But Twain's private
convictions and public ironies about race were lost in the swelling national
chorus of white stigmatizers.

For Booker T. Washington to be received and perceived as a gentleman,
on nearly equal terms with whites, was a dangerous kind of heroism for a
black man in the late nineteenth century. He learned how to exploit the
shame that whites imposed on human blackness to protect their paternalistic power and privilege. That strategy has led to many attacks on Washington's lack of manly independence. In chapter 3 of *The Souls of Black Folk*
(1903), W. E. B. Du Bois accuses Booker T. Washington of being "unmanly"
no fewer than seven times. Washington's "emasculating" effect (252) helped
to build a submissive, "servile caste" (247). Du Bois sees very clearly Washington's allegiance with the capitalist dynamics of "the rich and dominating
North" (246). The president of Tuskegee Institute "grasped the spirit of the
age . . . the speech and thought of triumphant commercialism" (241).[63] In

soliciting the money of northern whites, Washington sold out southern blacks—so runs the now familiar charge.

Du Bois's charge signals a clash in cultural constructions of manliness. Speaking from the privileged background that encouraged him to call for a "talented tenth," as if the other nine-tenths had no talents, Du Bois tried to constitute a black elite who would speak for all African Americans with dignity, honor, and sometimes paternalistic presumption. Washington, who rose from enslaved peasant beginnings, saw that national power was shifting to industrialists while southern power was returning to racist whites. Casting his lot with the new corporate elite, he gained power and cultural authority by accepting black segregation and service roles as the most that whites would tolerate.

Yet as I've emphasized in chapter 4, Washington resisted as well as accommodated white associations of the black male body with shameful dependence. He sought to preach and teach the dignity of physical labor. In his fund-raising, he continually countered the white-imposed shame of being seen as a beggar, or worse. With rigorous self-control, he presented the products of Tuskegee Institute as candidates for working-class employment, and himself as a candidate for incorporative white uplift. Proudly quoting a Boston philanthropist who thanks him for "doing *our* work" (185), he maneuvers within the new industrial elite's uses of race, shame, and philanthropy to reconstruct a "we" out of imposed abjection.[64]

Du Bois astutely suggests that giving the vote to African American men after the Civil War was a form of raced sacrifice. Yes, "a guilty nation" had to give black men the right to vote. It was also "the only method of compelling the South to accept the results of the war." As a result, "Negro suffrage ended a civil war by beginning a race feud. And some felt gratitude toward the race thus sacrificed in its swaddling clothes on the altar of national integrity."[65] Curiously, Washington's one blast of anger in *Up from Slavery* declares more specifically "that it was cruelly wrong in the central government" during Reconstruction "to fail to make some provision for the general education of our people" (83). From seemingly opposed perspectives of resistance and accommodation, each leader articulates how the United States set up the black race as a sacrifice, to secure a reunited white identity and preserve white dominance.

The internal costs of this group sacrifice have been very high. Arnold Rampersad has suggested that many black biographers remain "wary of psychology" in part because of "the overriding need, in a racist national culture, to keep black heroes scrubbed and shining and heroic, and to conceal any evidence that may 'tarnish' their reputations."[66] More generally, the threat of white shaming or brutality has encouraged masks of self-control to fend off either anger or unmanly vulnerability. Though Washington repeatedly argues that being a member of an "unpopular race" or "what is regarded as an inferior race" (52) just made him work harder to succeed, he also notes that the "burden" of presumed failure "pressed down on us, sometimes, it seemed, at the rate of a thousand pounds to the square inch" (145). Du Bois, too, speaks of the "double-aimed struggle of the black artisan . . . to escape white contempt" as well as poverty, in part by reaching "toward ideals that made him ashamed of his lowly tasks" (215–16).

I'll now risk some generalizations about racial ascriptions, shaming, and social groups. As Howells is about to enter that tenement apartment, he self-consciously invokes whiteness to characterize what he's leaving—"a beautiful white spring day." Mixing aloneness, self-alienation, and presumptive entitlement, Howells uses the adjective "white" to polarize and dichotomize. The momentary binary allows him to fend off his tangle of shaming and shame. Carnegie, sure of his founding membership in a new club of corporate millionaires, uses "race" more incorporatively, to shame other millionaires into exercising civic leadership, to mark Anglo-Saxon dominance, and to help deserving others gain capitalist success. Believing in democratic diversity, Addams shames Pullman without invoking whiteness at all—and can't get published. With a keen sense that rich white men ascribe shamefulness to male dependence, begging, and black male bodies, Washington gains power over black people and influence with white people by transforming his black begging body into an outsourced version of white managerial agency—"doing *our* work."

At the turn into the twentieth century, then, race becomes a visible shorthand for shaming dynamics that create imagined reciprocities in a national white community. From the outside, as a prominent member of a group banned from white privileges, Washington sees the conjunction between shaming and whiteness very clearly. From the inside, whiteness becomes visible when the writer senses a class threat to the dominance of corporate millionaires (Carnegie) or a personal threat to his entitlement (Howells). Addams, who affiliates with nondominant white social groups, doesn't highlight whiteness's links to privilege. Because Howells's sense of social belonging is shaky, he invokes whiteness to dichotomize rather than incorporate. For those seeking to rebuild elite community, consolidate group dominance, or prop up threatened norms of privilege and manliness, racialized language becomes a unidirectional, top-down signifier of who's in, who might get in, and who's out.

None of these texts invokes traditional patriarchal norms for group formation. Indeed, Addams excoriates Pullman's paternalism as wholly inappropriate for a modern democratic state. Instead, in very different ways, each writer except for Addams shows how race-ing or other modes of shaming can enhance feelings of reciprocal belonging in a postpatriarchal nation-state. Especially at the upper end, class functions not simply to display and enforce group dominance, but also to establish and discipline stratified communities of one's peers. These communities, real as well as imagined, can supply a sense of mutual recognition.[67] Our current critical emphasis on the play of desire and hybridities tends to miss or minimize this aspect of modern upper-middle-class life.

A long journey to some short conclusions. First, two that I hope are obvious: Howells needed a therapist, and shaming works better when it comes from the top. Second, race-ing is an intensified form of collective shaming to control the threat of an outsider group that now has some entitlement to get in. As my introduction has already noted, W. E. B. Du Bois observed in *The Souls of Black Folk* that "this is an age when the more advanced races are coming in closer contact with the less developed races, and the race-feeling is therefore intensified[.]"[68] To put it another way, race becomes foundational because, for the first time, white people found themselves in a world where race might not matter.

Third, rhetorics and practices of shaming not only police group boundaries, but also create class and subgroup coherence, at least among millionaires. Fourth, rhetorics and practices of incorporative whiteness similarly generate inclusive reciprocities as well as exclusionary discipline, while preserving paternalistic norms. They foster a double dynamic of expansive assimilation and contractive class re-formation. Fifth, gifts of surplus wealth aim to restore a sense of small-group belonging and recognition as well as to purify one's image, exercise power, and benefit the less fortunate.

Finally, by the early twentieth century, race-ing had become a collective shaming that consolidated white people's mutual recognition and reciprocity within a national paternalist imaginary. As one consequence of expanding the scope of paternalism from local to national scale, whiteness incorporates the father as the primary metonym for benevolence. In *The Golden Bowl,* Henry James shows how that incorporation is also a displacement. James capaciously dramatizes how a father awash with surplus wealth is supplanted by whiteness and a daddy's girl as spiritual grounds for the paternalistic authority that confers shaming and recognition.

7　The Golden Bowl:
The Daddy's Girl as Paternalist

In *The Golden Bowl* (1904), James transforms Isabel Archer's story to a non-Gothic mode. He uplifts a daddy's girl from naive good faith to the painful power of consciousness, while turning her rich and loving father into a bemused spectator, perhaps akin to the struggling reader.

Initially the novel looks like a full-scale retreat to nostalgia for a patrician world of leisured civility and private transgressions. It certainly is that, in part. Yet as if writing from the inside, James also shows the new industrial elite's uses of incorporative whiteness for class and group formation. James also shifts the center of paternalistic sensibility from the father's Carnegie-like benevolence to the daughter's consciousness. By using the threat of social shaming, Maggie Verver patches up a small elite group's sense of mutual belonging. Simultaneously, the growth of Maggie's consciousness parallels Jane Addams's daughterly progress from a subjectivity defined by filial deference to a mind alive with heterogeneous imaginings and social responsibilities.[1]

The plot is actually quite simple. *The Golden Bowl* recounts the drama of a rich father and daughter who try to assimilate two colorful outsiders into their family through marriage. But James expands the narration of Maggie's subjectivity beyond the benevolence that Carnegie grandiosely proclaims. To manage her inward heterogeneity, Maggie makes transcendent whiteness a necessary fiction of moral value and discipline as well as social decorum. As I've been arguing intermittently, race-ing is a kind of shaming to consolidate a diffuse dominant group. Mixing inclusion with exclusion, incorporative whiteness uses race-ing to generate conflicting energies of expansive assimilation and contractive class re-formation.[2] Maggie's consciousness enacts this double dynamic.

By implication, as I've argued in chapter 6, if blackness is a fiction imposed by the white gaze, then whiteness is a more comprehensive fiction of group coherence. If whiteness helped to further cross-class bonding, the dynamics of *The Golden Bowl* suggest that incorporative whiteness also helped to preserve paternalistic norms and consolidate the new industrial class.[3] As a national imaginary, whiteness helped corporate America to stimulate and accommodate greater social heterogeneity, while partially supplanting patriarchal domesticity as a central trope for manliness, benevolence, and entitlement.

As one result of her successful transformation from daddy's girl to paternalist, Maggie's character is riddled with contradictions that her critics tend to replicate. At one level she seems to be a ruthless, even sadistic capitalist who collects people for the profit of a family enterprise. At a contradictory, complementary level, she seems to welcome a private masochism that she associates with unstinting giving and loving. At a self-simplifying level, she is a daddy's girl who wants to keep her father and herself in a loving cocoon, perhaps to fend off the dangers of passion in their marriages. At an imperial level, she seems close to a dominatrix, with what Mark Seltzer has called a "colonizing empathy[.]"[4] At still another level, her heterogeneous consciousness outstrips the daughterly and paternalistic roles she plays. Finally, she performs what Marcel Mauss might call a spiritual potlatch. Fearful of having "to pay all" without her father's loving understanding (494), she finally does so, alone. She has "done all" (544), to refashion a sense of decorum and belonging in her fragmenting social group.[5] The tortured and self-torturing effects of her consciousness invite a great variety of critical ruminations about the narrative's pervasive mixture of empathy with sadism and masochism.

Recent critics have exposed the imperial and assimilative uses of race in *The Golden Bowl,* though the contractive uses of class have received less attention. Putting Adam Verver at stage center sotto voce, Thomas Peyser and Patricia McKee make his collecting for museums a metonym for capitalism's language of abstracted convertibilities and the Ververs' acquisition of two aliens, the Prince and Charlotte. Earlier critics, particularly Laurence Holland, focus on marriages, not museums, to show how Maggie's generosity of consciousness brings two fragmenting upper-class couples back to good family form. One could call these critical approaches the Foucauldians and the formalists, or the bonds of power and the bonds of love. In the last two decades other power-oriented critics, notably Carolyn Porter, Mark Seltzer, and Lynda Zwinger, have exposed the capitalist and patriarchal embeddedness of these characters' desires.[6] Yet in quasi-Maussian ways, Maggie's gifts restore the bonds of reciprocal community by lifting people beyond their desires, whether for sex, acquisitions, or power. Each approach articulates an aspect of the novel's split and contrary energies.

The missing link in both critical approaches is shaming. It's missing for good reason, since the ending turns on Maggie's renunciation of it, at least publicly. Instead, to her own mind and seemingly to the narrator's, she becomes a sacrificial scapegoat. At one point she sees others looking at her with pleading in their eyes, as if to say, "she was there, and there just *as* she was, to lift it off them and take it; to charge herself with it as the scapegoat of old" (487, James's emphasis). Yet to most readers and sometimes to Maggie herself, Charlotte becomes the more wrenching social sacrifice. Either way, whereas her father dreams of benevolently civilizing the American provinces, Maggie draws on precapitalist dynamics of honor and shame to recivilize her family group. The threat of shaming the Prince and Charlotte for their adultery suffuses the second half of the novel.

Dynamics of honor and shame also help to explain why Prince Amerigo, repeatedly associated with blackness and sometimes with a black beast-man, proves to be more absorbable than Charlotte Stant, a many-colored and hybridized New Woman, at least in her sexually transgressive aspects. The Prince, an Italian aristocrat in need of money, suggests an upscale personification of the immigrant. Yet he can be brought belatedly to a sense of honor, whereas Charlotte, the Prince's "huntress" and "muse" (73), has to be tamed, by bringing her sexual desire under her husband's paternal control. At the end, Maggie takes considerable pleasure in her painful imagination of Charlotte with Adam's "long silken halter looped round her beautiful neck" (523). Contemporary assimilationist discourses would mandate the opposite resolution, since an immigrant alien would be more threatening than a sexually transgressive white woman, especially a married upper-class woman.[7]

Throughout volume 2, Maggie's white lies ennoble or encage the Prince and Charlotte, whose furtive heterosexual exchanges reflect their entrapment by appetites that mix sexual desires with marketplace acquisitions. By contrast, Maggie's gifts can't be reduced to marketplace exchanges. As with other Jamesean heroines, her giving sustains what Carolyn Porter has called "a moral order of value" no longer relying on paternal authority, but instead "dependent upon the imagination[.]"[8] Yet Maggie's ultimate gift is not to give. By not relating what she knows, she preserves the intimate relationships of this four-person group. Maggie's consciousness, which seems guided by a policy of don't ask, don't tell, and imagine everything, also subsumes and finally relinquishes her own possessive desires for her father, to preserve him from the knowledge that he has been cuckolded, the ultimate patriarchal shame. As she says to her father, "where there's a great deal of pride there's a great deal of silence" (171).

Adam and the Prince

Adam Verver is a curiously unprepossessing billionaire, short, bald, paunchy, and self-effacing. He is a "little man," we're told a few too many times. "Barely taller than his daughter," who herself is frequently described as "little," Adam is "a small spare slightly stale person, deprived of the general prerogative of presence." He also has considerable "stoutness." Finally, "he had lost early in life much of his crisp closely-curling hair" (160), though that detail might subtly emphasize his potential for "highbrow" cultural activities.

In James Ivory's movie of *The Golden Bowl* (2001), Nick Nolte makes Adam look much too formidable and handsome. Nonetheless, Nolte evokes some qualities that it may take several readings of the novel to appreciate, especially Adam's quiet forcefulness of mind, and perhaps the serenity of his unspoken knowledge about the Prince and Charlotte. If so, Maggie's "unpenetrated parent" (420) keeps that knowledge from his readers as well as his daughter.[9] Every day he contentedly wears the same clothes, mixing black, white, and blue: "the same little black 'cutaway' coat . . . the same cool-looking trousers, chequered in black and white . . . a white-dotted blue satin necktie;" and "over his concave little stomach, . . . a white duck waistcoat" (161).

At the most obvious level of his characterization, Adam is a Carnegie-style philanthropist. Adam's "gift" to American City will be "civilisation condensed," a "museum of museums, a palace of art, . . . of treasures sifted to positive sanctity" (142–43), to raise the standards of the millions toward beauty and taste. "It's the work of his life and the motive of everything he does" (49), Maggie tells the Prince. Adam's philanthropy is the second stage of his "acquisition[.]" No longer afflicted with the "barren" prospects, "the bondage of ugliness[,]" and the "livid vulgarity" of money-making, he now feels "crowned" with his passionate imagination of "the religion he wished to propagate[.]" His "years of darkness" have become "years of light" (142–43). Yet James's drama keeps Adam in darkness, as the light shifts from "little" unconscious Adam to "little" conscious Maggie. Along the way, James racializes Maggie's triumph as the ability of pure androgynous whiteness to contain the hybrid colors and blackness represented by the Prince and Charlotte.[10]

At the start of the second book, as Adam tries to escape from Mrs. Rance, James remarks that "this amiable man" had never been refreshed by "the many-coloured human appeal." Rather, Adam liked how it "faded to the blessed impersonal whiteness for which his vision sometimes ached" (129–30). But Adam seems surrounded by colorful, predatory women, and he lacks the "force" to fend them off. "It pressed upon him hard . . . this attribution of power" (133). Seeing the besieged state of her seemingly unmanly, unforceful father, Maggie constitutes herself as his protector. She imagines that he could be shielded from the incessant threat of such women by marrying Charlotte, her former school friend, who now needs the money and stability that Adam could provide for her. Adam makes the same gift reciprocal, by marrying Charlotte to make his daughter less worried about having abandoned him. Significantly, as the two start to concoct this passionless marriage as a way of protecting him and their intimacy, they hide away in a garden enclave framed by "a small white gate, intensely white and clean" (152–53).[11]

Conversely, though the Prince shares with Adam a passive ease around forceful women, we learn only a few pages later that "the main seat of his affection" is his remaining property in Rome, "the big black palace, the Palazzo Nero" (156). From the beginning, the Prince is a dangerous mix. Though he is about to be married, the first paragraph notes "his arrests" at the "possibilities" in other women's faces as he strolls along what James pointedly names "Bond Street" (43). If the Prince seems skittish about his approaching bondage, he's also aware that as heir to the ancient Roman imperium and not much else, he needs the Ververs' multimillions. As his first name of "Amerigo" suggests, he will embrace New World gold.[12] Strangely, we never learn his last name, perhaps so that Maggie Verver never has to change her own last name's affiliation with her father, at least in readers' minds. More strangely, as Fanny Assingham tells her husband, Maggie's discovery that the Prince is named Amerigo awakens her desire for him, as if she wants to be swept off her feet by a "pushing man" like the one who became "godfather, or name-father, to the new Continent" (94). For his part, already steeped in the U.S. ethos of bargaining, the Prince is eager to marry money, much as his brother married a woman "of Hebrew race, with a portion that had gilded the pill" (53).

Yet the Prince also wants to rise above his racialized background. He frets about "how little one of his race could escape after all from history" (48). Musing about that history, he thinks that "he was somehow full of his race. Its presence in him was like the consciousness of some inexpugnable scent . . . some chemical bath[.]" He wants "some new history," an American one, to erase that taint (52). Much later, when Maggie ruminates about "the gold-and-brown, gold-and-ivory, of old Italian bindings[,]" she associates them with the "records of the Prince's race . . . the quality of her husband's blood, its rich mixture" (427).

The Prince's association with racialized identities and mixtures not only reflects the anxieties about immigration that Peyser exposes, but also indicts conventional masculinity. Though he tells Maggie that his historical self is a matter of public record, while "my single self" remains unknown to her (47), not until much later do we realize that his hidden self is maleness.[13] "All men were brutes," Charlotte ruminates after she receives the Prince's telegram; "the Prince's distinction was in being one of the few who could check himself before acting on the impulse." His "career" would be "uphill work for him, a daily fighting-matter on behalf of a good appearance" (244–45). The Prince might get drunk and beat her, Maggie playfully says to him, but other women's desires for him would "bring her round" (157).

Ironically, it's Charlotte's desire for the Prince that brings Maggie round to bringing him round. James frames the Prince's mixture of aristocratic passivity and dark brutal manhood in the conventions if not the language of sentimental women's novels. Like Mrs. Shelby in *Uncle Tom's Cabin*, Maggie has conscience enough for two, the Prince complacently reflects. If his wife lacks "perception[,]" the "substitute" would be "positively like a vicarious good conscience, cultivated ingeniously on his behalf" (274). After Maggie gains perception as well as conscience, she uses the Prince's good manners to shame him into suppressing his lustful responsiveness to Charlotte. At the beginning he has "no consistency of attention" (43); by the end, as he says to Maggie, "I see nothing but *you*" (580). Saving her man from himself, Maggie makes him ambiguously capable of loving her, by making him complicit with her white lies.

At the end of the first chapter, when the Prince famously invokes the passage about whiteness from Poe's *Narrative of Arthur Gordon Pym,* the context links whiteness to a "faith" and "goodness" inconceivable in his language of selfish bargaining. Though the Prince is not in love, with anybody, he's perplexed that Maggie's father wants to exhibit him as what Maggie calls "a part of his collection" (49). The Prince accepts that prospect because he understands the value of his own imperial acquisition, Maggie's gold. Yet for him, every gift carries a hidden bargain or exchange. Therefore he has to figure out the Ververs' unexpressed desire. Since he has made Maggie a little Princess, is that enough? What else do the Ververs want from him? "Who but a billionaire could say what was fair exchange for a billion?" (57). As Joseph Allen Boone has suggested, the Prince's "calculated passivity" makes him "waiting to be 'placed'" in someone else's narrative. To give that a more racialized reading, he wants and needs to know his place.[14]

It might be simply "to behave beautifully enough to make the beauty well-nigh an equivalent[,]" Fanny Assingham later surmises (229). But the Prince isn't sure. That mystery is "the shrouded object" (57) that impels him toward Fanny Assingham's, while his musings about Pym express his vexed and perplexed state of mind. "He had never known curtains but as purple even to blackness," he thinks. Now he approaches "a thickness of white air that was like a dazzling curtain of light[.]" The Ververs' minds, and Fanny's too, seemed "a great white curtain" to him (56).[15] Though the Prince walks and talks with sophisticated aplomb, inwardly he is Bigger Thomas at the Daltons.

Later, when the Prince finally yields to Charlotte's sexual pursuit, the narration suggests more than a little of what Gail Bederman has labeled the turn-of-the-century white phobia about the primal black rapist.[16] Sex with Charlotte, who is still a virgin, will be like deflowering the "rich white rose-bud" (290) on the front of her dress. That image strangely echoes Adam's memory of his hapless first wife, a "broken white flower" (140) who fortunately died before her tastes for shallow decoration dragged Adam's mind down too far from its "miraculous white-heat" (130). James takes care to emphasize "the mud . . . an unutterable dirty brown" framing Charlotte's "shabby" arrival at the inception of their affair (247–48). The dirty brown parallels the "low-browed" London fog (102) that frames the arrival of the Prince and Charlotte at the hybrid Jew's "rather low-browed" antique shop (113), where the Prince quickly realizes that the beautiful golden bowl is actually just cracked glass.[17]

Charlotte

Charlotte, not the Prince, represents the most disruptive mixture of hybridity and desire. If the Prince suggests a latently threatening black man, he also displays the potential for Adam's malleable passivity when faced with a strong woman, whether Charlotte or Maggie. "It takes Anglo-Saxon blood[,]" Charlotte says about her talent for initiating and organizing their affair. "'Blood'? he echoed. 'You've that of every race!'" (294). Inverting the Prince's mixture, she is an American born and raised in Florence. Like himself, the Prince muses, she has a "race-quality"; they are both "polyglot" (77–78), he thinks several times. As Laurence Holland was among the first to emphasize, Adam's purchase of Oriental tiles frames his proposal to Charlotte (178–99), and soon her "freedom" makes him feel "quite merged" in Jewish tribal rites (192).[18]

Seen through the Prince's eyes, Charlotte looks like a strong huntress or a muse, but also like "a cluster of possessions of his own" that he inventories and finds wanting. She seems "filled with gold pieces," he thinks, but she proves to be "empty[.]" Her "thick hair[,]" for instance, "was, vulgarly speaking, brown," he notes, though with "a shade of tawny autumn leaf in it for 'appreciation[.]'" That last word punningly mixes taste with enhanced financial value, grounded in a hierarchy of dark and not-so-dark colors. Another more ruthless pun comes a little later. Concluding his inventory with a detached assessment of her "flexible waist," the Prince sees the rest of Charlotte's body as a "silk purse, well filled with gold-pieces," yet "passed empty through a finger-ring[.]" As he sums up her net value, "It was as if, before she turned to him, he had weighed the whole thing in his open palm and even heard a little the chink of the metal" (72–73).

Here "chink" reverberates in rather nasty ways. Not only does the word reduce Charlotte to clinking, separable parts as well as pieces of gold, but it also means "crack" or "fissure," anticipating the crack in the golden bowl. Moreover, it carries a slang association degrading Charlotte to the social level of Chinese laborers. All that before these two old friends and near-lovers say their first words of greeting. Much later, when the novel has shifted from the Prince's framing consciousness to Maggie's, "chink" takes on a subtle transformation. As Maggie talks about her desire "to help every one" and her consciousness of being at "fault[,]" Fanny considers Adam's belief in his wife and thinks, "*That* way might safety lie—it was like a wider chink of light" (443, James's emphasis). Overtly the word slightly deflates Fanny's vain hope for safety. Yet the word also declares the possibility of a crack or fissure that lets in illumination, much as Maggie's mind moves toward a benevolent light that can suffuse any "fault" with love. Similarly, James's preface celebrates "the fields of light" available to the active imagination (30).

Like the Prince, Charlotte uses gifts as a form of bargaining. For her, a gift has to be an implicit "contract" (263) or exchange. She doesn't buy Maggie a gift, because she sees nothing in it for her. After Adam proposes, in a passionless dialogue saturated on both sides with explicit and implied double negatives (193–94), she finally accepts by saying, "'I'll give you . . . what you ask.'" (208). Like the Prince, she then puzzles over what the Ververs want in return, and concludes that "They had brought her in—on the crudest expression of it—to do the 'worldly' for them" (264).

Stateless, rootless, with no group to belong to, Charlotte becomes the novel's most threatening source of sexual desire. Correspondingly, she is also the most socially undiscriminating of the major characters. She implicitly faults herself for her interest in people such as the shopkeeper, with his "heterogeneous and not at all imposing" array (114). More admirably, she thinks, the Prince takes no notice. To "his advantage, . . . below a certain social plane, he never *saw*." Yet at least in her earlier passion for the Prince, she managed to preserve her virginity, and therefore her honor and virtue. As Fanny tells the Colonel, "nothing" finally happened between Charlotte and the Prince. "They fell in love with each other—but, seeing it wasn't possible, gave each other up" (89). As always, Charlotte led the way. Charlotte "left suddenly," and unexpectedly. "It was "a 'near' thing . . . The poor girl's departure was a flight—she went to save herself" (91).

After the Prince's approaching marriage stimulates Charlotte's competitiveness as well as desire, her return eventually leads to their passion's consummation. The description of the kiss that launches their adultery brilliantly highlights the mixing and merging that she invites, and the breakage that ensues. "Then of a sudden, through this tightened circle, as at the issue of a narrow strait into the sea beyond, everything broke up, broke down, gave way, melted and mingled" (259). As the "narrow strait" of their situation flows into the "sea" of desire, the identities of the Prince and Charlotte break down into indistinguishably reciprocal pronouns, nouns, and body parts: "Their lips sought their lips, their pressure their response and their response their pressure[.]" Finally, "with a violence that had sighed itself the next moment to the longest and deepest of stillnesses they passionately sealed their pledge." An oxymoronic sigh of violence leads them to what amounts to a contract, a "pledge" with a passionate physical seal.

By compelling Charlotte to be repossessed by Adam, Maggie learns how to contain Charlotte's possessive desire for the Prince. Charlotte may be "great," but Maggie is "good" (168), and from the start, as the Prince declares to his wife, "Goodness, when it's real, precisely, rather keeps people *in*" (46). The Prince learns to live the truth of that remark. Meanwhile Charlotte, trapped in her gilt cage (484, 521), looks to Maggie like a "creature imprisoned" (521), as if she were tethered at "the end of a long silken halter looped round her beautiful neck" (523). Her "silken noose" is controlled by Adam Verver's "firm prehensile thumbs," kept out of sight behind that frequently emphasized "white waistcoat" (536). Once Charlotte has been leashed to good patriarchal form, Maggie seems benevolently poised between sympathy and sadism, as if she were a witness at an execution. Her former friend has become a spectacle of humiliation, metaphorically roped for public view, somewhere between a pet monkey and a lynching.[19]

Maggie

Early on, Maggie talks to her father about her lack of experience with "wounds and shames" (171). "Do you realise, father, that I've never had the least blow? . . . Well, you'll realise when I *have* one!" Inconsistently, she says that "I don't *want* to know" about such experiences, which nonetheless "are sacred— . . . But one can always, for safety, be kind'" (171–72). These ambiguities and ironies frame the ending's indeterminacies. Ironically, Maggie tries to protect her father from the wound and the shame of her husband's sexual betrayal and his own wife's cuckolding. Ambiguously, her kindness signifies both her transcendent risk and her evasion, "for safety," of public anger and shaming. In either case, Maggie uses her tender, passionate consciousness as a gift that elevates almost everyone except Charlotte to their best selves. Her kindness elevates even the hybrid Jewish shopkeeper beyond bargaining (460–61) to offer her the crucial gift, his information about the Prince's and Charlotte's visit.[20]

To shield her father from shame, Maggie reduces Charlotte's "golden flame" to "black ashes" (553). The threat and the withholding of Maggie's shaming come together at the climactic moment, when Maggie says, "I accuse you—I accuse you of nothing" (498).[21] As many critics have noted, the pointed ambiguity puts Charlotte in a permanent bind. First she becomes a working woman, acting as tour guide for her husband's possessions. Then, like Madame Merle, she has to go to America. Meanwhile, Maggie's generosity of spirit elevates her to a "rapture" of religious loving. She sees herself and her father "floating" high above fragmentations of selfishness (506). Later, as Maggie's consciousness "floated her across the room" from Charlotte to "an early Florentine sacred subject, that [Adam] had given her on her marriage[,]" she sees the "tenderness" of her father's "sacrifice of such a treasure" as "a window for his spiritual face" (573).

Faced with Charlotte Stant's nonmonogamous sexual energy, Maggie restores the sacred power of paternalistic giving by sacrificing her father as well as taking over his role. Here I disagree with Lynda Zwinger, who says that at the end of the novel, "both daughters belong to the little patriarch, and an ocean intervening is no obstacle." At the end Maggie is in command. To preserve her little community, she relinquishes not only her daily access to her father, but also her chastely incestuous desire to please him by putting his needs before her own.[22] Perhaps Maggie is also to blame for her husband's affair, by leaving him alone too much. Though they may be rationalizing, the Prince and Charlotte see Maggie's postnuptial intimacy with her father as a "decree . . . forcing them against their will into a relation of mutual close contact that they had done everything to avoid" (244).[23] In any case, Maggie learns to suppress her own desires for revenge, to further the common good. She also becomes a canny in-fighter by learning how to use knowledge. Amid a good many metaphors of entrapment and bondage, she alerts each character "*that* she knows, but not *what* she knows."[24]

Maggie is a visionary capitalist, as Carolyn Porter has said. Yet Maggie is also a precapitalist aristocrat. From being "a little Princess," she becomes "a little queen" (351) who can command her Prince with "the very first clear majesty he had known her to use" (571), while controlling her wicked stepmother. Even while ruminating about her marriage, in midsentence, Maggie can fire a maid—"a new woman" no less—and stick a long pin into her hat, without breaking the flow of her thoughts about whether the Prince will leave her (381). Throughout, Maggie's growing consciousness as "erect commander" (473) depends on protecting her father from the shame of knowing he is a cuckold, though what Adam knows or doesn't know seems increasingly ambiguous.

Maggie's consciousness evolves through her remarkable capacity for imaginative similes. Twenty-five years ago, Ruth Yeazell persuasively argued that similes are Maggie's way of approaching and avoiding sexual knowledge.[25] Now we should add: *hetero*sexual knowledge, which implies capitalist dynamics of greed and acquisition. James's homoerotic dynamics, the focus of so much recent criticism, don't seem that terrifying or enticing here. It's intriguing, for instance, that Adam Verver tells the Prince he likes him because he's all "round. . . . It's the sort of thing in you that one feels—or at least I do—with one's hand." Thank goodness, Adam goes on, that the Prince has nothing "sticking out by itself[,]" "so damnable, for rubbing against, in a man" (137). If the gentleman doth protest too much, he does so in a pleasantly over-the-top way.

When James depicts heterosexual desire, he shows none of this homoerotic banter. Instead, he implies an intimate equivalence among heterosexual intimacy, racial mixture, and capitalist exchange. All three begin in greed and end in degradation, and James depicts all three with ironic detachment. In *Hawthorne,* twenty-five years earlier, James astutely suggests that Hawthorne is not obsessed with guilt. Instead, "He played with it, and used it as a pigment[.]"[26] Similarly, in *The Golden Bowl,* James treats heterosexual desire as a pigment to paint the most prevalent forms of capitalist degradation.

Maggie's proliferating similes not only invite and fend off heterosexual knowledge, but also use the language of color to purify dangerously interchangeable sexual and racial mixtures into whiteness. Her most celebrated simile is her vision of the mysterious relationship between the Prince and Charlotte as an "outlandish pagoda" plated with Oriental porcelain (327–28). Yet she twice thinks of it as an "ivory tower" (329, also 327). By the end Maggie has preserved "the polished old ivory of her father's inattackable surface" (532), while she has also preserved herself—or at least she thinks she has—from the danger of revenge for "the vulgar heat of her wrong" (489). As she thinks about that danger, in another well-known simile, she pictures such revenge as "a wild eastern caravan" with "crude colours . . . all a thrill, a natural joy to mingle with[.]" But Maggie forswears such lowbrow pleasures, in part because they would send her "plunging into other defiles"—a suitably low pun. Instead, she crafts a disembodied and secretly cracked form to enclose dark immigrant Italian men and sexual huntresses.

Not for nothing is Maggie a devout Catholic who wears a cross, as Fanny Assingham notes, "blest by the Holy Father, that you always wear, out of sight, next your skin" (402). Much more devout than innocent Adam, the daughter gives paternalism a final twist by sacrificing her father, ostensibly to save the United States from its sins of vulgarity and provinciality. In effect, she severs their actual daddy's girl relation to preserve its spiritual form, just as she recreates an imaginary "bowl without the crack" (475) after Fanny breaks the actual bowl into three pieces (447–48). Maggie relinquishes her daily intimacy with her father not simply to get her husband back, and not only to enforce the propriety of monogamy. Most deeply, she sacrifices her father for the sake of a deeper devotion, to restore "a kind of silver tissue of decorum" (351). One might paraphrase Andrew Carnegie's former worker and say, "Well, that was damned white of Maggie, wasn't it?"—except that the novel's last sentence buries her in darkness.

The Ending's Cracked Closure

The ending's hypercivilized fragility invites more vulgar readers to look through the cracks. As several critics have asked, what about the language of economic possession that accompanies the language of sacrifice and passionate giving? Cheek by jowl with the last scene's display of Maggie's capacity for tender empathy comes Adam's remark as they look at Charlotte and the Prince: "'*Le compte y est.* You've got some good things'" (574). Yes, they agree, Charlotte is "'great.' They could close upon it" (577). The novel's ending is a "closing" in several senses. Maggie's rapture of transcendent consciousness seems inseparable from her sadistic triumph over worldly Charlotte. Does she rise above capitalist exchanges or gain title to her conquests? Though I think Robert Pippin goes too far in saying the ending is "a moral as well as a personal disaster for all four of the principals," his exasperation sounds the right note.[27]

Nothing quite settles into the good form that Maggie aims for. By exalting the generous over the grasping, James sustains precapitalist ideals of leisured benevolence and family honor, though through a woman's imagination, rather than a father's authority. Yet Maggie's last scene presents a near-parodic pose of the little woman as shrinking violet, clinging to the man she has transformed into a protector. After the Prince says, "I see nothing but *you*[,]" Maggie sees "the truth of it" in his eyes and, "as for pity and dread of them, she buried her own in his breast" (580). As Carren Kasten points out, these final lines reduce the Prince to a romantic cliche, "I only have eyes for you."[28] Yet they also inflate the Prince to a Gothic father-lover, whereas Maggie seems to be performing another homage to a Poe story by burying herself alive.

Or perhaps Maggie performs contradictory cliches. When she buries her eyes "as for pity and dread[,]" does she pity him or dread him? More subtly, is that simile real or feigned, an Aristotelian catharsis or a performance? If it's a performance, is it an attempt to make the Prince feel protective and powerful, a relinquishment of her quest for insight, or a sign of her relief at repossessing her husband, with perhaps a little shame at her manipulations? Might it be James's deliberately inadequate gesture toward a melodramatic patriarchal resolution? And why does James conclude the novel with "in his breast" rather than "on his chest"? Has the Prince discovered his maternal side? Or is his emasculation what Maggie means moments before by thinking that "she had begun to be paid in full" (579)?[29] The finale leaves readers with an uncomfortably unresolvable mixture of maternal solicitude, ritual self-sacrifice, daughterly yielding, wifely repossession of the prodigal husband, and revenge against a designing woman.

These daddy's girl contradictions reflect larger contradictions in James's appropriation of paternalism to reconstitute social value beyond the marketplace, and his attempt to reconstitute the value of gifts beyond their exchange equivalents. Sara Blair and Ross Posnock celebrate how James opens his narratives to the fluid interplay of fragmenting identities and multicultural experience. But James embraces such experiences to contain them. Rescue fantasies are basic to the work of benevolence, and as Kenneth Warren has emphasized in *Black and White Strangers,* James's characteristic drama lies in "rescuing his subject from vulgarity[.]"[30] James's "subject" needs considerable glossing, because James also seeks to rescue his protagonists from possessive desire. By focusing on what Laurence Holland calls a constricted tribal kinship group, and by resituating the capacity for benevolence in a daughter's consciousness beyond the marketplace, *The Golden Bowl* restores threatened precapitalist values of honor and shame.[31]

Yet Blair and Posnock are right to emphasize how modern James is in his self-decenterings. Paradoxically, James's celebration of formal artifice responsively embraces the spirit of corporate capitalism, which erodes the traditional links among value, production, and patriarchal family structure. Now value must be created, to stimulate consumer desire. In her capacity to "pay all" (465), Maggie augments her social capital by creating civilized form and value from the fragmentations of vulgarity and desire. Her creator uses Maggie's consciousness to augment the cultural distinction of fiction-making.

Creating Value, Sustaining Sacrifice

Where can capitalist value be situated—in producers, consumers, or the exchange relation itself? James's unsettling answer is to expose the necessary fictionality in all constructions of value. To emphasize either the late nineteenth-century shift from producer to consumer capitalism or the tensions between moral and exchange values, as current criticism tends to do, isn't quite enough. As my first chapter takes up in more detail, James Livingston's *Pragmatism and the Political Economy of Cultural Revolution* provides a way beyond equating capitalist value with alienation from conditions of production. For Livingston, the New Woman represents "not only the principle of consumption but the promise of subjectivity" in the first age of surplus rather than necessity. Once consumer demand becomes more important than productivity as "the key variable in economic growth," value becomes "constituted by the varieties of subject positions or social relations required to appreciate goods, not measured by the quantities of labor-time required to produce commodities[.]"[32]

Neither Maggie nor Charlotte is a full-fledged New Woman, of course. Ostensibly Charlotte is a traditional temptress, whereas Maggie seems imprisoned in a daughterly mode, at least at first. Yet Maggie's mind finally embraces all the separating individualities in her intimate group, not only to control them, but also to reestablish their relational and therefore moral value. In that respect, *The Golden Bowl* becomes a modernist allegory of how modern subjectivity can be reconstituted. To quote Livingston once more, "the integrity of the self finally becomes a function of the modern subject's fragmentation and reconstruction." From a more philosophical vantage point, Robert Pippin makes a similar argument, that James creates mutual dependence and value from what Pippin calls the narcissistic void of modernity.[33]

As many of James's prefaces exultantly declare, form is the novelist's way of creating surplus value from his disparate materials. At one level, that imaginative effort embraces the spirit of corporate capitalism, since James-ean form stimulates readerly modes of consumer desire. Yet as Pippin argues in *Henry James and Modern Moral Life,* James also tries to establish the moral value of interdependence, at odds with consumer culture. It's not that Maggie is a heroine, he says; she "remains a defensive, cold, prim little nun" whereas Charlotte is "the only character . . . capable of generating real human heat." Rather, the "real hero, in any of James' stories, is a social entity of which men and women are constituents." To get there, readers have to get beyond the idea of meaning as property to be discovered and "individually owned[.]"[34] That "fantasy of resolution, answers, secrets revealed, . . . is better described as a kind of narcissism, . . . a refusal to accept the risks and uncertainties Jamesean modernity requires." The new morality, in effect a transformation of isolated consciousnesses into mutual reflectors, challenges both "individualist and traditional mental frameworks[,]" and remains "secured by no fixed or objective normative standard."[35] Perhaps one could call that moral vision Consciousness, Inc.—capitalism in yet another guise.

Along another axis, the novel also invites musings about the resurgent appeal of ancient sacrificial rites. The word "sacrifice" peppers the novel, especially toward the conclusion. Laurence Holland's reading highlights "the torture of the sacrifice" necessary to restore a "community of devotion[.]" If marriage represents a "flawed form" of "ideal communion[,]" as he argues, Maggie brings the Prince beyond his first "community of passion" with Charlotte, and beyond the "stiffened proprieties of marriage" as well. Their new commitment to passionate loving requires sacrificing Charlotte. With her father, too, Charlotte's "cry is the source of the communion Adam and Maggie share[.]"[36] Such communion and commitment demand cruelty as well as devotion.

Taking a larger view, Susan Mizruchi's *Science of Sacrifice* argues that when faced with heterogeneity, capitalist societies need sacrificial rites to fortify their social borders and justify their economic inequities. In her reading of James's 1899 novel, *The Awkward Age,* sacrifice restores not only boundaries and class distinctions, but also a sense of "completeness" and even "'holiness'" in a "demoralized social order[.]" Sacrifice is "essential in times of acute transition" because it acts as a rite of purification to "expel group sin." Sacrifice also plays a key role in "an elite's ability to control an emergent female sexuality." Finally, Mizruchi suggests that James's "maternal center" articulates pervasive anxieties about the downfall of paternal power, and about the inability of women in the modern world to "care for kin[.]"[37]

In short, to reduce *The Golden Bowl* to a comfortable cliche, James's portrait of Maggie as paternalist looks backward as well as forward. In dramatizing Maggie's reconstruction of fragile relationships, James exposes the transcendent artifice as well as the tenuousness of a social decorum not based on exchange and desire. By restoring her group's reciprocal bonds, Maggie's extravagant generosity creates bonds that can contain the dangers of diversity, not least in her own subjectivity. Lacking the bonds of belonging, anyone can fall prey to desire. Yet although Maggie's gift recreates her elite community with an imaginative version of incorporative whiteness, she also articulates a sense of stranded isolation that no material exchange can wholly assuage.

Like the golden bowl itself, the self-subsuming whole exists only as a difficult fiction of transcendence, hovering just above the desiring self's relentlessly heterogeneous cravings. If Charlotte most directly personifies these cravings, Maggie also finds them latent in herself, particularly in her impulses for revenge, and more profoundly in her desire to hold tight to her father. Perhaps her yearning for him is incestuous, as so many critics have sensed. Perhaps it's the opposite, providing a haven of filial safety from the dangers of adult passion. In either case, relinquishing that desire, whatever it is, and keeping her capacity for shaming in reserve, Maggie restores her group's tenuous reciprocity. Yet the bonds she has forged, in several senses, have not entirely suppressed the dangerous appeals of autonomy, diversity, and passionate possessiveness, for Maggie as well as Charlotte and the Prince.

More specifically, Maggie "keeps under the body," as Booker T. Washington would say, by sacrificing her desire for the daughterly recognition that only her father can supply. By the end, the Prince conveys his awed recognition of his wife's moral power. Her generosity has recreated her elite group out of its own debased fragments, without cutting out the newcomers. At the same time, Maggie ends with a very modern mixture of recognition and misrecognition. Her benevolent agency has left her stranded and isolated, in the midst of her communion.

If Carnegie gives his surplus wealth publicly to institutions, *The Golden Bowl* gives Maggie's surplus consciousness privately to the reader. Available as a potentially shaming attentiveness, it remains in excess of the roles she performs to bind her group together. That excess, often expressed through her melodramatic similes, creates her literary value, which depends in part on her evasion of all interpretive and moral categories. Only her readers fully recognize her, and most of us can't make up our minds about her. To quote Robert Pippin once more, the fact that James doesn't know what's going on either generates a "foot-stomping impatience" in many critics.[38]

James's preface to the 1909 edition emphasizes the honor involved in his own authorial giving, as well as his paternalistic ability to create novelistic value for the "passive" and "docile" reader (26). The Princess "duplicates, as it were, her value" by becoming a "compositional resource . . . as well as a value intrinsic" (21). She becomes a way for the writer and the reader to feel alive with consciousness "in the fields of light" (30).[39] To let the "accumulated good stuff" happen in prose that takes on the quality of poetry, the novelist has to let his own mind "give and give" (30–31). As James retrospectively contemplates his attempts "to scatter here a few gleams of the light" of his "unshamed" visions, he finds "absolutely no release to his pledged honour on the question of repaying that confidence" (34) of the trusting reader. Otherwise "the reader is, in the common phrase, 'sold'[,]" in a "really quite swindled state" (35).

That "swindled state" occurs when art replicates the marketplace, without any higher possibilities for the mind. It's as if James is warning his readers that we might all become like the Jewish shopkeeper, unless an artist can uplift us beyond our ordinary capitalist docilities. Only then can the reader be led by the "play of the *representational* values" toward "the spiritual and the aesthetic vision, the mind led captive by a charm and a spell, an incalculable art" (35, James's emphasis). Instead of sinking to the level of calculating shopkeepers, readers need magicians, and James presents himself as the most magisterial of those creative illusionists. The great writer can repair the "disconnected" state of ordinary life; "by his lightest touch the whole chain of relation and responsibility is reconstituted" (37). Only then, as his preface concludes, can "'connexions'" be "employable for finer purposes than mere gaping contrition" (37).

James's narrative as well as his preface give new life to the language of honor and shame, and therefore new life to paternalism. Throughout, honor implies giving greatly, while shame implies the tawdriness of self-isolation as well as possessive desire. The novel itself becomes James's extravagant gift to readers in need of self-transcending, self-sacrificing imagination. Such gestures of extravagant giving help to paper over the widening crack between paternalism and profits. By giving greatly, Andrew Carnegie and Adam Verver present themselves as noble civic leaders, using their money to rise above their money making. By giving greatly, Henry James uses art to rise above the baseness of his human materials. As James's culminating authorial gesture, *The Golden Bowl* reclaims the honor of paternalistic authorship through the value-creating, incorporative light and play of consciousness. To attain that end, his daddy's girl has to do the father's cultural work, and what she knows has to remain her private sacrifice.

8   *Tender Is the Night:*
Paternalism's Elegy

One of the great problems with reading *Tender Is the Night* (1934) is that the narrator presents his hero with keening empathy, though Dick Diver invites satire at every turn. These tensions come partly from Fitzgerald's autobiographical investments, which help to make the narration so strangely caressing and self-pitying. They also arise from incompatible grandiosities in Fitzgerald's allegorical aims, particularly his attempts to make Dick represent a Southern ideal of honor as well as a figure of national disunity and degeneration. More profoundly and powerfully, I think, the tensions expose the narcissistic aspects of paternalism.

Much like Maggie Verver at the end of *The Golden Bowl,* Dick begins with the ability to bring disparate and ordinary selves beyond themselves into a transcendent though momentary unity. In more prosaic terms, he can give a great party. As Dick's self-image deteriorates from the ideal host to a self-sacrificing martyr, the novel becomes an elegy for paternalism's failed promise. Yet Fitzgerald partially reveals what Dick's self-image avoids confronting: an emptiness, initially filled up with rescue fantasies, and eventually spilling out as bilious racism. To tell that double story of self-image and self-lack, Fitzgerald oscillates between admiration and projected self-pity. Perhaps that oscillation reflects his own narcissistic mixture of manic dreams and depressive lacks. Intermittently, Fitzgerald's ironic humor punctures the pretentious of various characters, especially those on the periphery of the story. More paradoxically, the narration's cherishing attentiveness to multicolored landscapes seems at odds with its ambivalent disdain for people of any color but white.

In several respects, the novel stands as a summa and coda for most of the issues I've been discussing. Yet the golden bowl, the daddy's girl, the New Woman, honor and shame, inadequate fatherhood, and incorporative whiteness appear here as aspects of Western culture's decline and fall. The world we loved is passing, Fitzgerald implies, and our "we" is passing too. The grandly civilized entitlements of the leisured white gentleman are yielding to aggressive women, homosexuals, and too many people of too many different colors. By recounting Dick's own fall, Fitzgerald tries to dramatize that vanishing grandeur, and to recoup it a little in the grandeur of Dick's yielding.

The drama doesn't quite work, at least for me, not simply because Dick often seems to be a shallow socialite, and not just because Dick's claims to self-sacrifice avoid self-knowledge. More crucially, his alleged greatness becomes revealed as an emptiness, filled only with a craving to be seen as great. For Dick, and for Fitzgerald too, that's the same as being loved. At bottom, Dick's unsatisfiable craving shows Fitzgerald's unsatisfiable need to reduce love to narcissism, in the name of the father.[1] Perhaps that's what happens to a man's paternalism when he loses his institutional supports.

"The golden bowl is broken"

We meet a reference to the golden bowl early on: "The silver cord is cut and the golden bowl is broken and all that" (58), Dick says.[2] It's unlikely that either Dick or Fitzgerald has James's novel in mind. Instead, the phrase invokes the source for James's title, Ecclesiastes 12:6. Ostensibly Dick is acting as tour guide, "full of excitement" as he talks to his friends about a World War I battlefield they are looking at. More surprisingly, at the moment when the novel first presents Dick's emotions, his throat is "straining with sadness" (56), and he uses the Biblical phrase to lament the war's destruction of civilized love. The allusion reverberates in several other directions as well, though Dick oddly excludes the Civil War. When Abe North says General Grant "invented this kind of battle at Petersburg in sixty-five[,]" Dick sharply disagrees. Grant "invented mass butchery," he replies. In contrast, this "tragic hill of Thiepval" witnessed "the last love battle" of two old European peoples, each passionate about their "sureties" and their "religion[,]" even their class distinctions. "All my beautiful lovely safe world blew itself up here with a great gust of high explosive love" (57).

As history, that assessment seems rather maudlin. As an entry to Dick's mind, it confirms Dick's view of himself as "an old romantic" (58) who mourns for a love that has been irretrievably "broken." More subtly, it announces his adherence to the tradition of white Southern honor, and therefore his displeasure with the results of the Civil War. Implicitly, only the losing side fought that war for love, and not for love of black people. Nonetheless, though Maggie Verver can turn a cracked golden bowl into a fiction of social value for a small elite group, Dick can't repair what the war has destroyed. Instead, he wistfully acknowledges "the broken universe of the war's ending" (245), and becomes a therapist who tries to mend the cracks in himself and his patients, including his wife. By the end of the novel, after Nicole has "cut the cord forever" between herself and her husband, Dick thinks to himself, "The case was finished. Doctor Diver was at liberty" (302). Solacing himself for his fall from grace, he claims what Maggie claims with a more imperious blend of suffering and self-aggrandizement, that he has repaired the broken cracks in Nicole at the cost of his own self-sacrifice.

The word "broken" recurrently defines Dick's world. Even at the outset of his temporarily distinguished career, Dick thinks to himself that he's not like the "clever men"; he's "less intact, even faintly destroyed. . . . though it'd be nice to build out some broken side till it was better than the original structure" (116). This passage pays homage to, or steals from, the celebrated passage five years earlier in Ernest Hemingway's *A Farewell to Arms:* "If people bring so much courage to this world the world has to kill them to break them, so of course it kills them. The world breaks every one and afterward many are strong at the broken places."[3] Fitzgerald's transposition of Hemingway stimulates a sequence of pointed invocations. Among them: the clinic is "a refuge for the broken, the incomplete, the menacing" (120), while the "weakness" of the psychiatric profession "is its attraction for the man a little crippled and broken" (137).[4] Later Dick breaks his nose in a fight (226). There's even a nice pun as Dick thinks about Nicole in the early stages of her therapy. While fretting about how to "divorce her from any obsession that he had stitched her together," he admires the way "she paused fractionally in front of the hall mirror" (137).

The Biblical context suggests still other ironic possibilities. "Remember now thy Creator in the days of thy youth," Ecclesiastes begins (12:1). God, of course, is the ultimate paternalist. By implication, only by renewing God's presence can the silver rod and the golden bowl be made whole again. In his work as therapist, husband, and host, Dick seeks to play the role of Creator, but his own emerging brokenness blocks his rescue fantasies from succeeding. Instead, his downward spiral parallels the descent in Ecclesiastes from the mysteriously mournful image of the golden bowl to the simple judgement two verses later: "Vanity of vanities, saith the preacher; all *is* vanity."

Daddy's Girls

The daddy's girl takes center stage right at the start, since young Rosemary Hoyt, who turns eighteen soon after she appears, has just starred in a movie called *Daddy's Girl.*[5] The film ends with father and daughter "united at last in a father complex so apparent that Dick winced for all psychologists at the vicious sentimentality" (69). Seemingly practicing in life what she plays in the movie, Rosemary becomes highly aroused by Dick's confident air of benevolent control: "He looked at her and for a moment she lived in the bright blue worlds of his eyes" (12). Soon her ruminations go further. "He seemed kind and charming[,]" she thinks; "his voice promised that he would take care of her, . . . open up whole new worlds for her, unroll an endless succession of magnificent possibilities" (16). Dick, already thirty-four and married, becomes reciprocally aroused by what he takes to be her adoring desire for him.[6]

Ironically, Rosemary is actually a mama's girl who already has an independent career. The daddy's girl is a role that her contract requires her to play on screen and in public (110).[7] Moreover, she's the first of the novel's many New Women. As her mother says to her, "You were brought up to work—not especially to marry. . . . economically you're a boy" (40). Soon Rosemary's heterogeneous desires start to stray, and the limitations of Dick's appeal become apparent. At first she delights in "the sense that Dick was taking care of her" (21), and she wants him to teach her about sex. "Take me. . . . take me, show me" (64). But she also has more frankly lustful desires for her director, Earl Brady, who is less paternal and more aggressive. With a "hard-boiled sparkle in his eyes . . . he refused the fatherly office" (31). Still later, Dick learns that Rosemary has done some heavy petting with a Yale undergraduate in a railway car.

Dick's mind returns to that imagined scene again and again. He can't bear to lose the illusory feeling of being her all in all. He wants to preserve the "tremendous illusions" of their first mutual rapture, when "the communion of self with self seemed to be on a plane where no other human relations mattered" (75). Now, as he obsesses about the scene in the railway car—"Do you mind if I pull down the curtain?" he says to himself five times—he begins to look less like a consummate paternalist and more like a needy flailer. Four years later, as he thinks of Rosemary again, the narcissism of his need shows more nakedly: "he wanted to hold her eloquent giving-of-herself in its precious shell, till he enclosed it, till it no longer existed outside him" (208). But that promise is gone now, he realizes. Mourning the loss of that all-in-all desire in both Rosemary and Nicole, he slowly degenerates into racist bigotries and helpless rages.

Much as Rosemary's ambitions and desires prove too multiple for Dick to accept, his wife rises from a much more sordid daddy's girl's past, that of incest victim, to gain confidence in her own heterogeneous desires. Nicole's experience of incest functions as a private and rather formulaic Freudian counterpoint to Rosemary's public daddy's girl role. What Rosemary plays at, Nicole has had to live. As we learn in part 2, Dick meets Nicole in Switzerland, where he becomes her therapist, another form of rescue fantasy. Though he rather scoffingly associates Nicole's first letters to him with "sprightly and sentimental epistolary collections" such as *Daddy-Long-Legs* (121), the connection between paternalistic sentiment and incestuous desires in both novels is more intimate than he realizes, particularly in himself. Both show how a powerful man's need to be loved gets subsumed in his need to control.

As with Rosemary, when Nicole grows stronger and Dick weakens, his imagined unity with her fractures. In their first months they signed their letters to each other with "Dicole" (103). At their first kiss, they became "an indissoluble mixture, with atoms joined and inseparable . . . he was thankful to have an existence at all, if only as a reflection in her wet eyes." Yet what's being reflected, and what arouses him so, is her affirmation of his protective, engulfing power. Nicole's body "curved in further and further toward him, with her own lips, new to herself, drowned and engulfed in love" (155). The moment evokes Poe's "Annabel Lee": "this maiden she lived with no other thought / Than to love and be loved by me."

Now, as Nicole grows toward equality and independence, Dick's desires for other young girls become indiscriminate and eruptive. "Nicole was his girl[,]" he keeps saying to himself right after he has "taken" Rosemary (213) at long last. But the "girl" has become a woman, and she sniffs the prospect of his new daddy's girls. She becomes enraged not because of Rosemary, who has only made her suspicious, but because of an accusation from a former patient that Dick seduced her daughter, whom Nicole angrily calls "a little dark girl . . . not more than fifteen" (190). While defending himself against Nicole's "straight hard gaze[,]" he remembers a ride into Zurich with a "flirtatious little brunette" whom he had kissed (187).

Soon he thinks of himself as a seeker after some hopelessly Platonic ideal. "He was in love with every pretty woman he saw now, their forms at a distance, their shadows on a wall" (201).[8] Why is it, he wonders, that he can't stop looking for "a wraith, a fragment of my desire? . . . To belittle all these years with something cheap and easy?" (202). A little later, drunk in an Italian police station, he accepts the angry crowd's identification of him with a man "who had raped and slain a five-year-old child" (234–35). On the last page, Dick has been run out of a New York town for getting "entangled with a girl who worked in a grocery store" (315).

More privately, Dick muses that "young and magnetic" Rosemary resembles his daughter, nine-year-old Topsy (207). He recurrently worries that since his daughter was "very fair and exquisitely made like Nicole," she might grow up to be like Nicole. That concern seems ambiguously poised between his daughter's body and Nicole's sexual history, perhaps with another sexually predatory father in the offing. Fortunately, he says to himself, Topsy has become "robust" in her physique (257). If Dick worries that he might become like Nicole's father, he doesn't acknowledge it. Instead, he shies away from making Topsy a daddy's girl, partly by giving more conversational time to his son, and partly by emphasizing paternal discipline rather than praise. "What do I care whether Topsy 'adores' me or not?" he says, it's not clear to whom, and it's not clear why. "I'm not bringing her up to be my wife" (257).

As a daddy's girl, Nicole seems to have a relatively simple narrative of psychological progress from incest victim to self-reliance. Yet Fitzgerald also gives her a more nasty narrative of descent, in which she begins as a beast-woman and ends by embracing anarchy. When she's first described, she's wearing a "bright red" dress, "her brown legs were bare[,]" and she "had thick, dark, gold hair like a chow's" (14). Soon Rosemary sees "her chow's hair foaming and frothing in the candlelight" (32). Though she keeps her mind hidden, outwardly she behaves as "an obedient retriever" (26). Her sister, Baby Warren, thinks of her as a "'gone coon'" (157), a phrase linking her to lower-class black people as well as raccoons.

All that comes while Nicole is mentally ill, and supposedly deserving of readers' sympathies. As she gets well, she slowly detaches herself from being a daddy's girl for Dick. More transgressively, she shows only intermittent interest in "bringing up children she could only pretend gently to love, guided orphans" (180). At one point she almost kills the children in a car accident, precipitated by her rage at Dick (192–93). Then, once she gains more strength of mind, she lets loose her adulterous desire for Tommy Barban, a mercenary soldier. A barbarian and a self-capitalizing adventurer, Tommy embodies the new world of imperial conquests that has replaced "love battles." Her lust justifies her last name of Warren; "She felt her face quiver like a rabbit's" (299). For Nicole, Tommy also represents an Orientalized anarchy: "She liked his bringing her there to the eastward vision . . . as if he had wolfed her away from Damascus and they had come out upon the Mongolian plain." As she grew "nearer to what she had been in the beginning, . . . she welcomed the anarchy of her lover" (298).

Dick has recoiled from her potential for anarchy. Right before their first kiss, her "impertinence, the right to invade implied, astounded him. Short of anarchy he could not think of any chance that Nicole Warren deserved." But he kisses her anyway, "possessed by a vast irrationality" (154). Always attracted by "rebels" who give her "vitality" (180), Nicole turns to Tommy partly because of his rough love, and partly because of "the foreignness of his depigmentation by unknown suns" (269). She even gives him her self as well as her body, at least for awhile. Now that she's "well again[,]" she tells him, "perhaps I've gone back to my true self—I suppose my grandfather was a crook and I'm a crook by heritage" (292). The victim of daddy's girl incest has grown up to be her grandfather's clone.

What looks like Nicole's descent into anarchy is also the narrative's indictment of consumer capitalism. When Nicole first tries to seduce Dick, she realizes her potential to become her grandfather, "Sid Warren, the horse-trader[.]" In that spirit, she could "confuse all values" by presenting herself as "a valuable property" (143). Though she doesn't do that then, her sister does it later. In one of the novel's most famous set pieces, the narrator describes Nicole as a consumer, "the product of much ingenuity and toil[,]" buying items made by workers from California to Brazil (55). Whether in her shopping or her adultery, Nicole comes to reflect what the narrator takes to be capitalism's devaluation of all values.

The New Woman

With admiring misogyny, Fitzgerald's narrative blames American women as well as capitalism for Dick's fall. Rosemary, Nicole, and especially Nicole's sister, Baby Warren, become different forms of the New Woman, and Baby's capitalist use-values reduce Dick from a heroic rescuer to a disposable commodity. Nicole's affair with her manly barbarian allegorizes the new United States, where the modern woman's unregulated sexual desires can couple with mercenary conquest. Faced with such fragmented products of his degraded and degrading country, Dick's capacity for chivalric leadership fades to a humiliated social spectacle.

The "young woman with the helmet-like hair" (83) who shoots her lover in the train station offers a preview of how women as well as war can destroy men's identities. As Fitzgerald takes care to emphasize, "she shot him through his identification card."[9] Later Dick's feminist patient, a painter who had once been "exceptionally pretty" but now has a mysterious skin disease, explains her case: "I'm sharing the fate of the women of my time who challenged men to battle" (183–84). Though Dick "wanted to gather her up in his arms, as he so often had Nicole, and cherish even her mistakes" (185), he can't restore her to her former beauty. Instead, she dies of "neurosyphilis" (243), as if punished for her sexual transgressions.

Other assertive women fare better, sometimes at Dick's expense. Rosemary's mother, Elsie Speers, gains Dick's admiration, mostly because she knows how to "wait" for men to finish their important business (165). Yet her last name signals what she has and what Dick has lost. "He had lost himself . . . the spear had been blunted" (201). Even Frau Gregorovius, the wife of his partner at the clinic, convinces her husband to ease Dick out of their joint ownership, bought with the Warrens' money, because Dick's alcoholism means he is no longer "a serious person" (242). They can replace Nicole's money with other sources, she says. Besides, she tells him, Nicole "only cherishes her illness as an instrument of power" (239). By the end of the novel, the only power over women that Dick can exercise comes when he kicks a cross-dressing lesbian Countess in the ass (306). To risk a bad pun, he becomes the more hapless butt in that incident, a figure of shame and ridicule.

The most vivid New Woman is Baby Warren, introduced by the narrator with startling snottiness.[10] She is "a compendium of all the discontented women who had loved Byron a hundred years before, . . . there was something wooden and onanistic about her" (151–52). Soon the narrative features her untouchable self-absorption. Though she "was a tall, fine-looking woman," she is "deeply engaged in being almost thirty." To the narrator, being "engaged" to herself rather than a man has given Baby "certain spinsters' characteristics—she was alien from touch," and "relished the foretaste of death, prefigured by the catastrophes of friends" (172). These descriptions resemble the relentlessly excessive disdain that the narrator of Stephen Crane's *The Monster* shows for the town's one independent woman, Martha Goodwin.

For Dick, Baby incarnates the specter of being owned by the Warrens' money. Festering in his imagined dependence, and "resenting her cold rich insolence[,]" he associates her with the "emergent Amazons" who don't understand "that a man is vulnerable only in his pride, but delicate as Humpty Dumpty once that is meddled with[.]" As he mulls over his "dread of breakage" (177), scapegoating Baby for his loss of manly independence allows him to remasculinize himself a little, by mixing "malice" with self-pity. Yet Dick also "admired something in her" (216), perhaps her forceful sense of self, even before she talks the American Consulate into getting him out of jail. With a mournful snideness, the narrator describes her moment of triumph over the Consul: "the American Woman, aroused, stood over him; the clean-sweeping irrational temper that had broken the moral back of a race and made a nursery out of a continent, was too much for him" (232).

As with Nicole, Baby has several contradictory narratives. The first dismisses her as a spinster. With more spleen, this passage presents her as the epitome of all the "clean-sweeping" and "irrational" American wives and mothers who have "broken the moral back" of men by keeping them in the "nursery," even though Baby is neither a wife, a mother, or for that matter a baby. A third narrative, Baby as capitalist predator, surfaces a few pages later. As a result of finding Dick publicly drunk and jailed, "she had the satisfaction of feeling that . . . they now possessed a moral superiority over him for as long as he proved of any use" (235). Dick's use-value, not his moral worth, is what counts in her mind, and what she can discount. As she says to Dick earlier, if Nicole might be happier with another husband, "it could be arranged" (215).

The presence of these three opposing narratives undermines Fitzgerald's repetitive dichotomizing of the New Woman vs. the Moral Man to explain Dick's decline into rage, racism, and promiscuity. But the narrator holds on to the binary, perhaps because anger against women preserves the last shreds of moral manliness. All the while, the narrative shifts the representation of strong selves from broken men to assertive women.[11]

Honor and Shame: "Good-by, all my fathers"

In a momentarily polemical mood, the narrator says Baby and her kind have "broken the moral back of a race." In a more recurrently wistful mood, he attributes the decline of Dick's manliness and honor to a quite different source, the attenuation of strong paternal traditions. That disappearance implies the loss of the white patriarchal South as a locus for moral value.

Dick's father emerges from nowhere midway through the narrative, and retreats to his grave four pages later. All we know about him before is that he was Dick's model for "the somewhat conscious good manners of the young Southerner coming north after the Civil War" (164). He surfaces again as Dick thinks about the loss of his own self-sufficiency. When Dick married Nicole, he was "thoroughly his own man" (201). Now, at least in his own mind, he has been "swallowed up like a gigolo" by his dependence on the Warrens' money. In that context, Dick suddenly recalls his father, a Southern clergyman who moved north from Virginia to Buffalo, amid many "struggles in poor parishes" (201). Though his father "was of tired stock[,]" he "raised himself" to the "effort" of becoming young Dick's "moral guide[,]" in part to save his son from the "spoiling" that his mother would have given him (203).

These reminiscences lead rather too swiftly to news of Reverend Diver's death. As Dick then reflects, though we've heard nothing about it before, "Dick loved his father—again and again he referred judgments to what his father would probably have thought or done" (203). He does so because his father had "a deep pride . . . that nothing could be superior to 'good instincts,' honor, courtesy, and courage." Unfortunately, Reverend Diver lacked the spark of Yankee enterprise. As people said, he was "very much the gentleman, but not much get-up-and-go about him." At the end of his father's funeral, Dick says to himself—or is it the narrator who says it to his readers?—"Good-by, my father—good-by, all my fathers" (205).

By making that quotation a separate paragraph, Fitzgerald transforms a privately muttered goodbye into a choral farewell to the Southern gentleman. Much later, near the end of the book, Dick muses that his need to be loved may be an attempt to preserve the virtues of a vanishing patriarchy. "[I]t had early become a habit to be loved, perhaps from the moment when he had realized that he was the last hope of a decaying clan" (302).

That's about it for good fathers. Of the two other fathers featured in the novel, one beats his homosexual son (244), while the other, Mr. Warren, has raped his daughter.[12] Faced with what he takes to be his shamefully gay male offspring, the Spanish-Chilean father agonizes over the loss of honor. That scene frames Dick's second and last brief encounter with Mr. Warren, now dying at fifty, and afflicted with guilt as well as shame. "I've been a bad man" (249), he says to Dick, before he mysteriously disappears. The only men who defend honor are Tommy Barban, who fights a duel with a tawdry guest to protect Nicole from imputations of insanity, and Hosain, or "Conte di Minghetti," a rich man with an "Asiatic title," an Asian-African background, and "two very tan children by another marriage" (259) before his current marriage to Abe North's widow. He departs in high dudgeon after the Divers accused his children of having diseases and, much worse, mistook his sister for a maid. "His honor makes it necessary" (263), Mary explains. Both these parodic instances show how honor has been outsourced to barbarians and foreigners, whereas Dick and Mr. Warren inhabit different kinds of shame.

Awash in multiplications of paternal decline, Dick looks back only briefly to the vestigial honor of his Southern fathers. His farewell to the Southern gentleman appears as a momentary blip in his consciousness, no more sustainable than the narrator's blast against Baby Warren's New Woman. Whether sentimental or polemical, neither of these rhetorical moments builds to an earned authenticity. They seem dropped down out of the blue, to explain Dick's internal failures of morality and will.

In the first part of the novel, Fitzgerald inflates Dick's social significance by making him the hero of two contradictory allegories. Dick temporarily remasculinizes his hapless father's Southern values of honor and courtesy, while he also brings dignity and "repose" (51) to the crass, ascendant North and West embodied in Abe North and Dick's own Buffalo background. It's Fitzgerald's own form of grandiosity, as if to say, Look at the meanings I'm making here!

If anyone could unify the South and the North, Dick seems to be the man. At his best, Dick incarnates "the diffused magic of the hot sweet South" (35)—ostensibly the Mediterranean climate, but with antebellum resonances. Faced with "the very deference of Dick's attention[,]" even McKisco, the most surly of his party guests, yields to Dick's charm, and everyone gets "lifted above conviviality into the rarer atmosphere of sentiment" (33–34). Dick epitomizes the leisured gentleman who can make each guest savor the experience of being uplifted to a shared fiction of mutual nobility. "The Divers' day was spaced like the day of the older civilizations to yield the utmost from the materials at hand, and to give all the transitions their full value" (21). As one of the gay guests says to him much later, "I've always thought of it as the most civilized gathering of people that I have ever known." Tellingly, Dick is so far from civilized at that point that he responds to that praise with "a crab-like retreat" (246).

Simultaneously, before his work ethic vanishes, Dick is a figure of national unity and imperial progress. His two childhood locations rather patly unify the South, the North, and the West of vanished buffaloes and Buffalo Bill. After graduating from Yale and getting a Rhodes Scholarship to Oxford, he goes to Johns Hopkins, then Vienna, and finally publishes a book in Zurich in 1920 (115–16). He exemplifies national prowess on an international scale. Yet he also exemplifies a brittle, vulnerable, and sometimes crude Americanness. Even in the "heroic period" of his life, he thinks of himself with a phallic joke out of American frontier humor: "Lucky Dick, you big stiff" (116).

As many critics have noted, Dick's name has a phallic charge, turning ironic as he goes limp.[13] Yet his name also evokes a curiously bland Americanness, stripped of any regional associations. It seems poised between thrusting and sinking. If he were still a Southerner, he would undoubtedly be called "Richard," perhaps even Richard d'Iver. But his upward mobility has left such claims to provincial status far behind. At the outset of his career, then, he appears to himself and others as a confident union of the Yankee and the patrician, the manly and the gentlemanly. Though he retains Southern roots in his code of chivalric social leadership, he is also a "hero, like Grant, . . . ready to be called to an intricate destiny" (118). By the last page, when Dick's connection to Grant surfaces again, the allusion has only a hollow pathos.[14]

The Divers' children, too, symbolize the possibilities of cross-racial national unity. Naming their son "Lanier" alludes to Sidney Lanier, a postbellum white Southern poet, while "Topsy" evokes the mischievous orphan black girl in Harriet Beecher Stowe's *Uncle Tom's Cabin* (1852). In uniting these contending elements, Dick performs a domestic version of E Pluribus Unum, though strangenesses accrue at the margins of his family's paternalistic unity. Lanier oddly calls him "Dick" at first (193), before turning to the more formal and conventional address of "father" (257) at a later stage of Dick's decline. Topsy's birth precipitated a renewed attack of her mother's insanity, Nicole recalls in a crazed monologue: "everything got dark again. . . . You tell me my baby is black—that's farcical, that's very cheap" (161). Yet Topsy is "very fair" (257), as if to belie or perhaps disown her novelistic namesake.

Paradoxically, one sign of Dick's failure to preserve his paternalistic ideal is his increasing attentiveness to his children. It's a sign of his neediness, not an affirmation of his powers. Dick has developed an "almost unnatural interest in the children" (257), Nicole thinks to herself. Later she decides that "he was seeking his children, not protectively but for protection" against awareness that he is "a deposed ruler" (280). The adjective carries a double charge: Dick has also been "de-posed." In that sense, his fathering becomes his last act. A weird violence suffuses his final goodbye to Lanier and Topsy: "he wanted to lift their beautiful heads off their necks and hold them close for hours" (311). Yet the sentimentality suffusing that farewell, as with the sentimentality in his farewell to his fathers, is really self-pity. Despite his clinging need for his children, he doesn't write, he doesn't call, he doesn't ask them to visit (315). His goodbyes to his fathers and his children show Dick's narcissistic inability to love.

Ultimately, to repeat one of my arguments in chapter 6, the move of Dick's father from Virginia to Buffalo mirrors the country's transformation from small-scale communities to a large-scale nation-state. There the many possibilities for transient relationships and mobilities make honor structurally dysfunctional, since honor serves in part to bond small hierarchical groups. Slowly forsaking his profession, where a drive for honor might secure his place in a competitive community of peers, Dick tries to regain the more traditional honor of a leisured gentleman by creating small social groups. Fending off the shame of not having the brilliant career he had imagined for himself, he plays the host with diminishing success and increasing references to self-sacrifice.

In that context, offering himself as the perfect "host" takes on a religious connotation. If in his best moments Dick "appeared so effortless that he still had pieces of his own most personal self for everyone" (77), that performance makes him a communion wafer being devoured. Yet unlike Christ's self-sacrifice, Dick's martyrdom leads to no one's redemption. Even his family starts to fall apart. Toward the end, Dick can make the Divers feel "unified again" only by joking that the father can divorce his child (265).

The Failure of Incorporative Whiteness

One of the most disorienting aspects of reading this narrative is the impasse between valuing colorful settings and devaluing people of color. Fitzgerald takes a cherishing delight in describing lavishly multicolored landscapes. At the same time, his characterizations and plotting quietly mock the multicolored human landscape that Dick periodically rails against.[15] Sometimes the narrative even lowers the visual status of white people who have been sunburned.

In the first pages, for instance, the description blends the colors of the Riviera landscape into a beautiful harmony. Moreover, the scene seems shaped by paternalistic order. "Deferential palms" cool the "facade" of a "large, proud, rose-colored hotel." Christian and Muslim, West and East, civilization and nature, even land and sea blend into a seamless unity: "The hotel and its bright tan prayer rug of a beach were one."[16] The "pink and cream of old fortifications, the purple Alp . . . lay quavering in the ripples and rings" of the Mediterranean. All the colors get incorporated into the imperial light: "the Mediterranean yielded up its pigments, moment by moment, to the brutal sunshine" (3–4).

As soon as people show up, the landscape disintegrates into lumpish or attractive body fragments and an anxious concern for whiteness. A nameless man applies the "chilly water" to his body with "much grunting and loud breathing[,]" and "floundered a minute in the sea." When Rosemary and her mother appear, the narrative takes a paragraph to inventory their body parts, from her mother's incipient "broken veins" to the "armorial shield" of Rosemary's hair and "the strong young pump of her heart." A "bald man in a monocle and a pair of tights, his tufted chest thrown out, his brash navel sucked in, was regarding her attentively." Soon, reaching the raft, Rosemary becomes "suddenly consciousness of the raw whiteness of her own body," as she sees "a tanned woman with very white teeth" looking down at her. "Not unpleasantly self-conscious," Rosemary checks out who has "flesh as white as her own" and who doesn't. "Between the dark people and the light, Rosemary found room" (5–6).

Dick uplifts these people into a temporary fiction of civilized unity. When Rosemary first sees him, Dick is "giving a quiet little performance for his group" (6). Like the hotel's "facade," Dick's performance eases and pleases. Soon, as they sit at a table, "person by person had given up something, a preoccupation, an anxiety, a suspicion, and now they were only their best selves and the Divers' guests." Only McKisco, "an arriviste who had not arrived[,]" had "contrived to be the unassimilated member of the party." But Dick draws him in, by drawing him out of himself. By creating "a detachment from the world" that makes everyone "subtly assured of their importance[,]" Dick's performance offers each guest a temporary absolution from being ordinary. As Rosemary intuits, Dick's arms are "full of the slack he had taken up from others, deeply merged in his own party" (32–33). A little later, Rosemary's appreciative gaze notes that Dick has the gift of making people feel chosen. He can "re-create the unity of his own party by destroying the outsiders" (52).

Abe North, an alcoholic composer, permanently dispels that unity. Abe's decline as a composer—he has written nothing for seven years—crudely anticipates Dick's incipient decline as a poser. It's hard to miss the allegorical baggage carried by his name: "Abe" for Abe Lincoln, and "North" for the unfortunate winner of the Civil War. Like a good post-Puritan, Abe talks to Rosemary with pompous irony about "his moral code" (34). Like a stereotypically benevolent abolitionist, he's all for freeing black people, but he can't tell them apart. Dick and Abe both think of Abe's black acquaintances as Indians (106, 110), and Abe also calls them "Senegalese" (108). As another sign of Abe's associations with debased polyglot identities, he has "the high cheekbones of an Indian" (9), and a hotel employee later refers to him as "Mr. Afghan North" (96). Moreover, Abe rights "injustice" by getting a black man named "Mr. Freeman" out of jail (97). When that act leads to Rosemary's discovery that another black man has been killed in Rosemary's bed, her first thought is "that it was Abe North" (109).

The anti-Yankee allegory here is exceptionally heavy-handed. It's as if to say, this is what happens when you free the slaves: they kill each other and blacken your honor.[17] Yet the irony cuts against Dick, too. As he says to Nicole, "it's only some nigger scrap" (110). Thereafter his racism pops out with less and less prompting. "He's a spic!" he shouts to Rosemary about her new lover (218). "You dirty Wops!" he shouts at his Italian jailers (228). "Why did you use your word spic in front of him?" Nicole asks after Dick's interchange with Hosain—not "the word," but "your word," implying its frequent use. Weakly disowning it, Dick responds, "I'm not much like myself any more" (260).

While the narrator poses as a good northern liberal in exposing Dick's racism, Fitzgerald's narrative seems to endorse it. A subtle recoil against racial mixing frames Dick's sexual consummation with Rosemary, "alone in her black pajamas" (209). More insistently, the narrator makes Dick blacker and blacker. Drunk at a bar, Dick slowly realizes that he has caused confusion rather than harmony, so he "drank a cup of black coffee" and heads back to his room to "lie down with his black heart" (223–24). "It's such a shame. . . . Oh, such a shame, such a shame[,]" Rosemary tells him a little earlier. "What's it all about anyhow?" "I guess I'm the Black Death," he replies. "I don't seem to bring people happiness any more" (219).

At the end whiteness returns to preside over the little kingdom from which Dick has been deposed. "A white sun, chivied of outline by a white sky, boomed over a windless day" (311–12). As Dick takes his final leave of the scene that he had done so much to create, he "raised his right hand and with a papal cross he blessed the beach from the high terrace" (314). Again the allegorizing is heavy-handed, since he parodically imitates the "Holy Father." Perhaps he is saying goodbye to his father again, this time with an Oedipal vengeance, since the papal cross rejects his own father's life as a Protestant clergyman. But Dick's gesture has much more pathos than belated rebellion, and in any case, it's just an act.

The momentary pose only exposes how little his paternalism can do now, and how far Dick has fallen from the honor he associates with white Southern patriarchy. As the gesture suggests, he hasn't ever really loved his father. Instead, just as he has yearned to possess a Platonic ideal of the Young Woman, he has loved a Platonic ideal of the Father. Dick has tried to incorporate himself as well as others into that paternalistic imaginary. Like his father, he has failed to measure up. When he realizes his failure, he welcomes and even courts shame to convince himself that he still exists, if only in negative relation to honor. Both the grandiose aspirations and the shame reveal Dick's inability or unwillingness to escape narcissism. Yet it's a narcissism steeped in dependence on a social code. Unable to love anything beyond his own performance, he feels emptied of self when his act no longer gains approval.

Paternalism's Narcissistic Emptiness

Near the end of the novel, Dick feels a surge of his old confidence, but it quickly turns into need. "[T]he old fatal pleasingness, the old forceful charm, swept back with its cry of 'Use me!'. . . . Wanting above all to be brave and kind, he had wanted, even more than that, to be loved" (302). Maybe, and maybe not. Earlier, as he rescues a "lost and miserable family" in Gibraltar, he confuses or conflates two similar states of feeling. "An overwhelming desire to help, or to be admired, came over him" (206). To be helpful, to be admired, to be loved, all become the same thing in Dick's mind. They solace his sense that honor is on the ropes, and ward off his looming feelings of emptiness.

So long as his guests completely enter Dick's world, he makes them feel extraordinary. His "exquisite consideration" and intuitive "politeness" makes them live once again "the proud uniqueness of their destinies, buried under the compromises of how many years" (27–28). Then, "at the first flicker of doubt . . . he evaporated before their eyes" (28). Much later, he thinks about the strange mixture of loneliness and inward absence underlying his ability to knit people and groups together. In the "broken universe" after the War, personalities "had seemed to press up so close to him that he became the personality itself—there seemed some necessity of taking all or nothing[.]" Yet he remained "only as complete as they were complete themselves."[18] There's "loneliness" in that, he concludes: "so easy to be loved—so hard to love" (245). Fitzgerald gives a grand spin to that fusion of benevolence with self-evaporation, and a good many critics have seized on it. Like Geneva's lake, Dick represents "the true centre of the Western World. . . . lost in the nothingness of the heartless beauty" (147).[19] My reading emphasizes a different allegory, more elegiac than ironic, more Southern than imperial. Dick discovers that he doesn't exist outside the shell of an emptied-out paternalism. "The strongest guard is placed at the gateway to nothing," Dick says, ostensibly about actors, actually about himself. "Maybe because the condition of emptiness is too shameful to be divulged" (70).

Is his feeling of emptiness genuine? Is it an aspect of his self-pity? Does it deflect recognition of Dick's shame that he hasn't measured up to an impossible paternal ideal? Or does it reflect his refusal to step outside the shell?

The narrative suggests all those possibilities as well as a more pragmatic one, that the absence of self enables Dick to give great parties. That last interpretation doesn't quite work, since his role as host depends on his ability to incorporate others into a collective superiority much like his own. Yet to choose from this spectrum of offered possibilities evades confronting Dick's narcissistic attachment to honor. Even embracing shame becomes a way for Dick to perpetuate honor in a negative mode. He holds onto it, and magnifies it, rather than venturing into the modern, mixed world of ordinary relationships and recognitions. As Nicole says to him, "you used to want to create things—now you seem to want to smash them up" (267). For Dick, acting on his destructive desires invites shame, which proves that he continues to exist in relation to his idealized code. Verbal or physical violence makes him feel momentarily alive. Even better, to act as the perfect host makes him feel that he has disappeared. Underneath both desires lies a fear that if he's really seen for who he is, he has no value.

As with King Lear, at least in Stanley Cavell's reading of him, Dick's search for love is an avoidance of love. On the surface, Dick's pleasure in being adored firms up his sense of momentary power. More deeply, it avoids his terror of being seen beyond the role he wants to perform. It may be, Cavell intimates, that Lear's shame reflects the incestuous nature of his love for Cordelia.[20] Perhaps Dick's promiscuous daddy's girl yearnings reflect that desire in more partially acknowledged form. Yet as we've seen in so many other daddy's girl texts, a father-figure's incestuous desires bespeak a lack. At the core of their narcissisms, King Lear and Dick Diver share a sense that for whatever reason, to be seen, known, and loved when stripped of authority and honor is unbearable. It's fear, rather than emptiness or shame, that grounds Dick's narcissism. His need to be loved for his paternalistic powers hides an unconscious conviction that he couldn't possibly be loved if he doesn't measure up to the paternal ideal.

Much safer, then, to yield to the romantic death wish implied in Fitzgerald's title, lifted from Keats's "Ode to a Nightingale." From beginning to end, *Tender Is the Night* remains a tender elegy for the hollowed-out honor of a leisured white patrician. The narrative empties out the antebellum ideal of the patriarchal Southern gentleman, without replacing it with anything else. By implication, it's better for a dishonored gentleman to rage, or as Dick does, to rage and fade, "Fade far away, dissolve, and quite forget . . ." Anything but mix with ordinary, heterogeneous people without the ability to command. In that respect, Dick becomes an attenuated version of what Jane Addams called "A Modern Lear."

Epilogue
Shirley Temple's *The Little Colonel:* Granddaddy's Girl

Even an academic book can have an uplifting ending; it's the American Way. Besides, the death of paternalism is certainly not the end of civilization, except perhaps as Dick Diver knows it. Playing very different changes on the theme, *The Little Colonel* (1935) gives us Shirley Temple's version of the daddy's girl role that Fitzgerald adapts for Rosemary's stardom. Shirley Temple is jaunty, she's bossy, she's hot-tempered, she's independent; she's little, she's cute, she's a great dancer, she needs her equally hot-tempered granddaddy's love. Like a little Maggie Verver, she mends her broken family relations. Like Nicole Diver and Alexandra Bergson, she's her grandfather's clone.

As in so many other fictions during the early corporate era, Shirley Temple's father is a hapless failure. Having bought worthless land salted with gold, he becomes an invalid for most of the movie. The plot's tensions focus on his wife's father, Colonel Lloyd (Lionel Barrymore), a former Confederate officer who has disowned his daughter for eloping with a man he doesn't approve of. Initially set in Kentucky in 1877, the movie shifts to a Western frontier village six years later, where the young couple's young daughter is acting the part of a "little Colonel," as if she were her grandfather, giving pleasure as well as orders to all the indulgent adults. When the family moves back to Kentucky, the little Colonel takes on the big Colonel. Slowly, under relentless and often comic assault from his uppity granddaughter, he edges back from anger to love for both his daddy's girls.[1]

In *Tender Is the Night*, Nicole's strength comes from her grandfather, who was a crook. In *O Pioneers!*, Alexandra Bergson's strength comes from her grandfather, without the despairing follies brought on by his terror of growing old. The little Colonel's strength matches her grandfather's in two ways: they're each bull-headed, and they each have an uncontrollable temper. "Some day your temper's going to split you wide open," a doctor says to the

Colonel, who is spluttering about his disobedient daughter. Later, when the Colonel finds a little white girl playing in the mud, he pokes her with a stick, and she flares up at him. "For a little girl, you've got a bad temper," he says sharply. "'Cause I'm so much like you," she replies, and throws mud on him. Only at that point does he discover she's his granddaughter. Finally, as they gingerly start to like each other, he lectures her about her family heritage. "You're a true Lloyd," he acknowledges. "You've got all the fire and courage our family's always had. You've got the same infernal temper that's been our curse. It's going to cause you a lot of unhappiness unless you learn how to control it. Will you try?" She looks at him warily. "I will if you will," she says.

Two other thematic issues complicate this pleasantly sentimental convergence of wills. Throughout their developing relationship, the little Colonel takes the North's side, whereas the Colonel passionately defends the Confederacy. At one point the two Colonels have a mock battle of Union and Confederate toy soldiers, and when she starts to lose, she knocks over the table. Second, and very much related, this little white girl likes black people, and loves to dance with an adult black male. She even has a black and white dog as a secret pet. She develops several friendships with black children, and goes to a black baptismal ceremony, where she baptizes one of her black friends. Most famously, the little Colonel has several tap-dancing sessions with Bill "Bojangles" Robinson, who plays one of the Colonel's servants.

The movie's liberal paternalism stays firmly in place, of course. The little white girl is always the superior force in her friendships. At the very end, after she has reconciled her grandfather and his daughter in front of the happy black servants, she coaxes the Colonel into towing a black child home in a rickety wagon. Then, in a final sentimental reversal, she gives a Confederate salute, while he gives a Union salute. Yet the crossovers remain more memorable than the paternalism. North and South, male and female, black and white begin as opposites, then converge with varying degrees of ease and speed. In the midst of the Depression, countering ubiquitous images of defeated and "forgotten" men, Shirley Temple plays a lovably bratty little girl who wears the pants in her family, dares to challenge a formidable elder on his turf, and wins. Her rages match her grandfather's, and her dancing matches Bojangles's dancing, in flair if not in sophistication. When out of her grandfather's sight, they dance up a storm, on equal terms. They leap out of their movie roles and become two Hollywood stars having a great time together. Uncle Tom and little Eva are on new social terrain.[2]

For me, the strangest moment in the movie comes in a peripheral dialogue toward the end, when a white villain says to the little girl, "Why good day, young lady. And how does your corporosity seem to segatuate, hm?" In the context of the movie, this bizarre question has no meaning that I can figure out. Intertextually, however, it's a spectacular racial crossover. In Pauline Hopkins's *Contending Forces* (1900), an ingratiating black man says to a white man, "Mornin, Cap'n, how's yer corporosity seem to segashiate?" The white man laughs uproariously, and gives the black man five dollars for entertaining him with such nonsensical pretentiousness. The black man pockets the money earned by his lucrative bit of signifying. As he tells his friends later, "By night I had twenty dollars in my pocket, an' everybody on the boat was a callin' me 'corporosity segashiate.' I've used that hoodoo ever since, an' I ain't found nary white gempleman can seem to git 'way from it without showing the color of his money."[3]

One could make a good deal of the mind-body tensions and the color-coded ironies in the phrase, and perhaps that's what attracted James Joyce, who snuck it into *Ulysses* (1922).[4] Fifteen years later, in *The Little Colonel*, a slightly altered version of a black man's joke comes out of a white man's mouth.

No doubt these crossovers show the persistence of white paternalistic appropriations. Yet to me, they also suggest the democratic possibilities inherent in cultural heterogeneity. For Fitzgerald, as for Colonel Lloyd, that social diversity represents social contamination. On the other hand, in tension with that recoil, Fitzgerald intermittently celebrates the ability of Dick Diver and his own narrative to embrace disparate human elements, if only to elevate them into an incorporated whiteness. In the novel, such fugitive embraces become even more transient than Dick's desires for younger women. In life, the heterogeneity in everyone's desires encourages crossover experimentations. No paternalistic mold can hold them back for long.

In any case, from Laura Hawkins to Shirley Temple, the daddy's girl became an American cultural icon. Then and now, she mixes a traditional daughterly appeal with the equal appeal of a young woman's audacious independence, beyond her father's control.

Notes

Introduction

1 My title also bows to Alan Trachtenberg's pioneering book, *The Incorporation of America: Culture and Society in the Gilded Age* (New York: Hill and Wang, 1982).

2 W. E. B. Du Bois, *The Souls of Black Folk,* in *Three Negro Classics,* ed. John Hope Franklin (New York: Avon Books, 1965, Du Bois's book 1st pub. 1903), 236. The sequence of "Thank you, mas'r" film clips at the end of Spike Lee's *Bamboozled* (2002) shows the paternalistic expectations framing many African American actors until the 1970s.

3 On Southern paternalism see Eugene D. Genovese's *Roll, Jordan, Roll: The World the Slaves Made* (New York: Pantheon Books, 1974), e.g., 3–7, 110–12, and 133–47 on reciprocal dependency. Genovese argues that because "all paternalism rests on a master-servant relationship" it is [therefore] "incompatible with bourgeois social relations" (661). I see early corporate paternalism as more mediated and mediating. See also Kenneth S. Greenberg's *Honor and Slavery* (Princeton: Princeton University Press, 1996), 46–47, 111–14, and a classic study, W. J. Cash's *The Mind of the South,* intro. Bertram Wyatt-Brown (New York: Vintage Books, 1991, 1st pub. 1941), esp. 209–15, 267–70, 389–95. Walter Johnson's *Soul by Soul: Life Inside the Antebellum Slave Market* (Cambridge, Mass.: Harvard University Press, 1999) emphasizes "the nuzzling violence that characterized slaveholding 'paternalism,'" with its "peculiar mixture of ostensible moderation and outright threat" (22–23, also 28–29 on its uses for white self-exculpation, 36 on slaves' strategic uses of white paternalism, and 108–13 on paternalism in slave markets.)

4 Donald VanDeVeer, *Paternalistic Intervention: The Moral Bounds on Benevolence* (Princeton, N.J.: Princeton University Press, 1986), 12–24 for examples and basic definitions, 81–87 on strong and weak paternalism, also 338–44 and 375–90 on John Rawls. VanDeVeer also discusses other philosophers and legal theorists from Kant and Mill to Ronald Dworkin, Gerald Dworkin, and H. L. A. Hart.

5 See especially Kevin K. Gaines, *Uplifting the Race: Black Leadership, Politics, and Culture in the Twentieth Century* (Chapel Hill: University of North Carolina Press, 1996).

6 On John Patterson, see Andrea Tone, *The Business of Benevolence: Industrial Paternalism in Progressive America* (Ithaca, N.Y.: Cornell University Press, 1997), 66–70, 224–25. Olivier Zunz's *Making America Corporate 1870–1920* (Chicago: University of Chi-

cago Press, 1990) and Angel Kwolek-Folland's *Engendering Business: Men and Women in the Corporate Office, 1870–1930* (Baltimore: Johns Hopkins University Press, 1994) describe paternalistic corporate practices. Kwolek-Folland also notes the "enlightened paternalism" manifested in public commercial architecture, mixing "civic duty and familial security" with "aristocratic grandeur" (101).

7 Mary R. Jackman, *The Velvet Glove: Paternalism and Conflict in Gender, Class, and Race Relations* (Berkeley: University of California Press, 1994). Jackman argues that benevolence provides an "ideological cocoon" of "love" to make the dominant group feel good while strengthening the group's control (14, also 15–16, 361–63, 381–83). From an ambivalently conservative perspective, Christopher Lasch's *The Culture of Narcissism: American Life in an Age of Diminishing Expectations* (New York: W. W. Norton, 1978) mourns the alleged collapse of traditional paternalism in the welfare state (52–70, 172–76, 218–36).

8 See Matthew Frye Jacobson, *Whiteness of a Different Color* (Cambridge, Mass.: Harvard University Press, 1998).

9 Charles Loring Brace, *The Dangerous Classes of New York, and Twenty Years' Work Among Them,* 3d ed. (New York: Wynkoop and Hallenbeck, 1880, 1st pub. 1872), i–iii.

10 Edward W. Said, *Orientalism* (New York: Vintage Books, 1978), 2. See also Louise Michele Newman, *White Women's Rights: The Racial Origins of Feminism in the United States* (New York: Oxford University Press, 1999).

11 Du Bois, *Souls of Black Folk,* 246. Cf. the introduction by Albion Small (!) to the first issue of the *American Journal of Sociology* (summer 1895): "Men are more definitely and variously aware of each other than ever before. They are also more promiscuously perplexed by each other's presence." Cited by Priscilla Wald, "Communicable Americanism: Contagion, Geographic Fictions, and the Sociological Legacy of Robert E. Park," *American Literary History* 14 (Winter 2002), 659.

12 Judith Sealander, *Private Wealth and Public Life: Foundation Philanthropy and the Reshaping of American Social Policy from the Progressive Era to the New Deal* (Baltimore: Johns Hopkins University Press, 1997), 30, 247.

13 Jane Addams, "A Modern Lear," rpt. in *The Social Thought of Jane Addams,* ed. Christopher Lasch (Indianapolis: Bobbs-Merrill Co., 1965), 107–23, quotation 117. 1st pub. in *Survey* 29 (November 2, 1912), 131–37. On Pullman's vault, see Carl Smith, *Urban Disorder and the Shape of Belief: The Great Chicago Fire, the Haymarket Bomb, and the Model Town of Pullman* (Chicago: University of Chicago Press, 1995), 277. Pullman left only $3,000 per year to his twin sons, whom he saw as irresponsible (277).

14 Sara Blair, *Henry James and the Writing of Race and Nation* (Cambridge: Cambridge University Press, 1996), esp. 193–94, 202.

15 Seth Mydans, "In Debris of Economic Crash: Thailand's Faith in Authority," *New York Times,* 10 August 1999, A1, A8, quotations A1.

16 Douglas Jehl, "Arab Honor's Price: A Woman's Blood," *New York Times,* 20 June 1999, 1, 8, quotation 1; Elisabeth Bumiller, "Deny Rape or Be Hated: Kosovo Victims' Choice," *New York Times,* 22 June 1999, A1, A13, quotation A1. On Pakistani families in northern England, see Warren Hoge, "Marked for Death, by Their Families," *New York Times,* 18 October 1997, A4. See also Sarah Lyall, "Lost in Sweden: A Kurdish Daughter Is Sacrificed," *New York Times,* 23 July 2002, A3, and Seth Mydans, "A Friendship Sundered by Muslim Code of Honor," *New York Times,* 1 February 2003, A4.

17 Gayatri Spivak, "Can the Subaltern Speak?" In *Colonial Discourse and Post-Colonial Theory: A Reader,* ed. Patrick Williams and Laura Chrisman (New York: Columbia University Press, 1994, 1st pub. 1988), 66–111, esp. 92–93, with complex qualifications.

18 In *Daddy's Girl: Young Girls and Popular Culture* (Cambridge, Mass.: Harvard Uni-

versity Press, 1997), Valerie Walkerdine explores the impact of Harold Gray's Little Orphan Annie (1924–68, when Gray died) and Shirley Temple's movies on British working-class culture.

19 Mark Twain, *A Connecticut Yankee in King Arthur's Court*, 103.

20 "A knowable self" transposes Raymond Williams's idea that novels provide "knowable communities." See Williams's *The Country and the City* (New York: Oxford University Press, 1973), 165.

21 Robert H. Wiebe, *The Search for Order, 1877–1920* (New York: Hill and Wang, 1967), 44–76.

22 Alan Trachtenberg, *The Incorporation of America: Culture and Society in the Gilded Age* (New York: Hill and Wang, 1982), chap. 6 (182–207); Amy Kaplan, *The Social Construction of American Realism* (Chicago: University of Chicago Press, 1988); "Romancing the Empire: The Embodiment of American Masculinity in the Popular Historical Novel of the 1890s," *American Literary History* 2 (1990): 659–90; *Cultures of United States Imperialism*, ed. Amy Kaplan and Donald E. Pease (Durham, N.C.: Duke University Press, 1993). Brook Thomas, *American Literary Realism and the Failed Promise of Contract* (Berkeley: University of California Press, 1997). Nancy Glazener, *Reading for Realism: The History of a U.S. Literary Institution, 1850–1910* (Durham, N.C.: Duke University Press, 1997).

23 Michael McKeon, "Historicizing Patriarchy: The Emergence of Gender Difference in England, 1660–1760," *Eighteenth-Century Studies* 28 (1995): 295–322; Stephen M. Frank, *Life with Father: Parenthood and Masculinity in the Nineteenth-Century American North* (Baltimore: Johns Hopkins University Press, 1998), 136, also 3 on spousal partnership. McKeon argues that "male domination and the subordination of women are constants . . . What changes is the form patriarchy takes" (300) as it shifts from "a sexual system of hierarchy to one of difference" (307) in which paternalistic benevolence embodied "patriarchy in other terms" (316).

24 James Livingston, *Pragmatism and the Political Economy of Cultural Revolution, 1850–1940* (Chapel Hill: University of North Carolina Press, 1994), esp. 70–75, 112; Kwolek-Folland, *Engendering Business*, 54.

25 Livingston, *Pragmatism*, 66–77; on the den, see Steven M. Gelber, "Do-It-Yourself: Constructing, Repairing and Maintaining Domestic Masculinity," *American Quarterly* 49 (March 1997): 66–112.

26 Tone, *Business of Benevolence*. See also chap. 1 of Zunz's *Making America Corporate*, 11–36, "Lost Autonomy": centralized bureaucratic hierarchies eroded the grounds for local paternalism as well as self-reliance among white men. Kwolek-Folland's *Engendering Business* highlights the feminization associated with corporate self-subordination. As defensive strategies of social control, corporate paternalistic practices preserved traditional ideals of womanhood while employing substantial numbers of women in nonfarm work for the first time in history. In "Are Women Business Failures?" (*Harpers Weekly*, 8 April 1905, 496), Edith Abbott notes statistics showing more than five million women wage earners in the United States, of whom two million were in domestic service. Of the remaining three million, "nearly one-half are factory employees, and the other half are divided between the professions, agriculture, trade and transportation, and other occupations."

27 Howard Horwitz, *By the Law of Nature: Form and Value in Nineteenth-Century America* (New York: Oxford University Press, 1991), 220.

28 Theodore Dreiser, *Sister Carrie* (New York: Signet Classic, 1961, 1st pub. 1900). Citations included in text.

29 Lynda Zwinger, *Daughters, Fathers, and the Novel: The Sentimental Romance of Heterosexuality* (Madison: University of Wisconsin Press, 1991).

30 Edith Wharton, *Summer* (New York: Harper and Row, 1980, 1st pub. 1917), 285.

31 Two exceptions to studies that relegate honor to the antebellum South or precapitalist cultures: Samuel Haber's *The Quest for Authority and Honor in the American Professions, 1750–1900* (Chicago: University of Chicago Press, 1991), and Joanne B. Freeman's *Affairs of Honor: National Politics in the New Republic* (New Haven: Yale University Press, 2001).

32 Philip Fisher, "Introduction," *New American Studies: Essays from Representations,* ed. Philip Fisher (Berkeley: University of California Press, 1991), xiii–xiv.

Chapter 1. Middle-Class Fatherhood and the Transformation of Work

1 Qtd. by Marjane Ambler, "The Long Tradition of Defying Selfishness," *Tribal College Journal* 7 (Winter 1995): 8–9.

2 Francis Paul Prucha, *The Great Father: The United States Government and the American Indians,* 2 vols. (Lincoln: University of Nebraska Press, 1994), 2:759.

3 Prucha, *Great Father,* vol. 2, 634–40, 669–71 on humanitarians and reformers. Louise Michele Newman's *White Women's Rights: The Racial Origins of Feminism in the United States* (New York: Oxford University Press, 1999), chap. 5, analyzes the career of Alice Fletcher, who helped to design the Dawes Act and doled out land parcels (119–24). Newman argues that racism was central to the feminism and "civilization-work" of these secular missionaries (52). As Frances Willard liked to repeat, "A white life for two" (66), implying racial as well as sexual purity.

4 Prucha, *Great Father,* vol. 2, 666–71, 872–79; quotations 667–68, 639–40 (vote); 1:594 (wards and dependents); 2:759, also 897 on "the discrepancy between citizenship and continuing wardship[.]" For Dawes' presumption that the Indian "race" would die out, see Harold Evans, with Gail Buckland and Kevin Baker, *The American Century* (New York: Alfred A. Knopf, 1999), 6–7. See also Eric Cheyfitz, "Savage Law: The Plot Against American Indians in *Johnson and Graham's Lessee v. M'Intosh* and *The Pioneers,*" in *Cultures of United States Imperialism,* ed. Amy Kaplan and Donald E. Pease (Durham, N.C.: Duke University Press, 1993), 113.

5 Stephen M. Frank, *Life with Father: Parenthood and Masculinity in the Nineteenth-Century American North* (Baltimore: Johns Hopkins University Press, 1998), 53, also 136.

6 Cheyfitz, "Savage Law," 110. After Marshall's decision, Jackson responded, "Let him enforce it," an impeachable abrogation of constitutional responsibility that led to the Cherokees' "Trail of Tears" in 1837.

7 See Prucha, *Great Father,* vol. 1, epigraphs.

8 On U.S. paternalism in the Philippines, see Vicente L. Rafael, "White Love: Surveillance and Nationalist Resistance in the U.S. Colonization of the Philippines," in *Cultures of United States Imperialism,* ed. Kaplan and Pease, 185–218. President William McKinley's policy emphasized "benevolent assimilation," analogous to the father's guidance of the son (185, also 211). On various patriarchal stances and rhetoric in Africa, see Donna Haraway, "Teddy Bear Patriarchy: Taxidermy in the Garden of Eden, New York City, 1908–1936," in *Cultures of United States Imperialism,* ed. Kaplan and Pease, 237–91, esp. 284 on the great white father as hunter; also Barbara Kingsolver, *The Poisonwood Bible* (New York: HarperFlamingo, 1998), a novel about a U.S. missionary's increasingly demented attempts to impose paternalistic controls on his wife, daughters, and natives of the Congo in the 1960s. In Phillip Noyce's movie, *Rabbit-Proof Fence* (2002), Kenneth Branagh portrays an Australian administrator in the 1930s who removes "half-caste" children from their aborigine families, ostensibly to improve their lives.

9 Mark Twain, *The Innocents Abroad or The New Pilgrims Progress* (New York: Signet

Classic, 1966, 1st pub. 1869), 398–99 (beginning of chap. 52). In Booth Tarkington's *Alice Adams* (New York: Grosset and Dunlap, 1921), the narrator remarks that an old gentleman at the door is "probably the last great merchant in America to wear the chin beard" (178).

10 On postbellum credit, see Lendol Calder, *Financing the American Dream: A Cultural History of Consumer Credit* (Princeton: Princeton University Press, 1999), 79–87.

11 Angel Kwolek-Folland, *Engendering Business: Men and Women in the Corporate Office, 1870–1930* (Baltimore: Johns Hopkins University Press, 1994), 77, also 188–89 and 70–93 on corporate tensions among restored patriarchy, manly rationality, and feminization. Andrea Tone, *The Business of Benevolence: Industrial Paternalism in Progressive America* (Ithaca, N.Y.: Cornell University Press, 1997), argues that corporations not only enforced separately gendered spheres in the workplace, but also reinforced traditional gender roles such as breadwinner (10–12, 168–69) to counter the shame men associated with workplace dependence on corporate paternalism (41–42, 235–37). In *The Emerson Effect: Individualism and Submission in America* (Chicago: University of Chicago Press, 1996), Christopher Newfield argues that Emersonian liberalism is "a transitional ideology" (218) reinforcing what he calls the "submissive individualism" characteristic of corporate employment (67–72, 84–88, 209–18). See also Olivier Zunz, *Making America Corporate 1870–1920* (Chicago: University of Chicago Press, 1990), chap. 1, on corporate tensions between individualism and hierarchical deference. In *The Incorporation of America: Culture and Society in the Gilded Age* (New York: Hill and Wang, 1982), Alan Trachtenberg notes that by 1900, one third of all adults in the United States were part of "the industrial labor force" (87).

12 Blanche Wiesen Cook, *Eleanor Roosevelt,* vol. 1 (New York: Penguin Books, 1992), 22.

13 Frank, *Life with Father,* 81.

14 "Yes, Virginia," an editorial in the *New York Sun,* 21 September 1897, was written by Francis P. Church and published anonymously. It has been widely reprinted.

15 Emily Dickinson to T. W. Higginson, 25 April 1862, in *The Letters of Emily Dickinson,* vol. 2, ed. Thomas H. Johnson and Theodora Ward (Cambridge, Mass.: Harvard University Press, 1958), 404.

16 Claudia Nelson, *Invisible Men: Fatherhood in Victorian Periodicals, 1830–1910* (Athens: University of Georgia Press, 1995), 200, also 180.

17 Oliver Wendell Holmes, *Elsie Venner: A Romance of Destiny* (Chicago: W. B. Conkey Co. [1861]), 112. Two minor novels by Jack London, *A Daughter of the Snows* (1902) and *Adventure* (1911), portray strong-willed young Anglo-Saxon heroines who have been raised by enterprising businessmen. I'm indebted here to Jonathan Auerbach.

18 Henry James, *The Portrait of a Lady* (New York: Signet Classic, 1963, based on 1881 ed.), 183.

19 F. Scott Fitzgerald, *Tender Is the Night* (New York: Scribner Paperback, 1995, 1st pub. 1934), 280.

20 Mitford M. Mathews, ed., *A Dictionary of Americanisms On Historical Principles* (Chicago: University of Chicago Press, 1951), 457.

21 See Richard L. Rapson, "The British Traveler in America, 1860–1935," Ph.D. dissertation, University of Michigan, 1969.

22 Ring W. Lardner, Jr., *The Young Immigrunts* (Indianapolis: Bobbs-Merrill, 1920), 10.

23 On "businessman," see Charles Sellers, *The Market Revolution: Jacksonian America 1815–1846* (New York: Oxford University Press, 1991), 237.

24 Gordon Wood, "Inventing American Capitalism," *New York Review of Books,* 9 June 1994, 44–49. See also Richard L. Bushman, *The Refinement of America: Persons, Houses, Cities* (New York: Alfred A. Knopf, 1992).

25 Sven Beckert, *The Monied Metropolis: New York City and the Consolidation of the American Bourgeoisie, 1850–1896* (Cambridge, Mass.: Harvard University Press, 2001), 256–57. Beckert emphasizes the new bourgeois elite's restriction of paternalism by distinguishing between the deserving and the undeserving poor, while supporting retrenchment of government services and accepting class divisions (213–26). For "business man" in the "Cross of Gold" speech, see *William Jennings Bryan: Selections*, ed. Ray Ginger (Indianapolis: Bobbs-Merrill, 1967), 40.

26 Antonio Gramsci, *An Antonio Gramsci Reader: Selected Writings, 1916–1935*, ed. David Forgacs (New York: Schocken Books, 1988), 293. Gramsci concludes, following Veblen: "The male industrialist continues to work even if he is a millionaire, but his wife and daughters are turning, more and more, into 'luxury mammals.'" On the work ethic, see Daniel T. Rodgers, *The Work Ethic in Industrial America, 1850–1920* (Chicago: University of Chicago Press, 1978), also Michael Kimmel, *Manhood in America: A Cultural History* (New York: The Free Press, 1996), 81–116, and E. Anthony Rotundo, *American Manhood: Transformations in Masculinity from the Revolution to the Modern Era* (New York: Basic Books, 1993), 175–76.

27 William Dean Howells, *A Modern Instance* (New York: Penguin, 1984, 1st pub. 1882), 49.

28 George Horace Lorimer, *Old Gorgon Graham: More Letters from a Self-Made Merchant to His Son* (London: Methuen, 1904), 234. Chapter 4 discusses Lorimer's two books of father-son letters.

29 See Brook Thomas, *American Literary Realism and the Failed Promise of Contract* (Berkeley: University of California Press, 1997), 234–35. Thomas notes that in *Hale v. Henkel* (1905), the Supreme Court granted corporations Fourth Amendment protections while denying Fifth Amendment protections. In the twenty-five years after the 1886 *Santa Clara* decision applied the Fourteenth Amendment's equal protection and due process clauses to corporations, over half the Fourteenth Amendment cases that reached the Supreme Court concerned corporations (312 of 607), whereas only thirty, including *Plessy v. Ferguson* (1896), concerned minority rights (235).

30 Mansel G. Blackford and K. Austin Kerr, *Business Enterprise in American History*, 3d ed. (Boston: Houghton Mifflin, 1994), 138, also 125–224.

31 Ambrose Bierce, *The Devil's Dictionary* (New York: Dover Publications, 1993, 1st pub. 1911), 19.

32 I'm indebted here to conversations and correspondence with Michael Millender, formerly a colleague in the Department of History and the Law School at the University of Florida. The *Dartmouth* case did not immediately free corporations from state control. Until the 1870s, when several states created "general incorporation" statutes, states retained power over corporations by reserving the right to repeal or amend corporate charters. For detailed histories, see Morton J. Horwitz, *The Transformation of American Law, 1870–1960* (New York: Oxford University Press, 1992), and Herbert Hovenkamp, *Enterprise and American Law 1836–1937* (Cambridge, Mass.: Harvard University Press, 1991). The second half of William E. Moddelmog's *Reconstituting Authority: American Fiction in the Province of the Law, 1880–1920* (Iowa City: University of Iowa Press, 2000) focuses on the "authority of property" in various novelists as well as in the law, especially for Dreiser (194, also 24, 191–216).

33 See Peter Dobkin Hall, *The Organization of American Culture, 1700–1900: Private Institutions, Elites, and the Origins of American Nationality* (New York: New York University Press, 1982), 90, also 174–84. See chap. 6, esp. 110–12 on the *Dartmouth* case, also 121–22 on the Supreme Court's 1844 ruling that Stephen Girard had the right to bequeath his property to set up a school for poor white orphans. Here Webster lost, argu-

ing for the heirs. Hall sketches how state and federal courts slowly affirmed corporate rights to manage property independent of the public will.

34 On *Beulah,* see Anne Goodwyn Jones, *Tomorrow Is Another Day: The Woman Writer in the South, 1859–1936* (Baton Rouge: Louisiana State University Press, 1981), 55–91.

35 Quoted by Ralph Waldo Emerson in his journal entry for October 6, 1836. See *Emerson in His Journals,* ed. Joel Porte (Cambridge, Mass.: Harvard University Press, 1982), 151.

36 Mary Ryan, *Cradle of the Middle Class: The Family in Oneida County, New York, 1790–1865* (Cambridge: Cambridge University Press, 1981), 184. See also Barbara Ehrenreich, *Fear of Falling: The Inner Life of the Middle Class* (New York: HarperCollins, 1989), on middle-class anxieties about falling into the working class.

37 Miles Orvell, *The Real Thing: Imitation and Authenticity in American Culture, 1880–1940* (Chapel Hill: University of North Carolina Press, 1989), 52, 71.

38 Philip Fisher, *Hard Facts: Setting and Form in the American Novel* (New York: Oxford University Press, 1987), 157–63, on *Sister Carrie.* In *Rethinking Class: Literary Studies and Social Formations,* ed. Wai Chee Dimock and Michael T. Gilmore (New York: Columbia University Press, 1994), Dimock's essay on "Class, Gender, and a History of Metonymy" argues for making class less metonymic by shifting attention from identity to discrepancies and "a series of momentary postures" (94). Also in *Rethinking Class,* Anne Janowitz's essay on English chartism argues that unlike race and gender, class has no "biological features." So it has meaning only as a category of social relationship, not of group taxonomy (239–40). Stuart Blumin notes that the middle class was "most likely to express awareness of its common values and beliefs as a denial of the significance of class"; see his "The Hypothesis of Middle-Class Formation in Nineteenth-Century America: A Critique and Some Proposals," *American Historical Review* 90 (April 1985): 309.

39 Edith Wharton, *The Custom of the Country* (New York: Collier Books, 1987, 1st pub. 1913), 182–84 (chap. 15).

40 Wharton, *Custom of the Country,* 181–82, 193–95.

41 William Dean Howells, "The Man of Letters as a Man of Business" (1893), qtd. by Amy Kaplan, *The Social Construction of American Realism* (Chicago: University of Chicago Press, 1988), 43.

42 John Locke, *Essay Concerning Human Understanding,* ed. and abridged by Maurice Cranston (New York: Collier Books, 1965, 1st pub. 1689), 144 (bk. 2, chap. 20); Albert O. Hirschman, *The Passions and the Interests: Political Arguments for Capitalism before Its Triumph* (Princeton: Princeton University Press, 1977), esp. 129–34.

43 Benjamin Franklin, "Information for Those Who Would Remove to America," rpt. in *The Norton Anthology of American Literature,* 5th ed., vol. 1, ed. Nina Baym et al. (New York: W. W. Norton, 1998, 1st pub. 1784), 511.

44 In *An Inquiry into the Nature and Causes of The Wealth of Nations,* ed. Edwin Cannan (New York: Modern Library, 1937, 1st pub. 1776), Adam Smith writes that "Labour, therefore, is the real measure of the exchangeable value of all commodities. The real price of every thing . . . is the toil and trouble of acquiring it" (30). Money's value derives from necessity: "The value of money is in proportion to the quantity of the *necessaries* of life which it will purchase" (836). Ultimately such exchange value equates useful "necessaries of life" with their equivalent in "toil and trouble." For Karl Marx, money represents exchange value alienated from the worker's labor: "The life he has given to the object confronts him as hostile and alien" (*Writings of the Young Marx on Philosophy and Society,* trans. and ed. by Lloyd D. Easton and Kurt H. Guddat [Garden City, N.Y.: Anchor Books, 1967], 290, also 265–76, 289–300). Here an implied metaphor of paternity justifies

Marx's presumption that a man's labor gives "life" to what he produces. In *Capital: A Critique of Political Economy,* 3d ed., ed. Frederick Engels, trans. Samuel Moore and Edward Aveling (New York: Modern Library, 1906, 1st pub. 1867), Marx again affirms that labor or production, not a commodity's exchangeability or use-value, determines true value (e.g., 46, 70, 83) until capitalism's emphasis on surplus value and profit cheapens the commodity's production value and therefore "the labourer himself" (351). "All surplus-value . . . is in substance the materialisation of unpaid labor" (585). Paternity, I'm suggesting, is the covert value legitimating the overt value of men's productive labor, for both Smith and Marx.

45 Richard Ohmann's *Selling Culture: Magazines, Markets, and Class at the Turn of the Century* (London: Verso, 1996), a genially informative neo-Marxist study of the rise of advertising and national mass culture from 1855 to 1910, declares that "the main engines of history are forces of production and the class conflict that develops with them" (76). Monopoly or marketing capitalism, he argues—the terms converge—separated women from their precorporate roles in semiautonomous productive units and (de)valued women primarily as consumers (74–76), while the middle-class home also shifted from a site of production to "a site of consumption and leisure" (91). Robert Seguin's *Around Quitting Time: Work and Middle-Class Fantasy in American Fiction* (Durham, N.C.: Duke University Press, 2001) also emphasizes class-linked modes of labor and production.

46 On Smith's views about patriarchy and scarcity, see Stewart Justman, *The Autonomous Male of Adam Smith* (Norman: University of Oklahoma Press, 1993), esp. 6–11, also 147–50, and 4–8 on stoicism as a manly replacement for patriarchy threatened by a feminized consumer society. Michael Perelman's *The Invention of Capitalism: Classical Political Economy and the Secret History of Primitive Accumulation* (Durham, N.C.: Duke University Press, 2000) a sophisticated neo-Marxist study, highlights Smith's hostility to the small producers that Perelman reveres (184, also 171–254).

47 Rotundo, in chap. 8 of *American Manhood,* emphasizes the growing congruence between work and male identity in the nineteenth century, unlike eighteenth-century merchants who gave considerable time to public and religious affairs as well as to their families (167–68).

48 George E. McNeill, *The Labor Movement* (1886), 484; qtd. by Michael Denning, *Mechanic Accents: Dime Novels and Working-Class Culture in America* (London: Verso, 1987), 172.

49 Martha Banta, *Taylored Lives: Narrative Productions in the Age of Taylor, Veblen, and Ford* (Chicago: University of Chicago Press, 1993); Mark Seltzer, *Bodies and Machines* (New York: Routledge, 1992); also Cecelia Tichi, *Shifting Gears: Technology, Literature, Culture in Modernist America* (Chapel Hill: University of North Carolina Press, 1987).

50 J. G. A. Pocock, *Virtue, Commerce, and History: Essays on Political Thought and History, Chiefly in the Eighteenth Century* (Cambridge: Cambridge University Press, 1985), 67–70, quotation 70.

51 Booker T. Washington, *Up from Slavery,* 146. See Calder, *Financing the American Dream.* Until the twentieth century, installment credit carried a "stigma" of femaleness, or unmanly dependence, while savings seemed manly. Then automobiles made credit more acceptable to men (180–86, 231–32, 258). Today the automobile is sparking a similar transformation in China.

52 Frank, *Life with Father,* 16. See also Ralph LaRossa, *The Modernization of Fatherhood: A Social and Political History* (Chicago: University of Chicago Press, 1997), who argues that in the nineteenth century men moved to the "periphery" of the home (29), but by the 1920s, the relatively predictable security of corporate salaries "gave many fa-

thers the freedom to focus more attention on their families" (35). LaRossa highlights the variety of U.S. fathering styles within, under, and against prescriptions for patriarchal manliness. Robert L. Griswold's *Fatherhood in America: A History* (New York: Basic-Books, 1993) notes that by 1900 "fatherly authority declined" in law as well (30). While chronicling the shift from the preindustrial patriarchal family to "breadwinners" and "providers" (3, 7), he argues that "patriarchal power increasingly came to lodge in the public rather than the private domain" (66, also 89–90).

53 Abraham Cahan, *The Rise of David Levinsky,* ed. Jules Chametzky (New York: Penguin, 1993, 1st pub. 1917), 2.

54 Warren I. Susman, "'Personality' and the Making of Twentieth-Century Culture," *New Directions in American Intellectual History,* ed. John Higham and Paul L. Conkin (Baltimore: Johns Hopkins University Press, 1979), 212–26.

55 Marcia Jacobson, *Being a Boy Again: Autobiography and the American Boy Book* (Tuscaloosa: University of Alabama Press, 1994), 112, 103 (Garland), 5, 16. See my essay review of books about childhood, "Tomboys, Bad Boys, and Horatio Alger: When Fatherhood Became a Problem," *American Literary History* 10 (Spring 1998): 219–36.

56 See Gail Bederman, *Manliness and Civilization: A Cultural History of Gender and Race in the United States, 1880–1917* (Chicago: University of Chicago Press, 1995); Christophe den Tandt, "Amazons and Androgynes: Overcivilization and the Redefinition of Gender Roles at the Turn of the Century," *American Literary History* 8 (Winter 1996): 639–64; Steven M. Gelber, "Do-It-Yourself: Constructing, Repairing and Maintaining Domestic Masculinity," *American Quarterly* 49 (March 1997): 66–112; Amy Kaplan, "Romancing the Empire: The Embodiment of American Masculinity in the Popular Historical Novel of the 1890s," *American Literary History* 2 (1990): 659–90.

57 Zunz, *Making America Corporate,* 60. In *The Fictional Republic: Horatio Alger and American Political Discourse* (New York: Oxford University Press, 1994), Carol Nackenoff notes that concerns with "power, agency, and manliness" arose as many people "lost the capacity to control their lives and work" (132). As one result, "Character formation was the nineteenth century version of a self-defense course" (45). On precapitalist ideals of manhood, see David D. Gilmore, *Manhood in the Making: Cultural Concepts of Masculinity* (New Haven: Yale University Press, 1990), 47, 217–24.

58 In *Nobody's Story: The Vanishing Acts of Women Writers in the Marketplace, 1670–1820* (Berkeley: University of California Press, 1994), Catherine Gallagher explores how the "nothing" at the center of marketplace exchange dynamics gave eighteenth-century English women writers access to the public sphere.

59 James Livingston, *Pragmatism and the Political Economy of Cultural Revolution, 1850–1940* (Chapel Hill: University of North Carolina Press, 1994), 62–83, quotation 71, also 75.

60 Livingston, *Pragmatism,* 77, 112, also 78: "the priority of the principle of class was determined by the development of capitalism." Sharon O'Dair's "Beyond Necessity: The Consumption of Class, the Production of Status, and the Persistence of Inequality," *New Literary History* 31 (Spring 2000): 337–54, critiques Livingston, emphasizing the fragmentation of status niches and diverse modes of inequality (345–47). Livingston also argues that pragmatism was a hopeful "postrepublican" response (273) to a society in which "men of property were becoming a minority" (276). He intimates the possibility of a socialist future for what he calls the new social self (275), as Alan Trachtenberg's preface emphasizes (xii). I think that prospect limits the possibilities for social and private subjectivity.

61 For Alan Greenspan's December 1999 speech, see Richard W. Stevenson, "Engineering the Nation's Longest Expansion: Greenspan and the Federal Reserve Re-examine

Some of the Basic Economic Assumptions About Jobs and Inflation," *New York Times,* 20 December 1999, C3.

62 Henry James, "Preface," *The Portrait of a Lady,* New York edition, ed. Robert D. Bamberg (New York: W. W. Norton, 1975, 1st pub. 1908), 3–15, quotations 7–9. In "Gender and Value in *The American,*" *New Essays on The American,* ed. Martha Banta (Cambridge: Cambridge University Press, 1987), 99–129, Carolyn Porter argues that James establishes a paternalistic, even patriarchal narrative tone in many of his novels to protect and control the moral value of consciousness against the pressures of exchange value.

63 For a lively account, see James B. Twitchell, *Living It Up: America's Love Affair with Luxury* (New York: Columbia University Press, 2002).

Chapter 2. Daddy's Girls and Upwardly Mobile Women

1 Mary Martin sang "My Heart Belongs to Daddy" in the show "Leave It to Me," and it made her a star, though Sophie Tucker had to explain the double entendres. See William McBrien, *Cole Porter: A Biography* (New York: Alfred A. Knopf, 1998), 220–21.

2 See Valerie Walkerdine, *Daddy's Girl: Young Girls and Popular Culture* (Cambridge, Mass.: Harvard University Press, 1997), for the impact of Shirley Temple, Little Orphan Annie, and other daddy's girl figures on working-class girls in contemporary England.

3 In "From Griffith's Girls to *Daddy's Girl:* The Masks of Innocence in *Tender Is the Night,*" *Twentieth Century Literature* 26 (Summer 1980): 189–221, Ruth Prigozy sketches the history of various daddy's girls scandals and cultural figures in the 1920s. She traces the motif back to D. W. Griffith's films of child-women.

4 On doctors' opposition to women riding safety bicycles in the early 1890s, see Ellen Gruber Garvey, *The Adman in the Parlor: Magazines and the Gendering of Consumer Culture, 1880s to 1910s* (New York: Oxford University Press, 1996), 112–17. Garvey identifies "the real threat . . . women on the loose, mobile and independent" (7–8).

5 G. Stanley Hall, *Adolescence,* 2 vols. (New York: D. Appleton, 1904), vol. 2, 391–92, qtd. by Joan Acocella, *Willa Cather and the Politics of Criticism* (Lincoln: University of Nebraska Press, 2000), 95 n. 3.

6 Claudia Nelson makes a related argument that stories of working-class incest in Victorian magazines served as cautionary tales for middle-class Englishmen. See *Invisible Men: Fatherhood in Victorian Periodicals, 1830–1910* (Athens: University of Georgia Press, 1995), 200, also 180.

7 Robert Hughes, "American Visions," *Time Special Issue,* May 1997, 22. See also Frances K. Pohl's *Framing America: A Social History of American Art* (New York: Thames and Hudson, 2002), 408: "Wood conceived of the couple as father and spinster daughter."

8 George Bernard Shaw's *Pygmalion* was first performed in Vienna in 1913, then in London in 1916. On why the *Pamela* plot became nonnarratable in nineteenth-century England, see Elizabeth Langland, *Nobody's Angels: Middle-Class Women and Domestic Ideology in Victorian Culture* (Ithaca, N.Y.: Cornell University Press, 1995).

9 Edmund Spenser, *The Faerie Queene,* Book 7, "Two Cantos of Mutabilitie," vi, 141, 138, 143–44. The unfinished cantos were published in 1609, ten years after Spenser's death.

10 Though "author" as published writer rather than cause doesn't appear in dictionaries until considerably later, Dante also plays with the possibility in his *Inferno,* 1: 85, when he first addresses Virgil.

11 See, for instance, Ann Louise Kibbie, "Monstrous Generation: The Birth of Capital in Defoe's *Moll Flanders* and *Roxana*," *PMLA* 110 (October 1995): 1023–34; also Terry Mulcaire, "Public Credit; or, The Feminization of Virtue in the Marketplace," *PMLA* 114 (October 1999): 1029–42. On capitalism and desire, see Regenia Gagnier, *The Insatiability of Human Wants: Economics and Aesthetics in Market Society* (Chicago: University of Chicago Press, 2000) and Walter Benn Michaels, *The Gold Standard and the Logic of Naturalism: American Literature at the Turn of the Century* (Berkeley: University of California Press, 1987). On creative destruction, a phrase coined by Joseph Schumpeter, see Philip Fisher, *Still the New World: American Literature in a Culture of Creative Destruction* (Cambridge, Mass.: Harvard University Press, 1999).

12 On the shifting roles of daughters in Western culture, see Linda E. Boose, "The Father's House and the Daughter in It: The Structures of Western Culture's Daughter-Father Relationship," *Daughters and Fathers,* ed. Linda E. Boose and Betty S. Flowers (Baltimore: Johns Hopkins University Press, 1989), 19–74; also Ramón Gutiérrez, *When Jesus Came, the Corn Mothers Went Away: Marriage, Sexuality, and Power in New Mexico, 1500–1846* (Stanford: Stanford University Press, 1991), 220–24, on the daughter as signifier of family honor or shame.

13 See, for instance, Amartya Kumar Sen, *On Economic Inequality* (Oxford: Clarendon Press, 1997) and *Development as Freedom* (New York: Alfred A. Knopf, 1999).

14 The ellipses are Wharton's. The fragment was written in 1919 but not published until R. W. B. Lewis included it as an appendix to *Edith Wharton: A Biography* (New York: Harper and Row, 1975). It was discovered by Cynthia Griffin Wolff, who also reprinted it in *A Feast of Words: The Triumph of Edith Wharton* (New York: Oxford University Press, 1977), 303–5; see also 299–308, comparing it to *Summer,* and 407–15 on dating it. For Lily's perception of Rosedale's "paternal" yet "predatory" presence, see *The House of Mirth* (New York: Signet, 1964, 1st pub. 1905), 258–59 (Bk. 2, chap. 6). For insightful discussions of Wharton, I'm indebted to a 1998 University of Florida honors thesis by Laurie Sizemore Dennison, "Dependence vs. Independence: The 'Daddy's Girl' Trope in Wharton's Novels." On "Beatrice Palmato," see Gloria C. Erlich, *The Sexual Education of Edith Wharton* (Berkeley: University of California Press, 1992), 36–39, who notes the passage's implication of their previous and frequent "mutual masturbation" (38).

15 John Updike, "Excellent Humbug," *New Yorker* 70 (5 September 1994): 105. Updike's review of Thomas Mallon's *Henry and Clara* parenthetically calls incest "the Romantics' ultimate daydream[.]"

16 Philip Barry, *The Philadelphia Story* (New York: Samuel French, 1942, 1st presented in 1939), 63–64 (philandering), 119–20 (love, goddess). George Cukor's movie (1940) keeps this speech.

17 T. Walter Herbert, *Sexual Violence and American Manhood* (Cambridge, Mass.: Harvard University Press, 2002), 199. Herbert derives the concept of compensatory pornographic enchantment from his observation of a therapy group for convicted pederasts.

18 Margaret Atwood, *Bodily Harm* (New York: Anchor Books, 1998, 1st pub. 1982), 145.

19 In *Child-Loving: The Erotic Child and Victorian Culture* (New York: Routledge, 1992), James R. Kincaid controversially argues that pedophilia is fine if it stays at the level of "an erotics of temptation and flirtation," since it brings out the adult's sense of play, while it also keeps the world eroticized. It "allows the adult to be more the child than the child is" (197, 196).

20 *Mark Twain's Aquarium: The Samuel Clemens Angelfish Correspondence 1905–1910,* ed. John Cooley (Athens: University of Georgia Press, 1991), quotations 23 (blots),

283. Twain "'collected'" a dozen young girls from elite families he met on his travels from 1905 to his death in 1910. Cooley notes that "there is no evidence to suggest real impropriety or scandal" (283), though one visit to a young girl's family in Bermuda may have lacked "restraint and discretion[,]" because Twain was upset that the "rapidly maturing Helen Allen" already had a boyfriend (281–82).

One of Twain's other private writings implies that he was in sexual decline after the age of 50. See *Letters from the Earth,* ed. Bernard DeVoto (New York: Harper and Row, 1962), letter 8, 37–42, esp. 40, where Satan says of the human male: "After fifty his performance is of poor quality, the intervals between are wide, and its satisfactions of no great value to either party; . . . his candle . . . can no longer stand, and is mournfully laid to rest in the hope of a blessed resurrection which is never to come." The puns on "laid" and "come" nicely frame "resurrection." See also Guy Cardwell, *The Man Who Was Mark Twain: Images and Ideologies* (New Haven: Yale University Press, 1991), 122–60, on Twain's complex sexual ambivalences.

21 Louisa May Alcott, *Little Women* (New York: Signet, 1983, 1st part pub. 1868, 2nd part pub. 1869), 75. Lynda Zwinger's *Daughters, Fathers, and the Novel: The Sentimental Romance of Heterosexuality* (Madison: University of Wisconsin Press, 1991) argues that in *Little Women,* Marmee trains Jo to be a daddy's girl (58), since to be a "little woman" is to do what mother does, curb her anger to please father or husband. As I argue in chapter 4, Jo strikes me as a blend of mama's girl and daddy's boy.

22 G. M. Goshgarian, *To Kiss the Chastening Rod: Domestic Fiction and Sexual Ideology in the American Renaissance* (Ithaca, N.Y.: Cornell University Press, 1992). For an astute analysis of Southern paternalism triumphant in *The Bostonians,* see Aaron Shaheen's "Henry James's Southern Mode of Imagination: Men, Women, and the Image of the South in *The Bostonians,*" *Henry James Review,* forthcoming.

23 Vladimir Nabokov, *Lolita* (New York: Penguin, 1995, 1st pub. 1955), 30.

24 On Phoebe Gloeckner, see Peggy Orenstein, "A Graphic Life," *New York Times Magazine,* 5 August 2001, 26–29. Cf. Elizabeth Freeman, "Honeymoon with a Stranger: Pedophiliac Picaresques from Poe to Nabokov," *American Literature* 70 (December 1998), 863–97. Freeman takes the stories more blithely: "the little girl as tour guide" (866) through a national landscape.

25 Irving Bacheller, *Keeping Up With Lizzie* (New York: Grosset and Dunlap, 1911). Citations included in text. Lendol Calder's *Financing the American Dream: A Cultural History of Consumer Credit* (Princeton: Princeton University Press, 1999), 213–17, analyzes the novel in relation to changing norms for credit.

26 Gene Stratton-Porter, *Her Father's Daughter* (New York: Grosset and Dunlap, 1921). Citations included in text.

27 Booth Tarkington, *Alice Adams* (New York: Grosset and Dunlap, 1921). Citations included in text.

28 Zwinger, *Daughters, Fathers, and the Novel;* also Margit Stange, *Personal Property: Wives, White Slaves, and the Market in Women* (Baltimore: Johns Hopkins University Press, 1998). Stange's chapter on "Papa's Girl" (104–27) argues that narratives of white slavery reinforced the seeming necessity for patriarchal authority, and, more problematically, that Jane Addams's "vision of . . . renovated patriarchal possessiveness" (115) "reflects the white slave house in reverse" (114). Dale Bauer's *Feminist Dialogics: A Theory of Failed Community* (Albany: State University of New York Press, 1988) turns the argument for patriarchal enforcements toward more open-ended ambivalence.

29 Henry James, Jr., *The American,* ed. William Spengemann (New York: Penguin, 1986, 1st pub. 1876–77 in *Atlantic Monthly;* pub. as book by Macmillan, 1879), 199. Carolyn Porter's "Gender and Value in *The American*" discusses James's tensions between

transcendent value and capitalist dynamics, with the daughter as the prime figure for value (126). See also Martha Banta, *Imaging American Women: Idea and Ideals in Cultural History* (New York: Columbia University Press, 1987), 22, and Stephanie A. Smith, *Conceived by Liberty: Maternal Figures and Nineteenth-Century American Literature* (Ithaca, N.Y.: Cornell University Press, 1994), 204.

30 Edith Wharton, *The Custom of the Country* (New York: Macmillan Publishing Company, 1987, 1st pub. 1913), 529. See also Wai-Chee Dimock, "Debasing Exchange: Edith Wharton's *The House of Mirth,*" *PMLA* 100 (October 1985): 54–63.

31 Elaine Hadley, *Melodramatic Tactics: Theatricalized Dissent in the English Marketplace, 1800–1885* (Stanford: Stanford University Press, 1995), e.g., 5, 15, 44, 89 (hierarchies, deference); 101, 111, 173 (patriarchy model); 136 (protest). Typically, villains enacted the evil self-interests and commodifications inherent in capitalist modernization (225).

32 I'm indebted here to Heather S. Nathan's paper at the 2001 American Literature Association Conference, "Too Good to be True: The Working Class Heroine and Popular Melodrama."

33 See William Veeder's fine discussion of names in *Henry James: The Lessons of the Master: Popular Fiction and Personal Style in the Nineteenth Century* (Chicago: University of Chicago Press, 1975), esp. 120–23. "Osmond" is the villain in Monk Lewis's *The Castle Spectre,* and Gilbert is Osmond's knave. The name also suggests a bloody British melodrama, *Osmond, the Great Turk,* as well as the worldliness implied in the French "monde." "Gilbert" also evokes artists such as Gilbert Stuart, and a painter named Gilbert in Susan Warner's *The Wide, Wide World.* "Pansy" was a popular children's magazine, and "Isabel" suggests various beset heroines, from Shakespeare's Isabella in *Measure for Measure* through Isabella in Horace Walpole's *The Castle of Otronto: A Gothic Story* (1764).

34 Henry James, *The Portrait of a Lady* (New York: Signet Classic, 1963; 1881 edition), 288 (convention), 282–83 (impress), 238 (knees). Tellingly, Ralph Touchett calls Osmond "'a sterile dilettante'" (319). On the "incestual economy" in the Osmond-Pansy and Osmond-Isabel relationships, see Smith, *Conceived by Liberty,* 189–210, esp. 203–7 on the "possessive paternalism" that links Osmond to Ralph and also to James.

35 James, *Portrait of a Lady,* 396, 398.

36 Ibid., 444.

37 Jack London's letter of 24 February 1914 is reprinted as an appendix to Joan London's baffled, yearning memoir, *Jack London and His Daughters,* intro. Bart Abbott (Berkeley: Heyday Books, 1990), 181–84, quotations 182–83. London ends this letter by saying that though "I do not like ruined colts[,]" when she needs money he'll send it, "if I have it at the time" (184). In *Jack London's Women* (Amherst: University of Massachusetts Press, 2001), Clarice Stasz recounts the stages of their relationship (94–96, 117–19, 150–56, 185–87 on that letter, 197–99, and 205–7 on her father's final visit and their final argument. At least two of London's novels portray young comrade-women who have been raised by their equally strong-willed businessmen fathers: *A Daughter of the Snows* (1902) and *Adventure* (1911). Both novels champion white racial superiority. Joan Lackland, the heroine of *Adventure,* was named in his daughter's honor (Stasz 205). I'm indebted to Jonathan Auerbach for pointing me to these novels and Stasz's study.

38 For an insightful discussion of this Cinderella pilgrimage, see Sandra M. Gilbert, "Plain Jane's Progress," in Charlotte Bronte's *Jane Eyre,* ed. Beth Newman (Boston: Bedford Books, 1996), 475–501.

39 Harriet Beecher Stowe, *Uncle Tom's Cabin or, Life Among the Lowly* (New York: Harper and Row, 1965, 1st pub. 1852). Citations included in text.

40 Kimberly G. Hébert suggests that Shirley Temple combines Topsy and Eva as the "'littlest minstrel'"; see her "Acting the Nigger: Topsy, Shirley Temple, and Toni Morrison's Pecola," *Approaches to Teaching Stowe's Uncle Tom's Cabin,* ed. Elizabeth Ammons and Susan Belasco (New York: MLA, 2000), 184–98, quotation 184, also 190.

41 Lydia Maria Child, *A Romance of the Republic,* ed. Dana D. Nelson (Lexington, Ky.: University Press of Kentucky, 1997, 1st pub. 1867), 6. Nelson's introduction emphasizes the father's failure (x).

42 Sylvia Plath, *Ariel* (New York: Harper and Row, 1966), 50.

43 Henry Wadsworth Longfellow, *Selected Poems,* ed. Lawrence Buell (New York: Penguin, 1988), 370–71. For the Bishop of Bingen explanation, I'm indebted to a 1997 talk by Eve Hershberger comparing "The Children's Hour" to James's *The Turn of the Screw.*

44 Newton Arvin, *Longfellow: His Life and Work* (Boston: Little, Brown, 1963), 139; Eve Hershberger, 1997 talk.

45 As Joanne J. Meyerowitz argues in *Women Adrift: Independent Wage Earners in Chicago, 1880–1930* (Chicago: University of Chicago Press, 1988), young working-class women earning wages "helped set patterns that other women later followed" (xxiii).

46 James, *Portrait of a Lady,* 53. "Too much imagination[,]" Mr. Touchett says, as if critiquing Isabel as well; "she couldn't have listened very attentively."

47 Edith Wharton, *Summer* (New York: Signet, 1993, 1st pub. 1917), 149. Dr. Merkle's working-class associations emerge in her dialect and her connections. "It ain't in my line," Dr. Merkle says when she bargains for the brooch. Later, bargaining again, she tells Charity she "heard all about the wedding from the minister's chore-man" (191).

48 William Dean Howells, *The Rise of Silas Lapham* (New York: Signet Classic, 1980, 1st pub. 1885). Citations included in text. See also 83, 154.

49 Wai-chee Dimock takes Pen's suffering more seriously, as an entry to analyzing capitalist limitations of moral liability for pain. See "The Economy of Pain: Capitalism, Humanitarianism, and the Realistic Novel," *New Essays on The Rise of Silas Lapham,* ed. Donald Pease (Cambridge: Cambridge University Press, 1991), 67–90.

50 Amy Kaplan, *The Social Construction of American Realism* (Chicago: University of Chicago Press, 1988), 41, referring to the opening interview. Kaplan also suggests that the realistic writer "becomes the necessary mediator" between readers and classes that "have become inaccessible to one another" (42, 41).

51 See John W. Crowley, *The Black Heart's Truth: The Early Career of W. D. Howells* (Chapel Hill: University of North Carolina Press, 1985).

52 Nathaniel Hawthorne, *The Marble Faun: or, the Romance of Monte Beni,* intro. Richard H. Brodhead (New York: Penguin Books, 1990, 1st pub. 1860). Citations included in text.

53 Brodhead's note (473) states that Beatrice Cenci probably lied about the incest, Guido Reni didn't paint the portrait, and Beatrice is probably not its subject.

54 This Arcadian scene evokes Poussin's painting, "Et in Arcadia Ego," with a skull in the midst of a pastoral paradise.

55 On Hawthorne's conflicts about Una's adolescent breakdown as the context for beginning *The Marble Faun,* see T. Walter Herbert, *Dearest Beloved: The Hawthornes and the Making of the Middle-Class Family* (Berkeley: University of California Press, 1993), 218–24, 234–83, also 152–53. Brodhead emphasizes the novel's functions as a tourist manual, and Nancy Glazener shows how emerging class stratifications in the United States affect Hawthorne's uses of allegory and his portraits of artists. See Brodhead, intro. to Penguin ed., and Glazener, *Reading for Realism: The History of a U.S. Literary Institution, 1850–1910* (Durham, N.C.: Duke University Press, 1997), 52–60, 64–66, 71–92. See also several essays in *Roman Holidays: American Writers and Artists in Nineteenth-*

century Italy, ed. Robert K. Martin and Leland S. Person (Iowa City, Iowa: University of Iowa Press, 2002). Richard Millington's "Where Is Hawthorne's Rome?: *The Marble Faun* and the Cultural Space of Middle-Class Leisure" (9–27) says the novel interrogates emerging American patterns of middle-class leisure (9–14). Other essays highlight sexual anxieties in the novel. I'm emphasizing Rome as a projection of Hawthorne's anxieties about aging.

Chapter 3. Daddy's Girls as Upwardly Mobile Women

1 Introduction by Marvin Felheim to Mark Twain and Charles Dudley Warner's *The Gilded Age: A Tale Of Today* (New York: Meridian Classic, 1985, 1st pub. 1873), vii. Further citations included in text.

2 Twain wrote the first eleven chapters; ibid., viii. Mr. Hawkins is called "Si" throughout the text, except for one mention of "Silas" (272).

3 For the associations to flag and disease, I'm indebted to Lynne Pulliam's unpublished essay, "Corporate Subjectivity in *The Gilded Age.*"

4 Twain is careless about Laura's age. If Laura were three (56–57) instead of five (49), she might not know she has been adopted.

5 "That was all" returns at her death, as a final attempt to reduce Laura to a label: "That was all. Merely heart disease" (421). I'm indebted here to Jenni Lieberman.

6 On Warner's authorship of the Selby sections, see Bryant Morley French, *Mark Twain and* The Gilded Age (Dallas: Southern Methodist University Press, 1965), 62–63. Twain wrote most of the chapters about Laura's roles in Washington and her end. In "Four Ways to Inscribe a Mackerel: Mark Twain and Laura Hawkins," *Studies in the Novel* 21 (Summer 1989): 138–53, Susan K. Harris analyzes Laura's "troubling characterization" (152) "as a figure of fallen innocence, as a victim of male power fantasies, as an American culture hero, and as a Mark Twain alter-ego" (138), until her story ends in a "reactionary mode" (140). Twain prevents Laura's "trickster" possibilities (151).

7 Ellen J. Goldner's thoughtful and historically rich article, "Tangled Webs: Lies, Capitalist Expansion, and the Dissolution of the Subject in *The Gilded Age,*" *Arizona Quarterly* 49 (August 1993): 55–92, focuses on Col. Sellers. She sees Laura's allegorical aspects more simply: Laura's "melodrama" presents "in burlesque form the death of the Old South" (69). She presumes, wrongly I think, that Laura's real father is a Southern gentleman (71). Goldner astutely associates Philip's last name of "Sterling" with the gold standard crisis (74), and links Col. Sellers to the transformation of value from use to future-oriented exchanges (64, 86–88).

8 Carol F. Karlsen, *The Devil in the Shape of a Woman: Witchcraft in Colonial New England* (New York: Vintage Books, 1987), 180, 247 (her emphasis).

9 William Congreve, *The Way of the World* (1700), IV, i.

10 Goldner, "Tangled Webs," 64, 86–88, on the dissolution of the subject as privileged observer.

11 María Amparo Ruiz de Burton, *Who Would Have Thought It?,* ed. Rosaura Sánchez and Beatrice Pita (Houston: Arte Público Press, 1995, 1st pub. anon., 1872), 28, 25.

12 Louisa May Alcott, *Work: A Story of Experience,* ed. Joy S. Kasson (New York: Penguin, 1994, 1st pub. 1873, serialized 1872). Further citations included in text.

13 I'm indebted here to Lynne Pulliam's unpublished essay, "Corporate Subjectivity in *The Gilded Age.*"

14 Theodore Dreiser, *Sister Carrie* (New York: Signet Classic, 1961, 1st pub. 1900). Citations included in the text. I prefer this edition to the less revised Pennsylvania edition.

For an opposing interpretation, see Robert Seguin's *Around Quitting Time: Work and Middle-Class Fantasy in American Fiction* (Durham, N.C.: Duke University Press, 2001), 19–55, which emphasizes Carrie's evasion of work; also, the motion of her hands as she rocks implies the sweatshop (34, also 40).

15 Walter Benn Michaels, *The Gold Standard and the Logic of Naturalism: American Literature at the Turn of the Century* (Berkeley: University of California Press, 1987), 35–52, contrasts *Sister Carrie* with *The Rise of Silas Lapham*. For Howells, character provides an autonomy that "resists fluctuation[,]" whereas Dreiser identifies character with speculative desire (44–45).

16 In *The Problem of American Realism: Studies in the Cultural History of a Literary Idea* (Chicago: University of Chicago Press, 1993), 155–65, Michael Davitt Bell suggests that Dreiser's often embarrassing tone of condescending sentimentalism is really a covert identification with his characters (159). Where Bell argues that Dreiser's "complex intermingling of normally antithetical perspectives" works to "collapse" narrative distance and class distinctions (162, 160), I argue that the oscillation between patronizing surveillance and sympathetic immediacy preserves the narrator's paternalistic authority.

17 "Adrift" has social resonance, particularly for young working-class women seeking urban jobs. See Joanne J. Meyerowitz, *Women Adrift: Independent Wage Earners in Chicago, 1880–1930* (Chicago: University of Chicago Press, 1988). "Carrie's unique adventures . . . sidestepped the hardships of living apart from family; most women adrift did not" (19–20, also 1).

18 The two most influential and exciting studies of Carrie's desire in relation to capitalist dynamics remain Michaels' *Gold Standard*, 31–35, 41–58, and Philip Fisher's *Hard Facts: Setting and Form in the American Novel* (New York: Oxford University Press, 1987), 155–78. Fisher, who is especially good on Carrie's "anticipatory self"(159), notes that even names become "frozen verbs" (161). Michaels emphasizes the congruence between Carrie's unsatisfiable desire and the capitalist "economy of powerful excess" (52). In *The Social Construction of American Realism* (Chicago: University of Chicago Press, 1988), 140–60, Amy Kaplan critiques Fisher and Michaels for overlooking contradictions and power relations that make Carrie's desire not only unsatisfiable but also "unreal" (151).

19 For Michaels, Hurstwood's lack of power shows his "inability to want badly enough. . . . Old age is a failure not of ability but of desire" (*Gold Standard*, 43–44). Old age before 40! Cf. Fisher, *Hard Facts*, 174, on "aging males whose stored energy in the form of money now disguises the actual exhaustion of their spirits." But aging isn't the only issue. In *Social Construction*, 147–48, Kaplan argues that like Carrie, Hurstwood plays dependent roles. At work, performing the role of a host who doesn't seem to be working, he is a manager with "no financial control[,]" not even allowed to "handle the money in the cash register." To his family, his "impotence" is not sexual but social, and Hurstwood's attraction to Carrie is a "compensation for his lack of authority at home."

20 In *Hard Facts*, Fisher suggests that Dreiser's "refusal to contrast acting with sincerity" makes him "the first novelist to base his entire sense of the self on the dramatic possibilities inherent in a dynamic society" (167). Hurstwood's inability to fuse desire with role-playing makes him an unusable waste product, suitable for recycling in Potter's Field, where bodies are replaced every 25 years. On maximizing capital flow through wasting nothing, especially in Chicago's meat-packing industry, see William Cronon's *Nature's Metropolis: Chicago and the Great West* (New York: W. W. Norton, 1991), e.g., 269, 378.

21 Irving Babbitt, *Literature and the American College: Essays in Defense of the Humanities* (Boston: Houghton Mifflin, 1908), 118–19.

22 In *Imaging American Women: Idea and Ideals in Cultural History* (New York: Columbia University Press, 1987), Martha Banta rightly observes that Carrie on stage is always the first role she plays, "forever Laura, the thwarted, put-upon heroine," though Banta reduces that role to "melodrama" (669–71). From the beginning, Carrie's daring independence adds to her appeal.

23 The Pennsylvania edition of *Sister Carrie* includes more sexually charged passages that Dreiser deleted before the novel was first published. Some argue that the pruning reflects censorship. To me the restorations make Carrie a more traditional character.

24 Edith Wharton, *The Custom of the Country* (New York: Collier Books—Macmillan, 1987, 1st pub. 1913), 39. Her mother calls her "Undie" too (41). Further citations included in the text. Mr. Spragg stands up to his daughter only once, when he orders her to return Peter Van Degen's gift of a pearl necklace "in a voice she did not know" (331). After momentarily submitting, she gets around his order by selling the necklace.

25 I'm indebted to Sophie Croisy for finding this allusion's source in the opening essay of *The Complete Essays of Montaigne*, vol. 1, trans. Donald M. Frame (Garden City, N.Y.: Anchor Books, 1960, 1st pub. 1578–80), 3: "Truly man is a marvelously vain, diverse, and undulating object." Undine's hair-waver and water-sprite aspects are both soulless.

26 As Howard Horwitz says in *By the Law of Nature: Form and Value in Nineteenth-Century America* (New York: Oxford University Press, 1991), Alexandra is "unique among capitalists in American literature" during this period. She's a woman who accumulates property, succeeds in business without bad behavior or catastrophe, and becomes "an accomplished land speculator" while loving the land (220–21).

27 Willa Cather, *O Pioneers!* (New York: Signet Classic, 1989, 1st pub. 1913), 18. Citations included in the text.

28 Marilee Lindemann's *Willa Cather: Queering America* (New York: Columbia University Press, 1999), 36–46, doesn't focus on this scene. She highlights Ivar's bare feet as part of his "'queer'" behavior, and the various responses to Emil's and Marie's bodies in their death "tableau" (41–43). Jonathan Goldberg's *Willa Cather and Others* (Durham, N.C.: Duke University Press, 2001) critiques Lindemann for reducing the novel's unstable cross-gendering to lesbian desire (14–22). For him, Alexandra becomes a "gleaming" unqueer entrepreneur, transcending liberal individualism's disembodied subjectivity (15).

29 Alexandra's vision also evokes Jesus; cf. Revelations 1:13–15.

30 After Alexandra's brothers try to prevent her from marrying Carl, they agree that their only mistake was to say she was forty years old. Yet Lou muses that "Alexandra ain't much like other women-folks. . . . Maybe she'd as soon be forty as not!" (129).

31 Jessica Benjamin, *The Bonds of Love: Psychoanalysis, Feminism, and the Problem of Domination* (New York: Pantheon Books, 1988).

32 Joan Acocella's "Cather and the Academy," *New Yorker* 71 (27 November 1995): 56, a polemic against readings of Cather that value lesbian erotics more than the work of writing, has been expanded into a book, *Willa Cather and the Politics of Criticism* (Lincoln, Neb.: University of Nebraska Press, 2000). Though Sharon O'Brien's *Willa Cather: The Emerging Voice* (New York: Oxford University Press, 1987) is Acocella's prime culprit, O'Brien's thoughtful reading of *O Pioneers!* also emphasizes Alexandra's work-centered subjectivity, and rightly sees some erotic dimensions (428–48). A visionary artist and a "gardener on an epic scale" (433–34), Alexandra can read nature's text, and transforms the land through love, not force (428–29).

33 Willa Cather, *The Song of the Lark* (New York: Bantam Classic, 1991, 1st pub. 1915). Citations included in text.

34 In *Willa Cather and Others*, Goldberg treats the novel's diva dynamics much more

sympathetically, emphasizing Cather's fascination with a Wagnerian soprano, Olive Frem-stad (43–84). As he notes, it's easy to miss that Ottenburg becomes Thea's husband at the very end (73, *Song of the Lark* 367).

35 The novel quotes the 1890 version of Emily Dickinson's "I asked no other thing"; cf. *The Complete Poems of Emily Dickinson*, ed. Thomas H. Johnson (Boston: Little, Brown, 1960), 306 (#621).

36 Robert Nathan, *Portrait of Jennie* (New York: Alfred A. Knopf, 1940). Citations included in the text.

37 Phillip Barrish, *American Literary Realism, Critical Theory, and Intellectual Prestige, 1880–1995* (New York: Cambridge University Press, 2001). Barrish argues that the incestuous dynamics in *Twilight Sleep* expose a widening gap between paternalist rules of conduct and the father's desire (104–5, 113–15).

Chapter 4. Daddy's Boys

1 As Louis Menand notes in *The Metaphysical Club* (New York: Farrar, Straus and Giroux, 2001), Jane Addams understood that the corporate transformation threatened "an old set of values, predicated on individualism and paternalism" (314).

2 Michael Moon, "'The Gentle Boy from the Dangerous Classes': Pederasty, Domesticity, and Capitalism in Horatio Alger," *Representations* 19 (Summer 1987): 87–110, esp. 95–99.

3 Several "Little Orphan Annie" websites give this information. Harold Gray's "Little Orphan Otto" first ran in the 1924 *Chicago Tribune*. After he changed it to "Little Orphan Annie," he introduced Daddy Warbucks in 1924, then Sandy in 1925. Gray was also writing another comic strip, "Little Joe."

4 Marjorie Kinnan Rawlings, *The Yearling* (New York: Charles Scribner's Sons, 1947, 1st pub. 1938), x; *Cross Creek,* directed by Martin Ritt (1983). With the guidance of his father, Jody tries to raise a fawn, until the family's increasingly desperate circumstances force father to say Jody has to kill the yearling, and he does. At the end, the weakening father gives his blessing as Jody becomes the man of the family. Apparently it's a myth that Rawlings drafted the novel about a girl. I'm indebted here to Kevin McCarthy.

5 Philip Fisher, *Still the New World: American Literature in a Culture of Creative Destruction* (Cambridge, Mass.: Harvard University Press, 1999): a "culture of invention" emerges when rapid workplace and social changes "destroy the value of intergenerational wisdom and increase the value of wisdom unique to each peer group" (182–83).

6 *Billy Budd* and *The Mysterious Stranger* were published posthumously, in unfinished states, and their texts are still unsettled. Written from 1886 to 1891, *Billy Budd, Sailor (An Inside Narrative)* was first published in 1924. Harrison Hayford and Merton M. Sealts, Jr., established a semidefinitive text in 1962 (Chicago: University of Chicago Press), though competing versions still exist. *The Mysterious Stranger* was published in 1916 as a hybrid taken from Twain's posthumous papers. Very different assemblages have since been published.

7 Susan L. Mizruchi, *The Science of Sacrifice: American Literature and Modern Social Theory* (Princeton: Princeton University Press, 1998), e.g., 26–28, also 204–5. In "The Father's Witness: Patriarchal Images of Boys," *Representations* 70 (Spring 2000): 115–41, David Lee Miller argues that sacrifices of sons in the Bible, Shakespeare, and many other texts show the father's need to display his fatherhood for a community of witnesses, to allay fears of his invisibility or his patriarchal inadequacy (129). In modern times, boys

"continue to signify fatherhood as the imaginary witness of identity[,]" but "they no longer rely on the father's witness to guarantee their existence" (137–38).

8 As Michael McKeon has noted in *The Origins of the English Novel, 1600–1740* (Baltimore: Johns Hopkins University Press, 1987), theatricalization is likely to occur "whenever social convention is raised to the level of self-conscious practice" (169). See also Elaine Hadley, *Melodramatic Tactics: Theatricalized Dissent in the English Marketplace, 1800–1885* (Stanford: Stanford University Press, 1995).

9 See, for instance, Magali Sarfatti Larson, *The Rise of Professionalism: A Sociological Analysis* (Berkeley: University of California Press, 1977), 148, on the obsessive status concerns of progressive engineers, who saw themselves as a middle group between capital and labor during the expansion of corporate capitalism and the public sector.

10 Eve Kosofsky Sedgwick, *Epistemology of the Closet* (Berkeley: University of California Press, 1990), and *Between Men: English Literature and Male Homosocial Desire* (New York: Columbia University Press, 1985); Moon, "Gentle Boy."

11 Thorstein Veblen, *The Theory of the Leisure Class: An Economic Study of Institutions* (New York: Modern Library, 1934, 1st pub. 1899), esp. chap. 4, arguing that each class emulates the standard of decency of the next higher class; Philip Fisher, *Hard Facts: Setting and Form in the American Novel* (New York: Oxford University Press, 1987), 157–63.

12 Ross Posnock has suggested that the dichotomizing of real and unreal reflects a fetishized bourgeois masculinity, whereas Michael Davitt Bell has emphasized how hegemonic pressures to be respectably masculine made male writers feel sissified or deviant. Posnock, *The Trial of Curiosity: Henry James, William James, and the Challenge of Modernity* (New York: Oxford University Press, 1991), esp. chaps. 7–9, also 298–99; Bell, *The Problem of American Realism: Studies in the Cultural History of a Literary Idea* (Chicago: University of Chicago Press, 1993), 33–37. On Howells and James as sissies, see Alfred Habegger's *Gender, Fantasy, and Realism in American Literature* (New York: Columbia University Press, 1982).

13 G. Stanley Hall, *Adolescence*, vol. 2 (1904), 391–92, qtd. by Joan Acocella, *Willa Cather and the Politics of Criticism* (Lincoln: University of Nebraska Press, 2000), 95.

14 Joanne B. Freeman's *Affairs of Honor: National Politics in the New Republic* (New Haven: Yale University Press, 2001) emphasizes honor's social usefulness in controlling elite men's competitiveness and political conflicts. Edmund S. Morgan's review-essay, "The Price of Honor," the *New York Review of Books* (May 31, 2001): 36–38, offers a helpful overview of how historians, particularly Bertram Wyatt-Brown, have developed the concept for the antebellum South. See Wyatt-Brown, *Southern Honor: Ethics and Behavior in the Old South* (Oxford: Oxford University Press, 1982), also Steven M. Stowe, *Intimacy and Power in the Old South: Ritual in the Lives of the Planters* (Baltimore: Johns Hopkins University Press, 1987), and Kenneth S. Greenberg, *Honor and Slavery* (Princeton: Princeton University Press, 1996).

In *Origins*, McKeon discusses the transformations of honor in post-Renaissance England, when status hierarchies conflicted with class formations (esp. 151–69). Honor derived from inherited rank or military prowess shifts to honor derived from "goodness of character" (156), or honor as virtue, particularly as embodied in the female chastity that enabled patrilineal transmission of property (157–58). Both progressives and conservatives began to think of honor as an "imaginary value" (212, also 205–6).

15 See Samuel Haber, *The Quest for Authority and Honor in the American Professions, 1750–1900* (Chicago: University of Chicago Press, 1991).

16 On the felt lack of groundedness as a source of the men's movement, see Marianna Torgovnick's "Tracking the Men's Movement," *American Literary History* 6 (Spring

1994): 163, also *Gone Primitive: Savage Intellects, Modern Lives* (Chicago: University of Chicago Press, 1990), 189–92 and 227–28.

17 Veblen, *Theory of the Leisure Class,* 24.

18 Michael Lewis, *Liar's Poker: Rising Through the Wreckage on Wall Street* (New York: Viking Penguin, 1989), 46, also 81, 184.

19 Jessica Benjamin, *The Bonds of Love: Psychoanalysis, Feminism, and the Problem of Domination* (New York: Pantheon Books, 1988), 84.

20 George Horace Lorimer, *Letters from a Self-Made Merchant To His Son* (Toronto: William Briggs, 1902, pub. under pseudonym of "John Graham"). Citations included in the text.

21 George Horace Lorimer, *Old Gorgon Graham: More Letters from a Self-Made Merchant to His Son* (London: Methuen, 1904).

22 Two derivative books by Charles Eustace Merriman try to capitalize on Lorimer's success: *Letters from a Son to His Self-Made Father* (Boston: New Hampshire Publishing, 1903), and *A Self-Made Man's Wife: Her Letters to Her Son: Being the Woman's View of Certain Famous Correspondence* (New York: G. P. Putnam's Sons, 1905). The father tells rural yarns, and the wife gives genteel advice.

23 William Dean Howells, *The Rise of Silas Lapham* (New York: Signet, 1980, 1st pub. 1885. Citations included in the text.

24 Frank Norris, *McTeague: A Story of San Francisco* (New York: Signet, 1964, 1st pub. 1899). Citations included in text. On his disdain for tea-party realism, see "Zola as a Romantic Writer" (1896), rpt. in *McTeague: A Story of San Francisco,* ed. Donald Pizer (New York: W.W. Norton, 1977), 308–10, esp. 309; also "A Plea for Romantic Fiction" (1901), rpt. Pizer, 313–16, esp. 314. June Howard's *Form and History in American Literary Naturalism* (Chapel Hill: University of North Carolina Press, 1985) astutely analyzes the opposition between civilization and primitivism in this and other texts as displaced class conflict. Introduced on p. 25, the "Other Dentist" may be a parody of Oscar Wilde, who toured the United States in 1882–83.

25 John F. Kasson, *Rudeness and Civility: Manners in Nineteenth-Century Urban America* (New York: Hill and Wang, 1990), 156; Warren I. Susman, "'Personality' and the Making of Twentieth-Century Culture," in *New Directions in American Intellectual History,* ed. John Higham and Paul L. Conkin (Baltimore: Johns Hopkins University Press, 1979), 212–26, also Susman, *Culture as History* (New York: Pantheon, 1984).

26 Amy Kaplan, *The Social Construction of American Realism* (Chicago: University of Chicago Press, 1988), 9. See also Alan Trachtenberg, *The Incorporation of America: Culture and Society in the Gilded Age* (New York: Hill and Wang, 1982), chap. 6, "Fictions of the Real," 182–207, also 121–22 on the shift from personal relations to impersonal market relations. Miles Orvell's *The Real Thing: Imitation and Authenticity in American Culture, 1880–1940* (Chapel Hill: University of North Carolina Press, 1989) discusses status elevation through displays of sham and appearances, e.g., 49–59.

27 Posnock makes a related point, in *Trial of Curiosity,* 319 n. 17. Judith Butler's *Gender Trouble: Feminism and the Subversion of Identity* (New York: Routledge, 1990) has stimulated a widespread critical debate about how gender is performed and staged.

28 Herman Melville, "Bartleby, the Scrivener," *Selected Tales and Poems by Herman Melville,* ed. Richard Chase (New York: Holt, Rinehart and Winston, 1950), 1st pub. 1853. Citations included in text.

29 Wyn Kelley, *Melville's City: Literary and Urban Form in Nineteenth-Century New York* (Cambridge: Cambridge University Press, 1996), 201–7. Several neo-Marxist studies emphasize the story's capitalist-labor conflicts, though without Kelley's problematizing of the narrator's relation to production and ownership. See Barbara Foley's "From

Wall Street to Astor Place: Historicizing Melville's 'Bartleby,'" *American Literature* 72 (March 2000): 87–116, which makes too much of Melville's alleged guilt about taking the conservative side in the Astor Place riots; David Kuebrich's "Melville's Doctrine of Assumptions: The Hidden Ideology of Capitalist Production in 'Bartleby,'" *New England Quarterly* 69 (1996): 381–405; and Stephen Zelnick's "Melville's 'Bartleby': History, Ideology, and Literature," *Marxist Perspectives* 8 (Winter 1979/80): 74–92, which highlights the narrator's relation to John Jacob Astor and Astoria.

30 Gilles Deleuze, "Bartleby; or, The Formula," in *Essays Critical and Clinical,* trans. Daniel W. Smith and Michael A. Greco (Minneapolis: University of Minnesota Press, 1997), 68–90, esp. 68–81, quotations 80–81. Deleuze argues that the American undermining of the father-function can liberate brotherly democratic possibilities.

31 Melville, *Billy Budd, Sailor (An Inside Narrative),* ed. Hayford and Sealts, citations included in text; Melville, "Bartleby," *Selected Tales;* Gilles Deleuze, "Bartleby," 81. In *Science of Sacrifice,* Mizruchi suggests that in trying to resemble a "professional sociologist" (151) and purify a society swelling with immigrants such as Claggart (152) and Billy (149), Vere, too, becomes a sacrificial victim (186).

32 Sedgwick, *Epistemology of the Closet,* 92–130, quotations 115–16, 121. See also Caleb Crain, *American Sympathy: Men, Friendship, and Literature in the New Nation* (New Haven: Yale University Press, 2001), 239–70. Mizruchi intriguingly notes that in 1810, British constables arrested the "Vere Street Coterie" at a London club for homosexual prostitution (*Science of Sacrifice,* 185–86).

33 Stephen Crane, *The Monster,* in *Great Short Works of Stephen Crane,* intro. James B. Colvert (New York: Harper and Row Perennial Classic, 1968, 1st pub. 1899), 190–247. Citations included in text.

34 See especially Lee Clark Mitchell, "Face, Race, and Disfiguration in Stephen Crane's *The Monster,*" *Critical Inquiry* 17 (Autumn 1990): 174–92. In "Value, Agency, and Stephen Crane's *The Monster,*" *Nineteenth-Century Fiction* 40 (June 1985): 76–93, Michael D. Warner argues that "it is precisely the idea of secret benevolence . . . that the story annihilates" (80).

35 Mark Twain, *A Connecticut Yankee at King Arthur's Court* (London: Penguin Books, 1986, 1st pub. 1889). Citations included in the text.

36 Later, when Hank's "boys are at the pump" (211), they make the water gush forth, and Hank's prose takes on overtones of oral sex. The people "saw the freed water leaping forth!" They would "kiss it; kiss it, and pet it, and fondle it" (212). I'm indebted to Jason Richards for this interpretation.

37 At an earlier point, Hank gripes about his diet: "a man can't keep his functions regular on spring chickens thirteen hundred years old" (113). Curiously, Hank's name is even more buried than Clarence's is. Not until p. 143 does Puss Flanagan call him "Hank!" in his reverie, and not until p. 353, in the middle of a newspaper article, do we discover that his name is "Hank Morgan" rather than "The Boss."

38 Martha Banta, "The Boys and the Bosses: Twain's Double Take on Work, Play, and the Democratic Ideal," *American Literary History* 3 (Fall 1991): 487–520, quotations 490, 502.

39 Mark Twain, *The Mysterious Stranger,* intro. Edmund Reiss (New York: Signet, 1980, 1st pub. in 1916 as a hybrid from Twain's posthumous papers), 151–253, quotation 253. I'm using the earlier form of the story, not more recent versions of "No. 44."

40 Henry James, "The Pupil," in *Tales of Henry James,* ed. Christof Wegelin and Henry B. Wonham (New York: W. W. Norton, 2003, 1st pub. 1891), 133–71. Citations included in text.

41 Cf. Terence Martin, "James's 'The Pupil': The Art of Seeing Through," *Modern Fic-*

tion Studies 4 (winter 1958–59), excerpted in *Henry James: Seven Stories and Studies,* ed. Edward Stone (New York: Appleton-Century-Crofts, 1961), 187–91. See also two essays rpt. in *Tales of Henry James.* Michael Moon's "A Small Boy and Others: Sexual Disorientation in Henry James, Kenneth Anger, and David Lynch" (*Comparative American Identities: Race, Sex, and Nationality in the Modern Text,* ed. Hortense Spillers [New York: Routledge, 1991], 148–51, rpt. 453–57) notes that "The Pupil" was "summarily rejected" by the *Atlantic Monthly* (454), perhaps because the story produced "discomfort" (454). Highlighting tensions among cleanliness, dirt, and erotic capture, he suggests that Morgan ends as "the sacrificial victim" of his mother and his tutor, now abjected as "members of a collapsed cult" (456). Philip Horne's excerpt from "Henry James: The Master and the 'Queer Affair' of 'The Pupil'" (*Henry James: The Short Fiction: Reassessments,* ed. N. H. Reeve [New York: St. Martins Press, 1997], 114–37, rpt. and excerpted 457–69) discusses Horace Scudder's rejection letter (465–69), recently discovered, and suggests that a homoerotic reading is in tension with other issues, among them "duty and sacrifice, money and honour" (466). Horne finds the tutor more "high-minded" (469) than I do.

42 See Thierry Bardini, *Bootstrapping: Douglas Engelbart, Coevolution, and the Origins of Personal Computing* (Palo Alto: Stanford University Press, 2001). In the early twentieth century, "bootstrap" meant either "unaided effort" or "a loop strap sewed at the side or on the rear top of a boot to help in pulling it on" (24). It morphed into a verb, then into "boot up," a process whereby, "in successive steps, the computer 'pulled itself up by its bootstraps' to a useful operating state" (238, also 169–72).

43 Horatio Alger, Jr., *Ragged Dick; or, Street Life in New York,* 1st serialized 1867, pub. as book 1868, rpt. in *Ragged Dick and Mark, the Match Boy* (New York: Collier, l962). Citations included in text.

44 In an unpublished essay, Jason Richards argues that Dick emerges from blackface minstrelsy traditions. Pauline Hopkins gives indirect support for that reading in the conclusion of her preface to *Contending Forces*: "I have introduced enough of the exquisitely droll humor peculiar to the Negro (a work like this would not be complete without it) to give a bright touch to an otherwise gruesome subject." *Contending Forces: A Romance Illustrative of Negro Life North and South,* intro. Richard Yarborough (New York: Oxford University Press, 1988, 1st pub. 1900), 16.

45 Kenneth S. Lynn, *The Dream of Success: A Study of the Modern American Imagination* (Boston: Little, Brown, 1955), 252–53. See also John G. Cawelti, *Apostles of the Self-Made Man: Changing Concepts of Success in America* (Chicago: University of Chicago Press, 1965), 101–23, which notes that chance and luck bring success in the novels, and that the benevolent businessman becomes "an ideal adoptive father" (113); also Michael Zuckerman, "The Nursery Tales of Horatio Alger," *American Quarterly* 24 (1972): 191–209, which emphasizes absent fathers and a craving for nurturance in the Alger tales. Carol Nackenoff's *The Fictional Republic: Horatio Alger and American Political Discourse* (New York: Oxford University Press, 1994) argues too simply that Alger's novels are political allegories of nostalgic paternalism and republican virtue deriving from his undergraduate essays. Her book usefully wanders from these arguments to many insights about social history and reader reception, for example, when she says that character formation was "the nineteenth-century version of a self-defense course" (45).

46 In *Confidence Men and Painted Women: A Study of Middle-Class Culture in America, 1830–1870* (New Haven: Yale University Press, 1982), 198–205, Karen Halttunen sees *Ragged Dick's* appropriation of the confidence man's theatricality as an add-on to traditional ideals of moral character. See also Judy Hilkey, *Character Is Capital: Success Manuals and Manhood in Gilded Age America* (Chapel Hill: University of North Carolina Press, 1997), e.g., 127.

47 At least twice Dick returns fraud for fraud, against the "drop-game" man and "Ephriam Smith" (79–83, 105–6). Instead of highlighting his dishonesty, the narrative admires Dick's self-control. On executive vs. clerkish behavior, as Olivier Zunz points out in *Making America Corporate 1870–1920* (Chicago: University of Chicago Press, 1990), middle-level corporate employees were "more dependent on the corporate career structure . . . than were the executives to whom they reported" (193, also 191–93 on the danger of complaining). In *Mechanic Accents: Dime Novels and Working-Class Culture in Nineteenth-Century America* (London: Verso, 1987), Michael Denning presents Alger as a "ventriloquist" (83, 171) who used the dime-novel genre to popularize middle-class values, especially good work habits and self-control. Alger rarely portrayed boys working in factories, for instance (170–72).

48 Edward Crapsey, *The Nether Side of New York; or, the Vice, Crime and Poverty of the Great Metropolis* (New York: Sheldon, 1872), 121, 125.

49 Ibid., 7–9, 75, 127. As Crapsey says of Wall Street (74), "There is little moral difference between the shrewd, driving business man and the scheming, restless scamp."

50 Moon, "Gentle Boy," 93.

51 Moon, "Gentle Boy," 95–99. Moon argues that Dick is both maternal and dominant (99), whereas Fosdick is effeminate, and their similar names suit them to each other (97). In the third volume, the two roommates adopt a child (99). On Alger's pederasty, see *The Lost Life of Horatio Alger, Jr.,* by Gary Scharnhorst with Jack Bales (Bloomington: Indiana University Press, 1985), 66–67. In early 1866, Alger was accused of molestation by a young boy, then by other boys. According to Edwin P. Hoyt, in *Horatio's Boys: The Life and Work of Horatio Alger, Jr.* (Radner, Penn.: Chilton, 1974), two boys confessed to their fathers that Alger had buggered them. Without denying the charges, Alger either left or was dismissed from the Unitarian ministry in Brewster, Mass., and went to New York, where *Ragged Dick* began to be serialized in January of 1867.

52 Glenn Hendler, *Public Sentiments: Structures of Feeling in Nineteenth-Century American Literature* (Chapel Hill: University of North Carolina Press, 2001), 107–8, 249 n. 87; Moon, "Gentle Boy," 107. Hendler's chapter on Alger (82–109) focuses on how the novels destabilize the public sphere by linking character to performance (97), publicity (109), yet also to republican virtue beyond the market (84, 94).

53 Moon, "Gentle Boy," 106–7.

54 Quoted in *The Home Book of Quotations Classical and Modern,* ed. Burton Stevenson (New York: Dodd, Mead, 1964), 829. According to the *Dictionary of National Biography,* Corwin said his career had been hurt because of his wit. His quotation continues, "All the great monuments are built over solemn asses."

55 Miller, "The Father's Witness," 119–21.

56 W. E. B. Du Bois, *The Souls of Black Folk,* rpt. in *Three Negro Classics,* ed. John Hope Franklin (New York: Avon Books, 1905), 1st pub. 1903; Ossie Davis, "Eulogy for Malcolm X," Faith Temple Church of God, Harlem (February 27, 1965), available at various Internet sites, for example, Google, "Malcolm X funeral."

57 Houston A. Baker, Jr., *Turning South Again: Re-thinking Modernism/Re-reading Booker T.* (Durham, N.C.: Duke University Press, 2001), 69, his italics, also 75, and 73: "there existed a deeply homoerotic bond between Booker T. Washington and *all* white men[,] and 27–29 on Baker's earlier assessments of Washington.

58 Booker T. Washington, *Up from Slavery,* intro. Louis R. Harlan (New York: Penguin, 1986), 1st pub. 1901. Citations included in text.

59 On the psychic cost of Washington's self-suppressions, see Maurice Wallace, "Constructing the Black Masculine: Frederick Douglass, Booker T. Washington and the Sublimits of African American Autobiography," in *Subjects and Citizens: Nation, Race, and Gender from Oroonoko to Anita Hill,"* ed. Cathy Davidson and Michael Moon (Durham,

N.C.: Duke University Press, 1995), 245–70. Wallace argues that black men's masks have been constructed to resist the ubiquity of white-imposed stereotypes, especially the symbiotic twins of the black rapist and the abjected or feminized Uncle Tom. For both Washington and Douglass, he says, manhood becomes a "phobic posture" renouncing the libidinal and the feminine (186–97, 194).

60 In *The Story of My Life and Work,* intro. Dr. J. L. M. Curry (Toronto: J. L. Nichols, 1900), written for black readers and sold door to door, Washington presents more of his early resistances, especially to Viola Ruffner, and describes women with more complexity. In a forthcoming essay for a University of Florida collection edited by Fitzhugh Brundage, "Booker T. Washington's Strategies of Manliness, for Black and White Audiences," I compare these texts in detail. For another comparison of the autobiographies, see Donald B. Gibson, "Strategies and Revisions of Self-Representation in Booker T. Washington's Autobiographies," *American Quarterly* 45 (September 1993): 370–93. Louis Harlan has disparaged *The Story of My Life and Work* as a "thoroughly bad book" produced by a "lazy and incompetent" young black journalist, Eugene Webber, whom Washington quickly fired; see *Booker T. Washington, 1856–1901,* vol. 1 (New York: Oxford University Press, 1972), 244–45. *Up from Slavery* was written with the assistance of a white Vermonter, Max Thrasher.

61 Letter of 1 October 1908 to R. Underwood Johnson, editor of the *Century,* qtd. by Carla Willard, "Timing Impossible Subjects: The Marketing Style of Booker T. Washington," *American Quarterly* 53 (December 2001): 655 (624–69). Washington is resisting white claims that mulattoes differ racially from darker blacks.

62 John F. Kasson, *Houdini, Tarzan, and the Perfect Man: The White Male Body and the Challenge of Modernity in America* (New York: Hill and Wang, 2001). Kasson analyzes the middle-class fascination with unclad, muscular white male bodies in the 1890s (8, 22), and the avidity for seeing manhood metamorphosize from weakness to physical virility, personified in Teddy Roosevelt as well as Tarzan and Sandow (e.g., 23, 32, 194).

63 In *Turning South Again,* Baker says the praise of President McKinley suggests "racial cross-dressing, homoerotic display and liaisons dangerous" (62). Later Baker links "'keep under the body'" to speculations that Washington died of syphilis (75). In a more plausible provocation, Baker memorably sexualizes Washington's broom (47–49). In *Uplifting the Race: Black Leadership, Politics, and Culture in the Twentieth Century* (Chapel Hill: University of North Carolina Press, 1996), Kevin K. Gaines notes "a none-too-subtle language of empire" in *Up from Slavery* (38, also 32–42 on Washington's "missionary" and elitist aspects, emulating Samuel C. Armstrong).

64 In *The Promise of the New South: Life after Reconstruction* (New York: Oxford University Press, 1992), 322–26, Edward L. Ayers highlights the drama of the Atlanta address. When the governor started to introduce Washington, for instance, the crowd applauded at the words "great Southern educator," then stopped abruptly when they realized the speaker was black (324). Ayers portrays Washington as a realistic tactician in a racial situation that was "impossible, and deteriorating" (326). On cultural resonances of the hand simile, see Eric J. Sundquist, *To Wake the Nations: Race in the Making of American Literature* (Cambridge, Mass.: Harvard University Press, 1993), 251–52.

65 It should be added that the alleged lack of bitterness appears in *Story's* reprinting of the Atlanta Exposition address. The second edition includes the story of the ex-slave who returns "to compensate his owner for his loss" (Gibson, "Strategies and Revisions," 382).

66 James Bryce, *The American Commonwealth,* 3d ed., vol. 2 (London: Macmillan, 1895), 508–9; Rev. J. C. Price, "Does the Negro Seek Social Equality?," *The Forum* 10 (January 1891): 558–64. On Washington's recycled metaphors, see Harlan, *Booker T. Washington,* vol. 1, 204. The first segregation laws in the 1880s arose from the visible presence of respectable, nonlaboring blacks in railroad cars (Ayers, *Promise,* 136–46).

67 Harlan, *Booker T. Washington,* vol. 1, 206.

68 W. D. Howells, qtd. by Harlan, intro. to *Up from Slavery,* xxix.

69 Mark C. Carnes, *Secret Ritual and Manhood in Victorian America* (New Haven: Yale University Press, 1989).

70 Sedgwick, *Epistemology of the Closet,* 145.

71 Lynda Zwinger, *Daughters, Fathers, and the Novel: The Sentimental Romance of Heterosexuality* (Madison: University of Wisconsin Press, 1991).

72 Ralph Ellison, *Invisible Man* (New York: Signet, 1953, 1st pub. 1952), chap. 2. Citations included in text.

73 In *By Silence Betrayed: Sexual Abuse of Children in America* (Boston: Little, Brown, 1988), John Crewdson links pedophilic and incestuous male behavior to "the abuser's fundamental narcissism" (200), also 60–69 on patterns of abuse and insecurity in their childhoods. James R. Kincaid's *Child-Loving: The Erotic Child and Victorian Culture* (New York: Routledge, 1992) takes a much more benign view of pedophilic desires: the child presents "a complex narcissistic image offering entry into a vision of play" (196, also 231, 303–38). *Father-Daughter Incest* (Cambridge, Mass.: Harvard University Press, 1981), by Judith Lewis Herman with Lisa Hirschman, doesn't focus on the psychology of seductive or incestuous fathering except to suggest that "male socialization within the patriarchal family" diminishes men's capacity for "affectionate relating" while increasing exploitive patriarchal tendencies (56), perhaps as compensations for feelings of inadequacy (71–76, 87–88, 91–94, 112).

74 Stuart Schneiderman attributes this formulation of obsessional and hysteric preoccupations to Serge Leclaire. See *Jacques Lacan: The Death of an Intellectual Hero* (Cambridge, Mass.: Harvard University Press, 1983), 59.

Chapter 5. Narrating the Corporation, 1869–1932

1 Alan Trachtenberg, *The Incorporation of America: Culture and Society in the Gilded Age* (New York: Hill and Wang, 1982), 5.

2 Ida M. Tarbell, *The History of the Standard Oil Company,* 2 vols. (London: William Heineman, 1905). Citations included in text.

3 Olivier Zunz, *Making America Corporate 1870–1920* (Chicago: University of Chicago Press, 1990), 33.

4 Clark Davis, *Company Men: White-Collar Life and Corporate Cultures in Los Angeles, 1892–1941* (Baltimore: Johns Hopkins University Press, 2000), 9–10, 148.

5 On America as a "sharp pyramid" where "big men" can triumph, see John F. Kasson, *Houdini, Tarzan, and the Perfect Man: The White Male Body and the Challenge of Modernity in America* (New York: Hill and Wang, 2001), 179, 171.

6 On corporate self-images as families, see Roland Marchand, *Creating the Corporate Soul: The Rise of Public Relations and Corporate Imagery in American Big Business* (Berkeley: University of California Press, 1998), esp. 102–14, 138–41.

7 Andrea Tone, *The Business of Benevolence: Industrial Paternalism in Progressive America* (Ithaca, N.Y.: Cornell University Press, 1997). In *Fatherhood in America: A History* (New York: BasicBooks, 1993), Robert L. Griswold argues that work structures made it very difficult for postbellum black fathers to be providers (22–23, 54).

8 William Graham Sumner, "The Absurd Effort to Make the World Over," rpt. in *Sumner Today: Selected Essays of William Graham Sumner, with Comments by American Leaders,* ed. Maurice R. Davie (New Haven: Yale University Press, 1940), 99–110, quotations 100–102. 1st pub. *Forum,* 17 (March 1894): 92–102.

9 Arthur W. Machen, Jr., "Corporate Personality," *Harvard Law Review* 24 (February 1911): 253–67. Citations included in text.

10 Machen defines a person as "a rational creature capable of feeling and willing" (262, also 263). In *The Gold Standard and the Logic of Naturalism: American Literature at the Turn of the Century* (Berkeley: University of California Press, 1987), Walter Benn Michaels critiques Machen's arguments from another angle (196–205).

11 Mansel G. Blackford and K. Austin Kerr, *Business Enterprise in American History*, 3d ed. (Boston: Houghton Mifflin, 1994), 163.

12 Charles Francis Adams, Jr., and Henry Adams, *Chapters of Erie* (Ithaca, N.Y.: Cornell University Press, 1956, 1st pub. as book in 1886; as essays, 1868–71. Henry Adams wrote the later essays. Citations included in text.

13 H[enry] D[emarest] Lloyd, "Story of a Great Monopoly," *The Atlantic Monthly*, 47 (March 1881): 317–34. Citations included in text.

14 For a lively history of these dealings, see John Steele Gordon, *The Scarlet Woman of Wall Street: Jay Gould, Jim Fisk, Cornelius Vanderbilt, the Erie Railway Wars, and the Birth of Wall Street* (New York: Weidenfeld and Nicolson, 1988), 220–22 on this episode.

15 Qtd. by Trachtenberg, *Incorporation*, 83. See Peter Dobkin Hall, *The Organization of American Culture, 1700–1900: Private Institutions, Elites, and the Origins of American Nationality* (New York: New York University Press, 1982), 110–12.

16 Herbert Hovenkamp, *Enterprise and American Law 1836–1937* (Cambridge, Mass.: Harvard University Press, 1991), 42–55; Martin Sklar, *The Corporate Reconstruction of American Capitalism, 1890–1916: The Market, the Law, and Politics* (Cambridge: Cambridge University Press, 1988), 49–52, 89–117; Brook Thomas, *American Literary Realism and the Failed Promise of Contract* (Berkeley: University of California Press, 1997), 234–35. Thomas suggests that corporations threatened liberal assumptions about the self by calling agency into question, in part through the logic of contracts (235–38).

17 Adams also supported regulatory controls for children's literature. See Glenn Hendler, *Public Sentiments: Structures of Feeling in Nineteenth-Century American Literature* (Chapel Hill: University of North Carolina Press, 2001), 88–91.

18 Henry George, *Progress and Poverty: An Inquiry into the Cause of Industrial Depressions, and of Increase of Want with Increase of Wealth. The Remedy*, 4th ed. (New York: Henry George, 1886, 1st pub. 1879). Citations included in text.

19 Norman Pollack, *The Humane Economy: Populism, Capitalism, and Democracy* (New Brunswick, N.J.: Rutgers University Press, 1990), 114.

20 Zunz, *Making America Corporate*, 100–101; Alfred D. Chandler, Jr., *The Visible Hand: The Managerial Revolution in American Business* (Cambridge, Mass.: Harvard University Press, 1977); James Livingston, *Origins of the Federal Reserve System: Money, Class, and Corporate Capitalism, 1890–1913* (Ithaca, N.Y.: Cornell University Press, 1986), 51.

21 Cf. Thomas, *Literary Realism*, 240–41.

22 Michaels, *Gold Standard*, 70.

23 Howard Horwitz, *By the Law of Nature: Form and Value in Nineteenth-Century America* (New York: Oxford University Press, 1991); James Livingston, *Pragmatism and the Political Economy of Cultural Revolution, 1850–1940* (Chapel Hill: University of North Carolina Press, 1994).

24 H[enry] D[emarest] Lloyd, *Wealth Against Commonwealth* (New York: Harper and Brothers, 1894). Citations included in text.

25 Thorstein Veblen, *The Theory of Business Enterprise* (New York: Scribner's, 1915, 1st pub. 1904). Citations included in text.

26 Robert D. Putnam, *Bowling Alone: The Collapse and Revival of American Community* (New York: Simon and Schuster, 2000), 276.

27 An individualistic warfare fantasy gaining popularity at this time is the beast-aristocrat—Tarzan, Batman, even Teddy Roosevelt—who rescues unmanly middle-class civilization from human predators. See my "The Last Real Man in America, from Natty Bumppo to Batman," *American Literary History* 3 (winter 1991): 753–81.

28 Rockefeller qtd. by Horwitz, *Law of Nature,* 186.

29 Louis D. Brandeis, *Other People's Money and How the Bankers Use It,* ed. Melvin I. Urofsky (Boston: Bedford, 1995), 1st pub. as book in 1914, as articles in 1913. Citations included in text.

30 Livingston, *Origins,* 63, 57.

31 Livingston, *Origins,* 232, also 49–67, 123–25, 228–33. See also Livingston's *Pragmatism,* 80–101.

32 Livingston, *Pragmatism,* 98–101. For him, the onset of corporate capitalism is "the first act of an unfinished comedy rather than the residue of tragedy" (98).

33 Kathleen Brady, *Ida Tarbell: Portrait of a Muckraker* (Pittsburgh, Penn.: University of Pittsburgh Press, 1989), 132, 153–54.

34 Surprisingly, Tarbell later advocated Taylorization and opposed careers for women. In *The Business of Being a Woman* (New York: Macmillan, 1912), she argues that career women become "atrophied" and "cold" (43), with a "perversion" of female qualities (46). A woman's business is to socialize the home (88), where she can "war" on wastefulness (69) and transform servant girls as well as children into "fit citizen[s]" (155). Nonreproductive women are "parasitical" and "irresponsible" (192–93), except for women such as Jane Addams (104–7, 224–37). Tarbell's *New Ideals in Business: An Account of Their Practice and Their Effects upon Men and Profits* (New York: Macmillan, 1916) celebrates Frederick Taylor's system of "scientific management": a workplace should be like "an army, moving in orderly, ordered ways, where every man is dependent on every other man . . . The spirit of the whole animates them" (165). See Martha Banta, *Taylored Lives: Narrative Productions in the Age of Taylor, Veblen, and Ford* (Chicago: University of Chicago Press, 1993), 136–38, 161–65, 168–69.

35 Michael Lewis, *Liar's Poker: Rising Through the Wreckage on Wall Street* (New York: Viking Penguin, 1989).

36 Adolf A. Berle, Jr., and Gardiner C. Means, *The Modern Corporation and Private Property* (New York: MacMillan, 1937, 1st pub. 1932). Citations included in text.

37 David D. Gilmore emphasizes this precapitalist function of manhood; see *Manhood in the Making: Cultural Concepts of Masculinity* (New Haven: Yale University Press, 1990), 47, 217–24.

Chapter 6. Giving and Shaming

1 Andrew Carnegie, "The Gospel of Wealth," in *The Gospel of Wealth and Other Timely Essays,* ed. Edward C. Kirkland (Cambridge, Mass.: Harvard University Press, 1962, 1st pub. 1900). Carnegie's essay was first published as "Wealth" in *North American Review* 148 (June 1889): 653–64; a second section, on "The Best Fields for Philanthropy," appeared in December 1889. After an English editor perhaps satirically republished "Wealth" as "The Gospel of Wealth," Carnegie adopted the title for both parts. Citations included in text.

2 Cited by Robert H. Bremner, *American Philanthropy* (Chicago: University of Chicago Press, 1960), 109. Bremner notes that at the start of the 1890s the New York *Tribune* said

there were 4,047 people in the millionaire class (109). A recent study by Judith Sealander, *Private Wealth and Public Life: Foundation Philanthropy and the Reshaping of American Social Policy from the Progressive Era to the New Deal* (Baltimore: Johns Hopkins University Press, 1997), concurs that most rich people gave primarily to their families (1). Sven Beckert, in *The Monied Metropolis: New York City and the Consolidation of the American Bourgeoisie, 1850–1896* (Cambridge: Cambridge University Press, 2001), notes the disappearance of public relief in New York from 1871 to 1875, as the belief in free markets and class divisions took hold among the new monied elite (227–28).

3 Matthew Frye Jacobson, *Whiteness of a Different Color: European Immigrants and the Alchemy of Race* (Cambridge, Mass.: Harvard University Press, 1998), 8. See also Michelle Brattain's *The Politics of Whiteness: Race, Workers, and Culture in the Modern South* (Princeton: Princeton University Press, 2001), which analyzes intersections between paternalism and white supremacy.

4 "The Era of Sociology," *American Journal of Sociology* 1 (July 1895): 1, 2, qtd. by Kenneth W. Warren, *Black and White Strangers: Race and American Literary Realism* (Chicago: University of Chicago Press, 1993), 39. As this editorial italicizes, "*the fact of human association is more obtrusive and relatively more influential than in any previous epoch*" (39).

5 Benedict Anderson, *Imagined Communities: Reflections on the Origins and Spread of Nationalism* (London: Verso, 1983), 139.

6 Joseph Frazier Wall, *Andrew Carnegie* (New York: Oxford University Press, 1970), 806; also Edward Chase Kirkland, *Dream and Thought in the Business Community, 1860–1900* (Ithaca, N.Y.: Cornell University Press, 1956, rpt. Chicago: Elephant Paperbacks, 1990),145–48. The editor is Allen Thorndike Rice.

7 On the transformation and consolidation of businessmen's values, see Robert H. Wiebe, *Businessmen and Reform: A Study of the Progressive Movement* (Chicago: Quadrangle Books, 1962), esp. 190–92 and 204–5 on ideals of leadership to preserve a classless society, and Wiebe's *The Search for Order 1877–1920* (New York: Hill and Wang, 1967), esp. chap. 6, "Revolution in Values."

8 The history of U.S. estate taxes is very complex. According to Martin McMahon, professor of tax law at the University of Florida (personal communication), an inheritance tax was enacted in 1797 or 1798, then repealed four years later. A more comprehensive tax exempting real estate was enacted in 1862 and repealed in 1870, reenacted in 1894, declared unconstitutional in 1895, reenacted differently in 1898, repealed in 1902, and reenacted in another form in 1916. The gift tax was enacted in 1924, repealed under pressure from Secretary of the Treasury Andrew Mellon in 1926, and reintroduced in 1932. Both taxes were dramatically increased in 1935.

9 Kirkland, *Dream and Thought,* 150.

10 As Olivier Zunz has described in *Making America Corporate 1870–1920* (Chicago: University of Chicago Press, 1990), centralized bureaucratic hierarchies in corporate work eroded the grounds for local paternalism as well as self-reliance, and established new forms of workplace deference for white men (11–36 on "Lost Autonomy"). Zunz and Angel Kwolek-Folland, in *Engendering Business: Men and Women in the Corporate Office, 1870–1930* (Baltimore: Johns Hopkins University Press, 1994), emphasize the ubiquity of paternalistic practices in the corporate workplace as defensive strategies of social control. In *The Business of Benevolence: Industrial Paternalism in Progressive America* (Ithaca, N.Y.: Cornell University Press, 1997), Andrea Tone analyzes how welfare capitalism emerged from several varieties of paternalism during the progressive era.

11 Raymond Williams, *The Country and the City* (New York: Oxford University Press, 1973), chap. 16, 165–81.

12 Andrew Carnegie, *Autobiography of Andrew Carnegie* [ed. John C. Van Dyke] (Boston: Houghton Mifflin, 1920), 235, 237.

13 Gerald Freund, *Narcissism and Philanthropy: Ideas and Talent Denied* (New York: Viking, 1996), 9; Jacobson, *Whiteness of a Different Color*, 78–88, on Davenport's leadership and Carnegie's funding of eugenics studies that advocated the Johnson Act's formula, 2 percent of each group in the 1890 census.

14 In *Whiteness of a Different Color*, Jacobson points out that during the debates about U.S. imperialism in the Philippines, anti-imperialists used a "more virulently racialist logic of civilization" because of their "racial fear for the republic" (210). Conversely, President McKinley justified his imperial policy as "benevolent assimilation."

15 Francie Ostrower, *Why the Wealthy Give: The Culture of Elite Philanthropy* (Princeton: Princeton University Press, 1995), 11, 39 on hierarchies of prestige, and 50–51 on philanthropy's role in establishing group identity. She concludes that "class identity overshadows ethnic identity" (63). Nancy Glazener, in *Reading for Realism: The History of a U.S. Literary Institution, 1850–1910* (Durham, N.C.: Duke University Press, 1997), makes a similar argument for the *Atlantic* group's uses of realism to produce class hierarchy, taste, and connoisseurship.

16 See also Bremner, *American Philanthropy*, 106, and Kathleen D. McCarthy, *Noblesse Oblige: Charity and Cultural Philanthropy in Chicago, 1849–1929* (Chicago: University of Chicago Press, 1982), 62–63 on Carnegie, also 99 on generational and class tensions between Gilded Age benevolence and more democratic ideas of civic stewardship.

17 As David Roberts argues in *Paternalism in Early Victorian England* (New Brunswick, N.J.: Rutgers University Press, 1979), classic patrician benevolence presumed that gentry charity, rather than laws administered by middle-class civil servants, can solve social problems.

18 See Thorstein Veblen, *The Theory of the Leisure Class: An Economic Study of Institutions* (New York: Modern Library, 1934, 1st pub. 1899), 68, 173–75.

19 See Thomas L. Haskell, "Capitalism and the Origins of the Humanitarian Sensibility," *American Historical Review* 90, pt. 1 (April 1985): 339–61, pt. 2 (June 1985): 551–66, also "Forum," *American Historical Review* 92 (October 1987): 797–878.

20 See Ron Chernow, *Titan: The Life of John D. Rockefeller, Sr.* (New York: Random House, 1998), 238–39, also 481–85 on John D. Rockefeller, Jr.'s accommodation to Southern segregationists. I'm indebted here to discussions with Houston A. Baker, Jr., who argues that black colleges stifled the possibility of training assertive black professionals by turning their students into "hands" once more. Atlanta University did give W. E. B. Du Bois a job for a decade after the failure of *The Crisis*. Nonetheless, as David Levering Lewis observes in *W. E. B. Du Bois: The Fight for Equality and the American Century, 1919–1963* (New York: Henry Holt, 2000), 137, black-run Morehouse College was the "single bright light" among white-run black colleges.

See also James D. Anderson, *The Education of Blacks in the South, 1865–1935* (Chapel Hill, N.C.: University of North Carolina Press, 1988), esp. 238–78 on northern philanthropists, also 72–78, 82–109, 248–49. As he emphasizes, black "Normal Schools" fostered moral rather than intellectual development, often against the wishes of African American students and parents, largely because northern white philanthropists agreed with southern whites that African Americans were "an inferior and childlike people" (92). Though claiming to offer "industrial education," schools such as Tuskegee Institute emphasized teacher training, but not the development of trade or farming skills (34, 59, 66, 75–77). The philanthropic goal of turning young African Americans into "contented common laborers in the South's caste economy" (92) fell apart in the 1920s, as whites competed for jobs that previously had been relegated to black people (228–29).

21 Bremner, *American Philanthropy,* 108; Chernow, *Titan,* 314. It took two years before Rockefeller separated himself from the University of Chicago, which he had founded. In 1910 advisors convinced him to display "'the fact of your entire disinterestedness.'" For Chernow, "the idea of subordinating his ego to some larger institutional end would also have appealed to his religious sense of self-denial" (496–97).

22 Chernow, *Titan,* 497, also 313–15 on Rockefeller and Carnegie.

23 Ibid., 675. In "The Gaze of Success: Failed Men and the Sentimental Marketplace, 1873–1893" (in *Sentimental Men: Masculinity and the Politics of Affect in American Culture,* ed. Mary Chapman and Glenn Hendler [Berkeley: University of California Press, 1999] 181–201), Scott Sandage analyzes the "begging letters" directed to Rockefeller. He concludes that the letters mix sentiment and rationality to reconstruct the writers' masculinity by making market relations a combination of gifts and transactions. "[B]eggars sought not charity but conversion" (188) and respect for their character and credibility.

24 On Rockefeller's father, see Chernow, *Titan,* 8–10, 28 and 43, also 459 on Ida Tarbell's discovery of the bigamy. Chernow emphasizes Rockefeller's buried shame, e.g., 29–30, and argues that he was reborn through work (46).

25 Carnegie, *Autobiography,* 33 (mother, Burns), 35 (struggles); intro., *Gospel of Wealth,* x (whine). Joseph Frazier Wall, *Andrew Carnegie* (New York: Oxford University Press, 1970), hesitantly provides an "amateur Freudian" analysis of why Carnegie could not marry until his mother died in 1886: "a weak, ineffectual father who had been unable to provide for his sons; a domineering, ambitious mother who *had* provided"; long sexual immaturity; competition with a younger brother for mother's affection; "a personal vanity so strong as to indicate latent narcissism" (417). Carnegie named his daughter Margaret, after his mother. More recently, James V. Catano argues that Carnegie's rhetoric of the self-made man is an instance of "full postoedipal individualism" denying various kinds of dependence. See *Ragged Dicks: Masculinity, Steel, and the Rhetoric of the Self-Made Man* (Carbondale, Ill.: Southern Illinois University Press, 2001), 58–88 on Carnegie, quotation 59, also 71–72.

26 A useful recent collection is *Scenes of Shame: Psychoanalysis, Shame, and Writing,* ed. Joseph Adamson and Hilary Clark (Albany: State University of New York Press, 1999), especially the intro., which links shame to dynamics of dominance, humiliation, and the failure of recognition (7–8). They also note shame's role "as a protective mechanism regulating human beings in their eagerness for communal life" (14). An excellent essay by Rita Felski, "Nothing to Declare: Identity, Shame, and the Lower Middle Class," *PMLA* 115, no. 1 (January 2000): 33–45, contrasts shame's "sense of failure or lack in the eyes of others" with guilt's "sense of inner badness caused by a transgression of moral values" (39), and also links shame to fears of humiliation. In *Intensely Family: The Inheritance of Family Shame and the Autobiographies of Henry James* (Madison: University of Wisconsin Press, 1995), Carol Holly argues that Henry James internalized his family's dynamics. See chap. 2, esp. 45–51.

27 J. G. Péristiany, ed., *Honour and Shame: The Values of Mediterranean Society* (Chicago: University of Chicago Press, 1966), intro., 11. Péristiany emphasizes "the insecurity and instability of the honour-shame ranking"; a man "is constantly 'on show'" to prove himself to his peers. By contrast, in the modern world of mobility and urbanization, "*who* are our peers and for how long?" (11–12, his emphasis). Intriguingly, at the University of Florida, this book is shelved in the Science Library, between *The Black Experience in America* and *Family Welfare Work in a Metropolitan Community.* A later collection, *Honor and Shame and the Unity of the Mediterranean,* ed. David D. Gilmore (Washington, D.C.: American Anthropological Association, 1987), emphasizes a spectrum of issues

that define male honor in "small atomistic kinship units" (7), though female chastity leads the list.

28 Marcel Mauss, *The Gift: The Form and Reason for Exchange in Archaic Societies,* trans. W. D. Halls (New York: W. W. Norton, 1990, 1st pub. 1950) quotation 65–66, also 36–41 on the potlatch as ostentatious giving to advance a man's rank and family honor by humiliating rivals. Further citations included in text. Mauss's essay on the gift was published in 1925.

29 Edmund S. Morgan, "The Price of Honor," *New York Review of Books,* 31 May 2001, 36–38, quotation 36. See also Alexis de Tocqueville, "Of Honor in the United States and in Democratic Communities," in *Democracy in America,* vol. 2, trans. Henry Reeve and Francis Bowen, ed. Phillips Bradley (New York: Vintage, 1954, 1st. pub. 1840), 242–55.

30 See Gilmore's intro. to *Honor and Shame and the Unity of the Mediterranean,* 2–17, esp. 7. On shifting roles of daughters, see Linda E. Boose, "The Father's House and the Daughter in It: The Structures of Western Culture's Daughter-Father Relationship," in *Daughters and Fathers,* ed. Linda E. Boose and Betty S. Flowers (Baltimore: Johns Hopkins University Press, 1989), 19–74. On preserving communities in times of scarcity, see Lewis Hyde, *The Gift: Imagination and the Erotic Life of Property* (New York: Vintage Books, 1983), 89. Lila Abu-Lughod's *Veiled Sentiments: Honor and Poetry in a Bedouin Society* (Berkeley: University of California Press, 1986) argues that poetry functions as an alternative to the ideology of honor, keeping intimacy alive (233–59).

31 See Samuel Egerton, *Pictures and Punishment: Art and Criminal Prosecution during the Florentine Renaissance* (Ithaca, N.Y.: Cornell University Press, 1985), 91. Egerton argues that these public spectacles of defamation and humiliation developed because old symbolic forms of punishment no longer functioned well, as an age of "communal faith" yielded to "an age of individual cynicism" (75, also 145).

32 Christopher Bracken, *The Potlatch Papers: A Colonial Case History* (Chicago: University of Chicago Press, 1997). The word "potlatch" first appears in parenthesis in 1875, amid several other words describing "aboriginal" gift-giving rituals (34–37). A law against the potlatch was passed by the Canadian legislature on January 1, 1885, without roll call or vote, and the first arrest was made on August 1, 1889 (83, 90). Twenty days later the Chief Justice invalidated the law because nobody could define the word (91–92). Another version became law in 1895, forbidding any "giving away," "giving back" or "payment" among aboriginal people (117–21, quotations 119). Though rituals of public gift-giving persisted, marking "the limit between whiteness and aboriginality" (191) at least to white enforcers, relatively few prosecutions occurred, mostly from 1919 to 1922, after an aggressive administrator shifted the venue from trial by jury to trial by a magistrate (209). One 1928 conviction was overturned on appeal, when judges wrote that the crown was still "unable to quote an authoritative definition of this word" (229). After 1922, "white officials lost their desire to enforce the law," which was repealed in 1936 (228–29). Further citations included in text.

33 Bracken, *Potlatch Papers,* 20, using Homi Bhabha's term, "colonial mimicry."

34 Using Derrida, Bracken critiques Mauss (140–41, 151–62), highlighting Mauss's "middle-of-the-road liberal socialism" (154) and his strange passages on sacrifice (162). Bracken also critiques Mauss's patriarchal presumptions, noting that women too staged potlatches (86, 147–48). One of Mauss's most startling claims is that Malinowski "throws a brilliant light upon all sexual relationships throughout humanity" by showing that the husband's gifts and "'constant' payments" to his wife are "a kind of salary for sexual services rendered" (73).

35 Intro. by "B. J. H." to *The Gospel of Wealth,* xxiii. Carnegie never told anyone of this one-page vow, not even his wife.

36 Chernow, *Titan,* 50. In *Bowling Alone: The Collapse and Revival of American Community* (New York: Simon and Schuster, 2000), Robert D. Putnam notes that "half of all charitable giving in America is religious in nature" (124). As Stephen Carter recently said, "We are Christians, and we are of the traditional Christian view that from those to whom much is given much is required. . . . we are supposed to give a lot of it [financial good fortune] away—and really a lot of it. That is just an absolute obligation of the faith." David Owen, "From Race to Chase: Yale's Stephen L. Carter Writes a Thriller," *New Yorker,* 3 June 2002, 50–57, quotation 57.

37 Merle Curti, "American Philanthropy and the National Character," *American Quarterly* 10 (winter 1958): 420–37, quotation 429, Bryce citation 423. As if bowing to Carnegie's spirit, Curti concludes that "In relieving class and group tensions . . . philanthropy has in a sense been the American equivalent for socialism" (436). Philanthropy is twice as common in the United States as it is in other countries (Putnam, *Bowling Alone,* 117).

38 See Peter Dobkin Hall, *The Organization of American Culture, 1700–1900: Private Institutions, Elites, and the Origins of American Nationality* (New York: New York University Press, 1982), 90, also 174–84, and 110–12 on the *Dartmouth* case; also Louis Menand, *The Metaphysical Club* (New York: Farrar, Straus and Giroux, 2001), 238–43, and Brook Thomas, *American Literary Realism and the Failed Promise of Contract* (Berkeley: University of California Press, 1997), 234–35.

39 See, for instance, Bertram Wyatt-Brown, *Southern Honor: Ethics and Behavior in the Old South* (Oxford: Oxford University Press, 1982), and Steven M. Stowe, *Intimacy and Power in the Old South: Ritual in the Lives of the Planters* (Baltimore: Johns Hopkins University Press, 1987). In *The Quest for Authority and Honor in the American Professions, 1750–1900* (Chicago: University of Chicago Press, 1991), Samuel Haber argues that recent studies of the rise of the professions underplay the centrality of honor as a social dynamic.

40 Two recent articles by Susan M. Ryan link the danger of being duped to mutually constitutive constructions of blackness and benevolent whiteness: "Charity Begins at Home: Stowe's Antislavery Novels and the Forms of Benevolent Citizenship," *American Literature* 72, no. 4 (December 2000): 751–82; and "Misgivings: Melville, Race, and the Ambiguities of Benevolence," *American Literary History* 12, no. 4 (winter 2000): 685–712.

41 In *Noblesse Oblige,* Kathleen McCarthy concludes that by the 1920s, impersonal giving had "destroyed the element of mutuality." In preindustrial cities, benevolent giving "entailed a mutual obligation of services and deference." Now there were technocrats to shield the rich from the poor (165, also 176–78). By the 1920s, "[s]tewardship and socializing were one," and "[t]he cash nexus reigned supreme" (171). Putnam's *Bowling Alone* includes a chapter on American philanthropy and volunteerism since the nineteenth century to support his sometimes untenable argument that civic involvements have declined (116–33, esp. 116–27). Putnam's title is a misrepresentation, or what he calls "poetic license" (113), since as he acknowledges, people in the United States aren't bowling alone; they're just not bowling in leagues.

42 Qtd. in McCarthy, *Noblesse Oblige,* 151. The tension between "liberal" generosity and expectations of "credit" or exchange has structured recent legal debates on giving. See Carol M. Rose, "Giving, Trading, Thieving, and Trusting: How and Why Gifts Become Exchanges, and (More Importantly) Vice Versa," *Florida Law Review* 44 (July 1992): 295–317, and 319–78 for five commentaries and response; also Melvin Aron

Eisenberg, "The World of Contract and the World of Gift," *California Law Review* 85 (July 1997): 821–66. Rose argues that the rhetoric of exchange depends on "humaneness" (378, also 316), whereas Eisenberg surveys three stages of legal scholarship before arguing for the role of "affective elements" in giving.

43 In "The Urban Picturesque and the Spectacle of Americanization," *American Quarterly* 52 (September 2000): 444–77, Carrie Tirado Bramen analyzes the varieties and hierarchies of whiteness used to depict European immigrants. "As whiteness became more inclusive it also became more segmented," partly to legitimate new immigrants "at the expense of African Americans" (450).

44 George Eliot (Mary Anne Evans), *Middlemarch,* ed. Gordon S. Haight (Boston: Houghton Mifflin. Riverside ed., 1956, 1st pub. as eight books in 1871–72, revised as one book, 1874), 553. Citations included in text.

45 Henry James, 1873 review, ibid., intro., v.

46 On gifts in the novel's market economy, see Wai-Chee Dimock, "Debasing Exchange: Edith Wharton's *The House of Mirth,*" *PMLA* 100 (October 1985): 783–92.

47 Edith Wharton, *Summer* (New York: Harper and Row, 1980, 1st pub. 1917). Citations included in text.

48 See Walter Benn Michaels, "The Contracted Heart," *New Literary History* 21 (spring 1990): 495–531. In *Gender and the Gothic in the Fiction of Edith Wharton* (Tuscaloosa: University of Alabama Press, 1995), Kathy Fedorko argues that Charity makes several independent choices at the end, to keep her child and reclaim Harney's brooch (81).

49 In *Noblesse Oblige,* Kathleen McCarthy describes four generations of civic stewardship in Chicago from 1849 to 1929: benevolent ladies and Christian gentlemen, who stressed voluntarism and personal involvement; Gilded Age plutocrats, who began the shift to institutional and managerial philanthropy that insulated themselves from the poor; progressive reformers, who democratized and decentralized institutional philanthropy, and Jazz Age donors and dilettantes in "the heyday of the technocrat" (177).

50 William Dean Howells, "Tribulations of a Cheerful Giver," *Impressions and Experiences* (New York: Harper and Brothers, 1909), 111–39. Citations included in text.

51 In *Reading for Realism,* Nancy Glazener argues that realism's paternalistic concern for nonelite characters converges with belletrism and philanthropy to consolidate the bourgeoisie's respectability (22, 28–29 on philanthropy).

52 Lincoln Steffens, *The Shame of the Cities,* intro. Louis Joughin (New York: Hill and Wang, 1957), 1st pub. as book in 1904, previously pub. as six magazine articles.

53 Jane Addams, "A Modern Lear," reprinted in *The Social Thought of Jane Addams,* ed. Christopher Lasch (Indianapolis: Bobbs-Merrill, 1965), 107–23, 1st. pub. in *Survey* 29 (2 November, 1912): 131–37; citations included in text.

54 Lasch quotes Lloyd's letter in his intro. to Addams, "A Modern Lear," 106. Allen F. Davis, *American Heroine: The Life and Legend of Jane Addams* (New York: Oxford University Press, 1973), notes that "*The Forum, North American Review, Century,* and *Atlantic Monthly,* among others, turned it down" (114). For Davis the essay is "mild" and balanced, blaming employees and labor organizers as well as Pullman (113–14).

55 Davis, *American Heroine,* 111–15; McCarthy, *Noblesse Oblige,* 100–102; Carl Smith, *Urban Disorder and the Shape of Belief: The Great Chicago Fire, the Haymarket Bomb, and the Model Town of Pullman* (Chicago: University of Chicago Press, 1995), 311–16; and Menand, *Metaphysical Club,* 306–16, discuss Addams's involvement in the Pullman strike. On Pullman, see Smith, *Urban Disorder,* 175–270. In the 1880s Pullman built a model suburb for his employees, to improve them as citizens and workers. The town had parks and recreation, though no bathtubs and only one water faucet for every

five units. Davis calls it a "feudal domain" (112). In the 1893 depression, the company laid off workers and reduced wages but not rents. The strike and riot occurred in early summer of 1894, and brought Eugene V. Debs to national prominence. The black porters refused to join the boycott because Debs' union wouldn't admit black workers (Menand, 374).

See also Janice L. Reiff, "A Modern Lear and His Daughters: Gender in the Modern Town of Pullman," *The Pullman Strike and the Crisis of the 1890s,* ed. Richard Schneirov, Shelton Stromquist, and Nick Salvatore (Urbana: University of Illinois Press, 1999), 65–86, emphasizing a second paternalism "of the male workers within their homes" (71). Several factors partially undermined these paternalisms. For one, "many, arguably most, Pullman women worked" (75). For another, "By 1892 almost half of the Pullman homes hosted at least one boarder[,]" and almost one fourth of the workers "lived in their own homes outside Pullman" (74). After the breakdown of Pullman's paternalism led to the strike (77), Pullman used gender strategically to break the strike, by bringing women back first, as laundresses (79).

56 Menand, *Metaphysical Club,* 307.

57 Lasch, intro. to *Social Thought,* xv–xvi; Davis, *American Heroine,* 13–5, 9, 160–61. Lasch contrasts her father's model of social service and moral rectitude with her stepmother's traditional pressures for womanhood. Yet Davis notes that her father discouraged Addams from career ambitions, whereas the stepmother encouraged her to think of herself as intelligent (9).

58 Davis, *American Heroine,* 57. In *Metaphysical Club* Menand argues that Addams grows from a do-gooder into a passionately democratic social scientist (312).

59 Sara Blair, *Henry James and the Writing of Race and Nation* (Cambridge: Cambridge University Press, 1996), 193–94, 202. Analyzing James's seemingly racist comment about the Pullman car, Blair teases out his complex mix of nostalgic racism, alienness from bourgeois norms, performative doubling of the porters' mobility and "inaptitude," and grudging acknowledgement of their new cosmopolitan status.

60 Anderson, *Imagined Communities,* 137.

61 McCarthy, *Noblesse Oblige,* 103.

62 Twain's letter, written on Christmas Eve, 1885, to the dean of Yale Law School and printed for the first time in Shelley Fisher Fishkin's *Lighting Out for the Territory: Reflections on Mark Twain and American Culture* (New York: Oxford University Press, 1997) 101; see also 99–107 on McGuinn. Chief Justice Taney qtd. in Brook Thomas's "Citizen Hester: The Scarlet Letter as Civic Myth," *American Literary History* 13 (summer 2001), 202. Responding to the contrast between "White City" and folk exhibits at the 1893 Chicago World's Fair, Frederick Douglass said, "As if to shame the Negro, the Dahomians are here to exhibit the Negro as a repulsive savage." Qtd. by Alan Trachtenberg, *The Incorporation of America: Culture and Society in the Gilded Age* (New York: Hill and Wang, 1982), 221.

Those who think this stigmatization no longer applies should consider the movie *Chicago* (2002), in which a hapless "cellophane" husband named Amos is frequently called "Andy" by his wife's lawyer. Implication: the husband is so shameful that he's interchangeable with Amos and Andy, classic black comedians.

63 W. E. B. Du Bois, *The Souls of Black Folk,* rpt. in *Three Negro Classics,* ed. John Hope Franklin (New York: Avon, 1965, 1st pub. 1903), chap. 3. Citations included in text. In *Race Men* (Cambridge, Mass.: Harvard University Press, 1998), Hazel Carby critiques Du Bois's patriarchal presumptions in making Washington "the metaphorical equivalent of the black mother (or the black female prostitute) who succumbs to the lust of white men" (39). Conversely, argues Ross Posnock, Washington enduringly stigmatized

black intellectuals as unmanly. See his *Color and Culture: Black Writers and the Making of the Modern Intellectual* (Cambridge, Mass.: Harvard University Press, 1998), 15, also 58–61 on Washington's complicity with "white terror of black literacy" (59), and 16, 222 linking Washington's stigmatizing to the Black Power movement.

64 Booker T. Washington, *Up from Slavery,* intro. Louis R. Harlan (New York: Penguin, 1986, 1st pub. 1901). Citations included in text. I develop these arguments further in chap. 4. In *The Death of Reconstruction: Race, Labor and Politics in the Post—Civil War North, 1865–1901* (Cambridge, Mass.: Harvard University Press, 2001), Heather Cox Richardson argues that by 1877, most northern whites thought African Americans were disaffected and discontented workers, not the more positive examples of a free labor ideology that ex-slaves had seemed to be after the Civil War (121, 205). In the context of what Richardson calls "The Un-American Negro" (183), Washington tried to reestablish the free labor image of black people, "a holding action that ultimated failed" (241, and 225–41).

65 Du Bois, *Souls of Black Folk,* 238.

66 Arnold Rampersad, "Psychology and Afro-American Biography," *Yale Review* 78 (autumn 1988): 1–18, quotation 16.

67 My emphasis on recognition draws on Jessica Benjamin's *The Bonds of Love: Psychoanalysis, Feminism, and the Problem of Domination* (New York: Pantheon, 1988).

68 Du Bois, *Souls of Black Folk,* 246 (chap. 3).

Chapter 7. *The Golden Bowl*

1 Allen F. Davis, *American Heroine: The Life and Legend of Jane Addams* (New York: Oxford University Press, 1973) 160, suggests a parallel to *The Golden Bowl*: Addams similarly represents herself as, in James's words, a "passionately filial" daughter of a "peculiarly paternal" father.

2 On the double dynamic, see Matthew Frye Jacobson, *Whiteness of a Different Color* (Cambridge, Mass.: Harvard University Press, 1998), e.g., 75: as immigrants, "peoples such as Celts, Italians, Hebrews, and Slavs were becoming less and less white . . . and yet were becoming whiter and whiter in debates over who should be granted the full rights of citizenship."

3 David Roediger, *The Wages of Whiteness: Race and the Making of the American Working Class* (New York: Verso, 1991). In *Whiteness of a Different Color,* Jacobson concludes that between 1840 and 1920, "the discourse of empire and the conservative racial logic of naturalization law stabilized and kept afloat the otherwise battered notion of monolithic, indivisible whiteness" (202).

4 Mark Seltzer, *Henry James and the Art of Power* (Ithaca, N.Y.: Cornell University Press, 1984), 89. For Margery Sabin, "Maggie's sadomasochistic rapture with Charlotte in the garden surpasses any moment of passion with Amerigo." "Henry James's American Dream in *The Golden Bowl,*" *The Cambridge Companion to Henry James,* ed. Jonathan Freedman (Cambridge: Cambridge University Press, 1998), 220, also 214 on the "almost intolerable ambiguity" of mixing salvation and torture.

5 Henry James, *The Golden Bowl,* intro. Gore Vidal (New York: Penguin, 1987, 1st pub. 1904, rev. 1909). Citations included in text. The 1909 New York Edition has small revisions in spelling and punctuation. The 1966 Penguin edition uses the 1904 version.

6 Thomas Peyser, *Utopia and Cosmopolis: Globalization in the Era of American Lit-*

erary Realism (Durham, N.C.: Duke University Press, 1998), 135–68; Patricia McKee, *Producing American Races: Henry James, William Faulkner, Toni Morrison* (Durham, N.C.: Duke University Press, 1999), 64–98; Laurence B. Holland, *The Expense of Vision: Essays on the Craft of Henry James* (Baltimore: Johns Hopkins University Press, 1982, 1st pub. 1964, 331–407; Carolyn Porter, *Seeing and Being: The Plight of the Participant Observer in Emerson, James, Adams, and Faulkner* (Middletown, Conn.: Wesleyan University Press, 1981), 130–53, also 40–43; Seltzer, *Henry James*, 59–95; Lynda Zwinger, *Daughters, Fathers, and the Novel: The Sentimental Romance of Heterosexuality* (Madison: University of Wisconsin Press, 1991), 76–95.

7 Edith Wharton's *The House of Mirth* (New York: Signet Classic, 1964, 1st pub. 1905) shows how adulterous Bertha Dorset easily remains at the center of her social set, while the set's reluctant inclusion of the Jewish businessman Simon Rosedale disgusts the narrator as well as Lily Bart.

8 In "Gender and Value in *The American*," *New Essays on The American*, ed. Martha Banta (Cambridge: Cambridge University Press, 1987), 99–129, Carolyn Porter argues that in a world in which the pressures of capitalist exchanges have undermined paternal authority, James is "devoted to sustaining a moral order of value . . . dependent upon the imagination" (104–5). From *The Portrait of a Lady* onward, he transfers that imaginative power to female protagonists, while "reinscribing patriarchal power in the author" (126).

9 Though various critics have asserted that Adam may well know what Maggie is trying to keep him from knowing, I didn't see that possibility until my third reading, and one has to read beyond Maggie's consciousness to sense his agency. See, for instance, 509–15, when in the midst of Maggie's complex anxieties about "sacrifice," Adam suggests he and Charlotte move to American City; or 362, when Adam suddenly resolves Maggie's anxieties about leaving the Prince alone with Charlotte by saying he and Maggie won't go to Spain after all; also 383–87, 392, 445, and 524. "So many things her father knew that she even yet didn't!" (554).

10 In *Utopia and Cosmopolis*, Peyser astutely analyzes the novel's anxieties about "the assimilation of the foreigner, the stranger, the survivor from a previous age" (138). The Ververs' "free-floating, cosmopolitan model of selfhood" triumphs over "Charlotte's desire to claim an identity firmly determined by race" (154). In that respect, Maggie enables the Prince to escape his own racial construction.

11 In "Roman Springs and Roman Fevers: James, Gender, and Transnational Dis-ease," *Roman Holidays: American Writers and Artists in Nineteenth-Century Italy,* ed. Robert K. Martin and Leland S. Person (Iowa City: University of Iowa Press, 2002), 140–58, Priscilla L. Walton shows links among Italy, illness, and "racialized characters and constructions" (141) in several of James's narratives, and intriguingly associates *The Golden Bowl* with Typhoid Mary (153–54).

12 James exploits the increasing tendency of impoverished European aristocrats to marry rich young American women. Ruth Brandon, in *The Dollar Princesses: Sagas of Upward Nobility* (New York: Alfred A. Knopf, 1980), gives the details. Starting in the 1870s, by 1915 there were 52 American princesses, 17 duchesses, 32 viscountesses, 33 marchionesses, 64 baronesses, and 136 countesses (1), among others.

13 Here I differ from McKee, who in *Producing American Races* links the Prince's darkness to the distinction of his European aristocratic background (98). Peyser emphasizes the Prince's role as an amoral "alien," associated with Machiavelli and the rising tide of immigration (141–42, 155).

14 Joseph Allen Boone, *Tradition/Counter/Tradition: Love and the Form of Fiction* (Chicago: University of Chicago Press, 1987), 193.

15 Cf. McKee, *Producing American Races,* 85–87: the blank whiteness makes the Prince feel "'left out,' but what is left out is an inner self" (86). I'm arguing that the Prince has several levels of inner self: a canny bargainer on the surface, a raced male underneath.

16 Gail Bederman, *Manliness and Civilization: A Cultural History of Gender and Race in the United States, 1880–1917* (Chicago: University of Chicago Press, 1995).

17 In "The Poetics of Cultural Decline: Degeneracy, Assimilation, and the Jew in James's *The Golden Bowl*" *American Literary History* 7 (fall 1995): 477–99, Jonathan Freedman suggests that the Jewish shopkeeper is Amerigo's "double" (493–94); each is an "unassimilable alien" (482), though Maggie brings both aliens toward "conversion" (492). Carren Kasten and David McWhirter develop Laurence Holland's suggestion that the Jew resembles James, treating "'My Golden Bowl'" with tenderness and ceremony. See Kasten, *Imagination and Desire in the Novels of Henry James* (New Brunswick, N.J.: Rutgers University Press, 1984), 153–54; McWhirter, *Desire and Love in Henry James: A Study of the Late Novels* (Cambridge: Cambridge University Press, 1989), 158–59.

18 Holland, *Expense of Vision,* notes the irony of Adam's passionless proposal, "with Adam breathing more intimately on the cheek of the tiles he buys than on Charlotte" (362, also 359–63). Peyser, *Utopia and Cosmopolis* (145) compares Adam's latent imperial violence here to Conrad's Kurtz. My reading emphasizes Adam's receptivity to Charlotte's energy.

19 In *Professions of Taste: Henry James, British Aestheticism, and Commodity Culture* (Stanford: Stanford University Press, 1990), Jonathan Freedman notes Maggie's sadistic intensity (237) and "absolute punitive authority" (239). To Peyser, Charlotte becomes "a virtual stand-in for a conquered race" (*Utopia and Cosmopolis,* 160).

20 Peyser, *Utopia and Cosmopolis* says the Jew's repentance seems "practically unmotivated" (156); McKee, *Producing American Races,* says the shopkeeper is really enacting "an eye for an eye[,]" since in redeeming himself he betrays the Prince, who had wronged him earlier (92).

21 Cf. Holland, *Expense of Vision,* 393.

22 Zwinger, *Daughters, Fathers, and the Novel,* 7. In *Feminist Dialogics: A Theory of Failed Community* (Albany: State University of New York Press, 1988), Dale Bauer agrees that although in the first book Maggie depends on her father's voice and code, Adam finally relinquishes authority to Maggie, who "rejects her father's powerful univocal discourse" of patriarchal possession for a more dialogic sense of desire, power, and intimacy (54).

23 Laurence Holland first pointed out that Maggie may have created the marriage problems; see *Expense of Vision,* 368, also 381–82.

24 Freedman, *Professions of Taste,* 236.

25 Ruth Bernard Yeazell, *Language and Knowledge in the Late Novels of Henry James* (Chicago: University of Chicago Press, 1976), 100–130.

26 Henry James, *Hawthorne,* fwd. Dan McCall (Ithaca, N.Y.: Cornell University Press, 1997, 1st pub. 1879), 46.

27 Robert B. Pippin, *Henry James and Modern Moral Life* (Cambridge: Cambridge University Press, 2000), 16–17, 66–82 on *The Golden Bowl,* quotation 87 n.18. For him, the novel's resolution "rests on a tissue of lies," and everyone, including James, knows "that this is bad" (87).

28 Kasten, *Imagination and Desire,* 172. Kasten notes the "suffocating restriction of real and metaphoric sight" (177) that concludes Maggie's journey toward insight. Many critics have commented on the problematic ending, for example, Paula Marantz Cohen, who calls Maggie's triumph "bizarre and morally dubious." See *The Daughter's Dilemma: Family Process and the Nineteenth-Century Domestic Novel* (Ann Arbor: University of Michigan Press, 1991), 179.

29 In *Producing American Races,* McKee argues that the Prince "claims adultery as his means of fending off castration" (92), and that later, while the Prince thinks "his good form functions as a cover, hiding his abjection[,]" Maggie values his mixture of abjection and pride (90).

30 Kenneth W. Warren, *Black and White Strangers: Race and American Literary Realism* (Chicago: University of Chicago Press, 1993), 28; Sara Blair, *Henry James and the Writing of Race and Nation* (Cambridge: Cambridge University Press, 1996); Ross Posnock, *The Trial of Curiosity: Henry James, William James, and the Challenge of Modernity* (New York: Oxford University Press, 1991).

31 Holland, *Expense of Vision,* 333.

32 James Livingston, *Pragmatism and the Political Economy of Cultural Revolution, 1850–1940* (Chapel Hill: University of North Carolina Press, 1994), 71, 112.

33 Livingston, *Pragmatism,* 112; Pippin, *Henry James and Modern Moral Life.* Pippin argues that the novel brings separated, self-absorbed, often self-deceiving minds into "tight relations of dependence and mutual reflection . . . however uncertain and constantly self-forming" (67–68). The context is modernism's "void or vacancy" (5, 27–28) of cultural authority, with money as the source of value and the cause of social change (34).

34 Pippin, *Henry James and Modern Moral Life,* 80 (heat), 147 (hero), 85 (meaning, also 123–24).

35 Ibid., 111 (narcissism), 74–75 (secured). Moreover, as Pippin argues, such moral dependence can be "both redemptive and destructive, often at the same time; . . . no choice is ever fully right" (178). "Offstage, James is more scratching his head . . . than wagging his finger" (4).

36 Holland, *Expense of Vision,* 393 (torture), 350 (devotion), 363 (flawed form), 398 (cry). "The abject surrender which Maggie is willing to perform makes her the scapegoat she has imagined being, for she takes on herself the burden of the wrongs done her[.]" Yet Charlotte is "the scapegoat who pays the most in deprivation" (397). James was influenced by Holman Hunt's painting, *Scapegoat,* which he saw in 1858 (394).

37 Susan L. Mizruchi, *The Science of Sacrifice: American Literature and Modern Social Theory* (Princeton: Princeton University Press, 1998), 26–27 (heterogeneity), 204 (holiness), 195 (transition), 197 (sin), 213 (sexuality) 268 (maternal).

38 Pippin, *Henry James and Modern Moral Life,* 86 n. 16.

39 This phrase was adopted by Reuben Brower for *The Fields of Light: An Experiment in Critical Reading* (New York: Oxford University Press, 1962), a classic book on how to do close readings.

Chapter 8. *Tender Is the Night*

1 I'm indebted here to Stanley Cavell's extraordinary essay on King Lear, "The Avoidance of Love: A Reading of *King Lear,*" *Must We Mean What We Say? A Book of Essays* (New York: Charles Scribner's Sons, 1969), 267–353.

2 F. Scott Fitzgerald, *Tender Is the Night* (New York: Scribner's, 1995, 1st pub. 1934). Citations included in text. Fitzgerald wrote seventeen drafts of the novel, only to rethink its structure after it was published. He then decided that the story should begin with part 2, with Dick at the top of his career, then turn to the Rosemary section, where he starts to decline. As Milton Stern puts it, Fitzgerald wanted to narrate "the long, steady 'dying fall' of Dick Diver from his transcendent possibilities[,]" and never settled on how to do that. Like most readers, I prefer the earlier version, because its dramatization of Dick's daddy's

girl yearnings both inflates and undermines the appeal of Dick's paternalism, and because part 1 shows him at what Matthew Bruccoli calls "the peak of his charm[.]" See Stern, "*Tender Is the Night* and American History," in *The Cambridge Companion to F. Scott Fitzgerald*, ed. Ruth Prigozy (Cambridge: Cambridge University Press, 2002), 97–98, quotation 98, and Matthew J. Bruccoli, *Some Sort of Epic Grandeur: The Life of F. Scott Fitzgerald* (New York: Harcourt Brace Jovanovich, 1981), 371–73, quotation 373.

3 Ernest Hemingway, *A Farewell to Arms* (New York: Charles Scribner's Sons, 1929), 249.

4 In *The Talking Cure: Literary Representations of Psychoanalysis* (New York: New York University Press, 1985), Jeffrey Berman uses this and other passages to emphasize Dick's choice of psychiatry as a way "to hold in check the inner forces ultimately leading to his ruin" (66–67). Berman highlights Dick's countertransference relation to Nicole.

5 Ruth Prigozy, in "From Griffith's Girls to *Daddy's Girl*: The Masks of Innocence in *Tender Is the Night*," *Twentieth Century Literature* 26 (Summer 1980): 189–221, shows Fitzgerald's indebtedness to various daddy's girl figures and scandals in the 1920s, from Little Orphan Annie (193–94), Mary Pickford, and Theda Bara (208) to Charlie Chaplin's marriage to a sixteen-year-old pregnant girl nicknamed "Lolita," and President Warren G. Harding's fathering of a daughter with a mistress who told all in a 1927 best-seller (192). She traces the cinematic motif back to D. W. Griffith's films "featuring child-women" (198, also 198–208).

6 Dick's age doesn't become apparent until much later, when he mulls over being less attractive to Rosemary than he was four years before. "Eighteen might look at thirty-four through a rising mist of adolescence; but twenty-two would see thirty-eight with discerning clarity" (208, also 181).

7 Prigozy notes the movie industry's "identical pattern: the actresses who were so tied to their fathers on the screen were . . . thoroughly dominated by their mothers" (196).

8 The "shadows on a wall" alludes to Plato's allegory of the cave, *The Republic*, book 7.

9 For Milton Stern, this is the key scene in which Dick "loses dominance as the omnipotent manager of all situations." Stern, "*Tender Is the Night*," 107.

10 In *Talking Cure*, Berman notes that Fitzgerald's original title was *The Boy That Killed His Mother*. Though he eventually abandoned that idea, "he did not entirely succeed in disguising the misogyny that underlies the story" (80).

11 In "Feeling 'Half Feminine': Modernism and the Politics of Emotion in *The Great Gatsby*," *American Literature* 68 (June 1996): 405–31, Frances Kerr analyzes Fitzgerald's fears of being taken for a "fairy" by other men (417). As he remarked of himself as a writer, "'I am half feminine—at least my mind is'" (qtd. 406). Michael Nowlin draws on Kerr's study to argue that though Dick attempts "to redeem the character of paternal authority" threatened by woman-oriented consumer capitalism, he "is finally exposed as a Father-impostor and as 'feminized' a subject as any of his patients." "'The World's Rarest Work': Modernism and Masculinity in Fitzgerald's *Tender is the Night*," *College Literature* 25 (Spring 1998): 58–77, quotation 59. I'm arguing that although the novel invites readers to blame strong women for castrating Dick, the novel also admires their seemingly greater forcefulness.

12 Several critics have argued that the incest motif shows Dick's loss of allegiance to the moral code of his father. See Berman, *Talking Cure*, 79.

13 In "Modernism and Masculinity," Nowlin brings out the Lacanian implications of Dick's "rather commonplace narcissistic attachment to the penis" (67). Nowlin argues that Dick's phallic dreams focus on having a "rare vocation" that can "supplant his father . . . and rival the father of psychoanalysis" (67). I see less Oedipal and workplace ri-

valry in Dick's self-measuring, and more identification with the antebellum tradition of Southern honor.

14 In *F. Scott Fitzgerald: The Last Laocoön* (New York: Oxford University Press, 1967), Robert F. Sklar analyzes the military aspects of Dick's associations with Grant (272–73), and notes the "Lincoln-Grant relationship between Abe and Dick" (278).

15 As John F. Callahan notes, "Paradoxically, the more dissociated Diver becomes from places, . . . the more intensely, vividly, unbearably Fitzgerald renders the natural world." "'France Was a Land': F. Scott Fitzgerald's Expatriate Theme in *Tender Is the Night*," *French Connections: Hemingway and Fitzgerald Abroad*, ed. J. Gerald Kennedy and Jackson R. Bryer (New York: St. Martin's Press, 1998), 173–86, quotation 183.

16 In "The Occidental Tourist: The Counter-Orientalist Gaze in Fitzgerald's Last Novels," *Style* 35 (Spring 2001): 111–25, James Bloom argues that the opening scene, especially the prayer rug metaphor, "establishes the narrative's commitment to discredit national, cultural, and ethnic boundaries." Although Bloom rightly emphasizes the great variety of Orientalized imagery in the novel, he more problematically finds that the images celebrate a counter-Orientalist perspective that exposes how the West, personified by Dick, is "losing its bearings, its authority to arbitrate and judge" (113). For me, most of the instances carry a negative charge.

17 As Felipe Smith observes of the dead man, Jules Peterson, "Peterson perishes in what amounts to Fitzgerald's restaging of America's post-Civil War Reconstruction as a riot by newly emancipated blacks." "The Figure on the Bed: Difference and American Destiny in *Tender Is the Night*," in *French Connections*, 187–213, quotation 208. Smith also argues that finding Peterson's body in Rosemary's bed anticipates Dick's blackening after he sleeps with Rosemary (209). In *Imagining Paris: Exile, Writing, and American Identity* (New Haven: Yale University Press, 1993), J. Gerald Kennedy sees Peterson "as the black counterpart of Devereux Warren," functioning as a "scapegoat" for Warren's incest with Nicole by being sacrificed as an innocent substitute "in the bed of Daddy's girl" (216).

18 From a different angle, Kennedy emphasizes Dick's "composite personality," and Fitzgerald's interest in "unconscious incorporation" to blend personalities. When Dick emerges on the beach in Nicole's "transparent black lace drawers" (*Tender,* 21), this "transvestite performance" begins "the pattern of gender reversal which runs through the novel" (*Imagining Paris,* 199). This scene prefigures the "sexual transformation" that Nicole has to "effect" in Dick "to free herself from the dominating father" (200).

19 Mitchell Breitwieser, in "Jazz Fractures: F. Scott Fitzgerald and Epochal Representation," *American Literary History* 12 (Fall 2000): 359–81, reads the nothingness more positively as an invitation to a loneliness that frees subjectivities from nationalisms and "the burden of symbolizing" (378), much as Fitzgerald searches in his late writings to articulate "desire that is not a suburb of commodity-fetishism, labor politics, uninhibited capitalism" (376). In *The Last Laocoön*, Sklar sees Dick's feelings of nothingness and self-disintegration as instances of a "genteel romantic hero" who "had attained an erotic fulfillment which implied castration" (285).

20 Cavell, "The Avoidance of Love," 299. "Lear's dominating motivation . . . is *to avoid being recognized*" (274). Cavell links that fear to shame, "the specific discomfort produced by the sense of being looked at" (278), and later calls shame "the experience of unacceptable love" (296). In *Talking Cure*, Berman reads Dick quite differently as someone who has "a desire to love so intensely as to both engulf and be engulfed. . . . Dick's insatiable quest for love paradoxically drains him, rendering him broken and incomplete" (72). Though Berman focuses on pre-Oedipal possibilities and transference relations, rather than narcissism, he illuminates the "rescue fantasy in which he desires to cure his patients through love, rather than self-awareness" (77).

Epilogue. Shirley Temple's *The Little Colonel*

1 In *Daddy's Girl: Young Girls and Popular Culture* (Cambridge, Mass.: Harvard University Press, 1997), Valerie Walkerdine discusses the impact of Shirley Temple and Little Orphan Annie as cultural icons during her own working-class girlhood in England. Citing various films in which Shirley Temple plays an orphan, Walkerdine suggests that those films were made to oppose Annie's working-class appeal. The filmmakers "were deliberately out to present a little girl who would be more acceptable to the liberal bourgeoisie" (94). At least in *The Little Colonel,* Shirley Temple is more of a fighter.

2 Kimberly Hébert argues that Shirley Temple's minstrel performances in *The Little Colonel* and other movies combine the appeal of Topsy and Little Eva. She calls Temple "a 'passing' Topsy." See "Acting the Nigger: Topsy, Shirley Temple, and Toni Morrison's Pecola," *Approaches to Teaching Stowe's* Uncle Tom's Cabin," ed. Elizabeth Ammons and Susan Belasco (New York: MLA, 2000), 184–98, quotation 190, also 191 on *The Little Colonel.*

3 Pauline Hopkins, *Contending Forces: A Romance Illustrative of Negro Life North and South,* intro. Richard Yarborough (New York: Oxford University Press, 1988, 1st pub. 1900), 137.

4 For Joyce's use of the phrase, see Tamara Olaivar, "'Your Corporosity Segaciating OK?': *Ulysses* and Pauline Hopkins," *James Joyce Quarterly* 34 (Fall-Winter 1996–97): 173–74; James Joyce, *Ulysses,* ed. Hans Walter Gabler (New York: Vintage Books, 1986, 1st pub. 1922), 347, lines 1482–83, toward end of episode 14.

Index

R